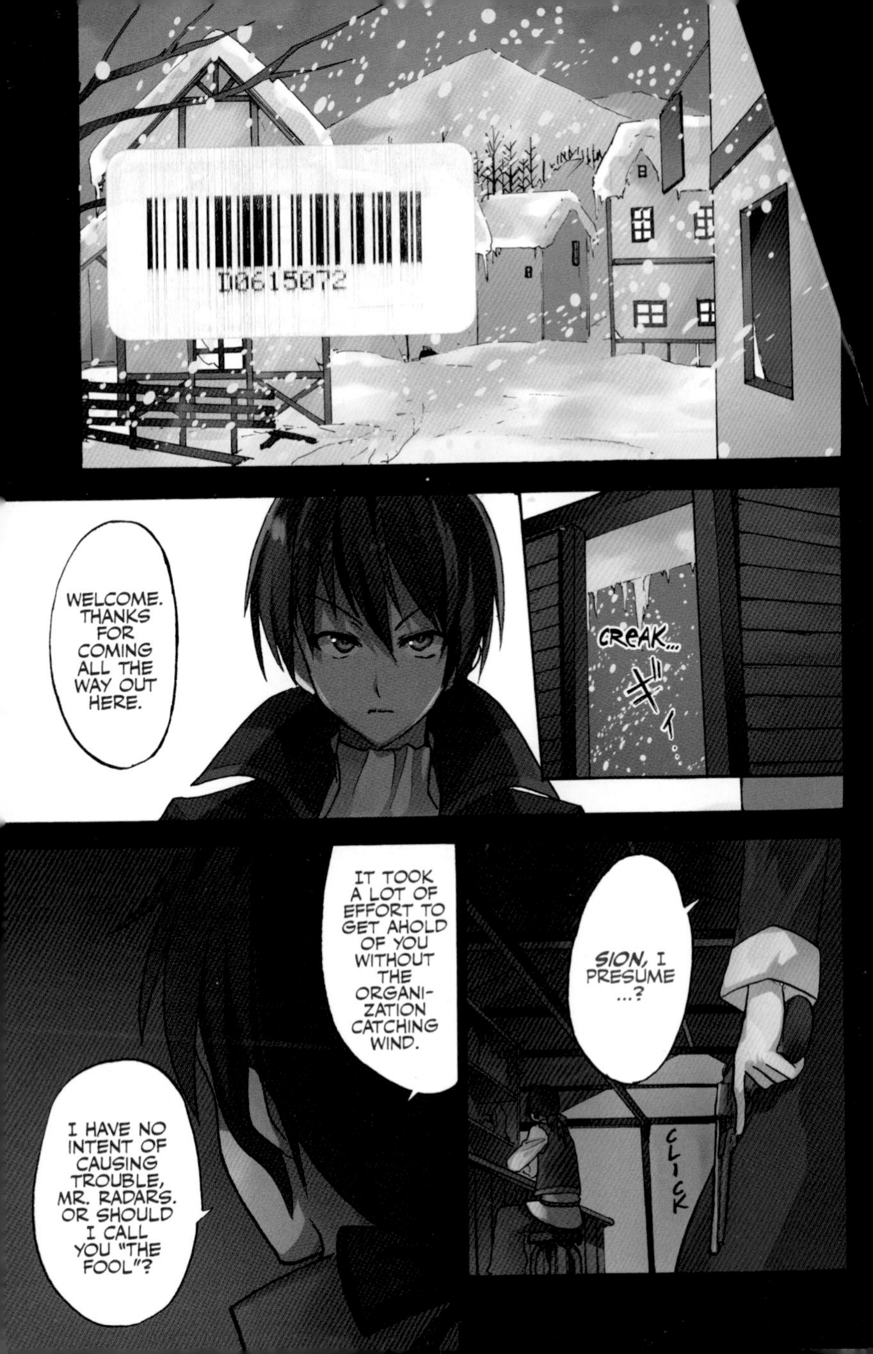
CREAK...
ギイ…
WELCOME. THANKS FOR COMING ALL THE WAY OUT HERE.
SION, I PRESUME ...?
CLICK
IT TOOK A LOT OF EFFORT TO GET AHOLD OF YOU WITHOUT THE ORGANI-ZATION CATCHING WIND.
I HAVE NO INTENT OF CAUSING TROUBLE, MR. RADARS. OR SHOULD I CALL YOU "THE FOOL"?

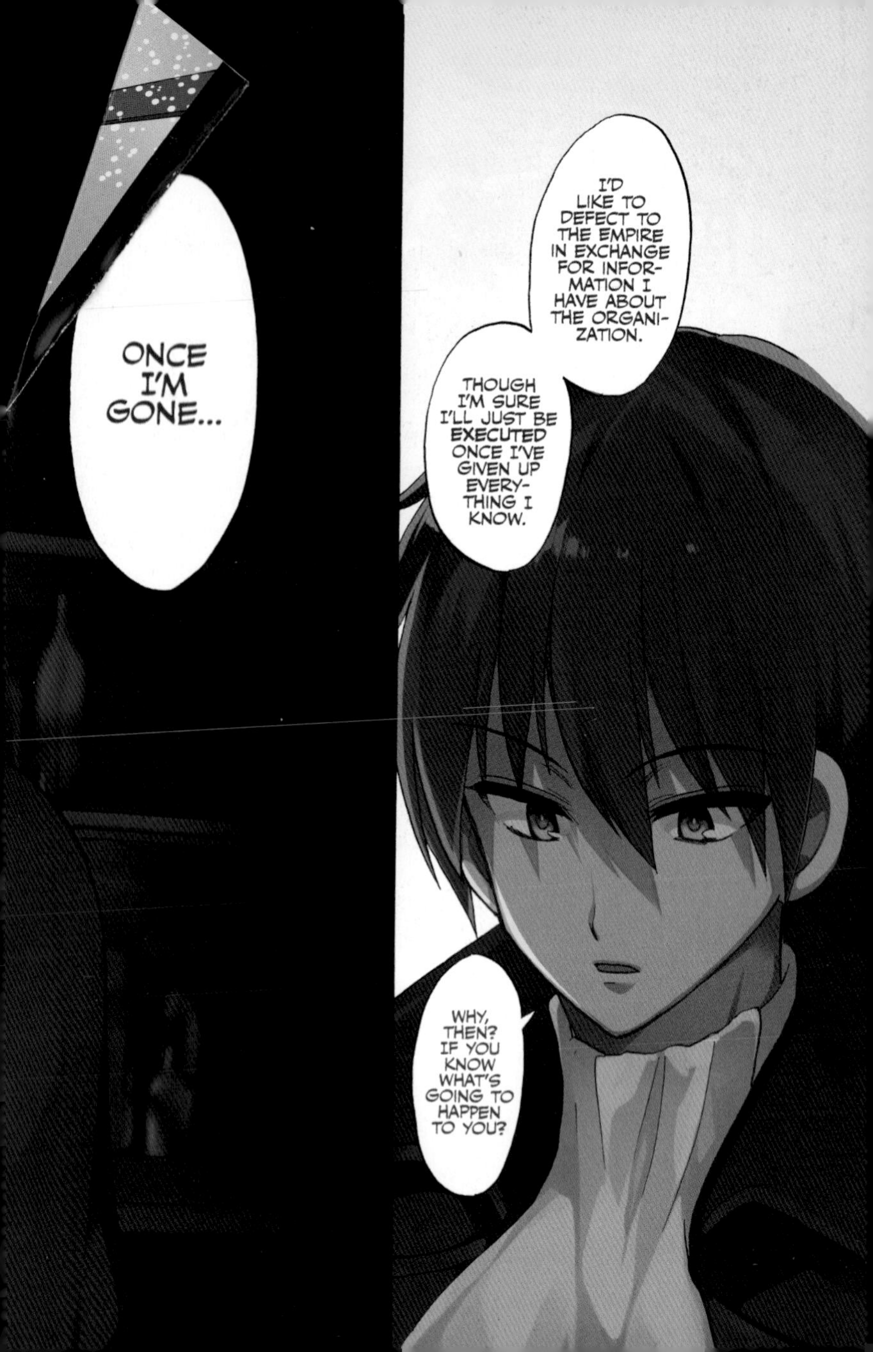
I'D LIKE TO DEFECT TO THE EMPIRE IN EXCHANGE FOR INFORMATION I HAVE ABOUT THE ORGANIZATION.
THOUGH I'M SURE I'LL JUST BE **EXECUTED** ONCE I'VE GIVEN UP EVERYTHING I KNOW.
WHY, THEN? IF YOU KNOW WHAT'S GOING TO HAPPEN TO YOU?
ONCE I'M GONE...

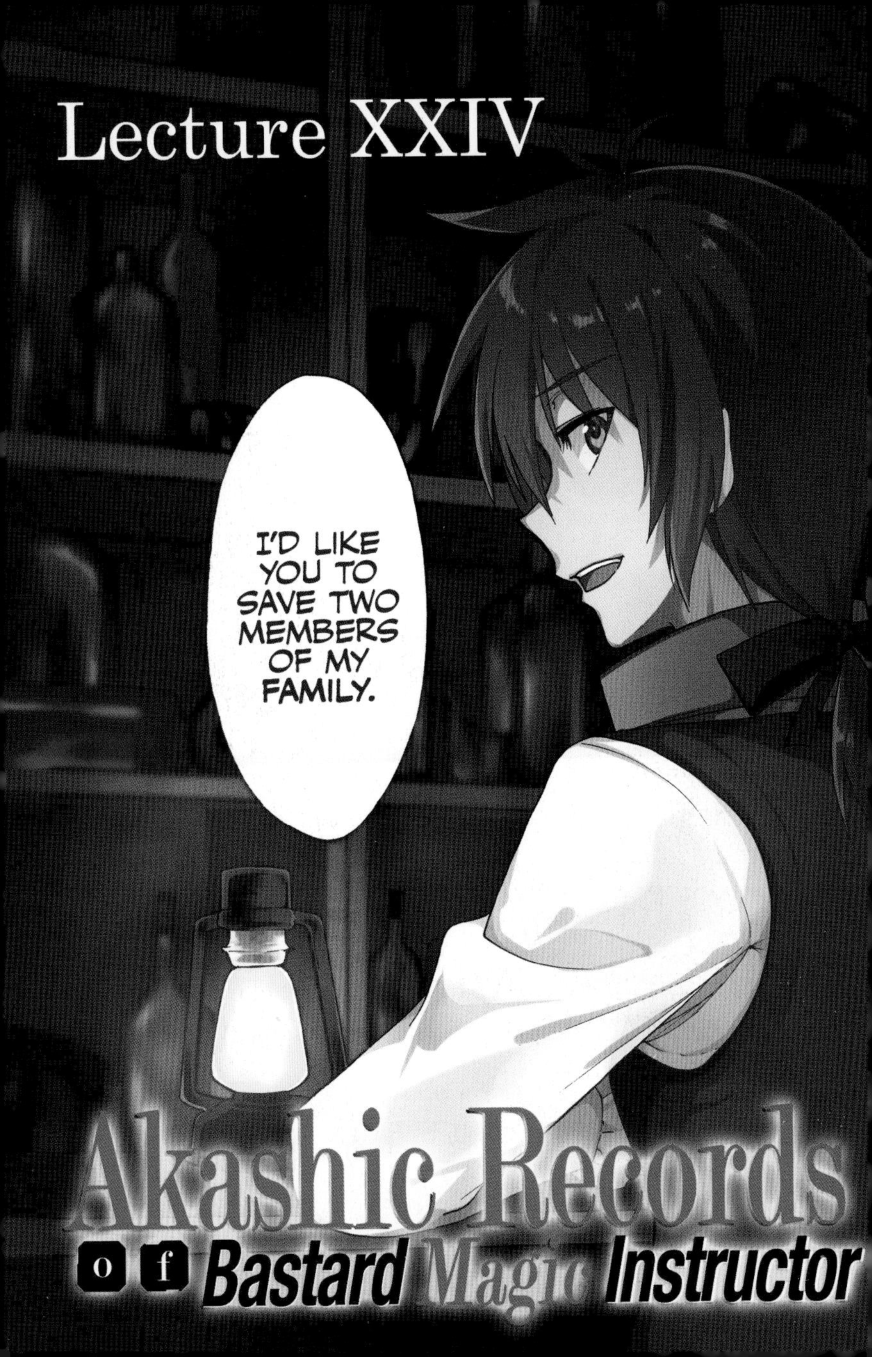
Lecture XXIV
I'D LIKE YOU TO SAVE TWO MEMBERS OF MY FAMILY.
Akashic Records of Bastard Magic Instructor

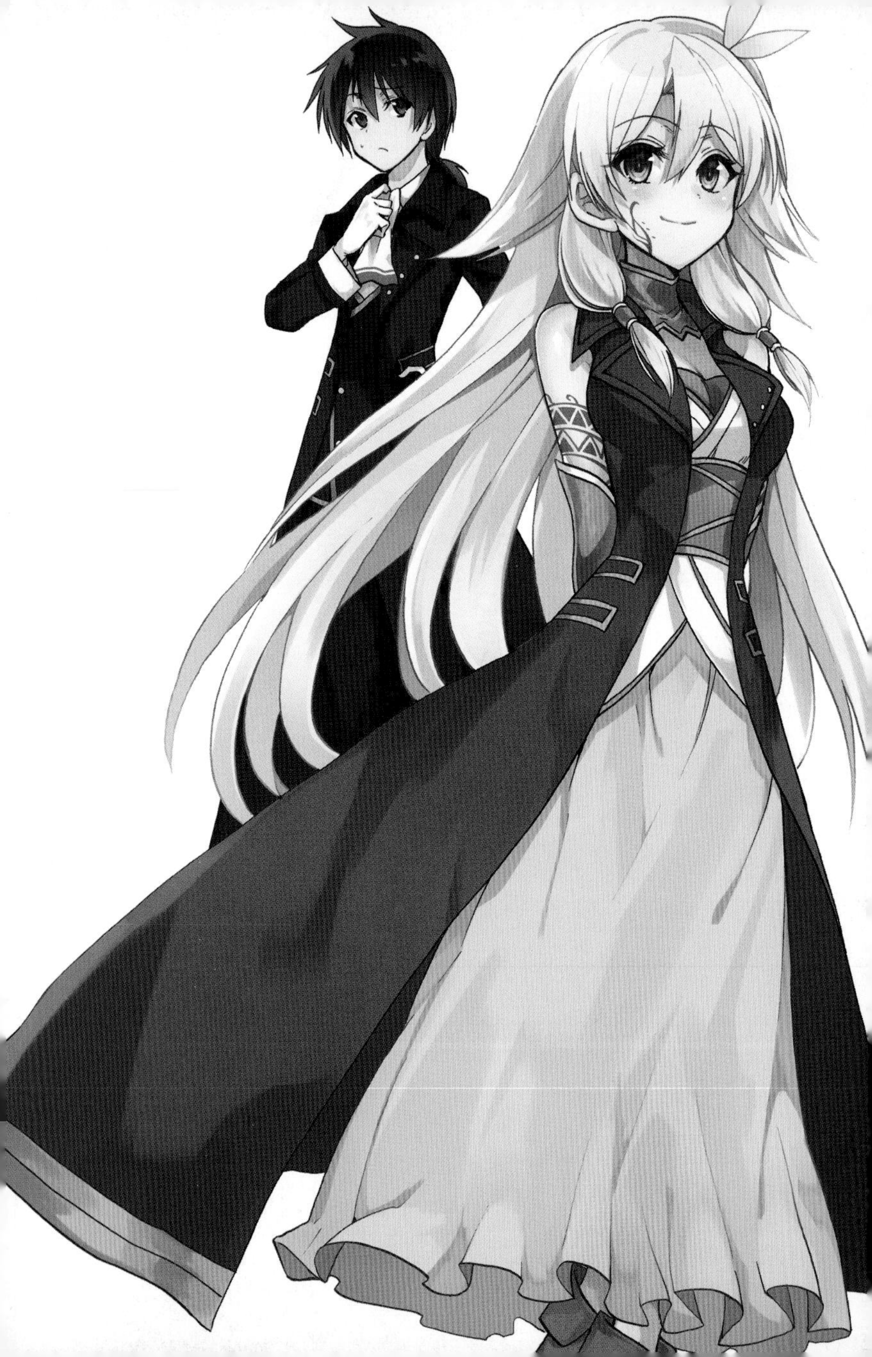

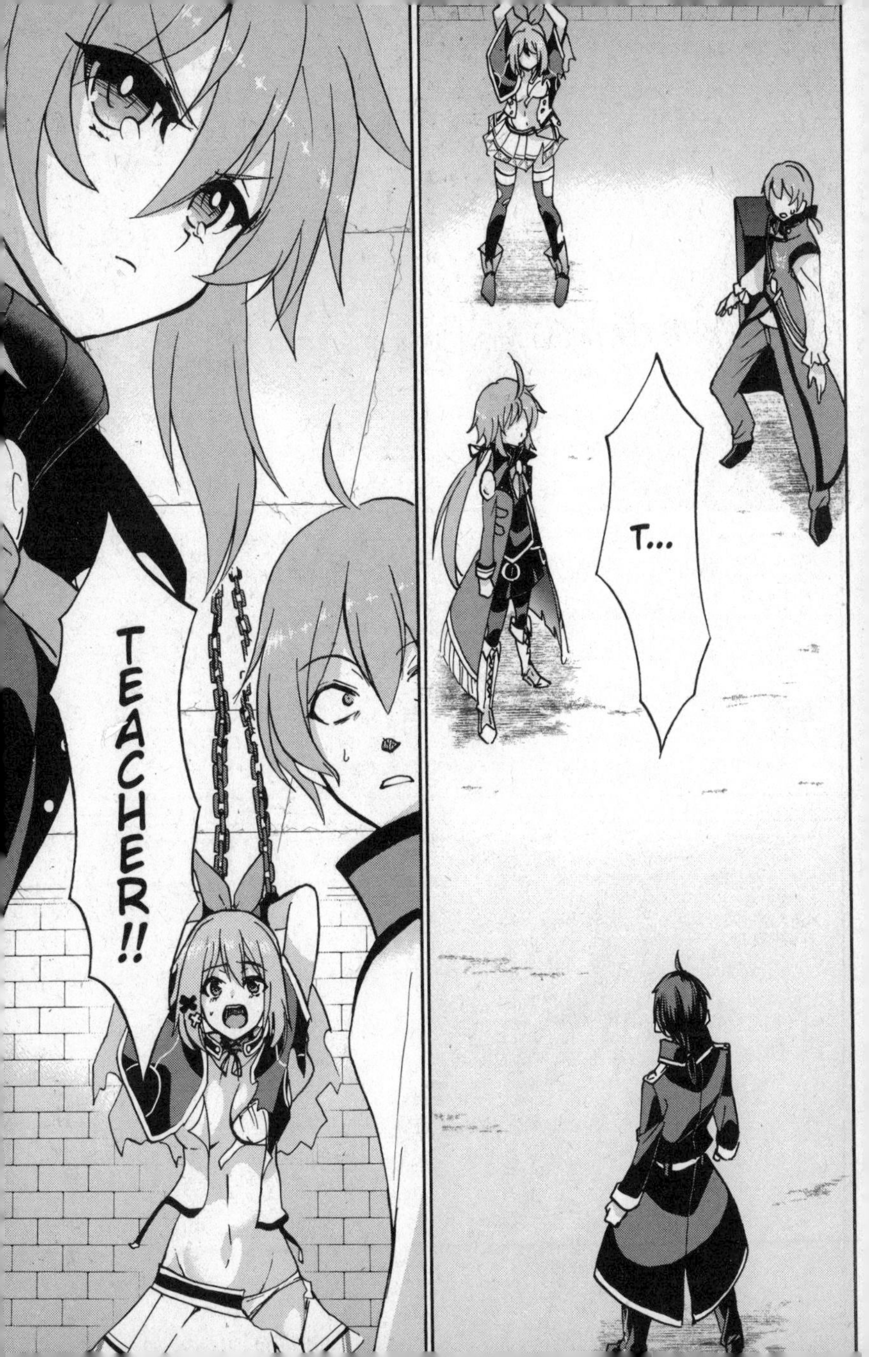
T...
TEACHER!!

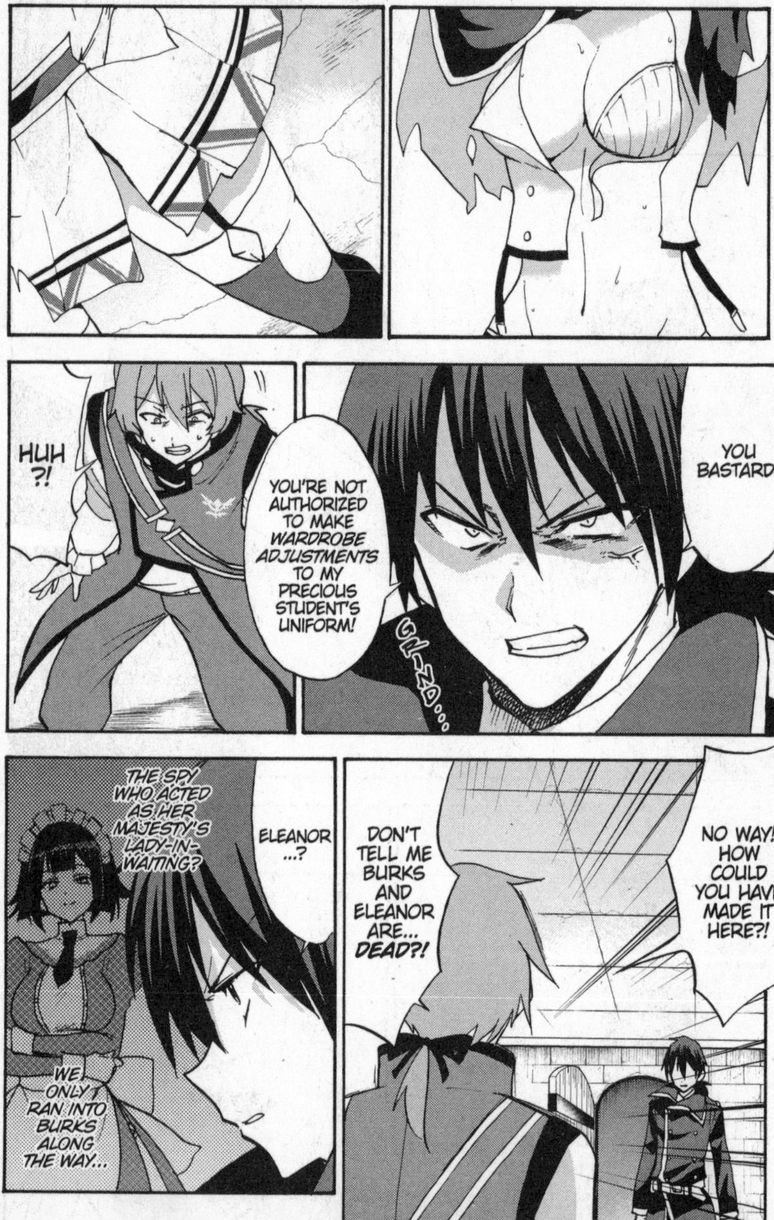
YOU BASTARD!
YOU'RE NOT AUTHORIZED TO MAKE WARDROBE ADJUSTMENTS TO MY PRECIOUS STUDENT'S UNIFORM!
GRIND...
HUH ?!
NO WAY! HOW COULD YOU HAVE MADE IT HERE?!
DON'T TELL ME BURKS AND ELEANOR ARE... DEAD?!
ELEANOR ...?
THE SPY WHO ACTED AS HER MAJESTY'S LADY-IN-WAITING?
WE ONLY RAN INTO BURKS ALONG THE WAY...

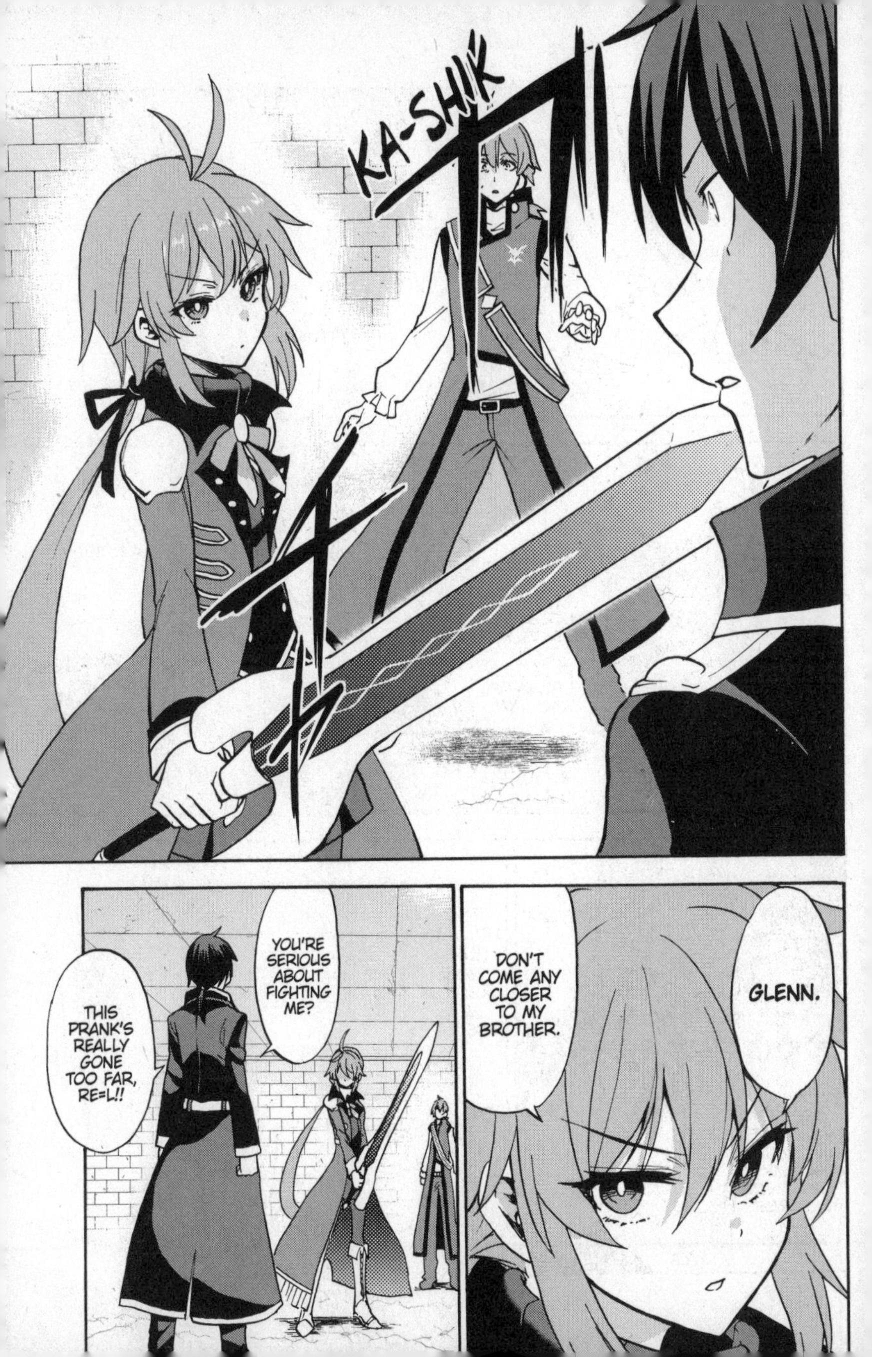
KA-SHIK
GLENN.
DON'T COME ANY CLOSER TO MY BROTHER.
YOU'RE SERIOUS ABOUT FIGHTING ME?
THIS PRANK'S REALLY GONE TOO FAR, RE=L!!

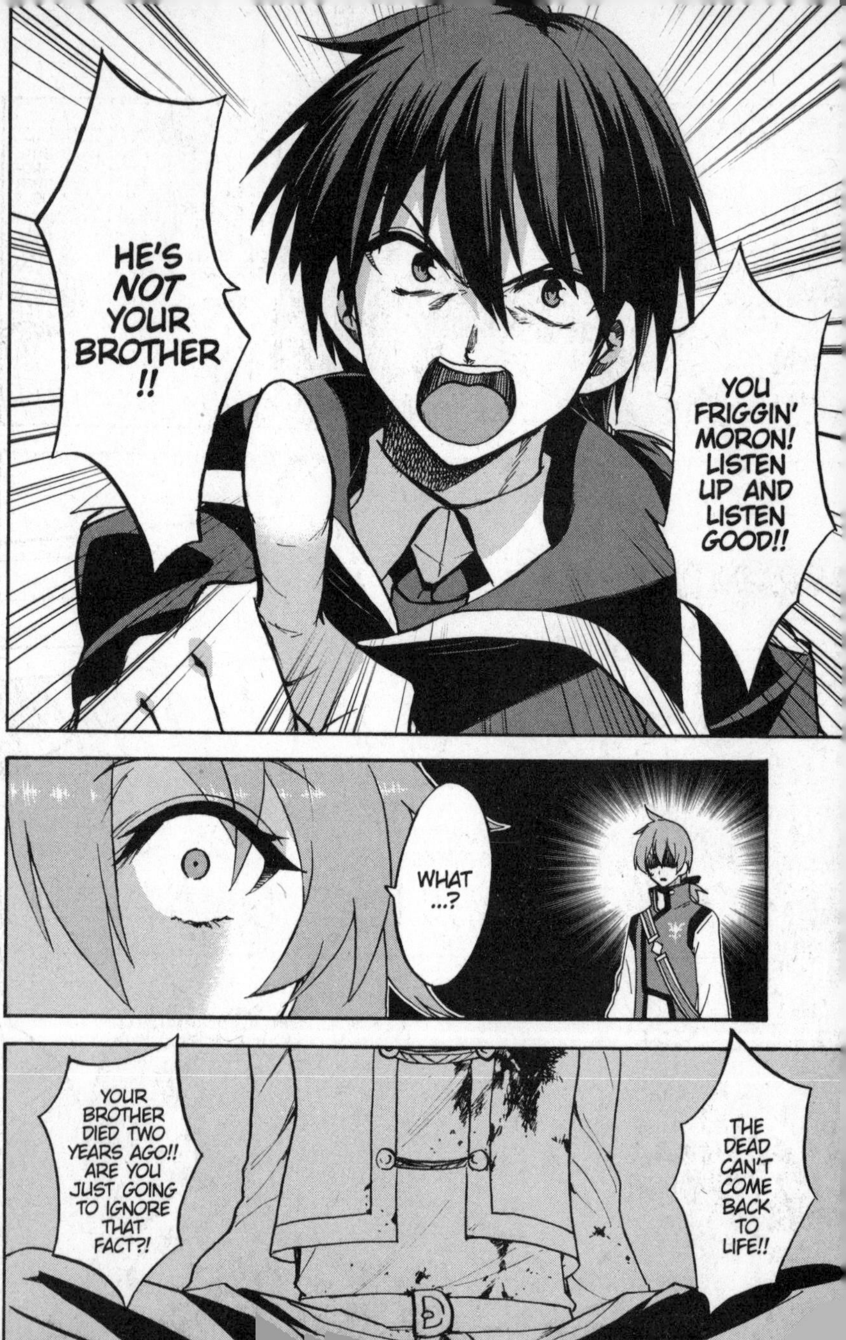
YOU FRIGGIN' MORON! LISTEN UP AND LISTEN GOOD!!
HE'S *NOT* YOUR BROTHER!!
WHAT ...?
THE DEAD CAN'T COME BACK TO LIFE!!
YOUR BROTHER DIED TWO YEARS AGO!! ARE YOU JUST GOING TO IGNORE THAT FACT?!

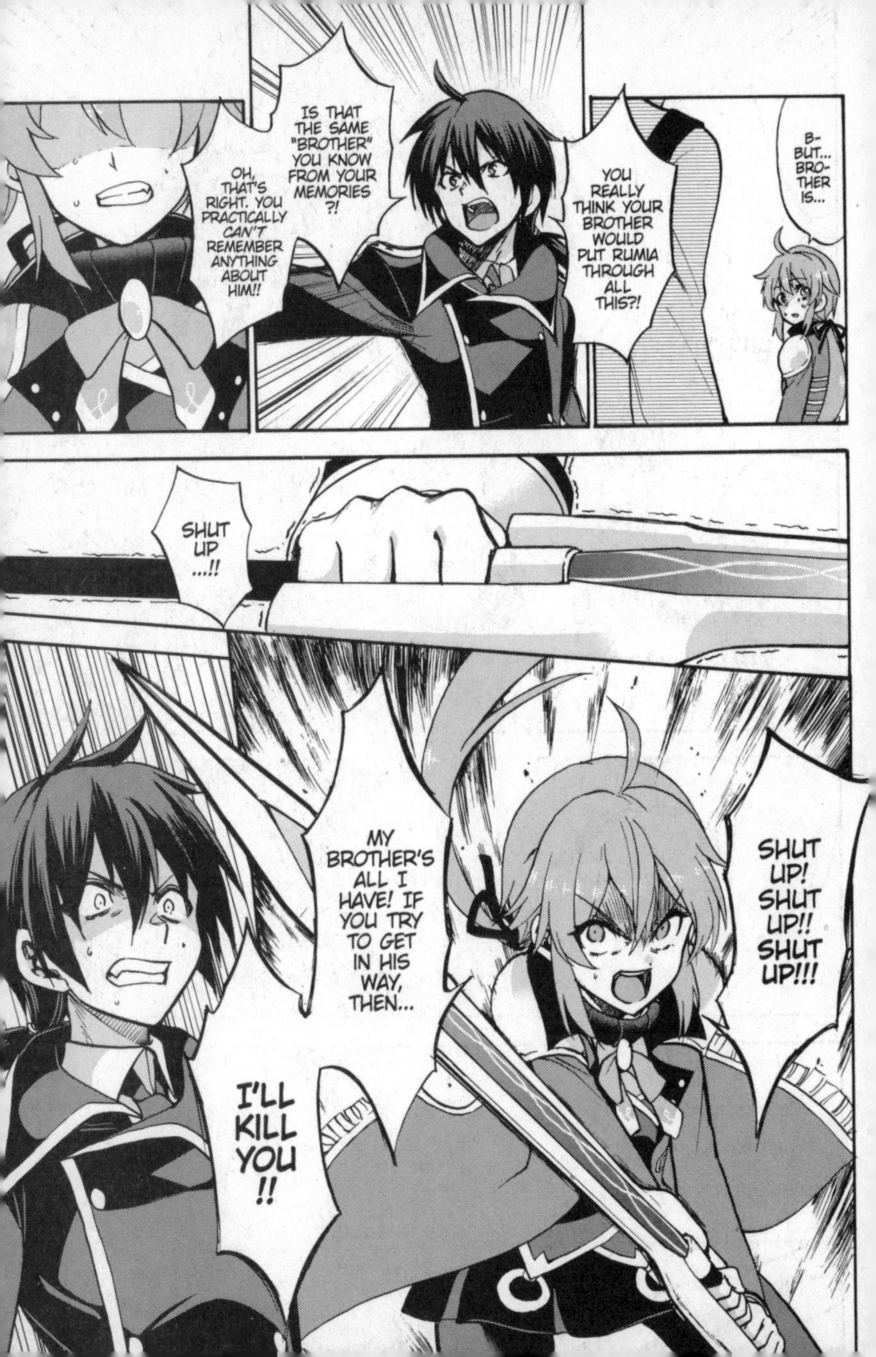
B-BUT... BROTHER IS...
YOU REALLY THINK YOUR BROTHER WOULD PUT RUMIA THROUGH ALL THIS?!
IS THAT THE SAME "BROTHER" YOU KNOW FROM YOUR MEMORIES?!
OH, THAT'S RIGHT. YOU PRACTICALLY CAN'T REMEMBER ANYTHING ABOUT HIM!!
SHUT UP...!!
SHUT UP! SHUT UP!! SHUT UP!!!
MY BROTHER'S ALL I HAVE! IF YOU TRY TO GET IN HIS WAY, THEN...
I'LL KILL YOU!!

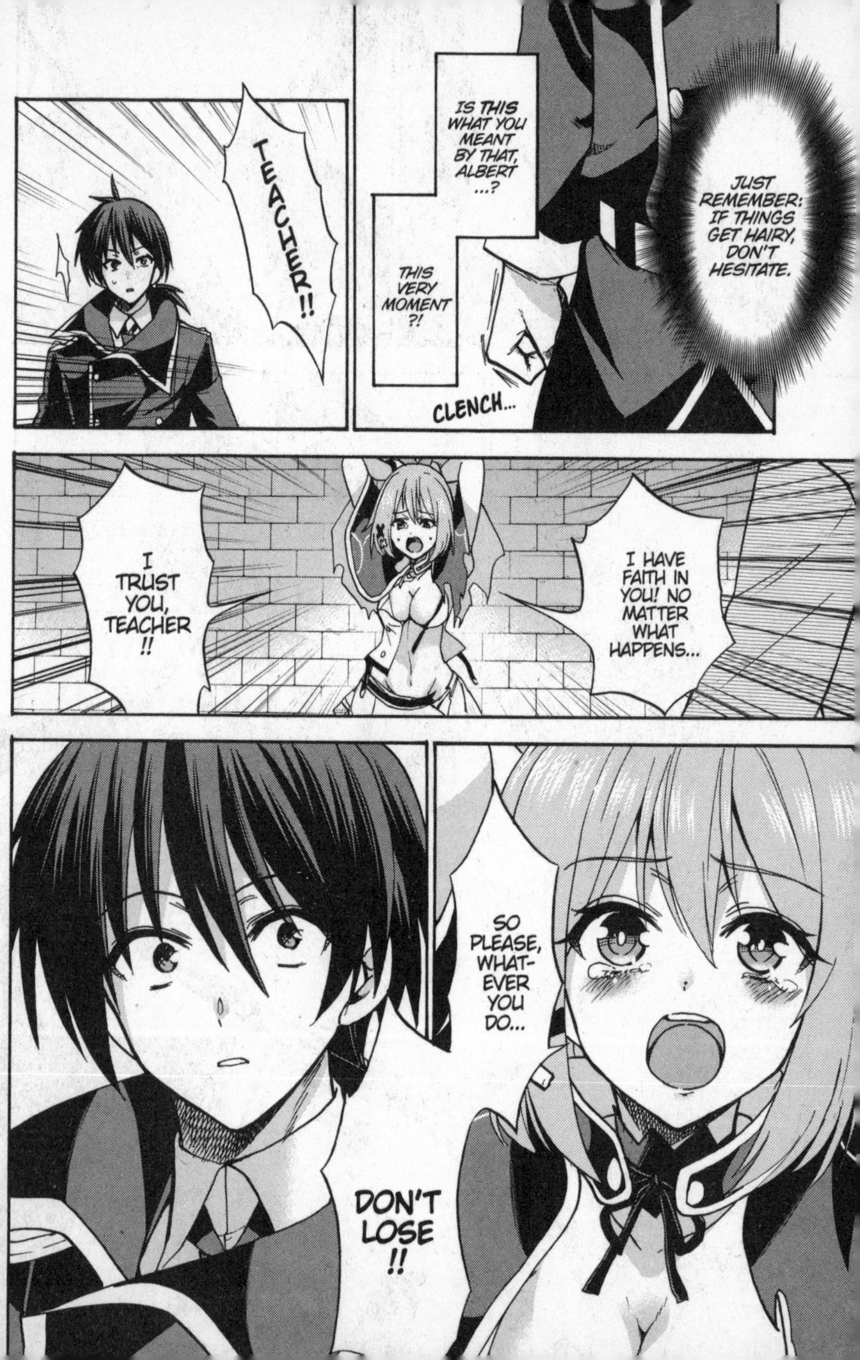
JUST REMEMBER: IF THINGS GET HAIRY, DON'T HESITATE.
IS THIS WHAT YOU MEANT BY THAT, ALBERT ...?
THIS VERY MOMENT ?!
CLENCH...
TEACHER!!
I HAVE FAITH IN YOU! NO MATTER WHAT HAPPENS...
I TRUST YOU, TEACHER !!
SO PLEASE, WHAT-EVER YOU DO...
DON'T LOSE !!

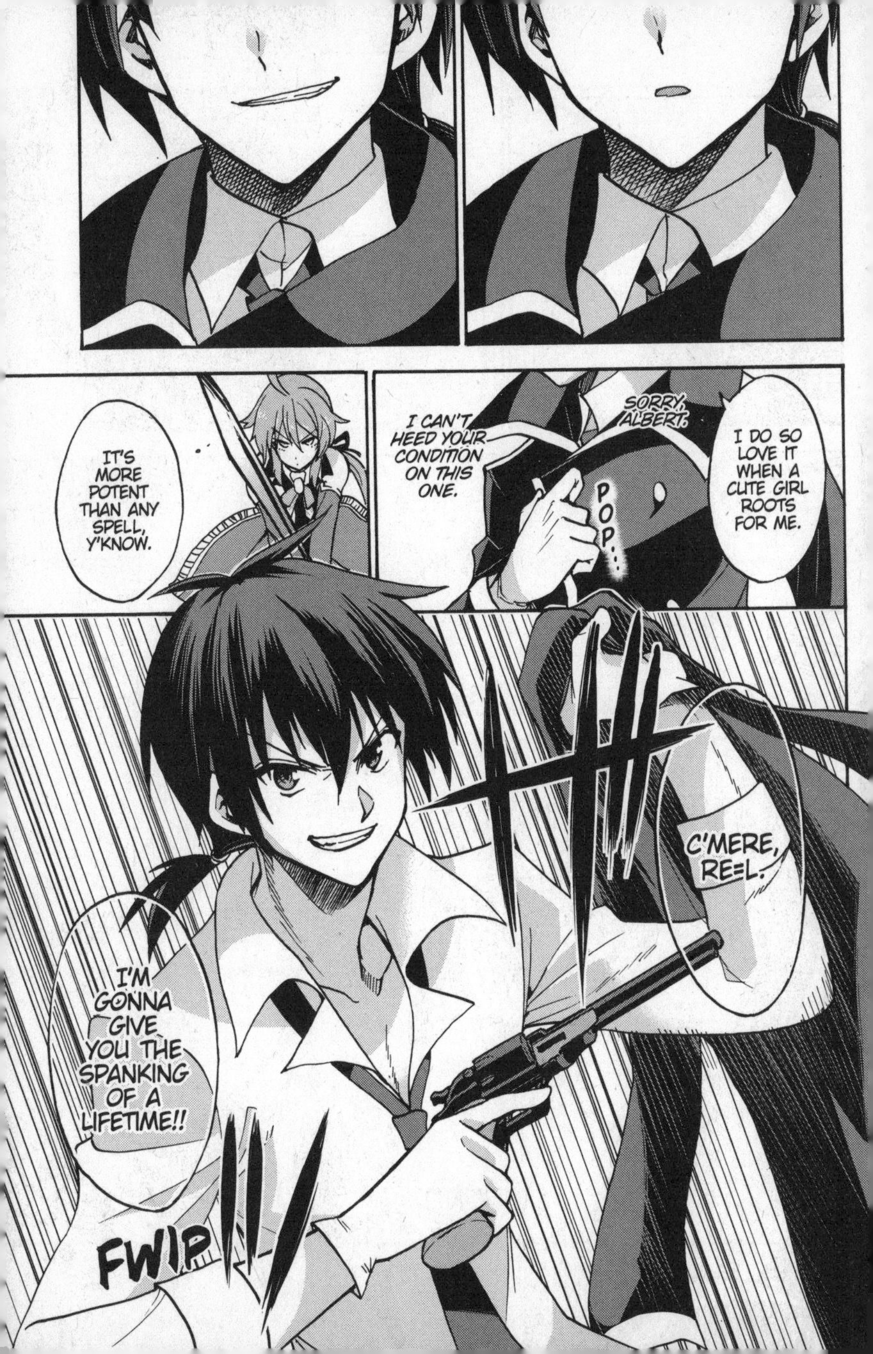
I DO SO LOVE IT WHEN A CUTE GIRL ROOTS FOR ME.
SORRY, ALBERT.
POP...
I CAN'T HEED YOUR CONDITION ON THIS ONE.
IT'S MORE POTENT THAN ANY SPELL, Y'KNOW.
C'MERE, RE=L.
I'M GONNA GIVE YOU THE SPANKING OF A LIFETIME!!
FWIP

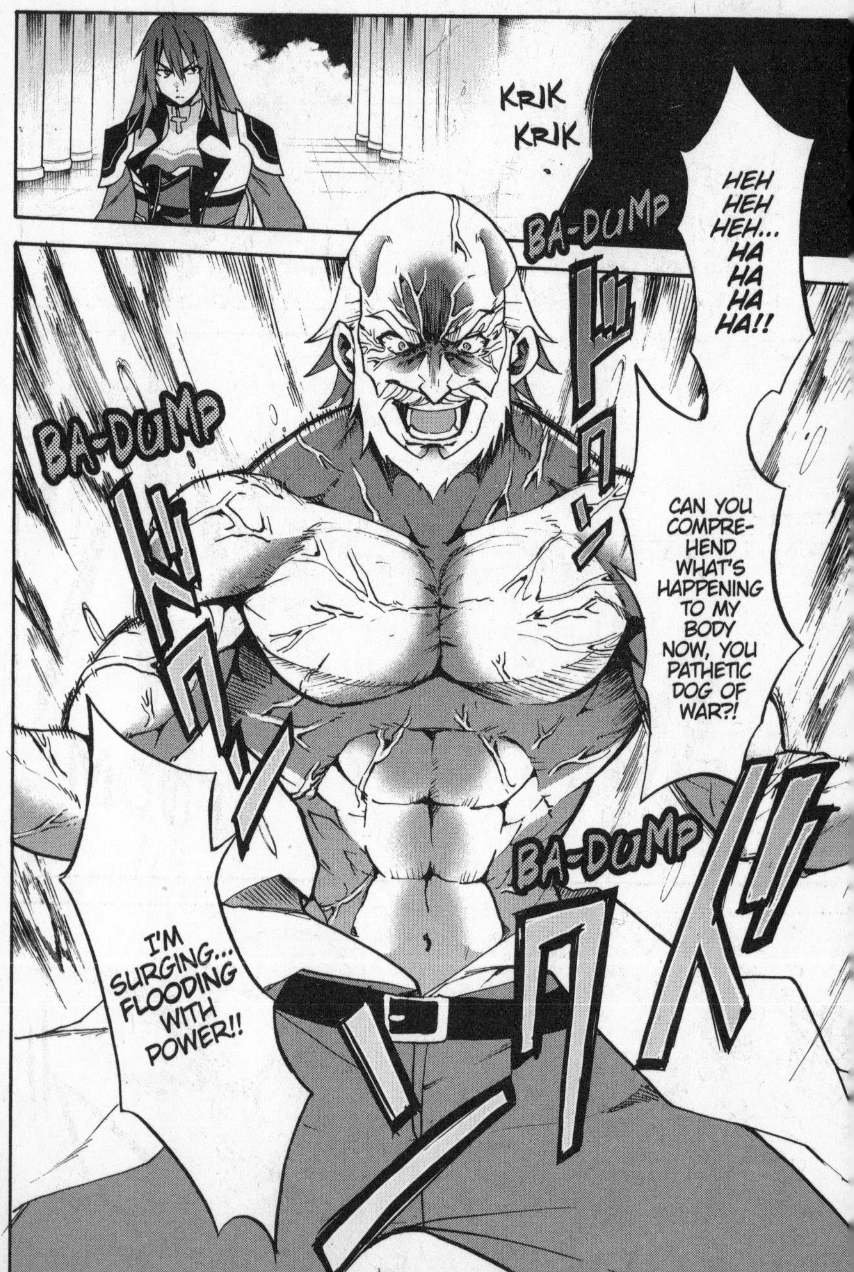
KRIK
KRIK
HEH HEH HEH... HA HA HA HA HA!!
BA-DUMP
CAN YOU COMPRE-HEND WHAT'S HAPPENING TO MY BODY NOW, YOU PATHETIC DOG OF WAR?!
BA-DUMP
BA-DUMP
I'M SURGING... FLOODING WITH POWER!!

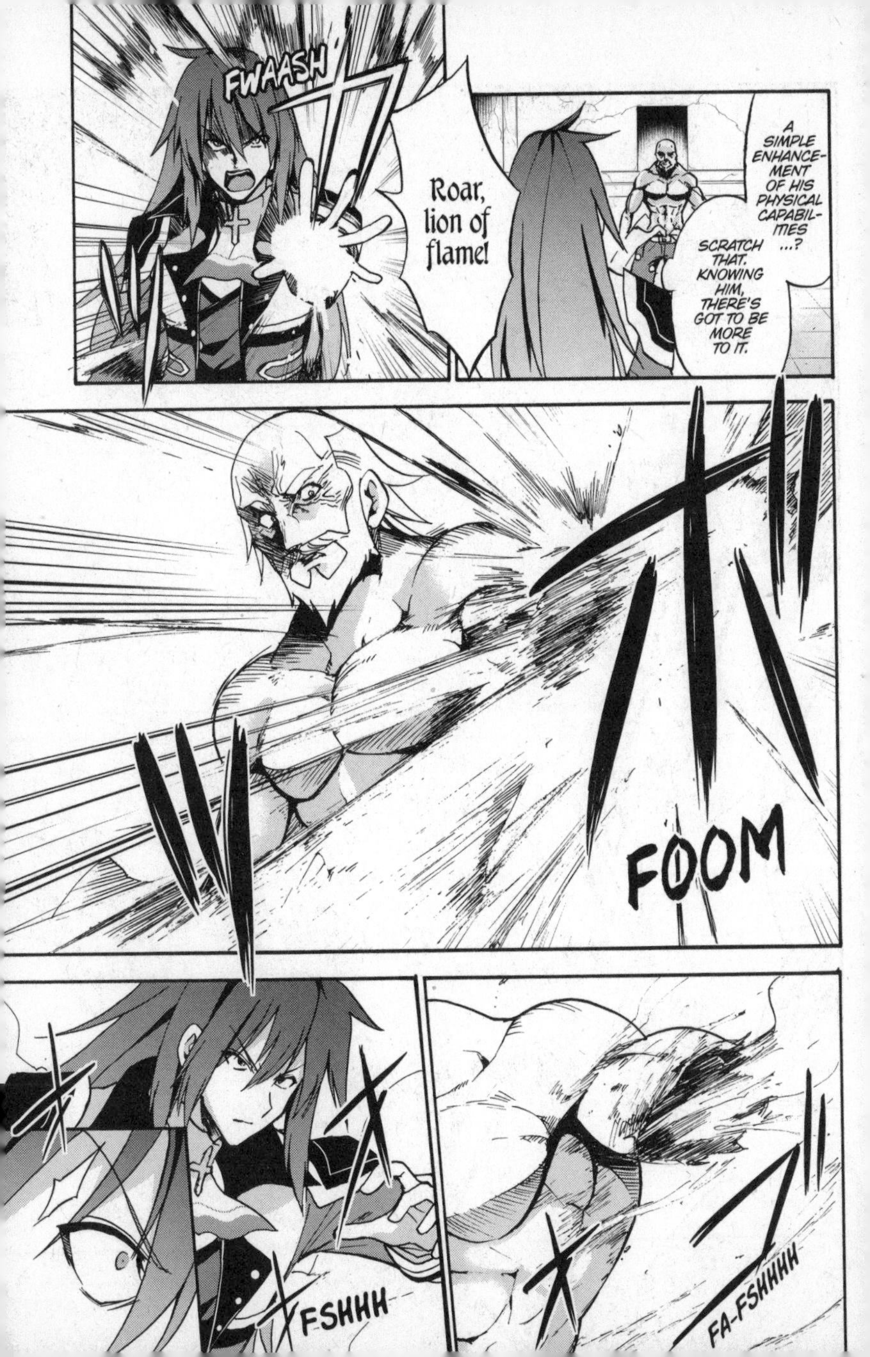
A SIMPLE ENHANCEMENT OF HIS PHYSICAL CAPABILITIES ...?
SCRATCH THAT. KNOWING HIM, THERE'S GOT TO BE MORE TO IT.
Roar, lion of flame!
FWAASH
FOOM
FA-FSHHHH
FSHHH

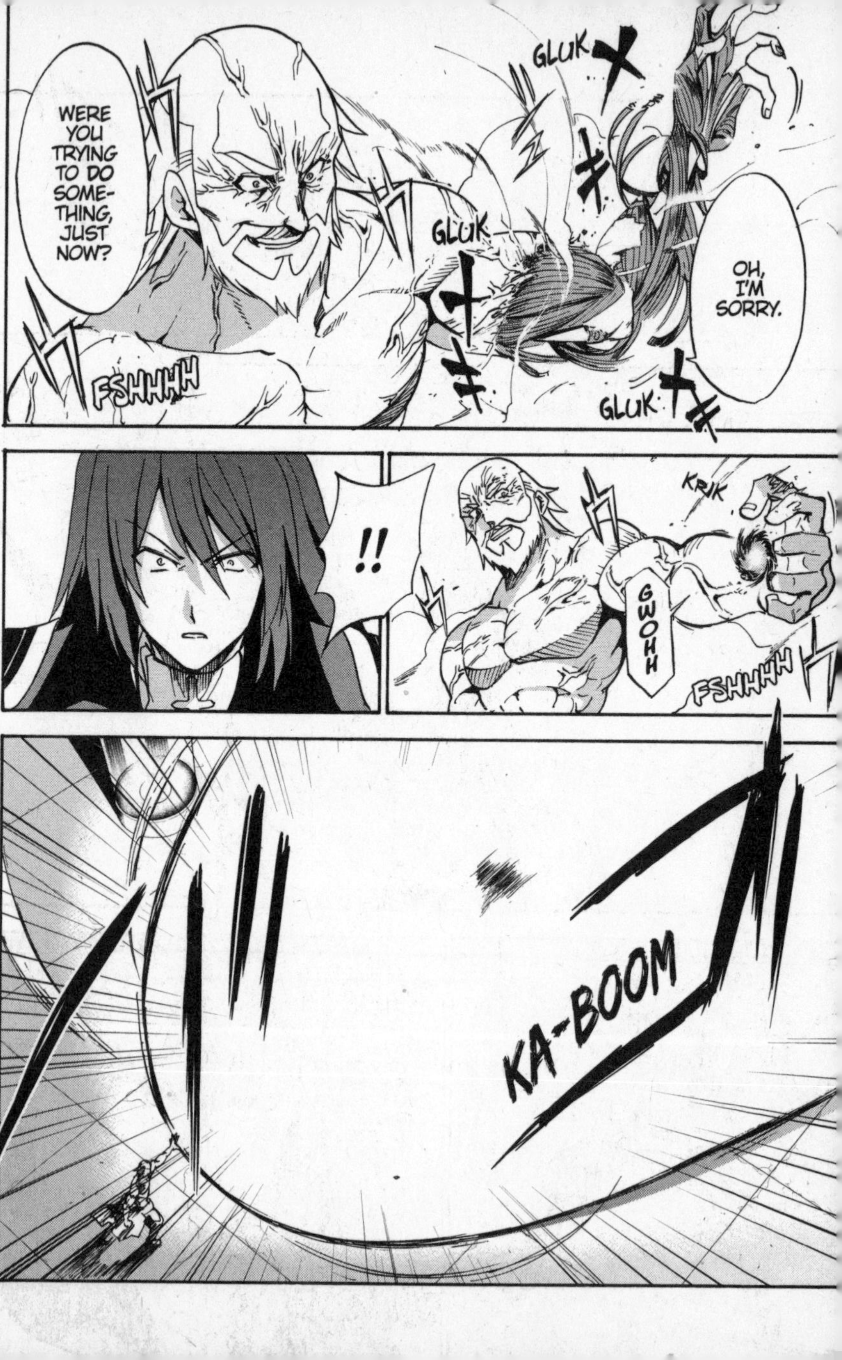
GLUK
OH, I'M SORRY.
GLUK
GLUK
WERE YOU TRYING TO DO SOME-THING, JUST NOW?
FSHHHH
KRIK
GWOHH
FSHHHH
!!
KA-BOOM

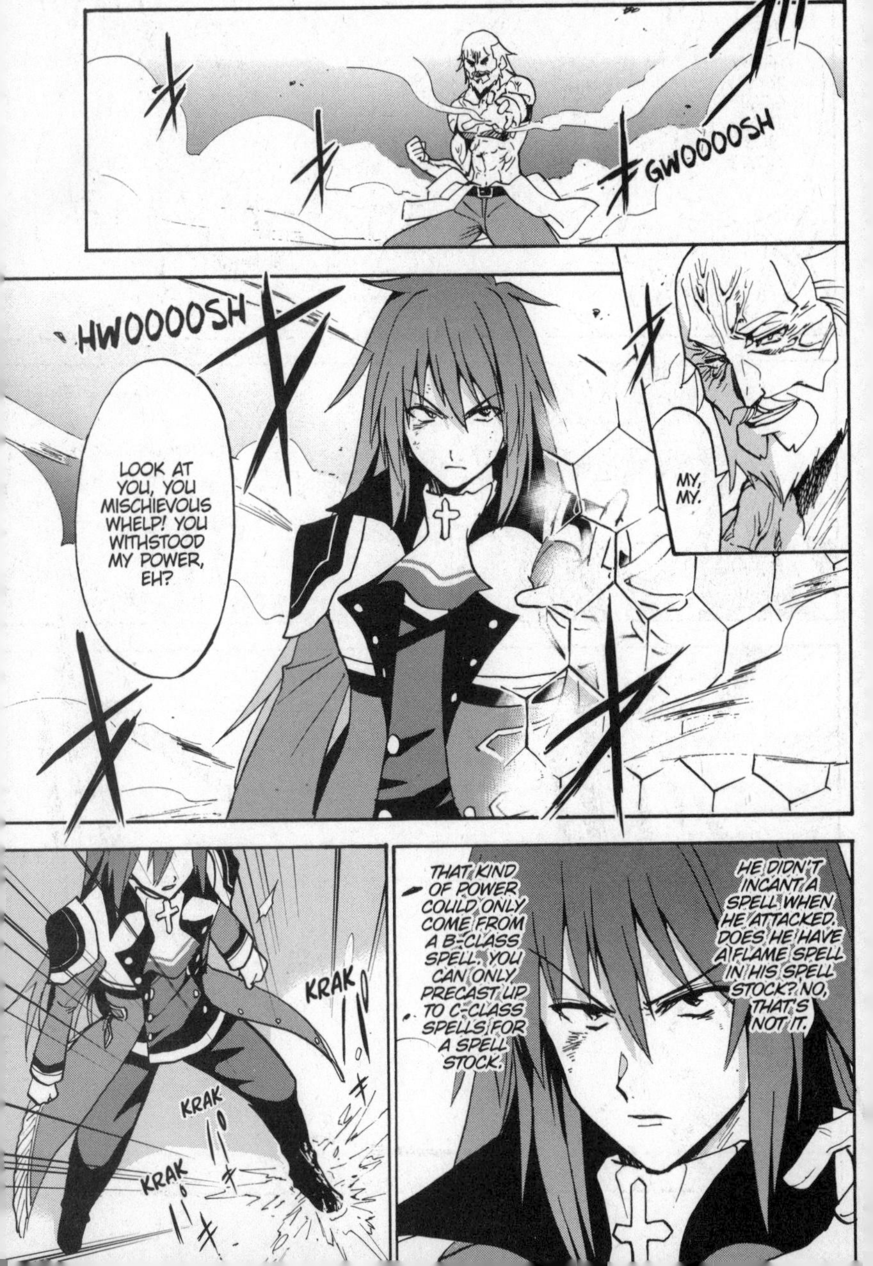
GWOOOOSH
MY, MY.
HWOOOOSH
LOOK AT YOU, YOU MISCHIEVOUS WHELP! YOU WITHSTOOD MY POWER, EH?
HE DIDN'T INCANT A SPELL WHEN HE ATTACKED. DOES HE HAVE A FLAME SPELL IN HIS SPELL STOCK? NO, THAT'S NOT IT.
THAT KIND OF POWER COULD ONLY COME FROM A B-CLASS SPELL. YOU CAN ONLY PRECAST UP TO C-CLASS SPELLS FOR A SPELL STOCK.
KRAK
KRAK
KRAK

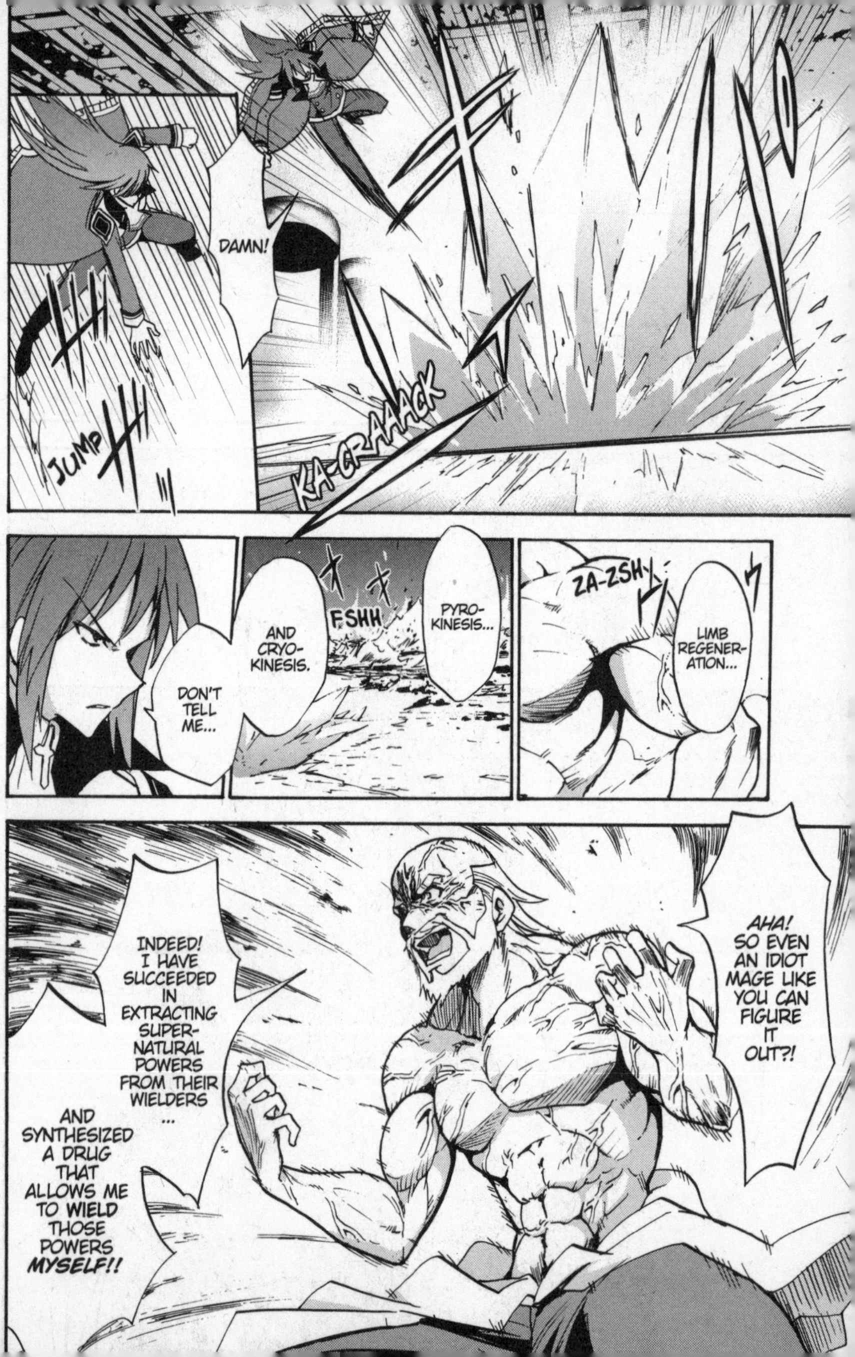
DAMN!
KA-CRAAACK
JUMP
ZA-ZSH
LIMB REGENER-ATION...
PYRO-KINESIS...
FSHH
AND CRYO-KINESIS.
DON'T TELL ME...
AHA! SO EVEN AN IDIOT MAGE LIKE YOU CAN FIGURE IT OUT?!
INDEED! I HAVE SUCCEEDED IN EXTRACTING SUPER-NATURAL POWERS FROM THEIR WIELDERS ...
AND SYNTHESIZED A DRUG THAT ALLOWS ME TO WIELD THOSE POWERS *MYSELF!!*

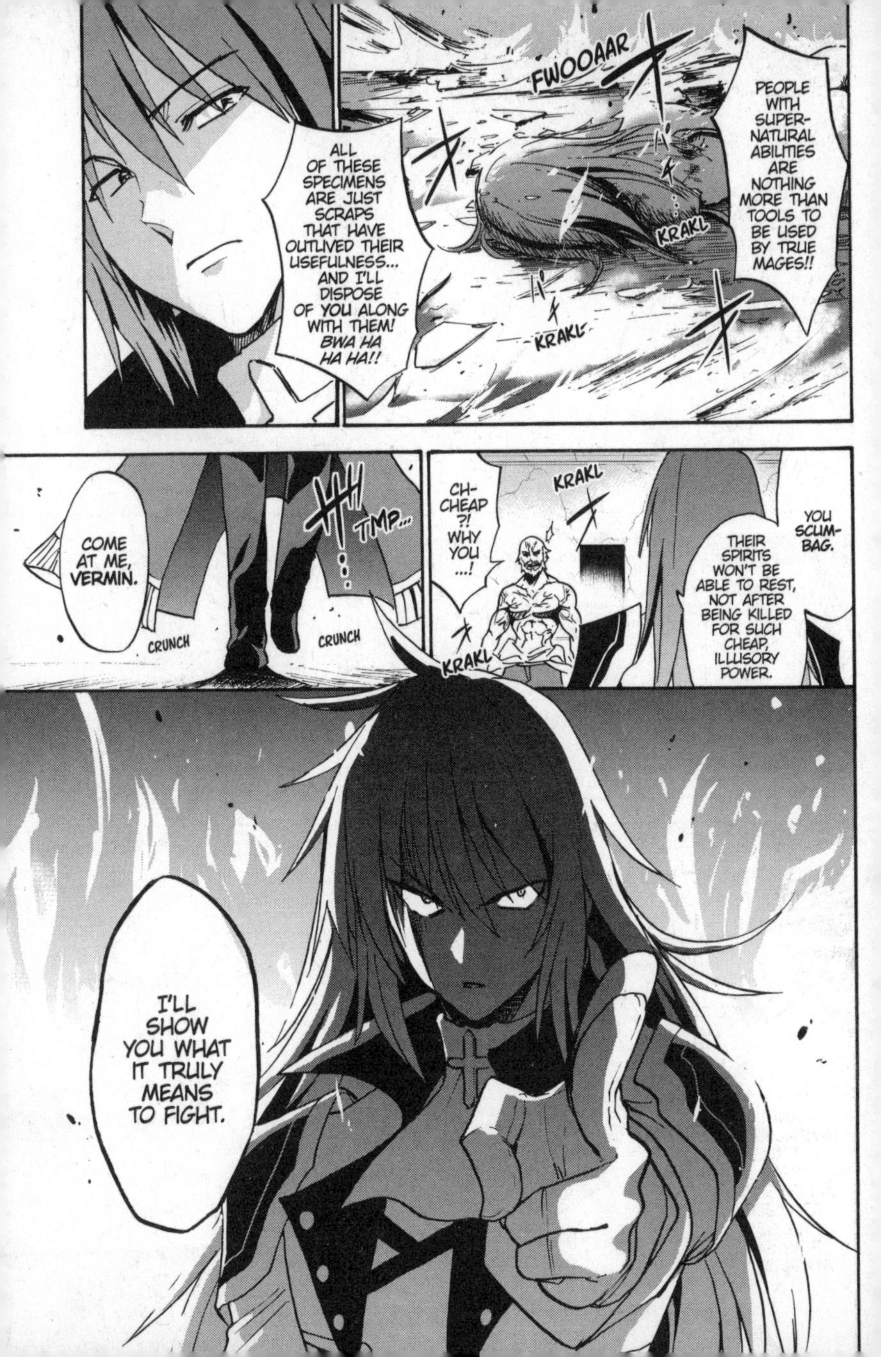
FWOOAAR
PEOPLE WITH SUPER-NATURAL ABILITIES ARE NOTHING MORE THAN TOOLS TO BE USED BY TRUE MAGES!!
KRAKL
KRAKL
ALL OF THESE SPECIMENS ARE JUST SCRAPS THAT HAVE OUTLIVED THEIR USEFULNESS... AND I'LL DISPOSE OF YOU ALONG WITH THEM! *BWA HA HA HA!!*
YOU SCUM-BAG.
THEIR SPIRITS WON'T BE ABLE TO REST, NOT AFTER BEING KILLED FOR SUCH CHEAP, ILLUSORY POWER.
KRAKL
CH-CHEAP?! WHY YOU...!
KRAKL
TMP...
CRUNCH
CRUNCH
COME AT ME, VERMIN.
I'LL SHOW YOU WHAT IT TRULY MEANS TO FIGHT.

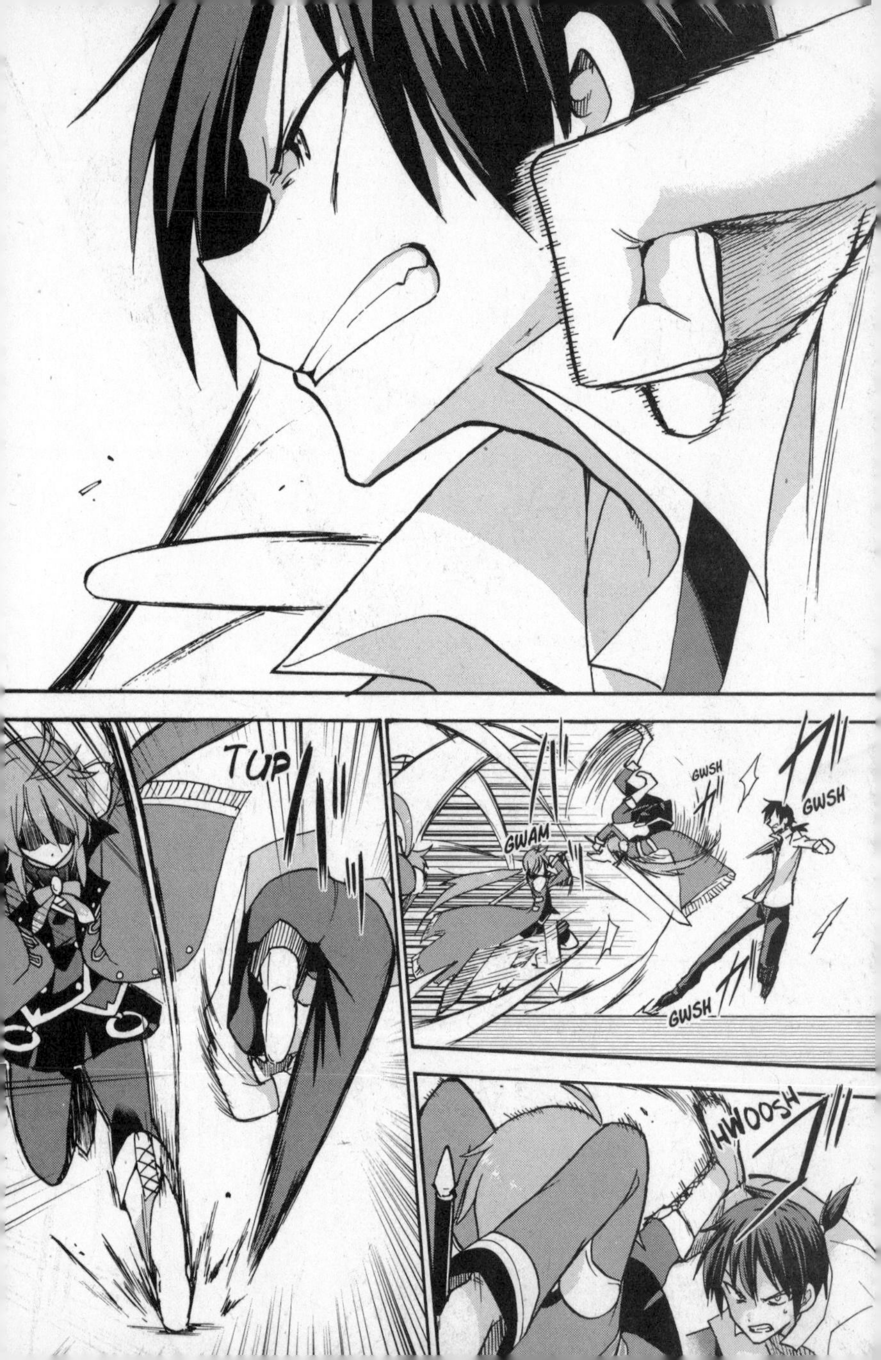
GWSH
GWSH
GWAM
GWSH
HWOOSH
TUP

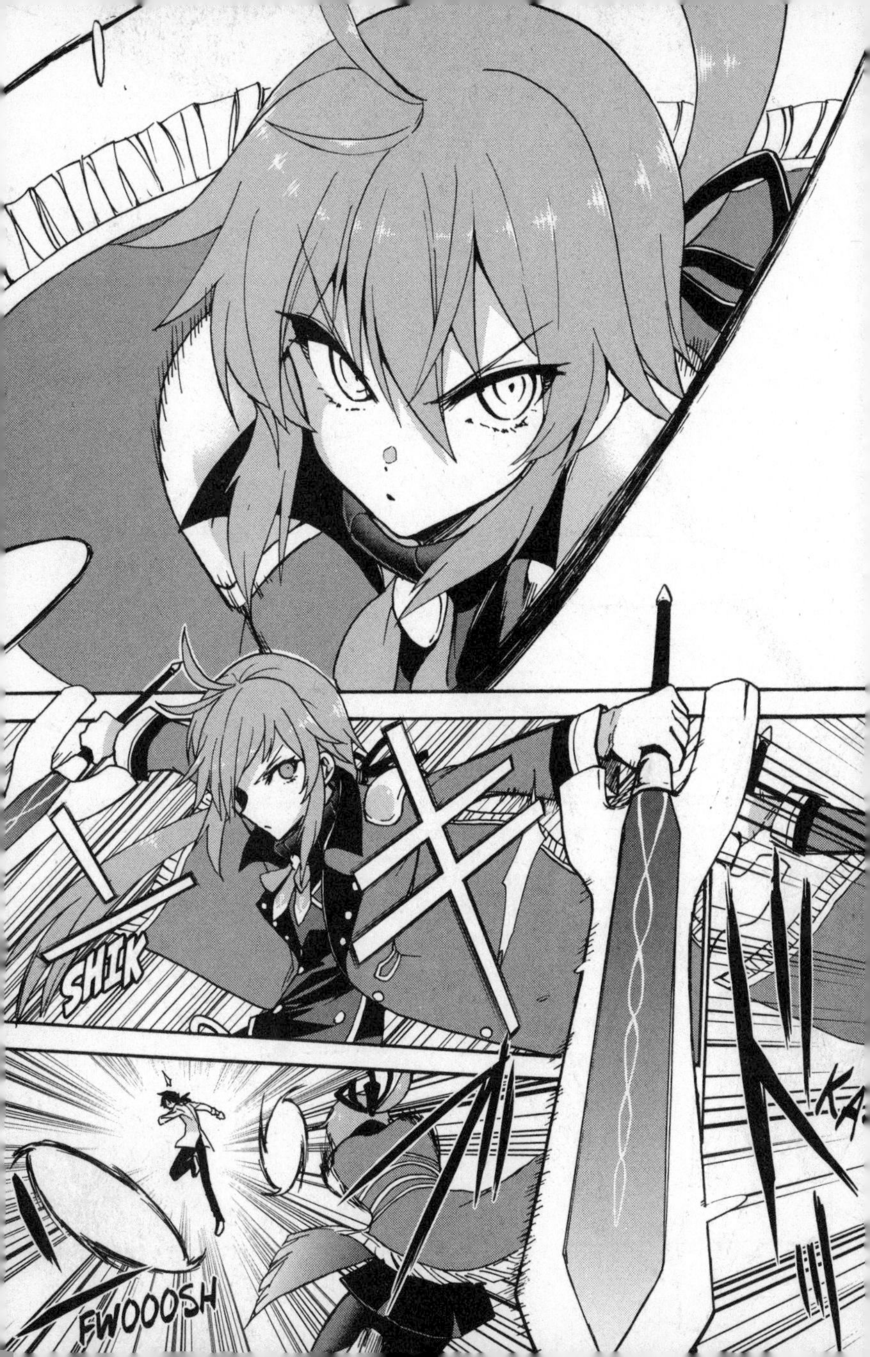
SHIK
KA
FWOOOSH

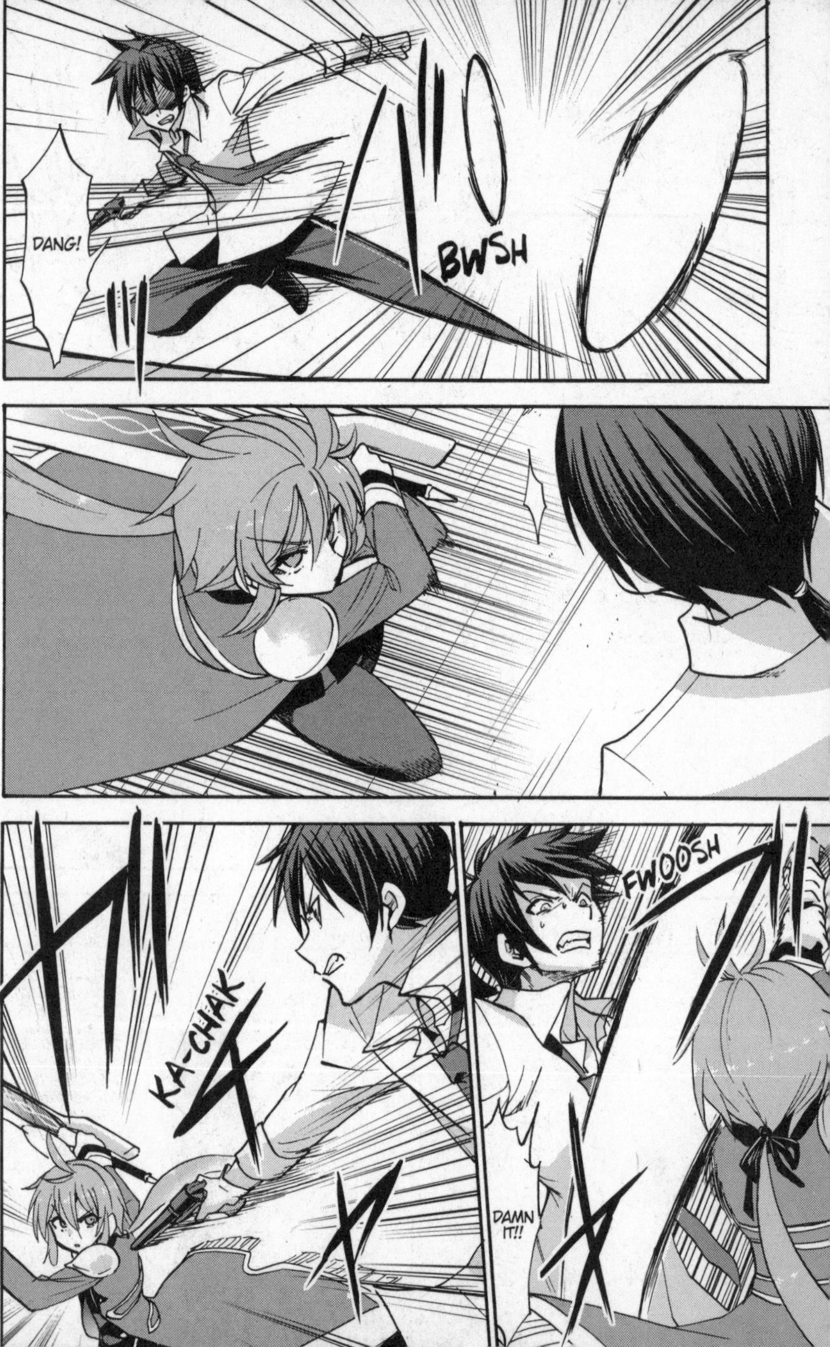
BWSH
DANG!
FWOOSH
DAMN IT!!
KA-CHAK

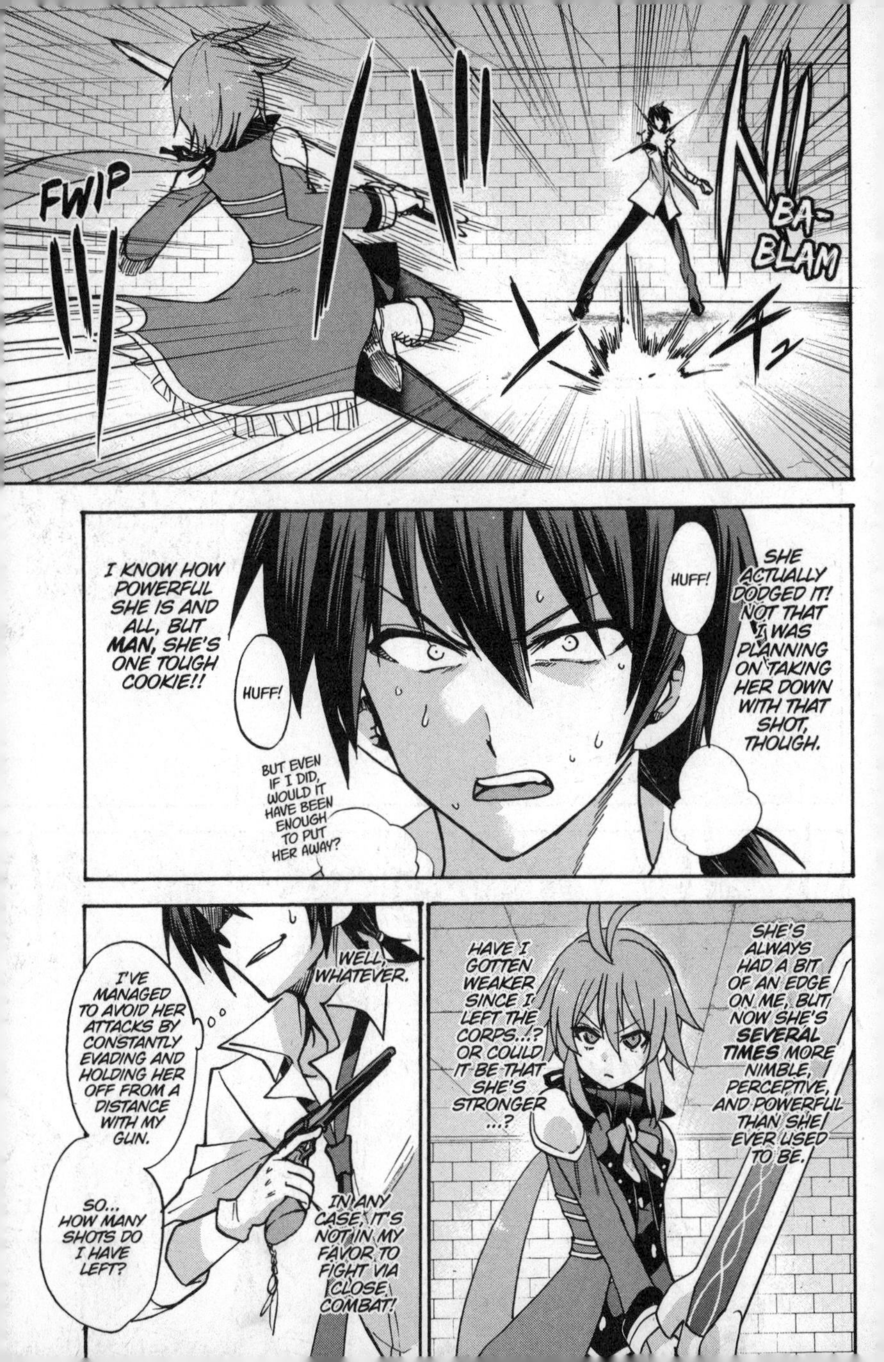
BA-BLAM
FWIP
SHE ACTUALLY DODGED IT! NOT THAT I WAS PLANNING ON TAKING HER DOWN WITH THAT SHOT, THOUGH.
HUFF!
BUT EVEN IF I DID, WOULD IT HAVE BEEN ENOUGH TO PUT HER AWAY?
HUFF!
I KNOW HOW POWERFUL SHE IS AND ALL, BUT **MAN**, SHE'S ONE TOUGH COOKIE!!
SHE'S ALWAYS HAD A BIT OF AN EDGE ON ME, BUT NOW SHE'S **SEVERAL TIMES** MORE NIMBLE, PERCEPTIVE, AND POWERFUL THAN SHE EVER USED TO BE.
HAVE I GOTTEN WEAKER SINCE I LEFT THE CORPS...? OR COULD IT BE THAT SHE'S STRONGER ...?
WELL, WHATEVER.
I'VE MANAGED TO AVOID HER ATTACKS BY CONSTANTLY EVADING AND HOLDING HER OFF FROM A DISTANCE WITH MY GUN.
IN ANY CASE, IT'S NOT IN MY FAVOR TO FIGHT VIA CLOSE COMBAT!
SO... HOW MANY SHOTS DO I HAVE LEFT?

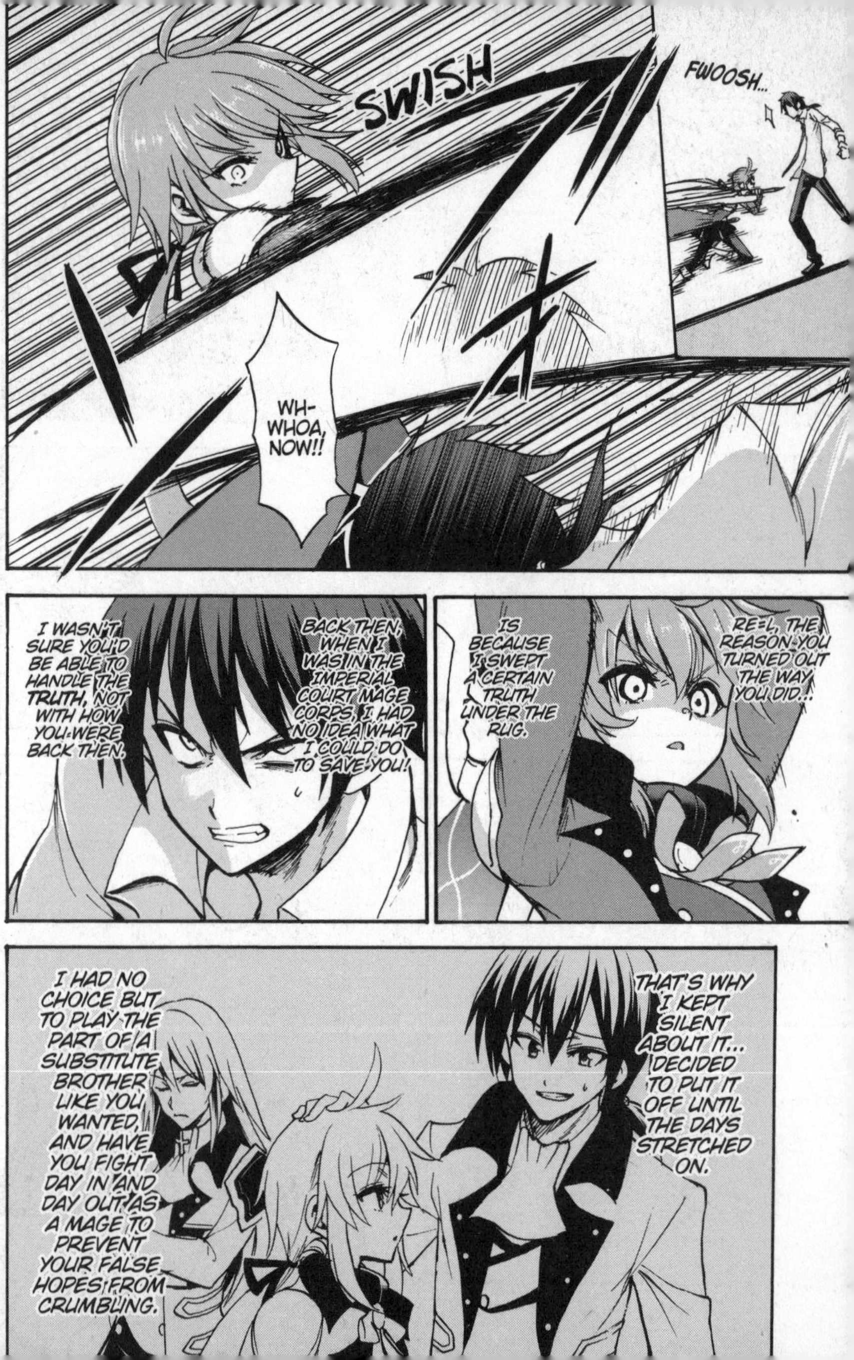
FWOOSH...
SWISH
WH- WHOA, NOW!!
RE=L, THE REASON YOU TURNED OUT THE WAY YOU DID...
IS BECAUSE I SWEPT A CERTAIN TRUTH UNDER THE RUG.
BACK THEN, WHEN I WAS IN THE IMPERIAL COURT MAGE CORPS, I HAD NO IDEA WHAT I COULD DO TO SAVE YOU!
I WASN'T SURE YOU'D BE ABLE TO HANDLE THE TRUTH, NOT WITH HOW YOU WERE BACK THEN.
THAT'S WHY I KEPT SILENT ABOUT IT... DECIDED TO PUT IT OFF UNTIL THE DAYS STRETCHED ON.
I HAD NO CHOICE BUT TO PLAY THE PART OF A SUBSTITUTE BROTHER LIKE YOU WANTED, AND HAVE YOU FIGHT DAY IN AND DAY OUT AS A MAGE TO PREVENT YOUR FALSE HOPES FROM CRUMBLING.

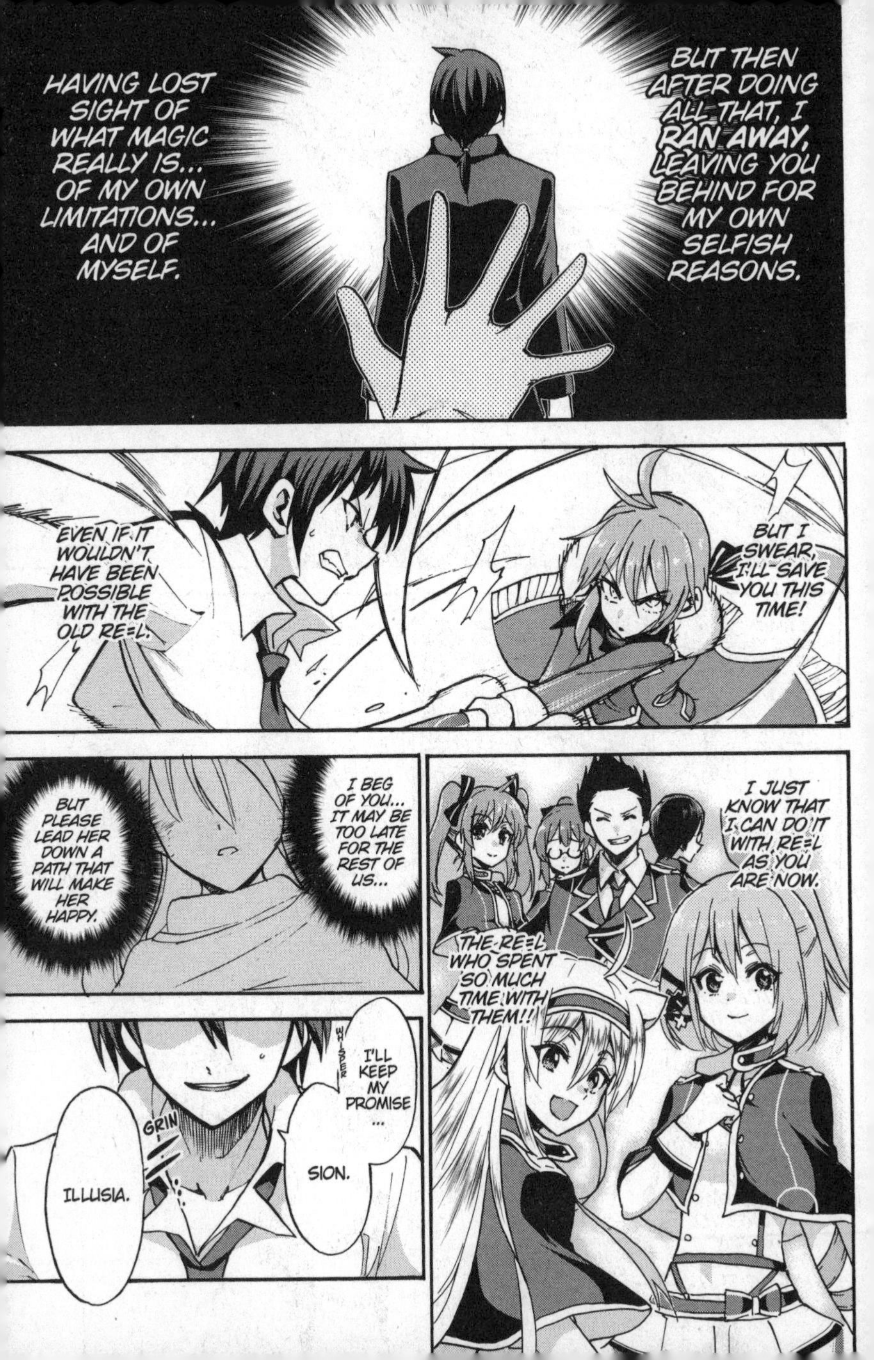
BUT THEN AFTER DOING ALL THAT, I **RAN AWAY,** LEAVING YOU BEHIND FOR MY OWN SELFISH REASONS.
HAVING LOST SIGHT OF WHAT MAGIC REALLY IS... OF MY OWN LIMITATIONS... AND OF MYSELF.
BUT I SWEAR, I'LL SAVE YOU THIS TIME!
EVEN IF IT WOULDN'T HAVE BEEN POSSIBLE WITH THE OLD RE=L.
I JUST KNOW THAT I CAN DO IT WITH RE=L AS YOU ARE NOW.
THE RE=L WHO SPENT SO MUCH TIME WITH THEM!!
I BEG OF YOU... IT MAY BE TOO LATE FOR THE REST OF US...
BUT PLEASE LEAD HER DOWN A PATH THAT WILL MAKE HER HAPPY.
WHISPER
I'LL KEEP MY PROMISE...
SION.
GRIN
ILLUSIA.

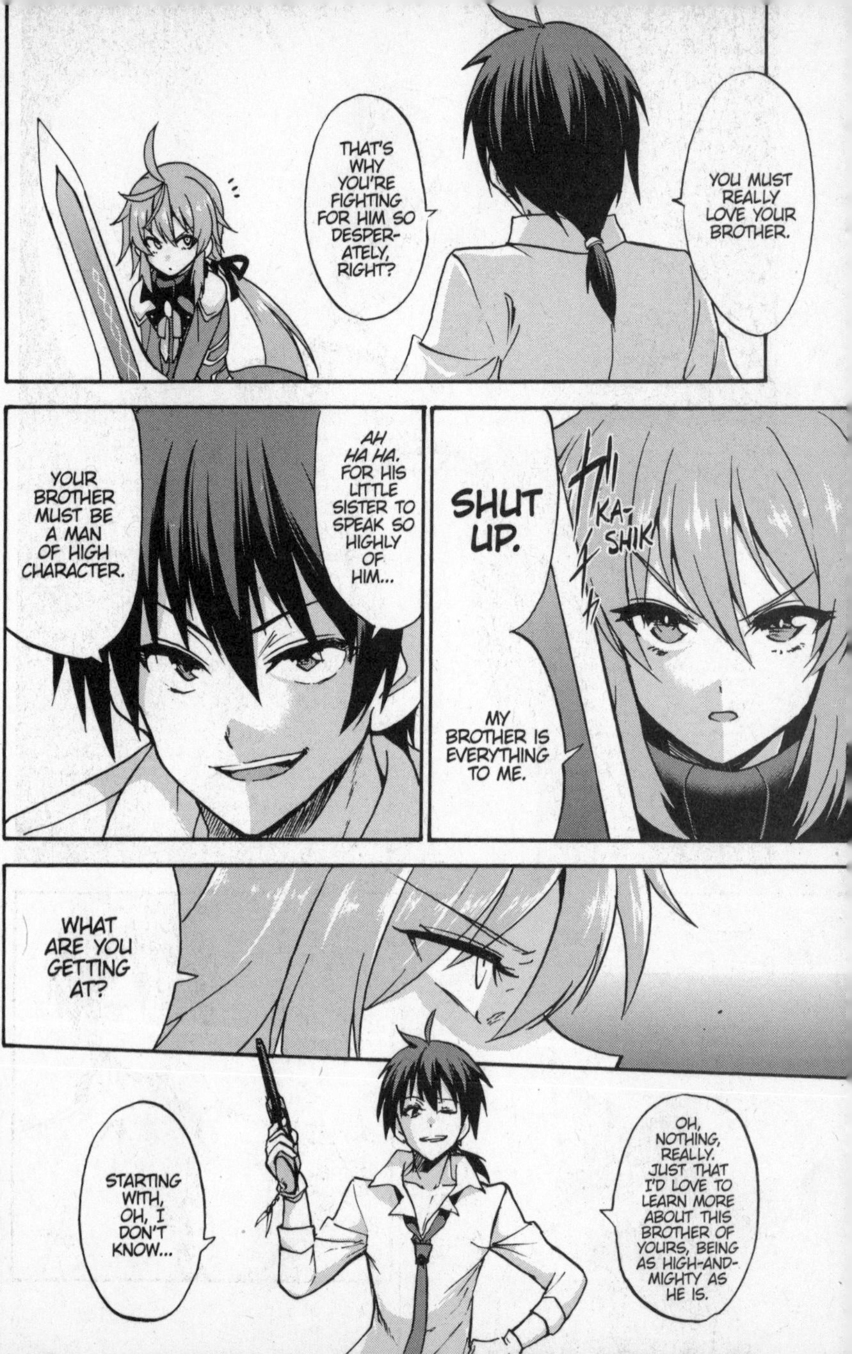
YOU MUST REALLY LOVE YOUR BROTHER.
THAT'S WHY YOU'RE FIGHTING FOR HIM SO DESPERATELY, RIGHT?
KA-SHIK
SHUT UP.
MY BROTHER IS EVERYTHING TO ME.
AH HA HA. FOR HIS LITTLE SISTER TO SPEAK SO HIGHLY OF HIM...
YOUR BROTHER MUST BE A MAN OF HIGH CHARACTER.
WHAT ARE YOU GETTING AT?
OH, NOTHING, REALLY. JUST THAT I'D LOVE TO LEARN MORE ABOUT THIS BROTHER OF YOURS, BEING AS HIGH-AND-MIGHTY AS HE IS.
STARTING WITH, OH, I DON'T KNOW...

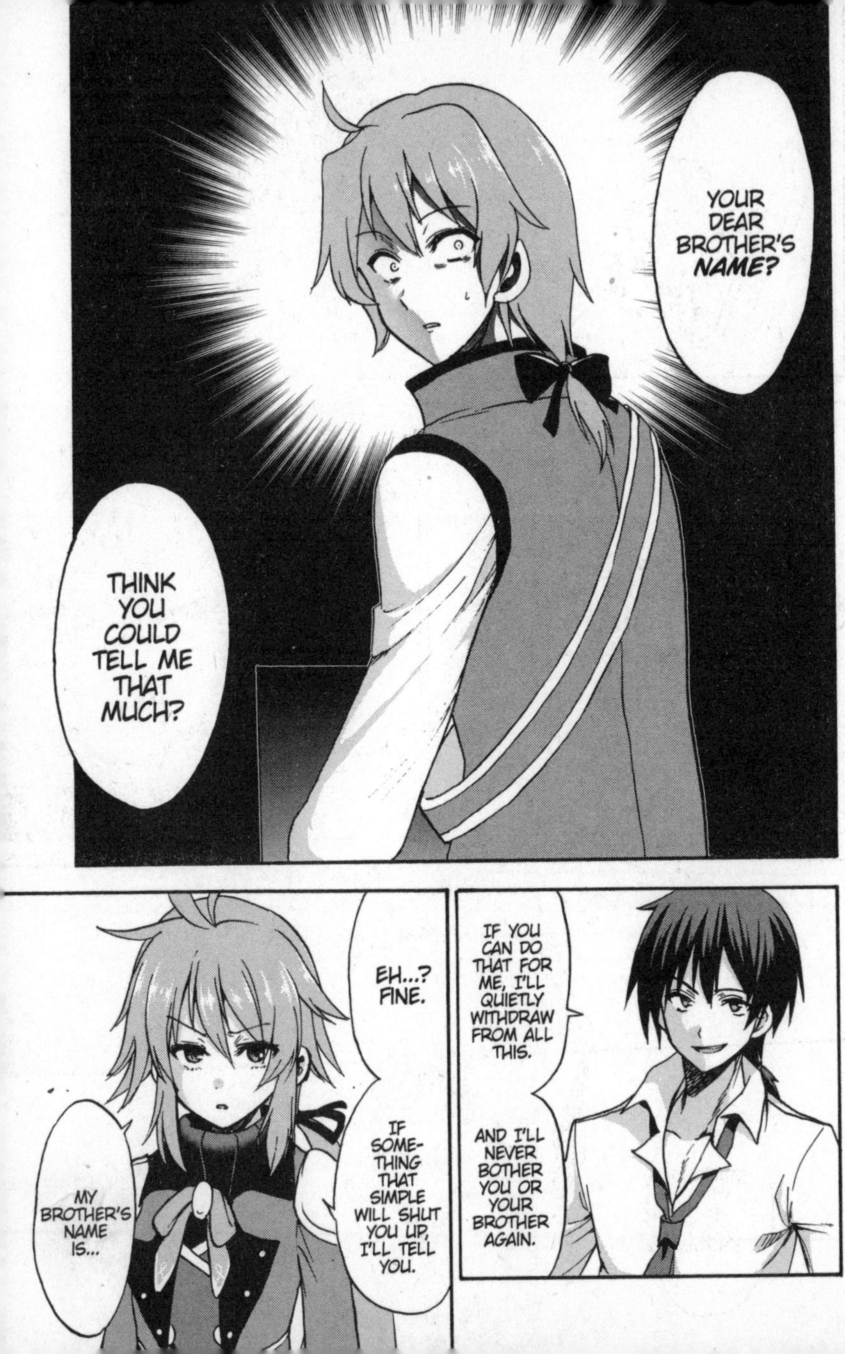
YOUR DEAR BROTHER'S *NAME?*
THINK YOU COULD TELL ME THAT MUCH?
IF YOU CAN DO THAT FOR ME, I'LL QUIETLY WITHDRAW FROM ALL THIS.
AND I'LL NEVER BOTHER YOU OR YOUR BROTHER AGAIN.
EH...? FINE.
IF SOME-THING THAT SIMPLE WILL SHUT YOU UP, I'LL TELL YOU.
MY BROTHER'S NAME IS...

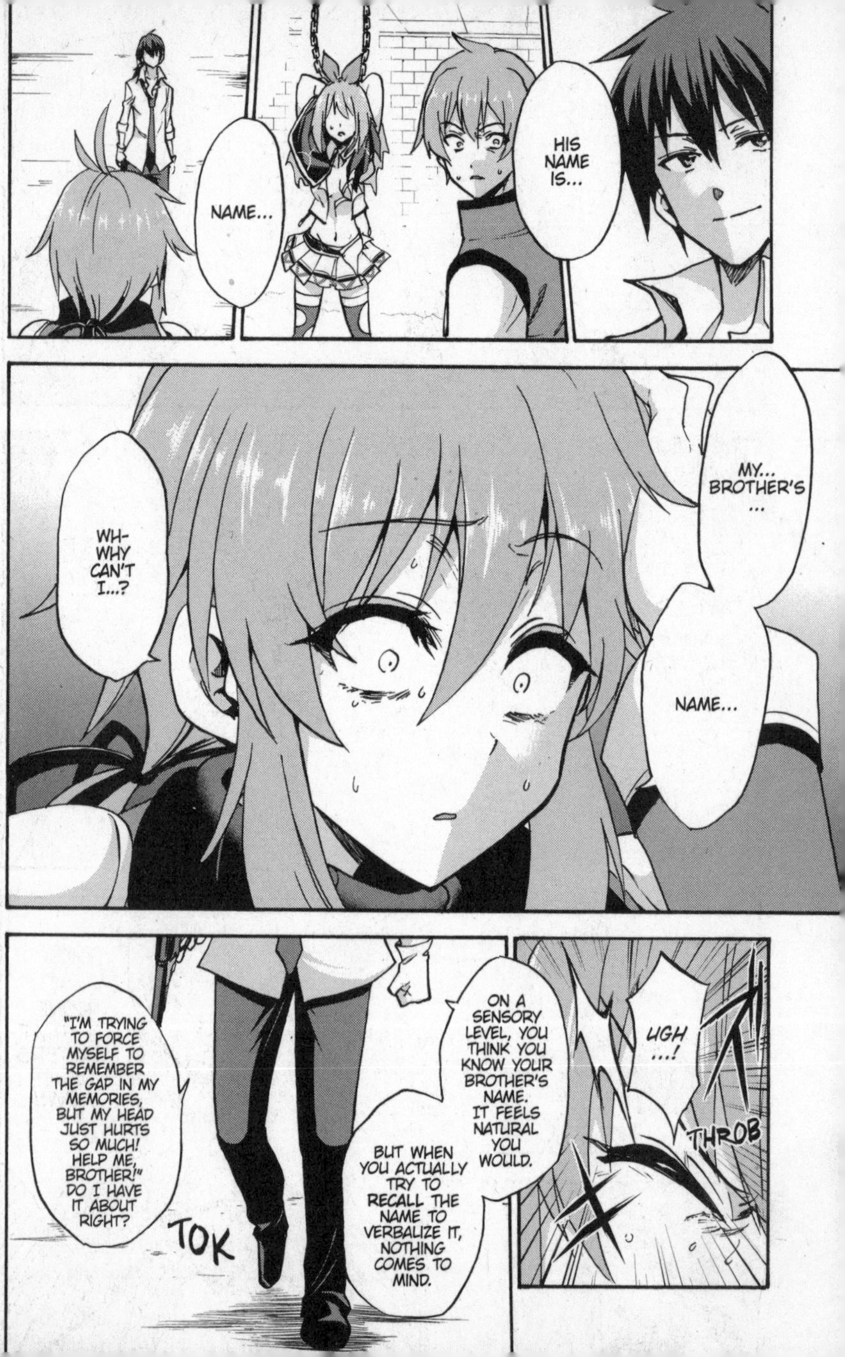
HIS NAME IS...
NAME...
MY... BROTHER'S ...
NAME...
WH- WHY CAN'T I...?
UGH ...!
THROB
ON A SENSORY LEVEL, YOU THINK YOU KNOW YOUR BROTHER'S NAME. IT FEELS NATURAL YOU WOULD.
BUT WHEN YOU ACTUALLY TRY TO RECALL THE NAME TO VERBALIZE IT, NOTHING COMES TO MIND.
"I'M TRYING TO FORCE MYSELF TO REMEMBER THE GAP IN MY MEMORIES, BUT MY HEAD JUST HURTS SO MUCH! HELP ME, BROTHER!" DO I HAVE IT ABOUT RIGHT?
TOK

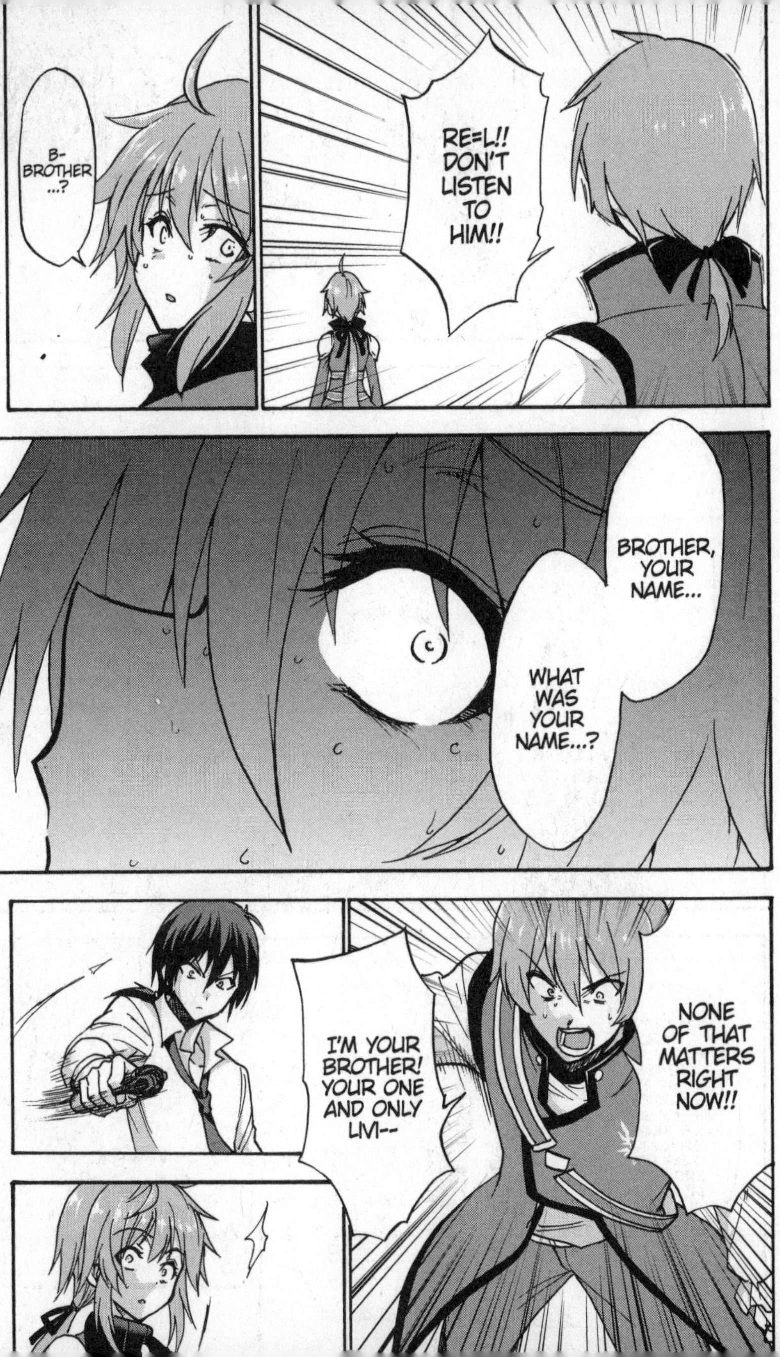
RE=L!! DON'T LISTEN TO HIM!!
B-BROTHER ...?
BROTHER, YOUR NAME...
WHAT WAS YOUR NAME...?
NONE OF THAT MATTERS RIGHT NOW!!
I'M YOUR BROTHER! YOUR ONE AND ONLY LIVI--

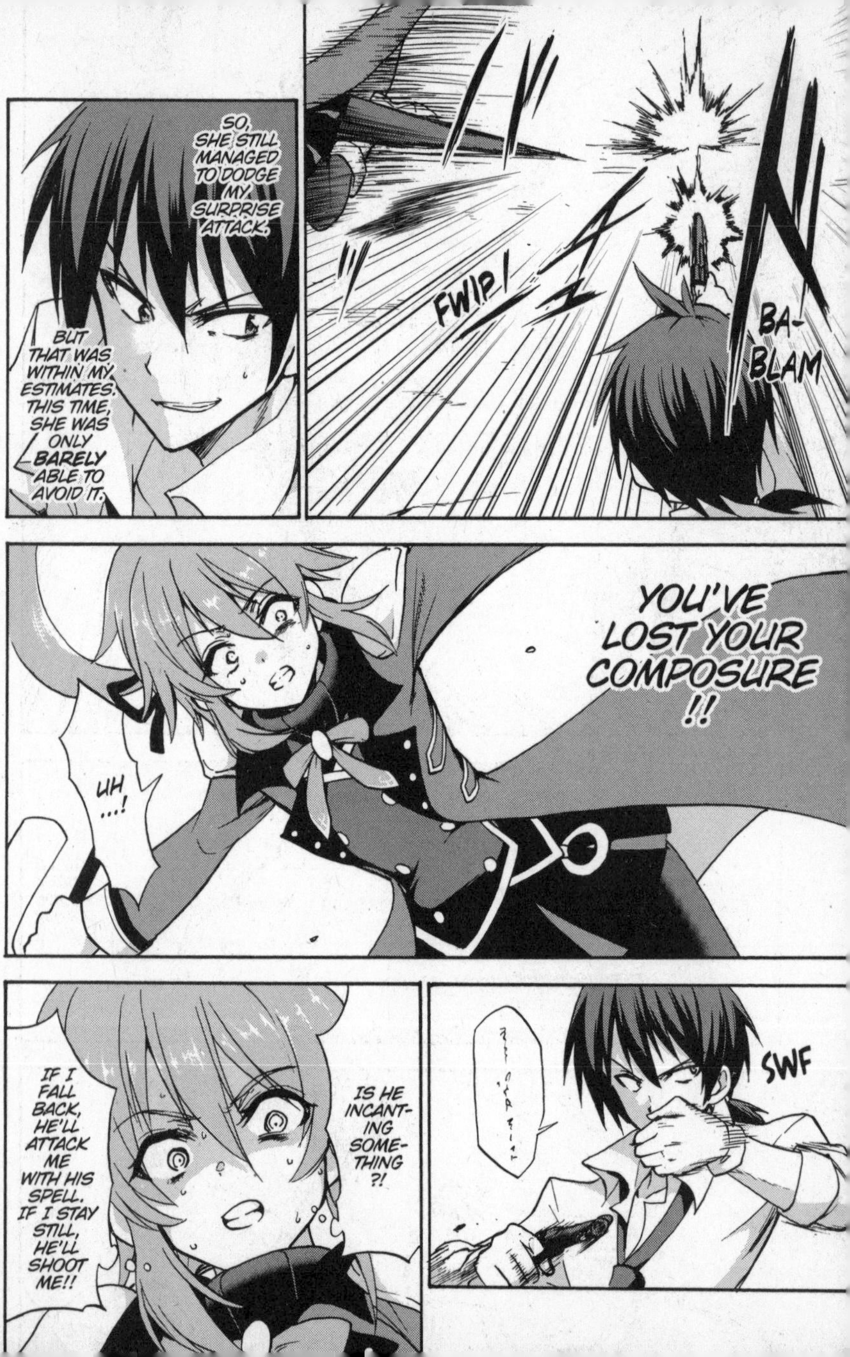
FWIP!
BA-BLAM
SO, SHE STILL MANAGED TO DODGE MY SURPRISE ATTACK.
BUT THAT WAS WITHIN MY ESTIMATES. THIS TIME, SHE WAS ONLY BARELY ABLE TO AVOID IT.
YOU'VE LOST YOUR COMPOSURE!!
UH...!
SWF
IS HE INCANTING SOMETHING?!
IF I FALL BACK, HE'LL ATTACK ME WITH HIS SPELL. IF I STAY STILL, HE'LL SHOOT ME!!

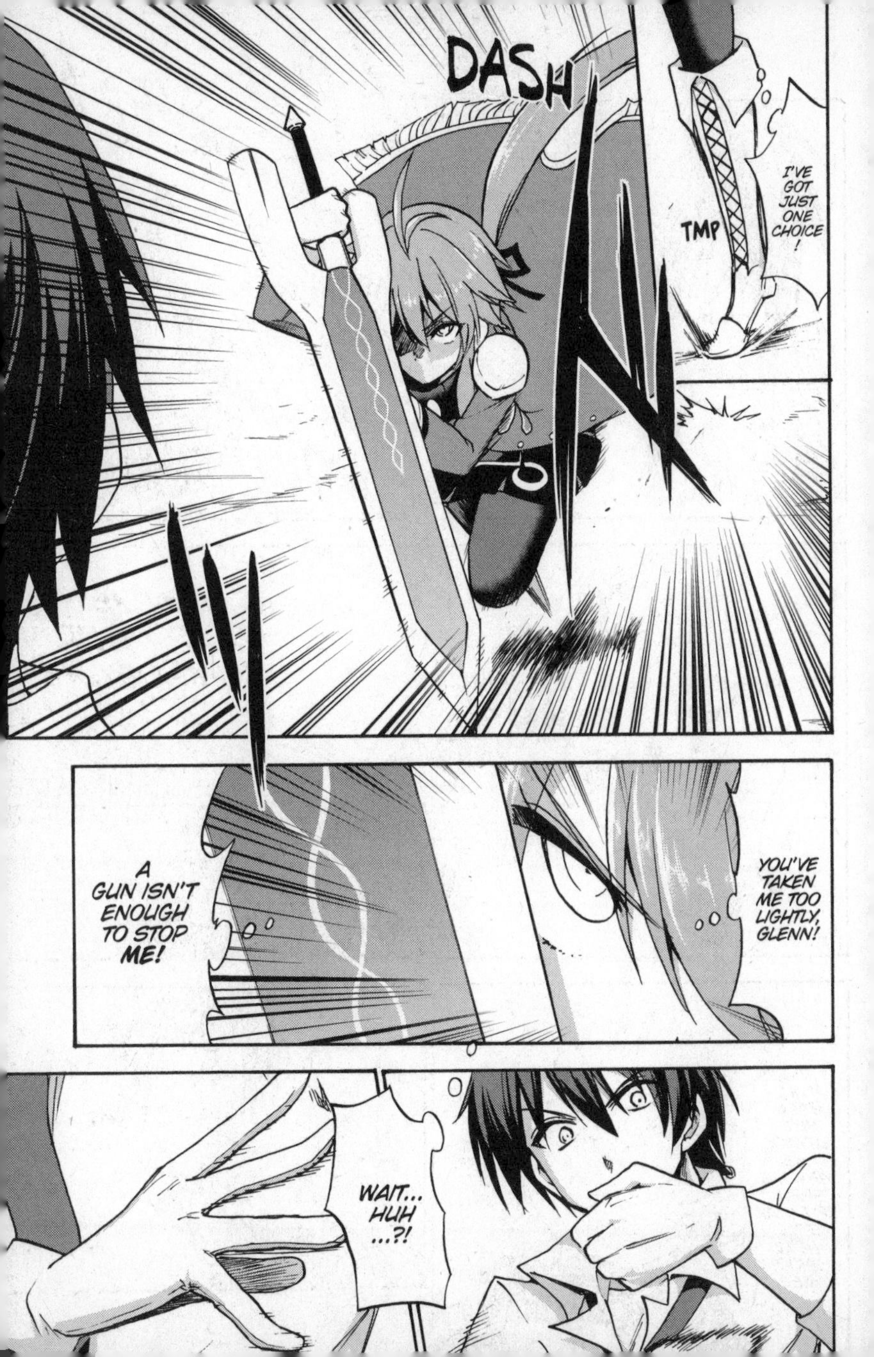
I'VE GOT JUST ONE CHOICE!
DASH
TMP
YOU'VE TAKEN ME TOO LIGHTLY, GLENN!
A GUN ISN'T ENOUGH TO STOP ME!
WAIT... HUH ...?!

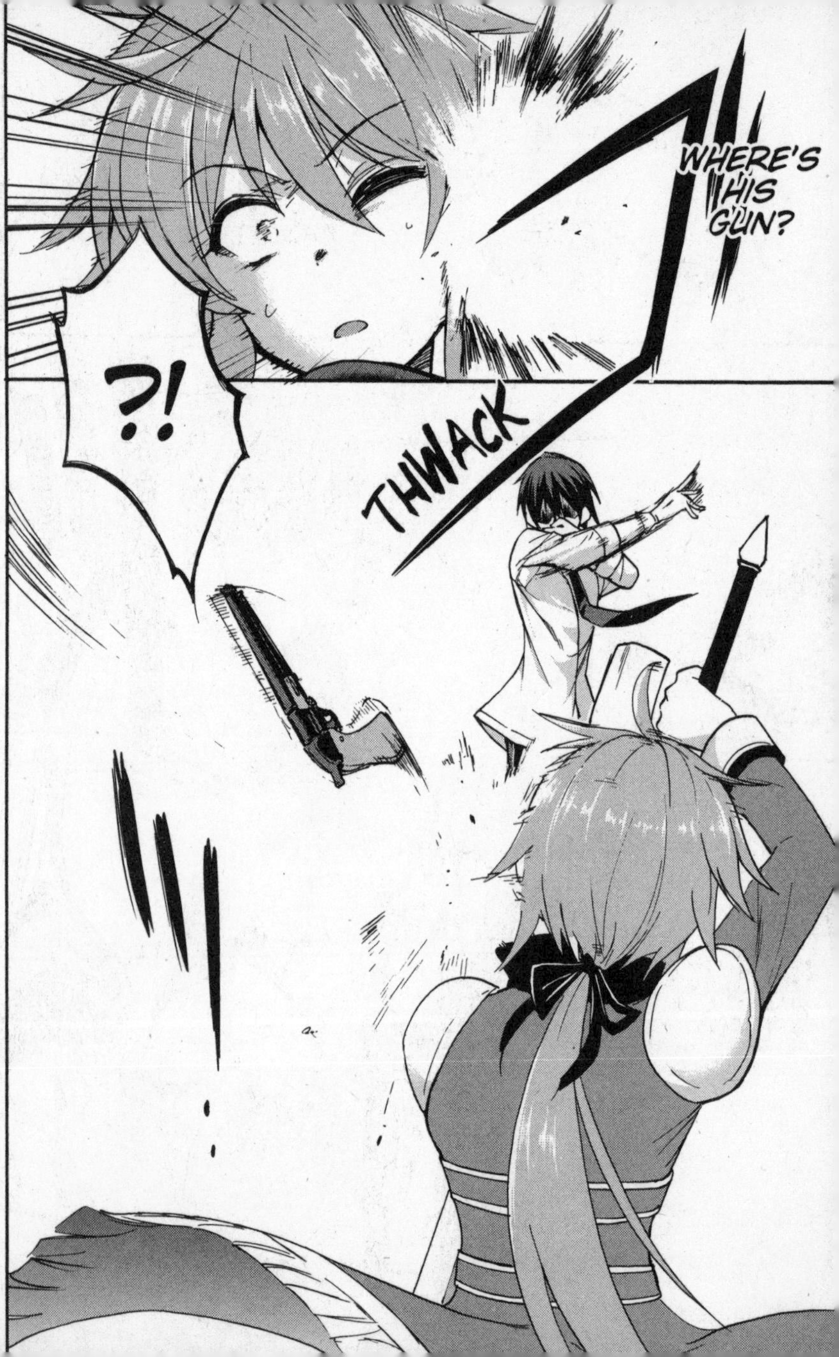
WHERE'S HIS GUN?
?!
THWACK

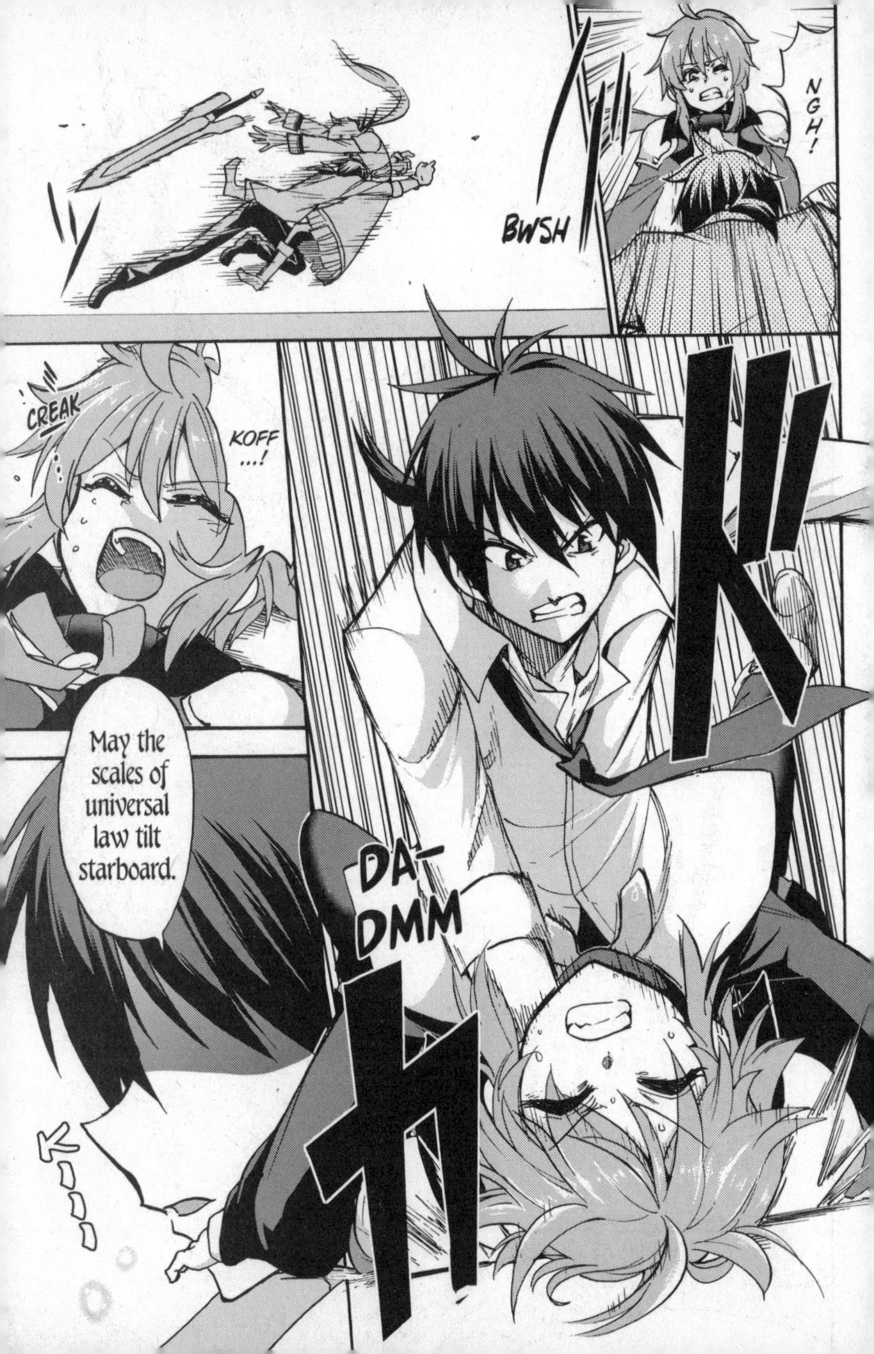
NGH!
BWSH
DA-DMM
CREAK
KOFF ...!
May the scales of universal law tilt starboard.

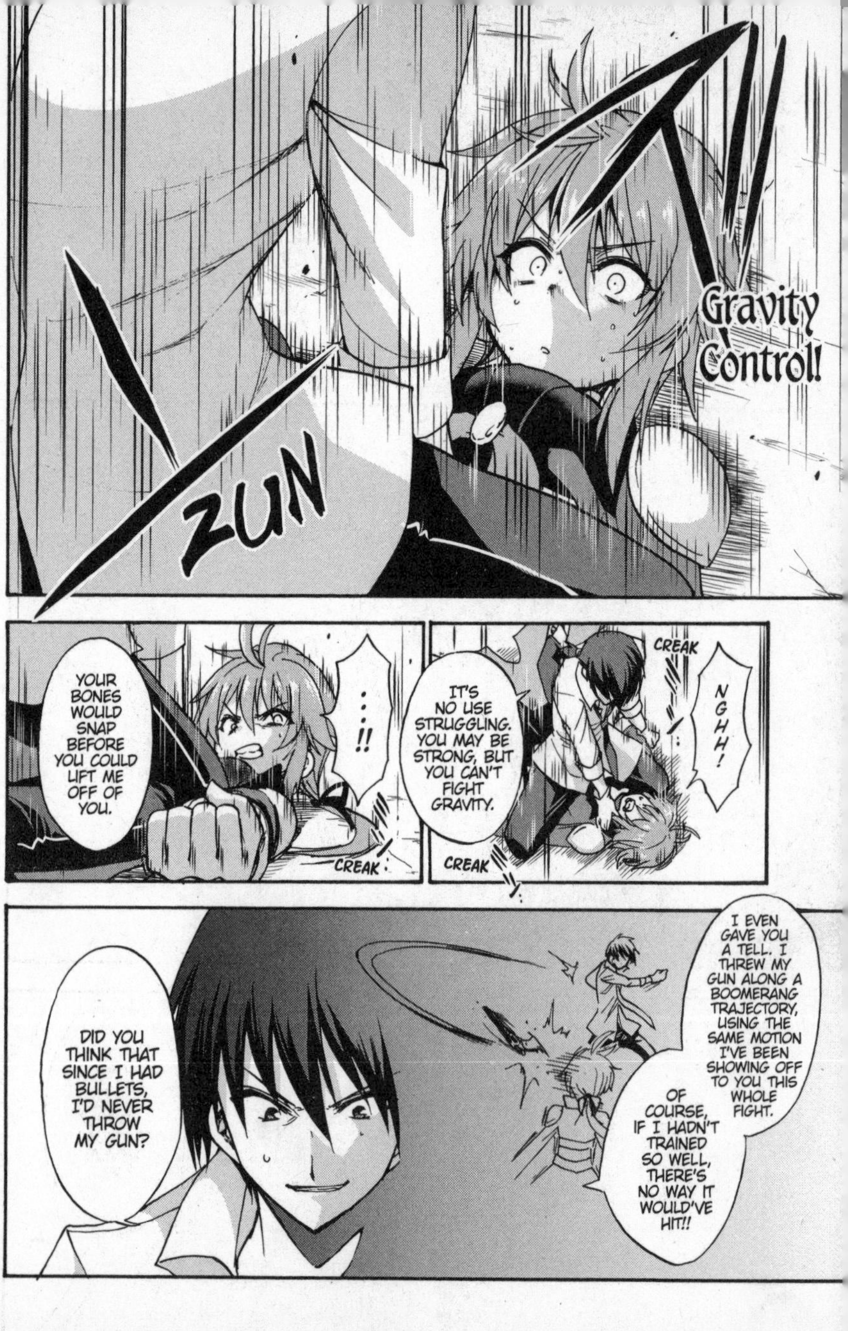
Gravity Control!
ZUN
CREAK
NGHH!
IT'S NO USE STRUGGLING. YOU MAY BE STRONG, BUT YOU CAN'T FIGHT GRAVITY.
CREAK
...!!
YOUR BONES WOULD SNAP BEFORE YOU COULD LIFT ME OFF OF YOU.
CREAK
I EVEN GAVE YOU A TELL. I THREW MY GUN ALONG A BOOMERANG TRAJECTORY, USING THE SAME MOTION I'VE BEEN SHOWING OFF TO YOU THIS WHOLE FIGHT.
OF COURSE, IF I HADN'T TRAINED SO WELL, THERE'S NO WAY IT WOULD'VE HIT!!
DID YOU THINK THAT SINCE I HAD BULLETS, I'D NEVER THROW MY GUN?

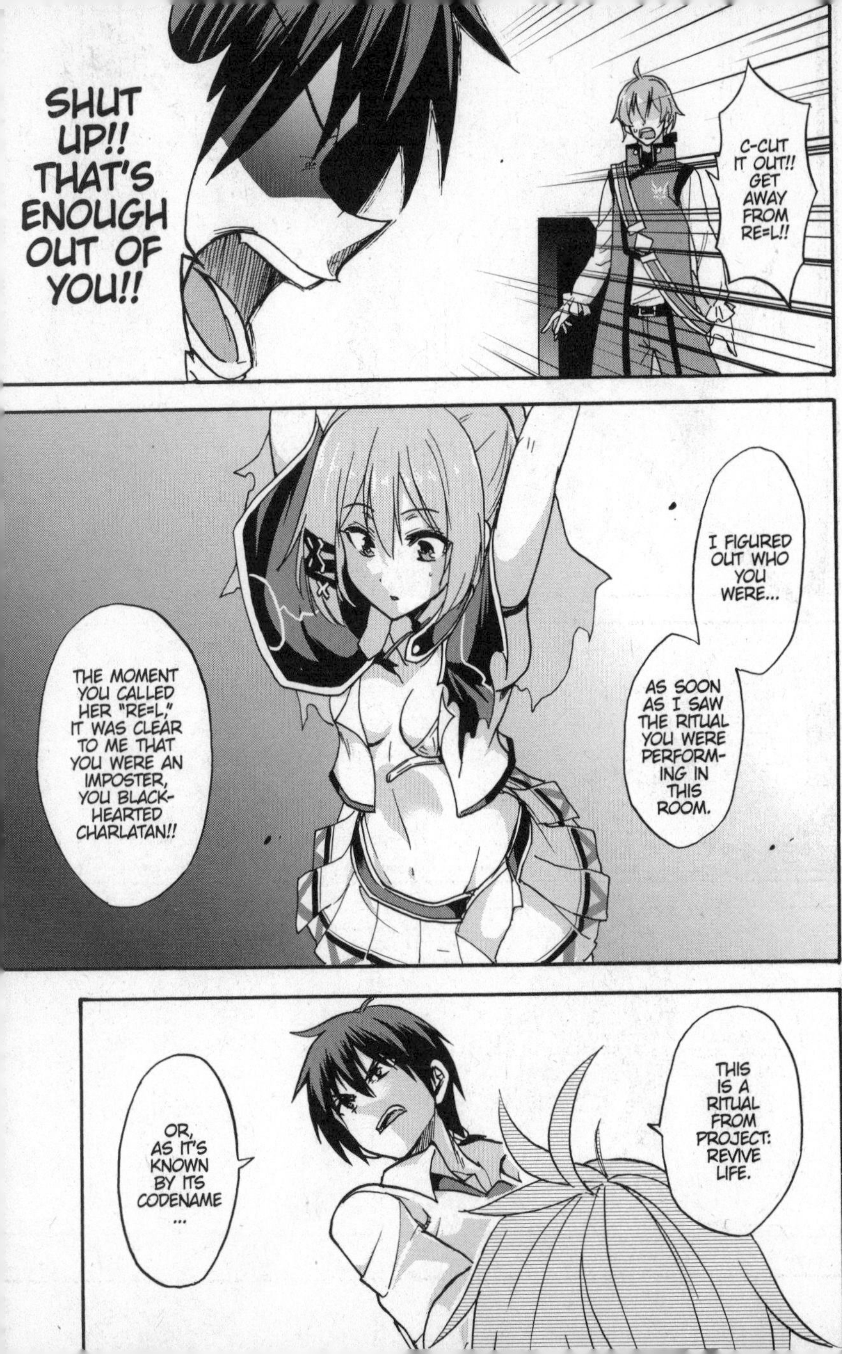
C-CUT IT OUT!! GET AWAY FROM RE=L!!
SHUT UP!! THAT'S ENOUGH OUT OF YOU!!
I FIGURED OUT WHO YOU WERE...
AS SOON AS I SAW THE RITUAL YOU WERE PERFORMING IN THIS ROOM.
THE MOMENT YOU CALLED HER "RE=L," IT WAS CLEAR TO ME THAT YOU WERE AN IMPOSTER, YOU BLACK-HEARTED CHARLATAN!!
THIS IS A RITUAL FROM PROJECT: REVIVE LIFE.
OR, AS IT'S KNOWN BY ITS CODENAME ...

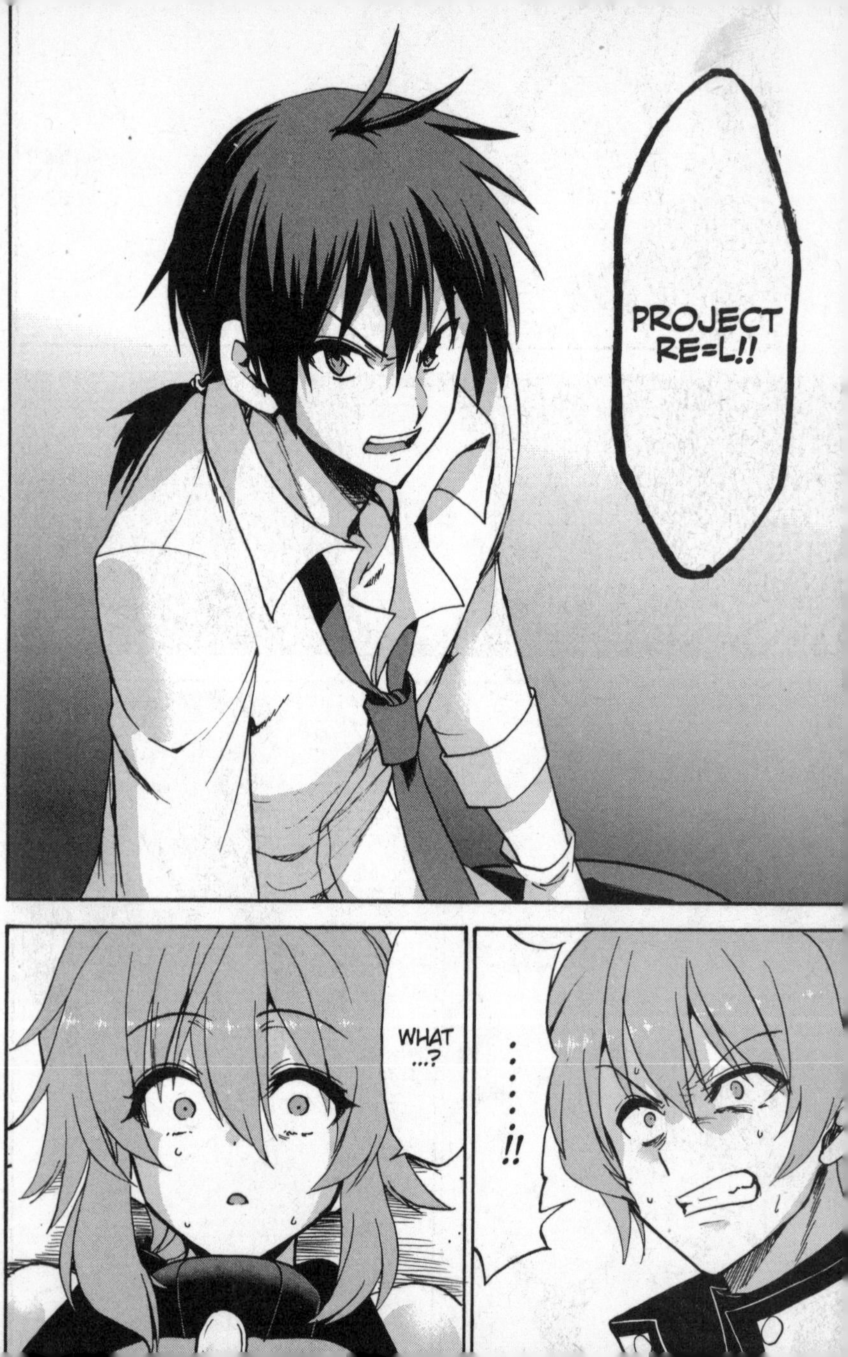
PROJECT RE=L!!
......!!
WHAT ...?

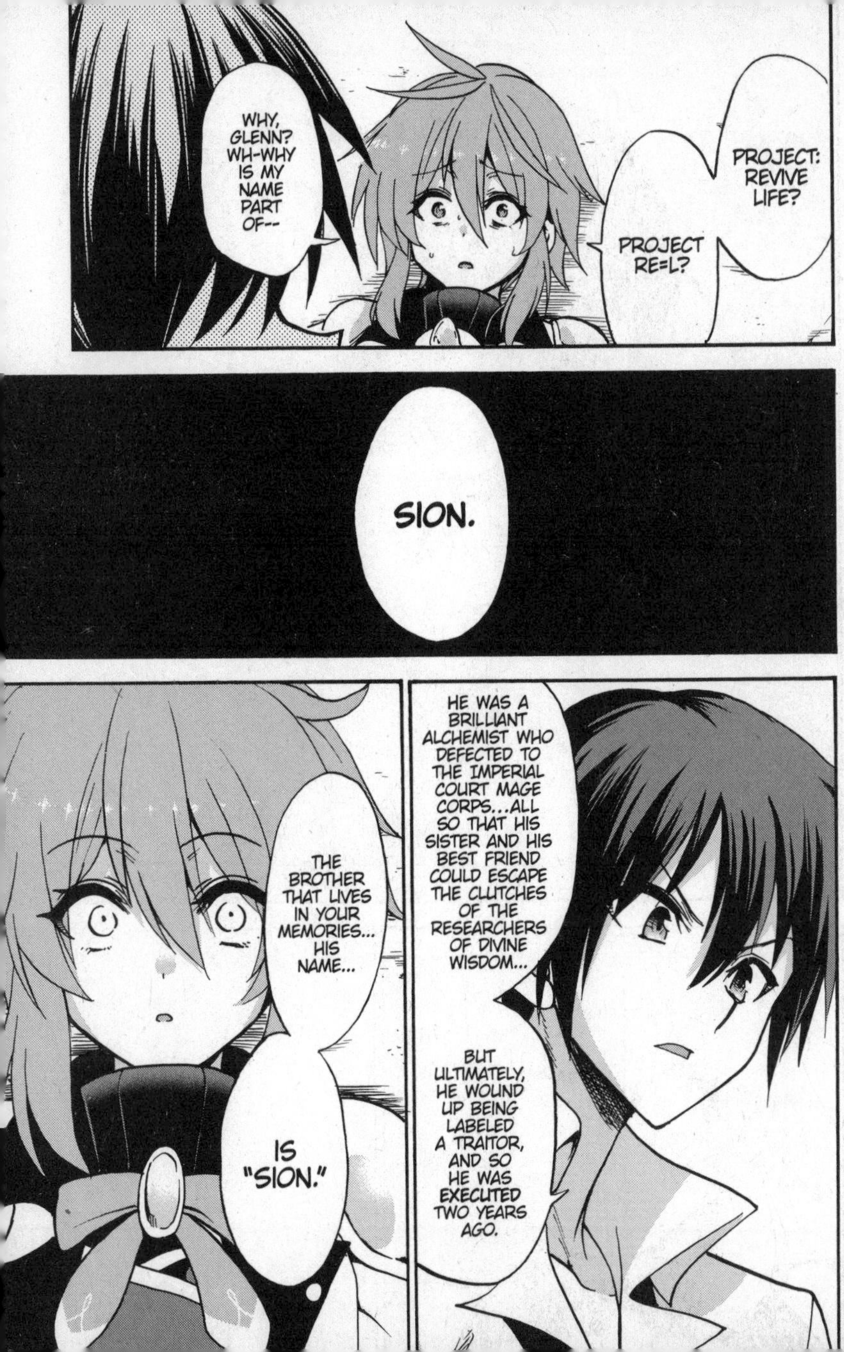
PROJECT: REVIVE LIFE?
PROJECT RE=L?
WHY, GLENN? WH-WHY IS MY NAME PART OF--
SION.
HE WAS A BRILLIANT ALCHEMIST WHO DEFECTED TO THE IMPERIAL COURT MAGE CORPS...ALL SO THAT HIS SISTER AND HIS BEST FRIEND COULD ESCAPE THE CLUTCHES OF THE RESEARCHERS OF DIVINE WISDOM...
BUT ULTIMATELY, HE WOUND UP BEING LABELED A TRAITOR, AND SO HE WAS EXECUTED TWO YEARS AGO.
THE BROTHER THAT LIVES IN YOUR MEMORIES... HIS NAME...
IS "SION."

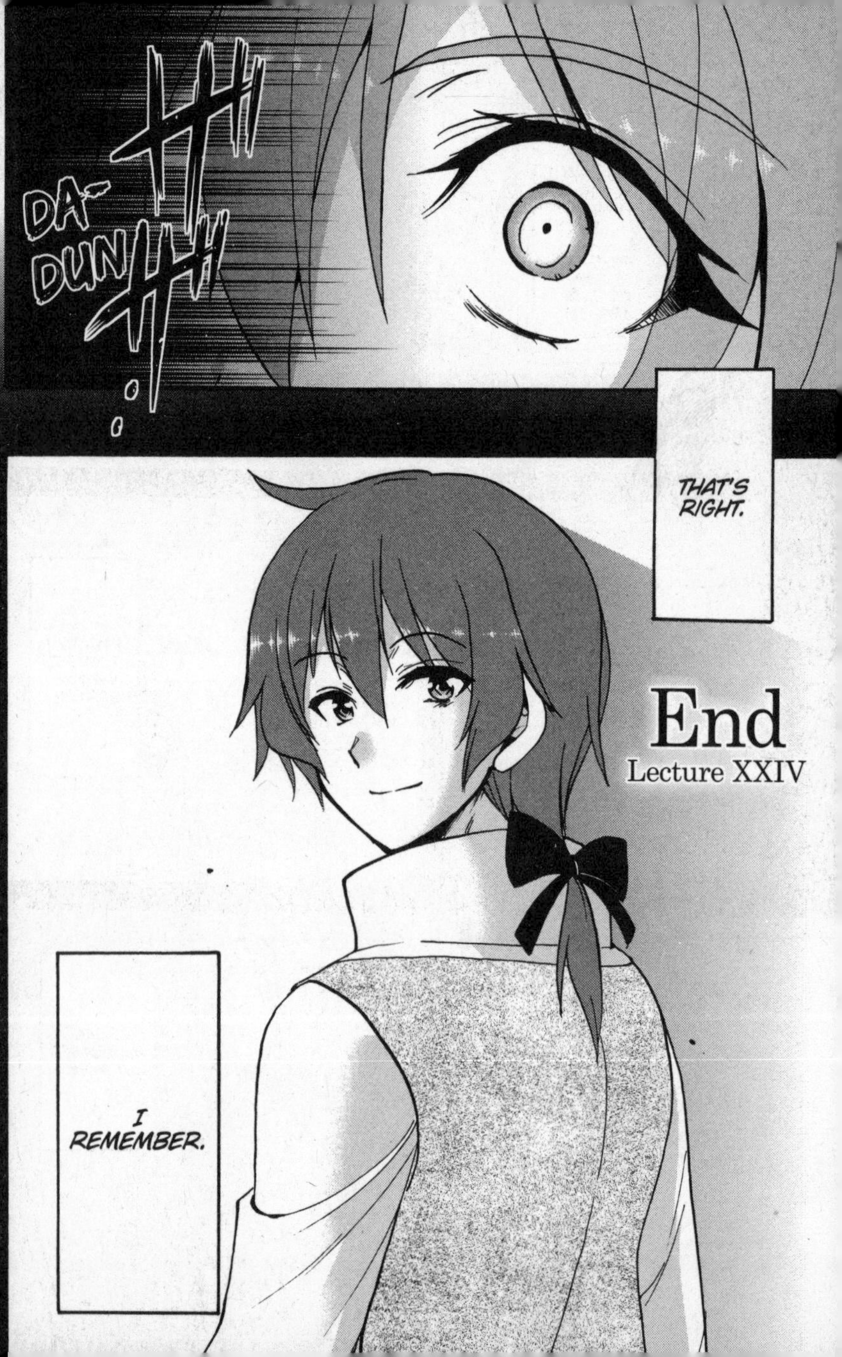
DA-DUN
THAT'S RIGHT.
End
Lecture XXIV
I REMEMBER.

Lecture XXV

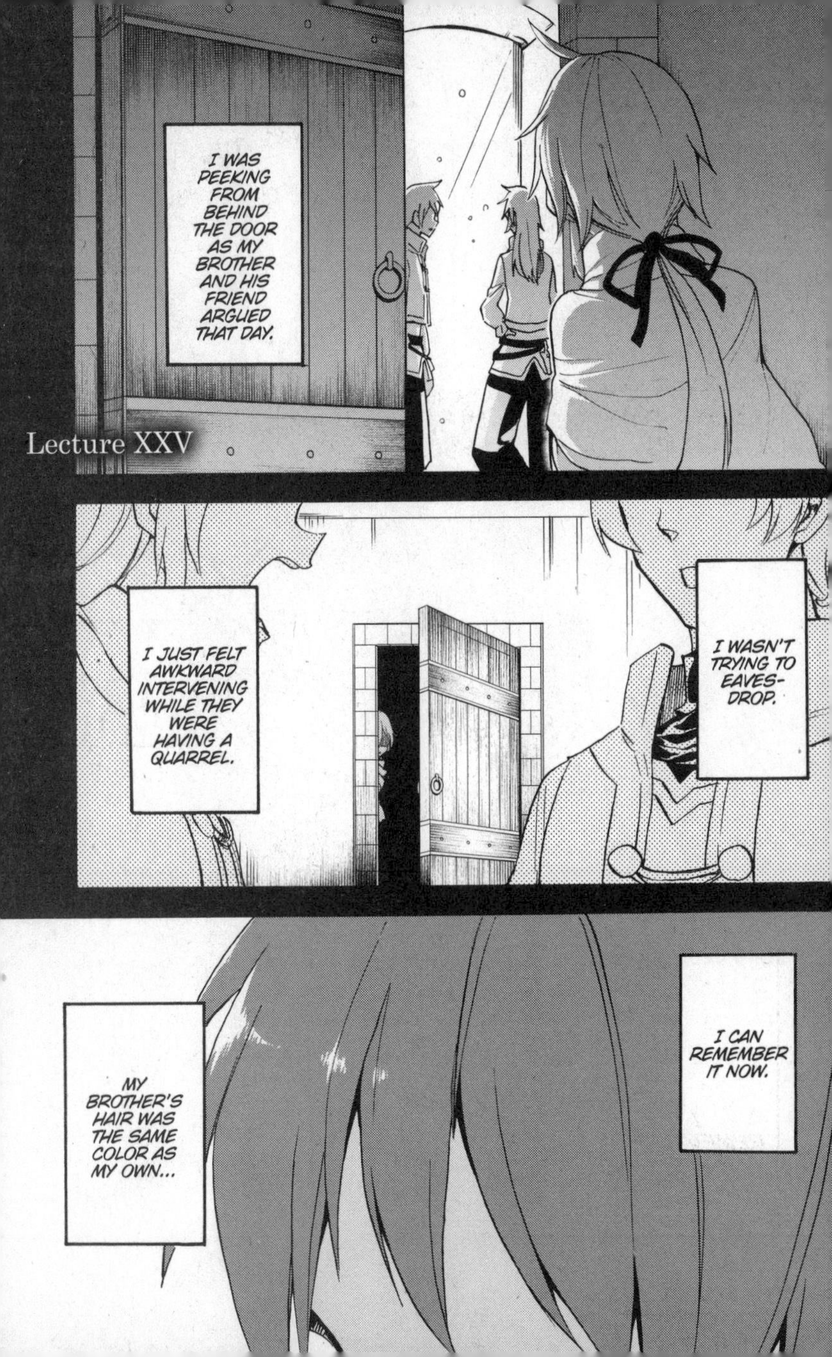
I WAS PEEKING FROM BEHIND THE DOOR AS MY BROTHER AND HIS FRIEND ARGUED THAT DAY.
I WASN'T TRYING TO EAVES-DROP.
I JUST FELT AWKWARD INTERVENING WHILE THEY WERE HAVING A QUARREL.
I CAN REMEMBER IT NOW.
MY BROTHER'S HAIR WAS THE SAME COLOR AS MY OWN...

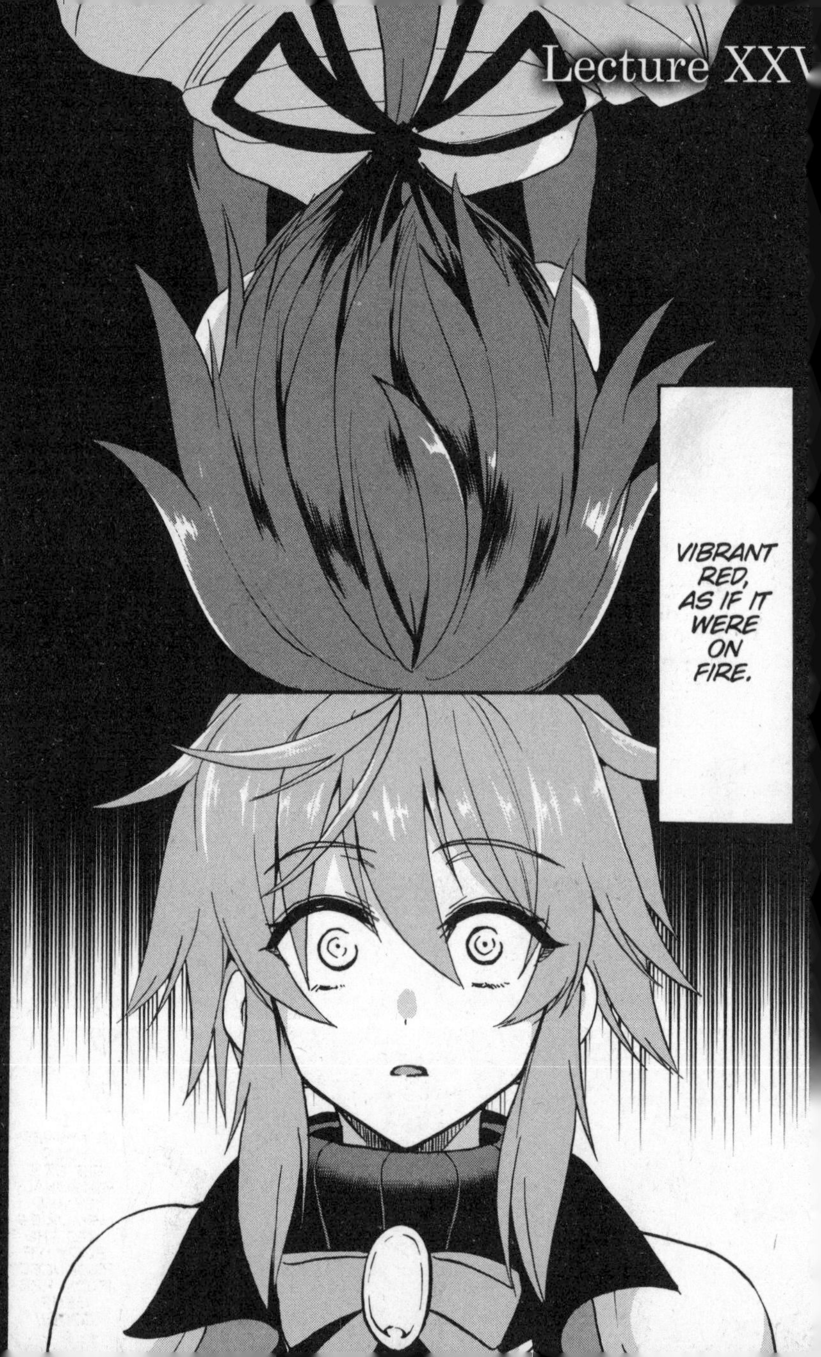
Lecture XXV
VIBRANT RED, AS IF IT WERE ON FIRE.

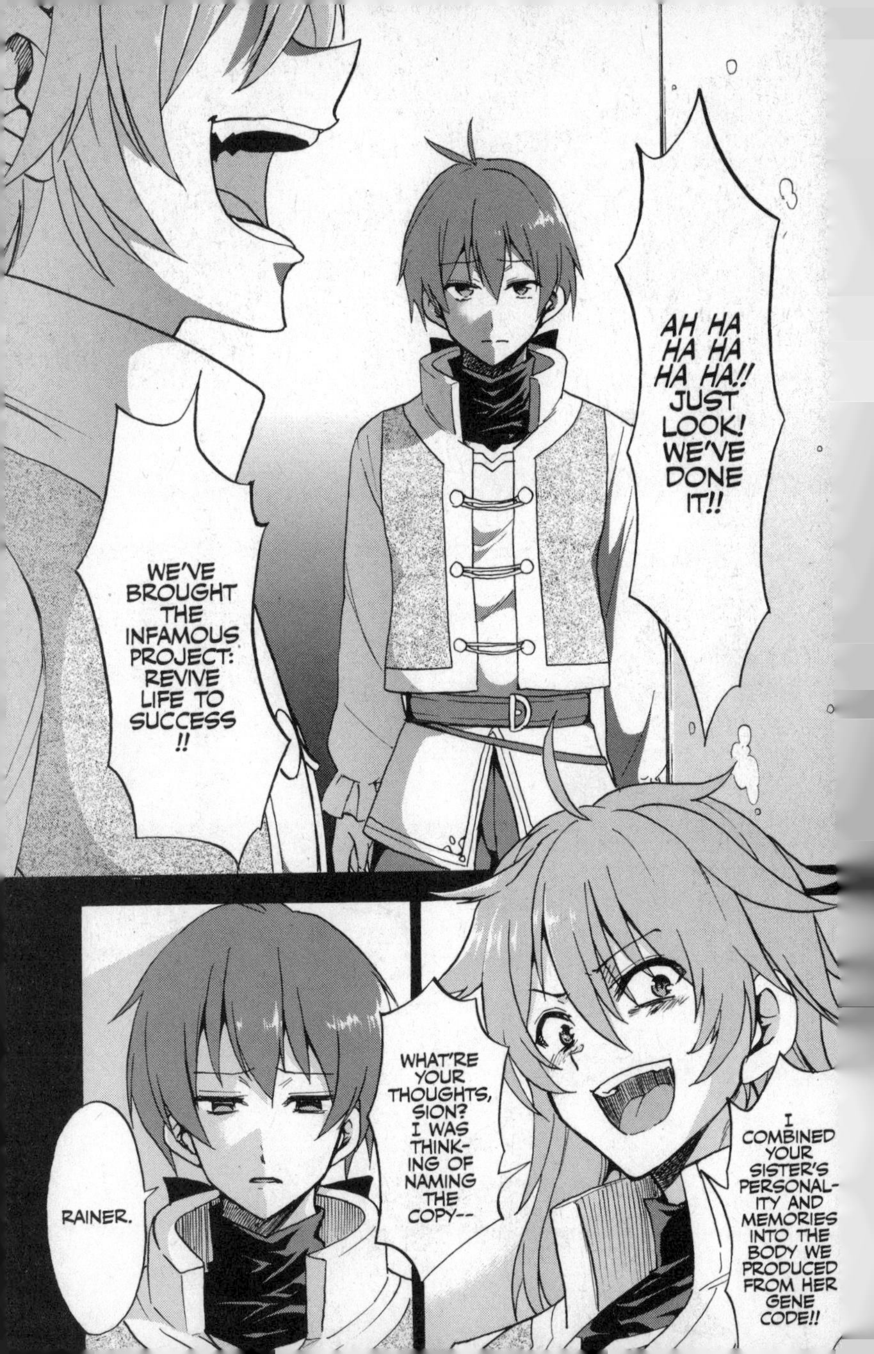
AH HA HA HA HA HA!! JUST LOOK! WE'VE DONE IT!!
WE'VE BROUGHT THE INFAMOUS PROJECT: REVIVE LIFE TO SUCCESS!!
I COMBINED YOUR SISTER'S PERSONALITY AND MEMORIES INTO THE BODY WE PRODUCED FROM HER GENE CODE!!
WHAT'RE YOUR THOUGHTS, SION? I WAS THINKING OF NAMING THE COPY--
RAINER.

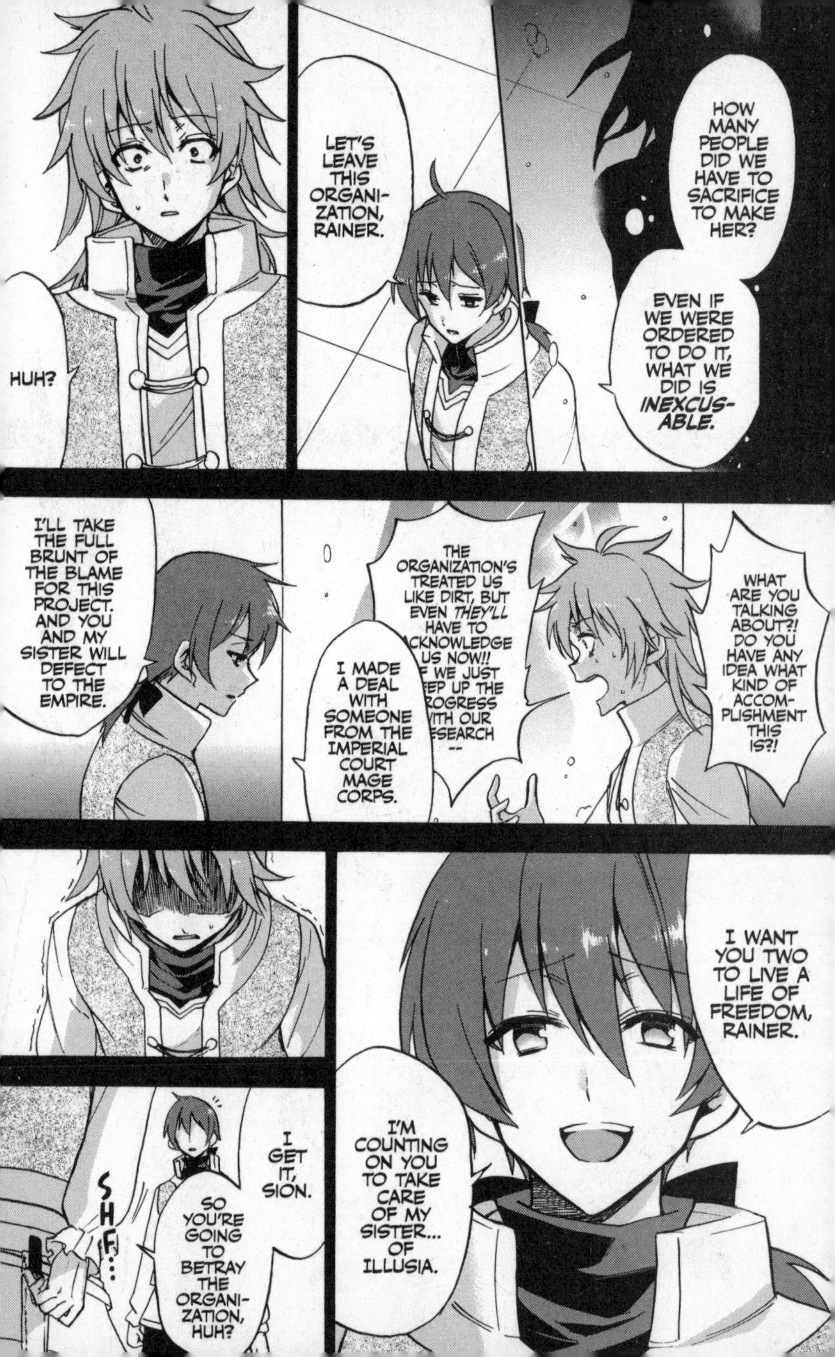
HOW MANY PEOPLE DID WE HAVE TO SACRIFICE TO MAKE HER?
EVEN IF WE WERE ORDERED TO DO IT, WHAT WE DID IS *INEXCUSABLE.*
LET'S LEAVE THIS ORGANIZATION, RAINER.
HUH?
WHAT ARE YOU TALKING ABOUT?! DO YOU HAVE ANY IDEA WHAT KIND OF ACCOMPLISHMENT THIS IS?!
THE ORGANIZATION'S TREATED US LIKE DIRT, BUT EVEN *THEY'LL* HAVE TO CKNOWLEDGE US NOW!! F WE JUST EEP UP THE ROGRESS ITH OUR ESEARCH --
I MADE A DEAL WITH SOMEONE FROM THE IMPERIAL COURT MAGE CORPS.
I'LL TAKE THE FULL BRUNT OF THE BLAME FOR THIS PROJECT. AND YOU AND MY SISTER WILL DEFECT TO THE EMPIRE.
I WANT YOU TWO TO LIVE A LIFE OF FREEDOM, RAINER.
I'M COUNTING ON YOU TO TAKE CARE OF MY SISTER... OF ILLUSIA.
I GET IT, SION.
SO YOU'RE GOING TO BETRAY THE ORGANIZATION, HUH?
SHF...

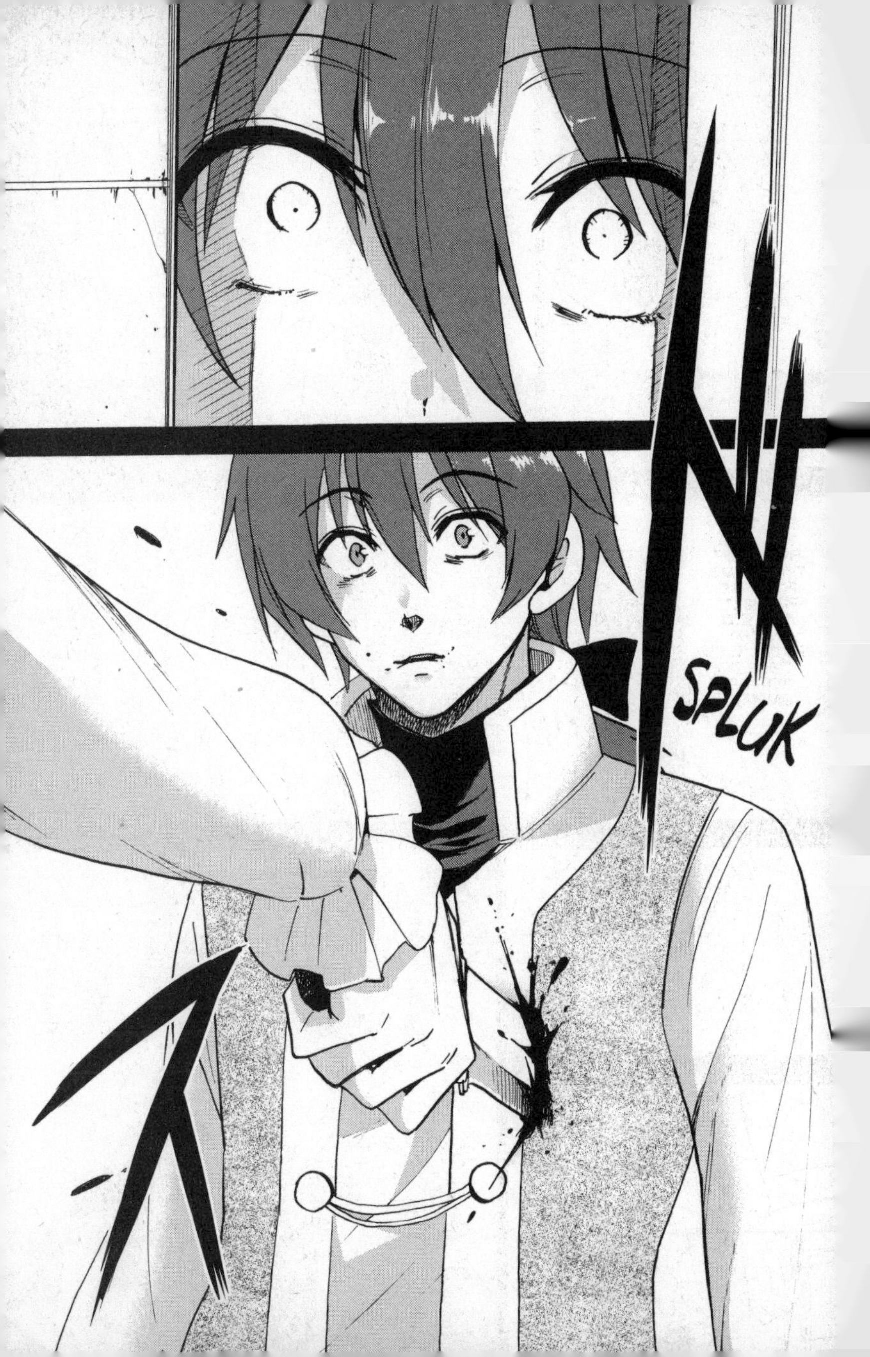
SPLUK

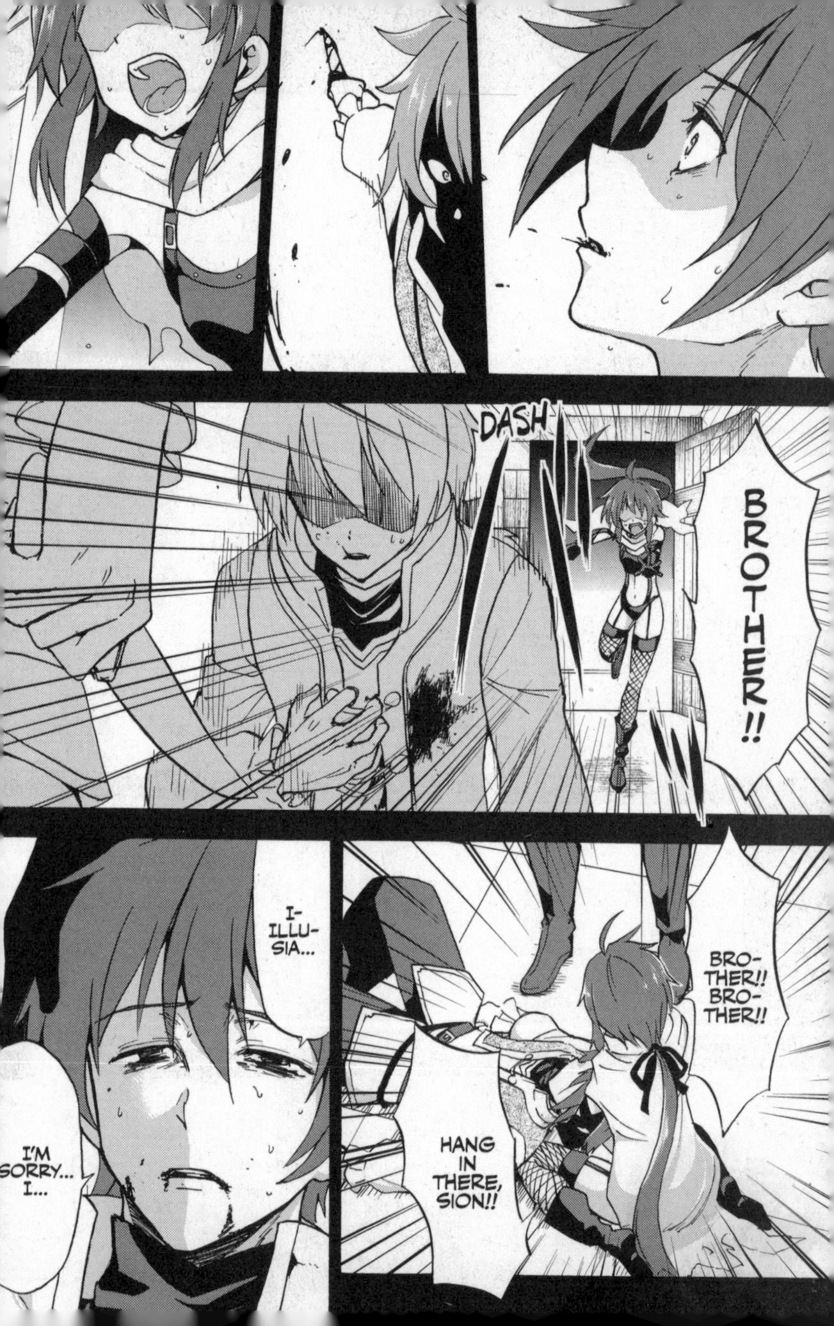
BROTHER!!
DASH
BROTHER!! BROTHER!!
HANG IN THERE, SION!!
I-ILLUSIA...
I'M SORRY... I...

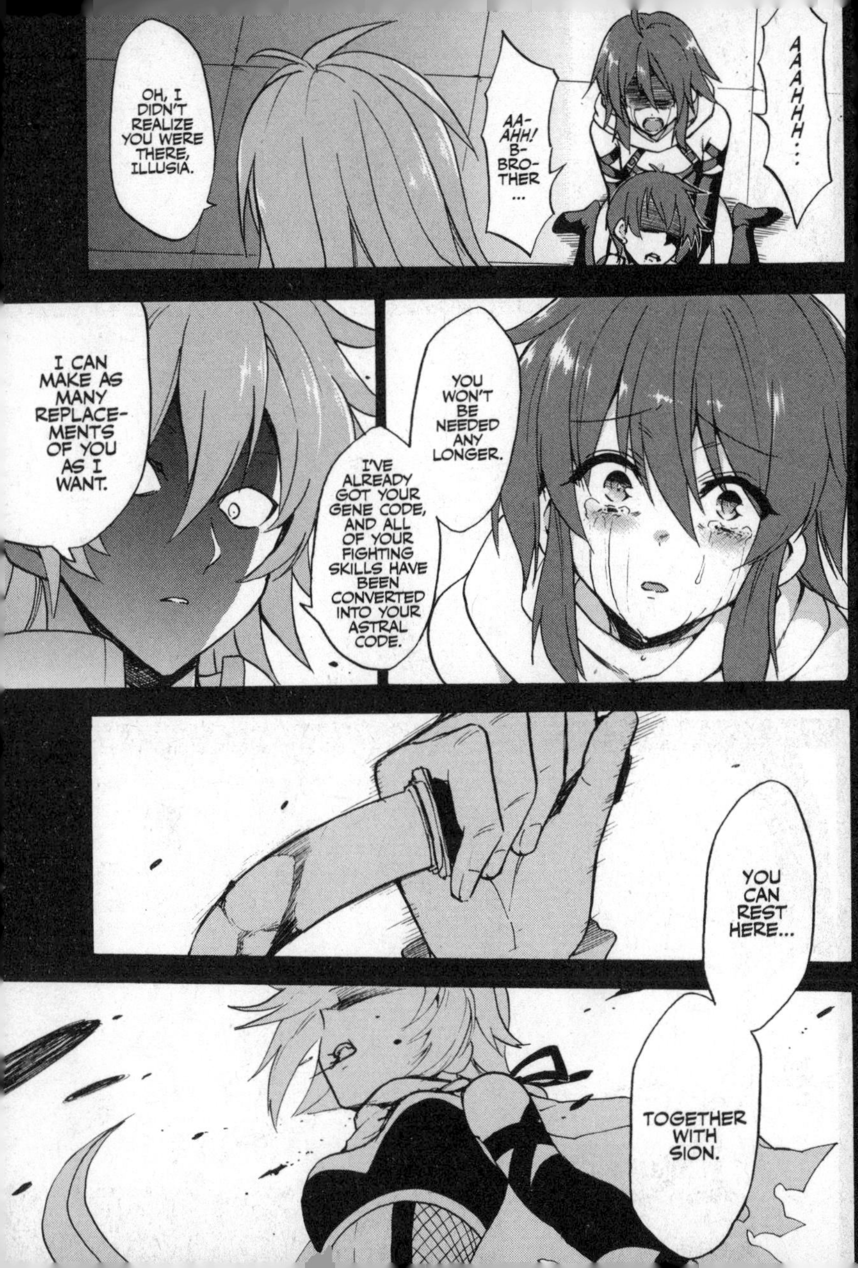
AAAAHHH...
AA-AHH! B-BROTHER...
OH, I DIDN'T REALIZE YOU WERE THERE, ILLUSIA.
YOU WON'T BE NEEDED ANY LONGER.
I'VE ALREADY GOT YOUR GENE CODE, AND ALL OF YOUR FIGHTING SKILLS HAVE BEEN CONVERTED INTO YOUR ASTRAL CODE.
I CAN MAKE AS MANY REPLACEMENTS OF YOU AS I WANT.
YOU CAN REST HERE...
TOGETHER WITH SION.

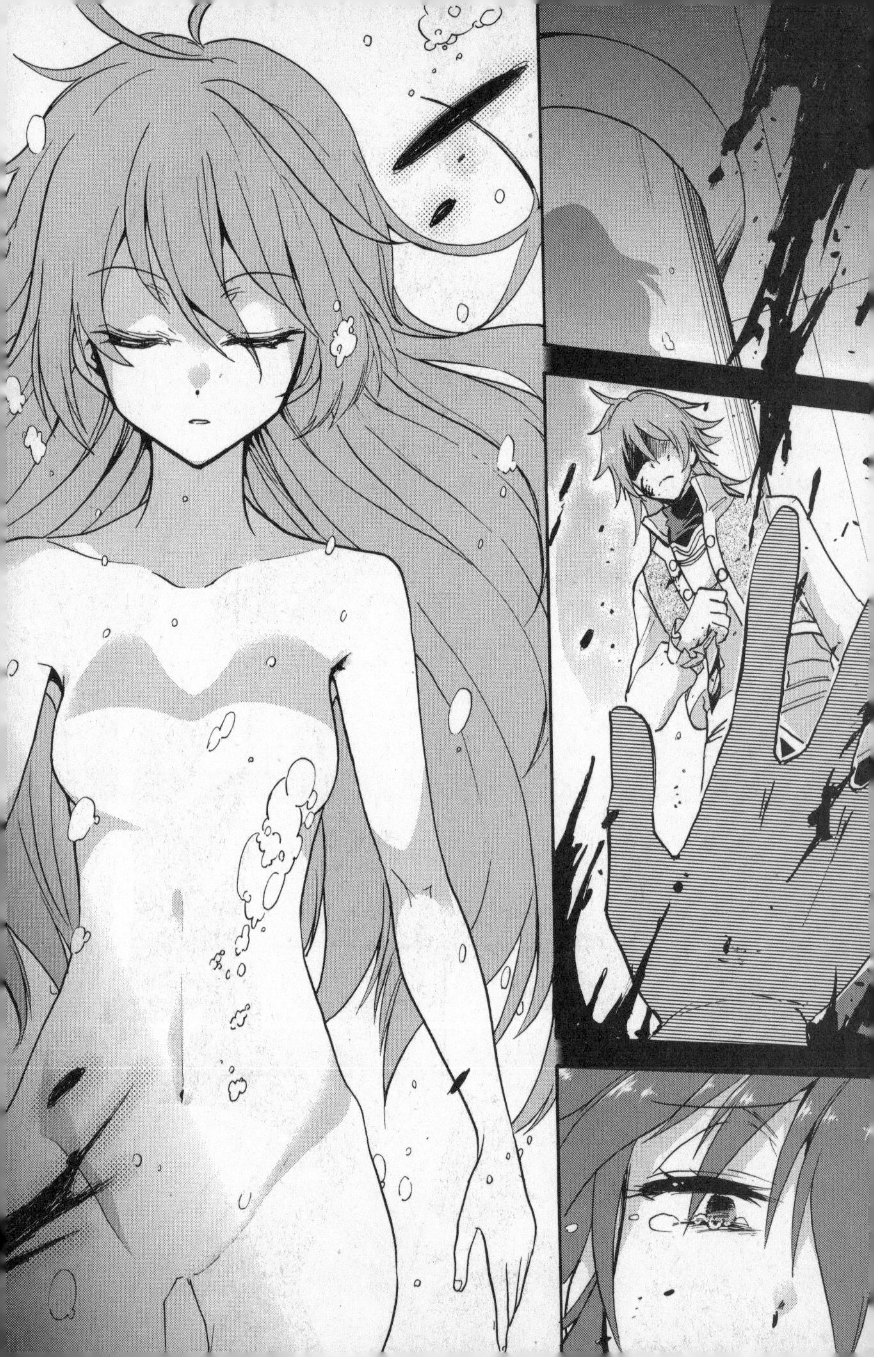

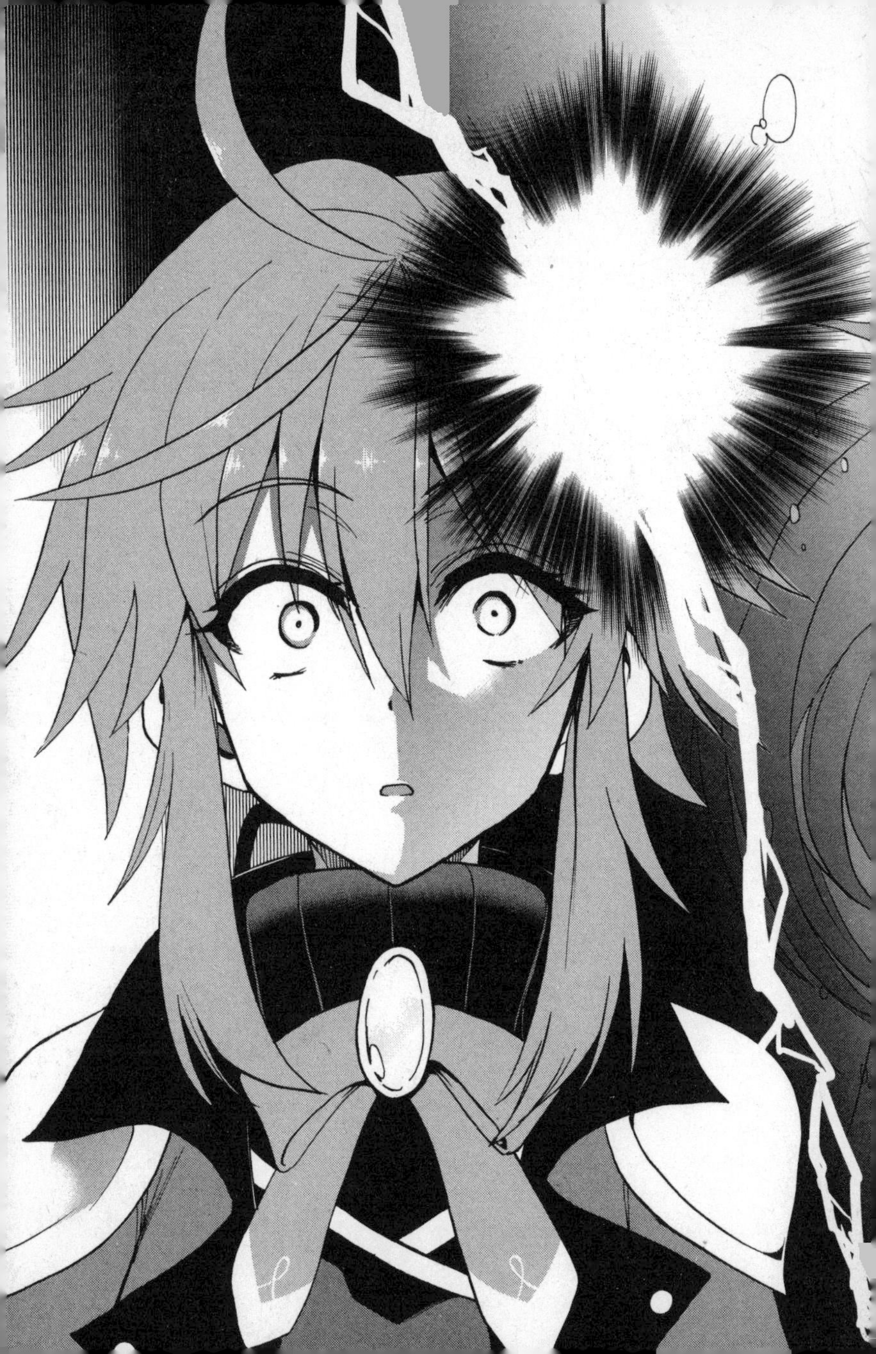

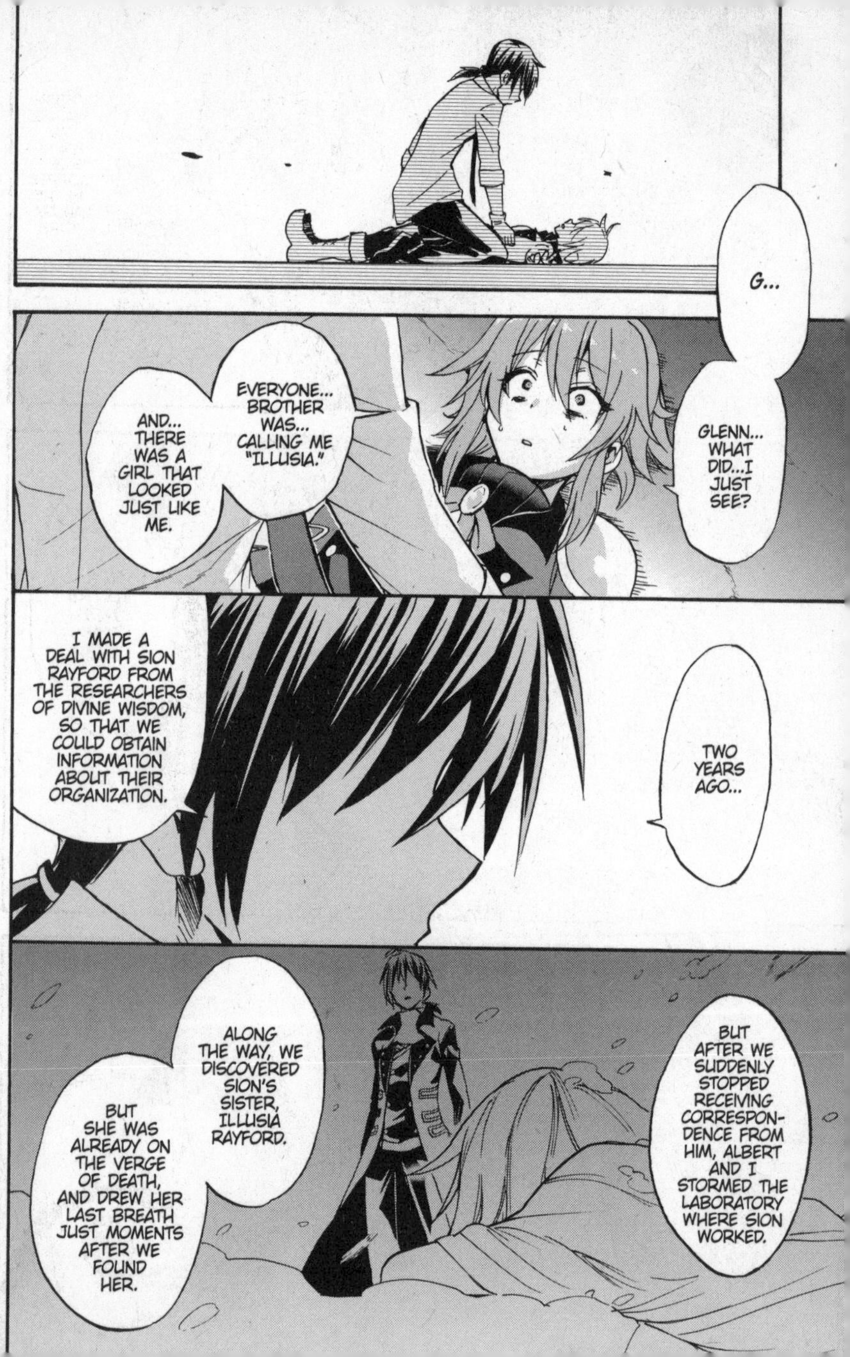
G...
GLENN... WHAT DID...I JUST SEE?
EVERYONE... BROTHER WAS... CALLING ME "ILLUSIA."
AND... THERE WAS A GIRL THAT LOOKED JUST LIKE ME.
TWO YEARS AGO...
I MADE A DEAL WITH SION RAYFORD FROM THE RESEARCHERS OF DIVINE WISDOM, SO THAT WE COULD OBTAIN INFORMATION ABOUT THEIR ORGANIZATION.
BUT AFTER WE SUDDENLY STOPPED RECEIVING CORRESPON-DENCE FROM HIM, ALBERT AND I STORMED THE LABORATORY WHERE SION WORKED.
ALONG THE WAY, WE DISCOVERED SION'S SISTER, ILLUSIA RAYFORD.
BUT SHE WAS ALREADY ON THE VERGE OF DEATH, AND DREW HER LAST BREATH JUST MOMENTS AFTER WE FOUND HER.

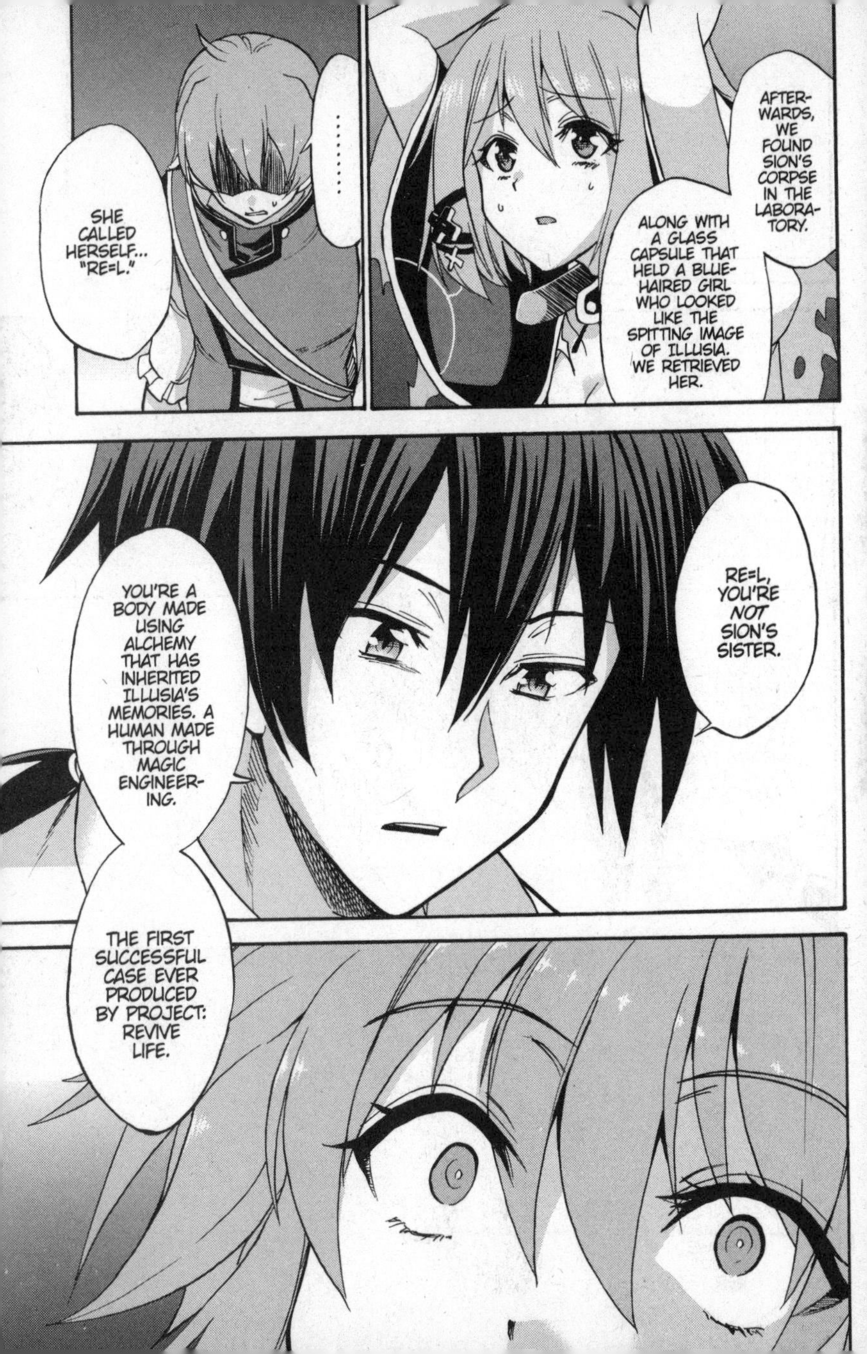
AFTER-WARDS, WE FOUND SION'S CORPSE IN THE LABORA-TORY.
ALONG WITH A GLASS CAPSULE THAT HELD A BLUE-HAIRED GIRL WHO LOOKED LIKE THE SPITTING IMAGE OF ILLUSIA. WE RETRIEVED HER.
......
SHE CALLED HERSELF... "RE=L."
RE=L, YOU'RE *NOT* SION'S SISTER.
YOU'RE A BODY MADE USING ALCHEMY THAT HAS INHERITED ILLUSIA'S MEMORIES. A HUMAN MADE THROUGH MAGIC ENGINEER-ING.
THE FIRST SUCCESSFUL CASE EVER PRODUCED BY PROJECT: REVIVE LIFE.

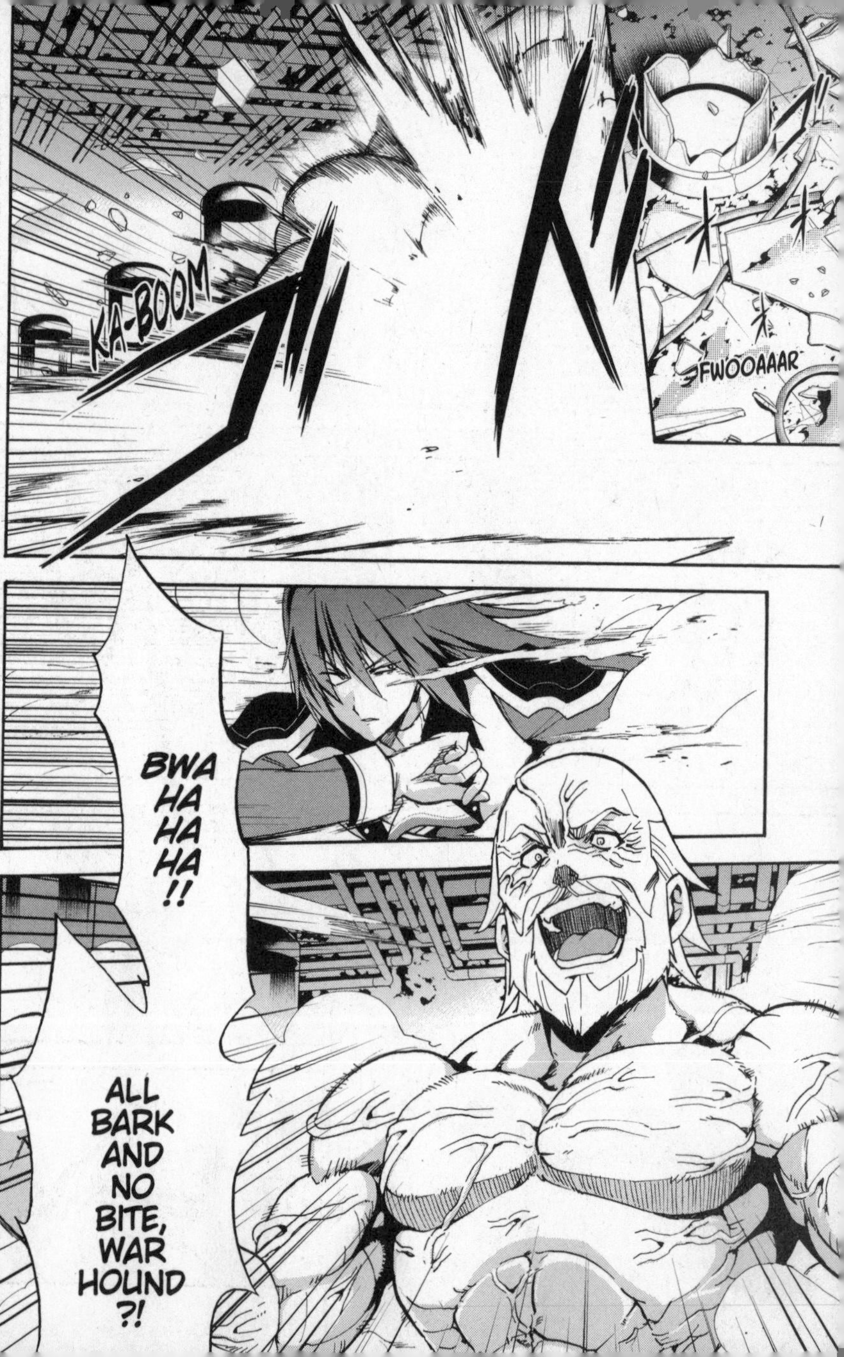
FWOOAAAR
KA-BOOM
BWA HA HA HA!!
ALL BARK AND NO BITE, WAR HOUND?!

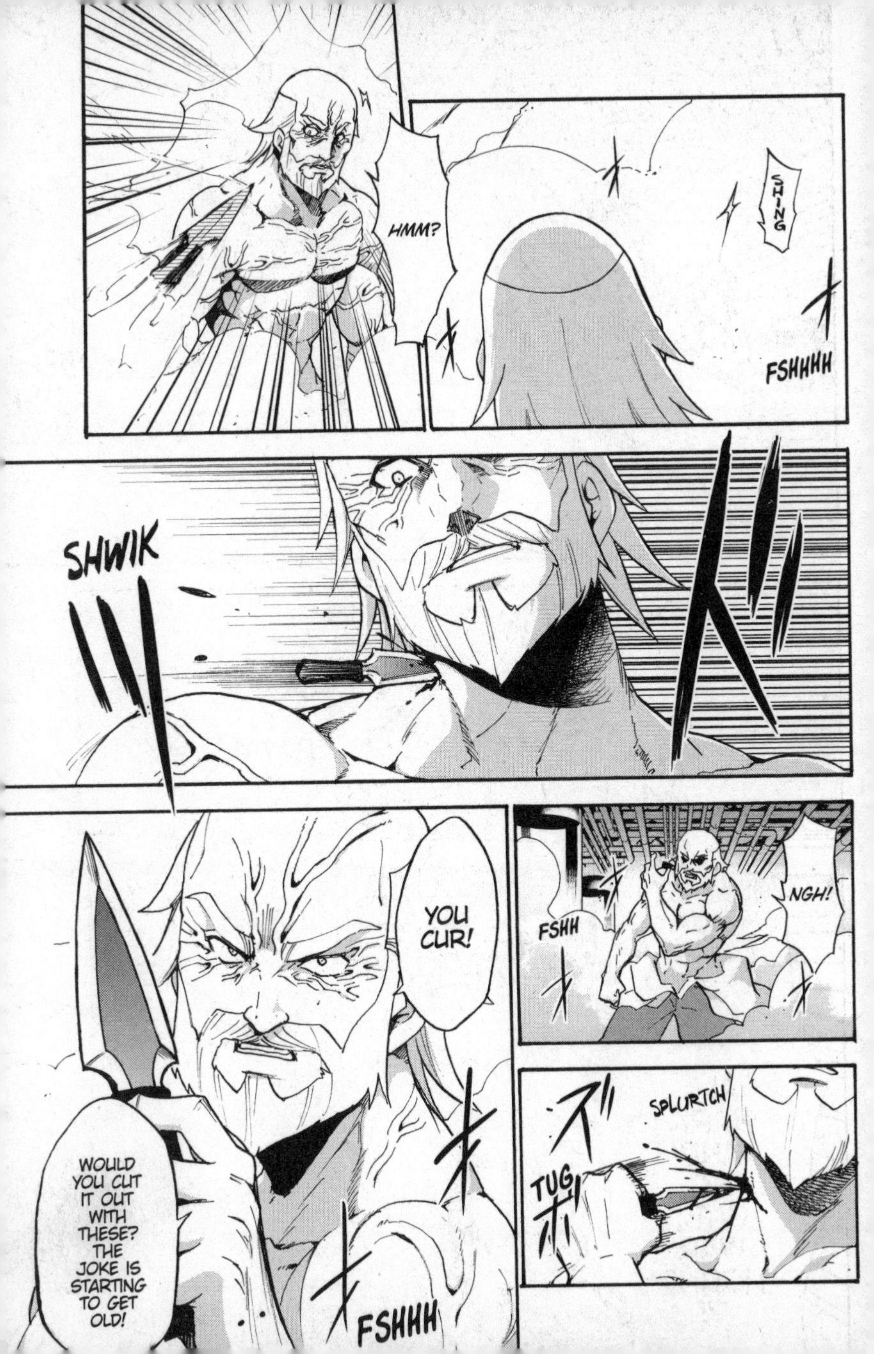
SHING
HMM?
FSHHHH
SHWIK
NGH!
FSHH
SPLURTCH
TUG
YOU CUR!
WOULD YOU CUT IT OUT WITH THESE? THE JOKE IS STARTING TO GET OLD!
FSHHH

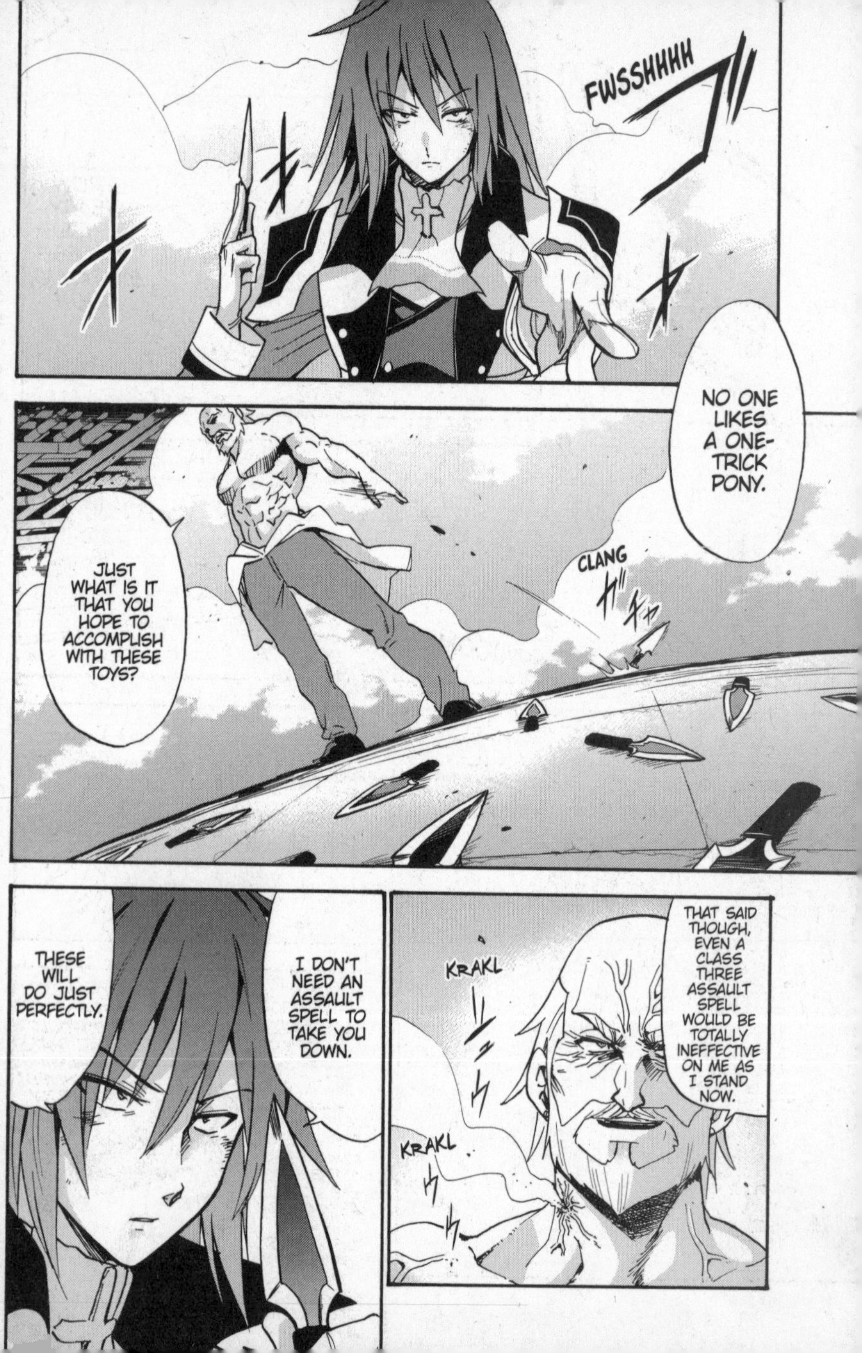
FWSSHHHH
NO ONE LIKES A ONE-TRICK PONY.
CLANG
JUST WHAT IS IT THAT YOU HOPE TO ACCOMPLISH WITH THESE TOYS?
THAT SAID THOUGH, EVEN A CLASS THREE ASSAULT SPELL WOULD BE TOTALLY INEFFECTIVE ON ME AS I STAND NOW.
KRAKL
KRAKL
I DON'T NEED AN ASSAULT SPELL TO TAKE YOU DOWN.
THESE WILL DO JUST PERFECTLY.

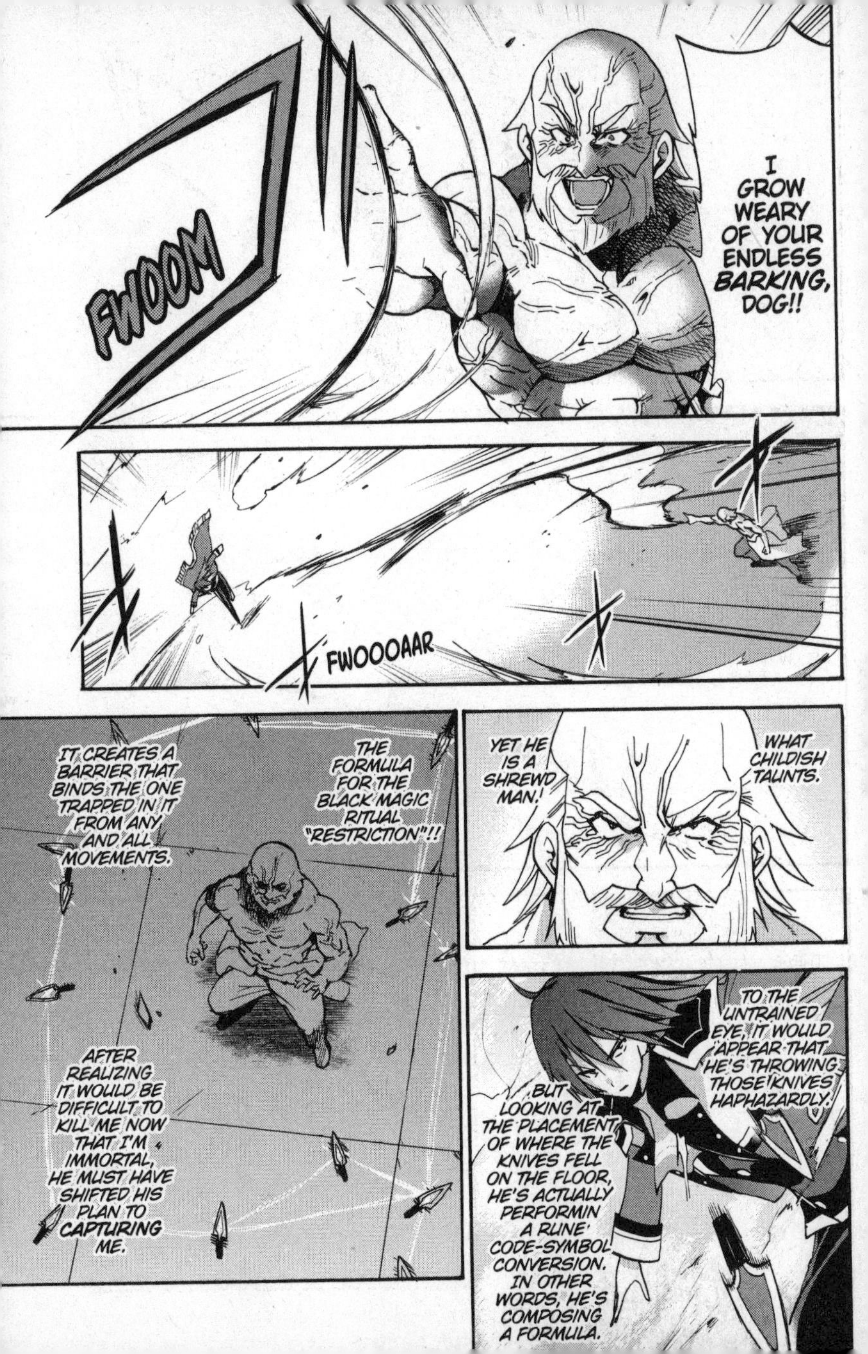
I GROW WEARY OF YOUR ENDLESS BARKING, DOG!!
FWOOM
FWOOOAAR
WHAT CHILDISH TAUNTS.
YET HE IS A SHREWD MAN!
TO THE UNTRAINED EYE, IT WOULD APPEAR THAT HE'S THROWING THOSE KNIVES HAPHAZARDLY.
BUT LOOKING AT THE PLACEMENT OF WHERE THE KNIVES FELL ON THE FLOOR, HE'S ACTUALLY PERFORMIN A RUNE CODE-SYMBOL CONVERSION. IN OTHER WORDS, HE'S COMPOSING A FORMULA.
THE FORMULA FOR THE BLACK MAGIC RITUAL "RESTRICTION"!!
IT CREATES A BARRIER THAT BINDS THE ONE TRAPPED IN IT FROM ANY AND ALL MOVEMENTS.
AFTER REALIZING IT WOULD BE DIFFICULT TO KILL ME NOW THAT I'M IMMORTAL, HE MUST HAVE SHIFTED HIS PLAN TO CAPTURING ME.

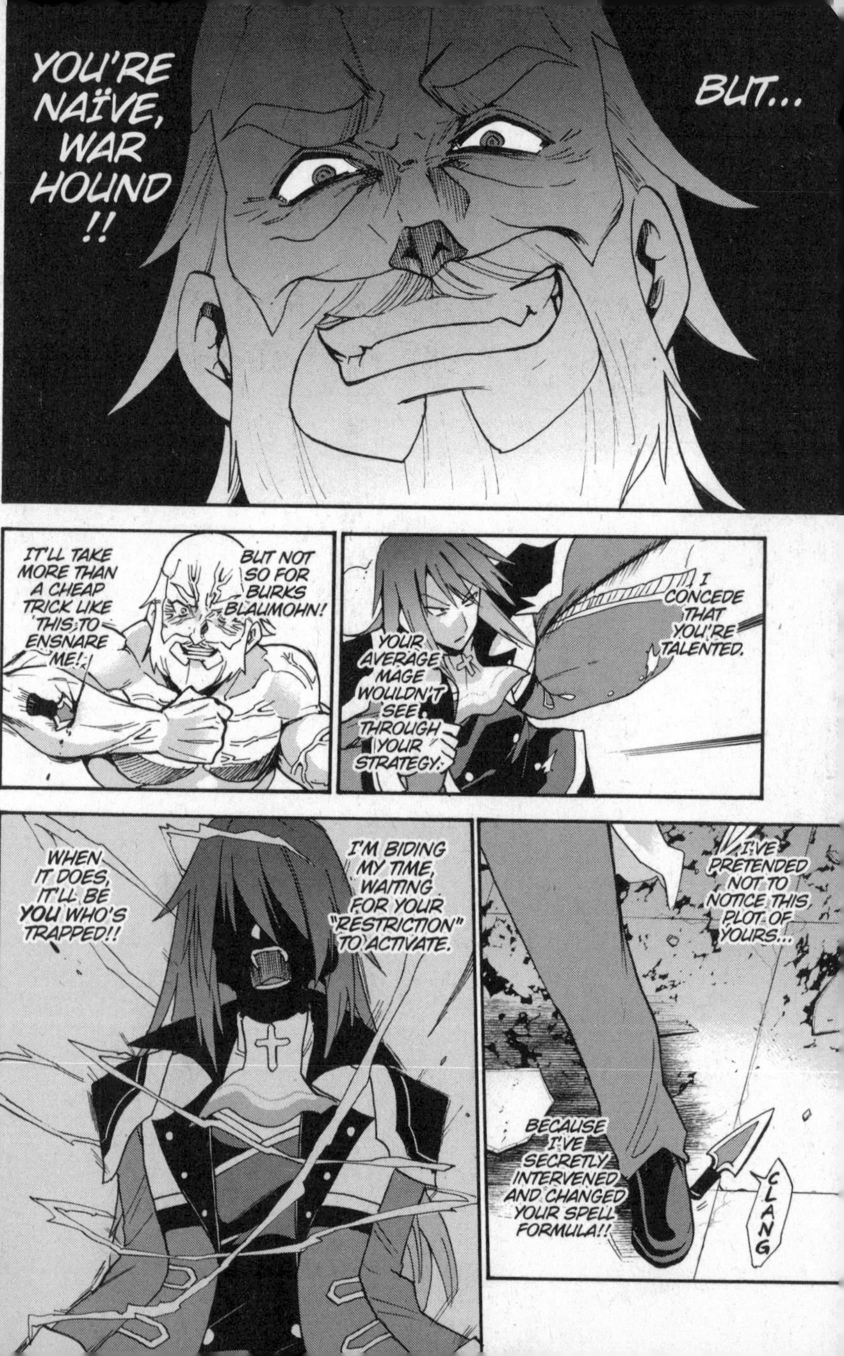

BUT...
YOU'RE NAÏVE, WAR HOUND!!
I CONCEDE THAT YOU'RE TALENTED.
YOUR AVERAGE MAGE WOULDN'T SEE THROUGH YOUR STRATEGY.
BUT NOT SO FOR BURKS BLAUMOHN!
IT'LL TAKE MORE THAN A CHEAP TRICK LIKE THIS TO ENSNARE ME!
I'VE PRETENDED NOT TO NOTICE THIS PLOT OF YOURS...
BECAUSE I'VE SECRETLY INTERVENED AND CHANGED YOUR SPELL FORMULA!!
CLANG
I'M BIDING MY TIME, WAITING FOR YOUR "RESTRICTION" TO ACTIVATE.
WHEN IT DOES, IT'LL BE YOU WHO'S TRAPPED!!

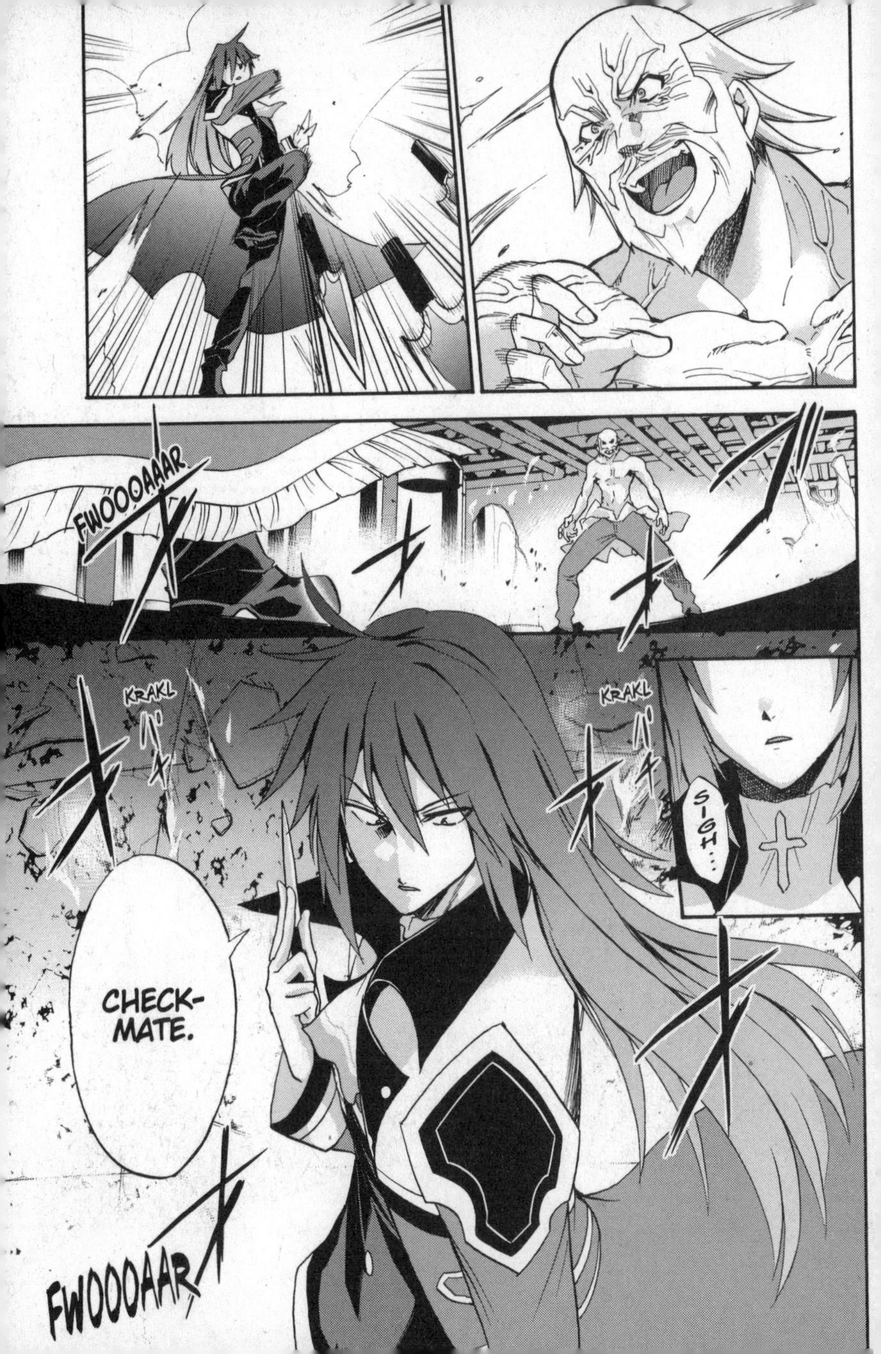
FWOOOAAAR
KRAKL
SIGH...
KRAKL
CHECK-MATE.
FWOOOAAR

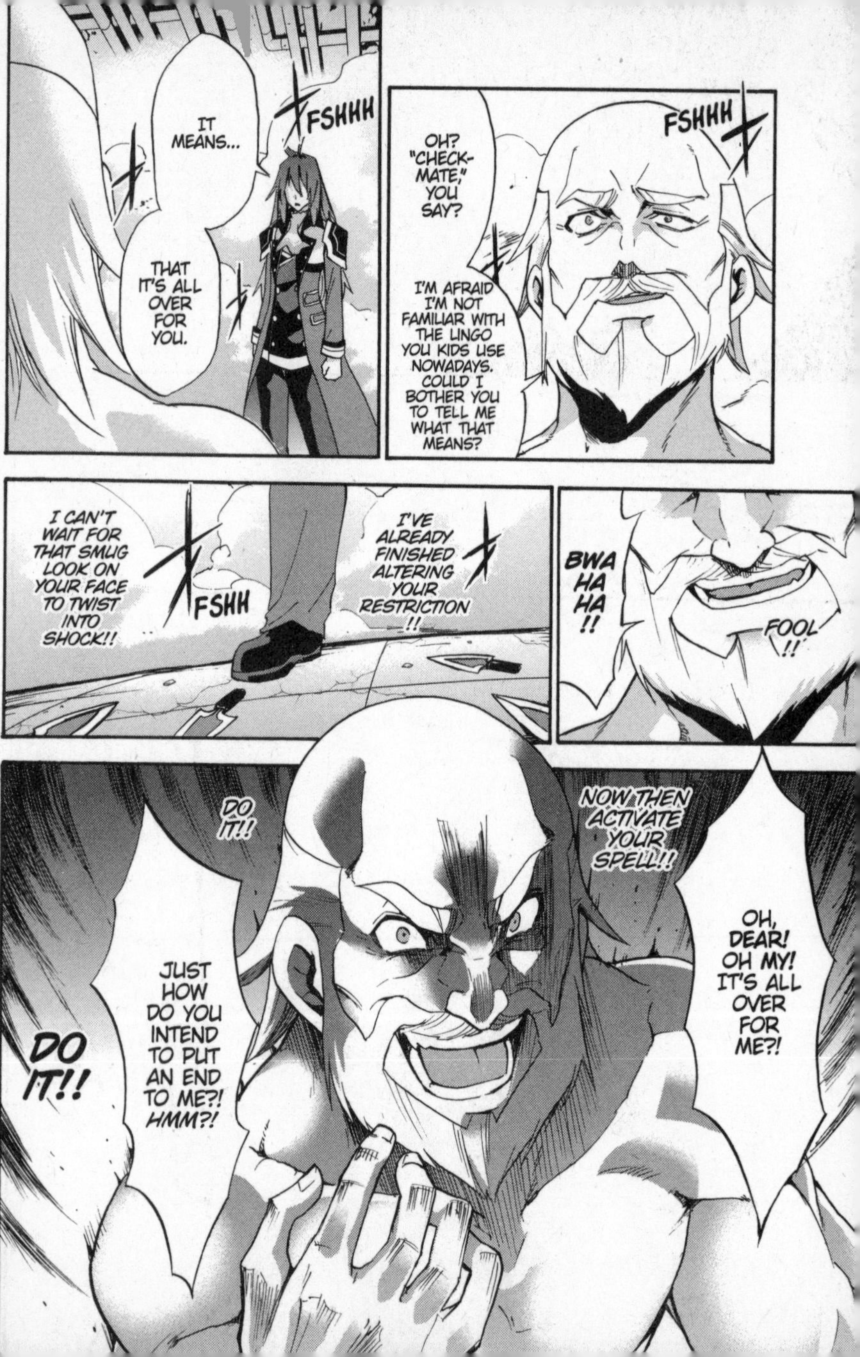
FSHHH
OH? "CHECK-MATE," YOU SAY?
I'M AFRAID I'M NOT FAMILIAR WITH THE LINGO YOU KIDS USE NOWADAYS. COULD I BOTHER YOU TO TELL ME WHAT THAT MEANS?
FSHHH
IT MEANS...
THAT IT'S ALL OVER FOR YOU.
BWA HA HA!!
FOOL!!
I'VE ALREADY FINISHED ALTERING YOUR RESTRICTION!!
FSHH
I CAN'T WAIT FOR THAT SMUG LOOK ON YOUR FACE TO TWIST INTO SHOCK!!
OH, DEAR! OH MY! IT'S ALL OVER FOR ME?!
NOW THEN ACTIVATE YOUR SPELL!!
DO IT!!
JUST HOW DO YOU INTEND TO PUT AN END TO ME?! HMM?!
DO IT!!

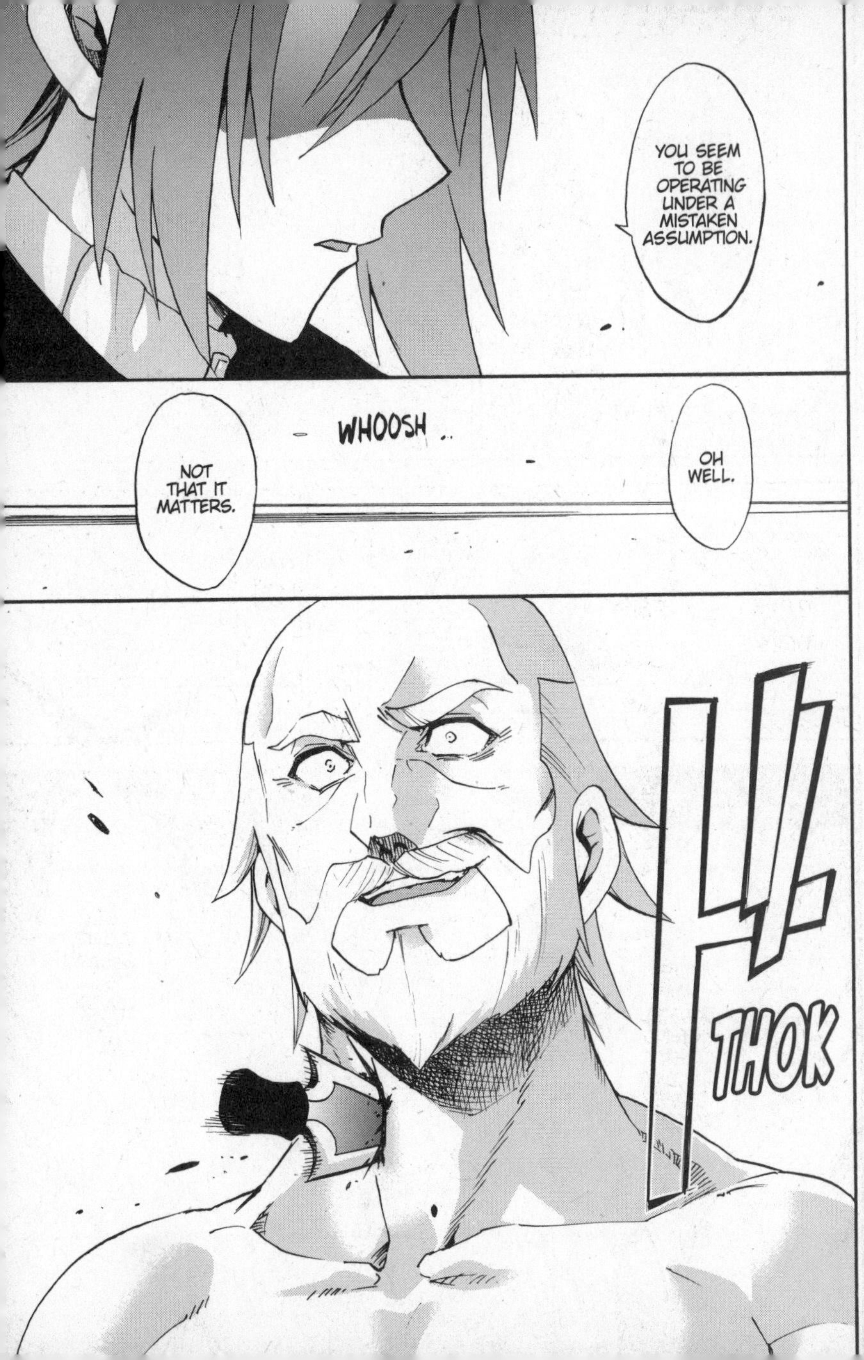
YOU SEEM TO BE OPERATING UNDER A MISTAKEN ASSUMPTION.
OH WELL.
WHOOSH
NOT THAT IT MATTERS.
THOK

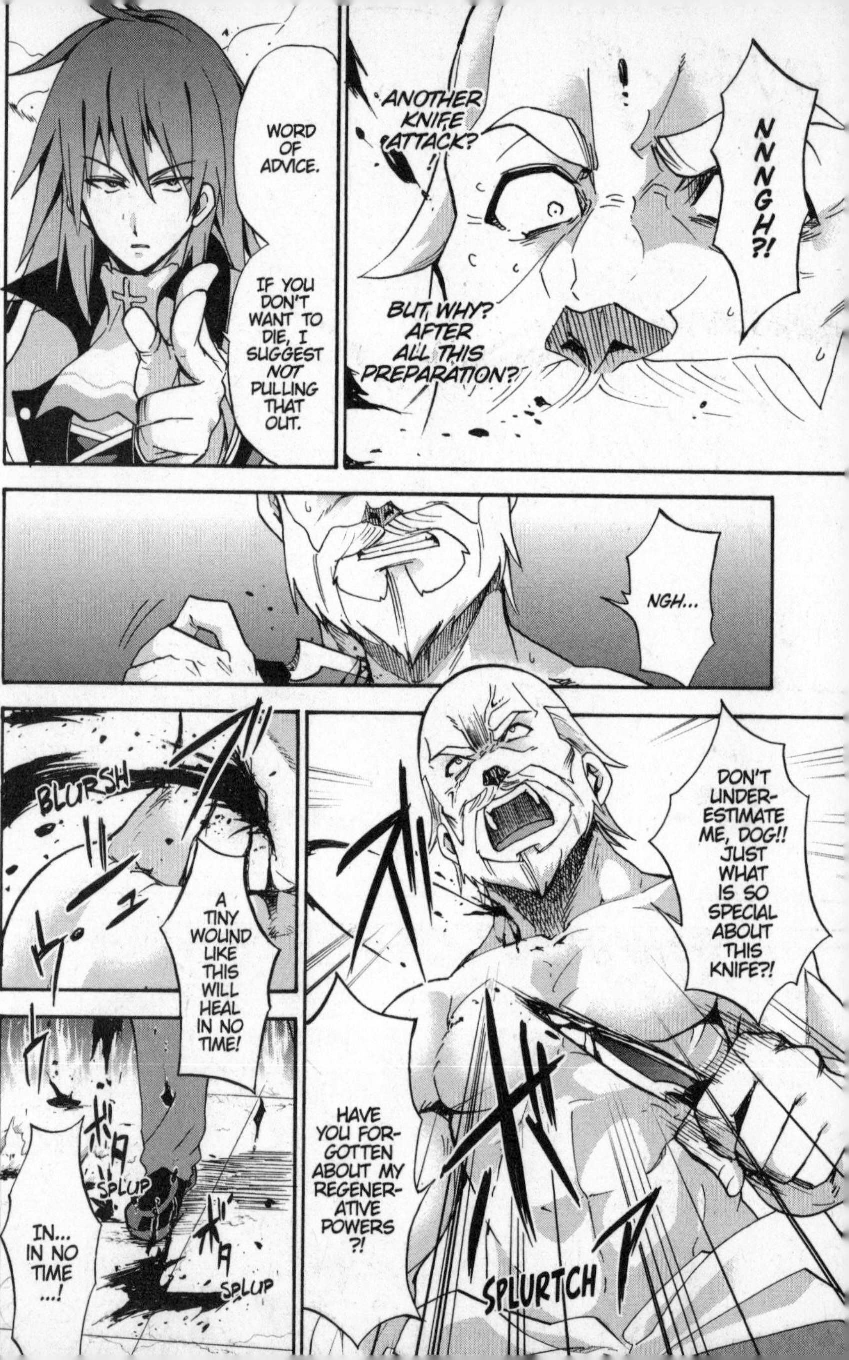
NNNGH?!
ANOTHER KNIFE ATTACK?
!
BUT WHY? AFTER ALL THIS PREPARATION?
WORD OF ADVICE.
IF YOU DON'T WANT TO DIE, I SUGGEST NOT PULLING THAT OUT.
NGH...
DON'T UNDER-ESTIMATE ME, DOG!! JUST WHAT IS SO SPECIAL ABOUT THIS KNIFE?!
HAVE YOU FOR-GOTTEN ABOUT MY REGENER-ATIVE POWERS?!
A TINY WOUND LIKE THIS WILL HEAL IN NO TIME!
SPLURTCH
BLURSH
SPLUP
SPLUP
IN... IN NO TIME ...!

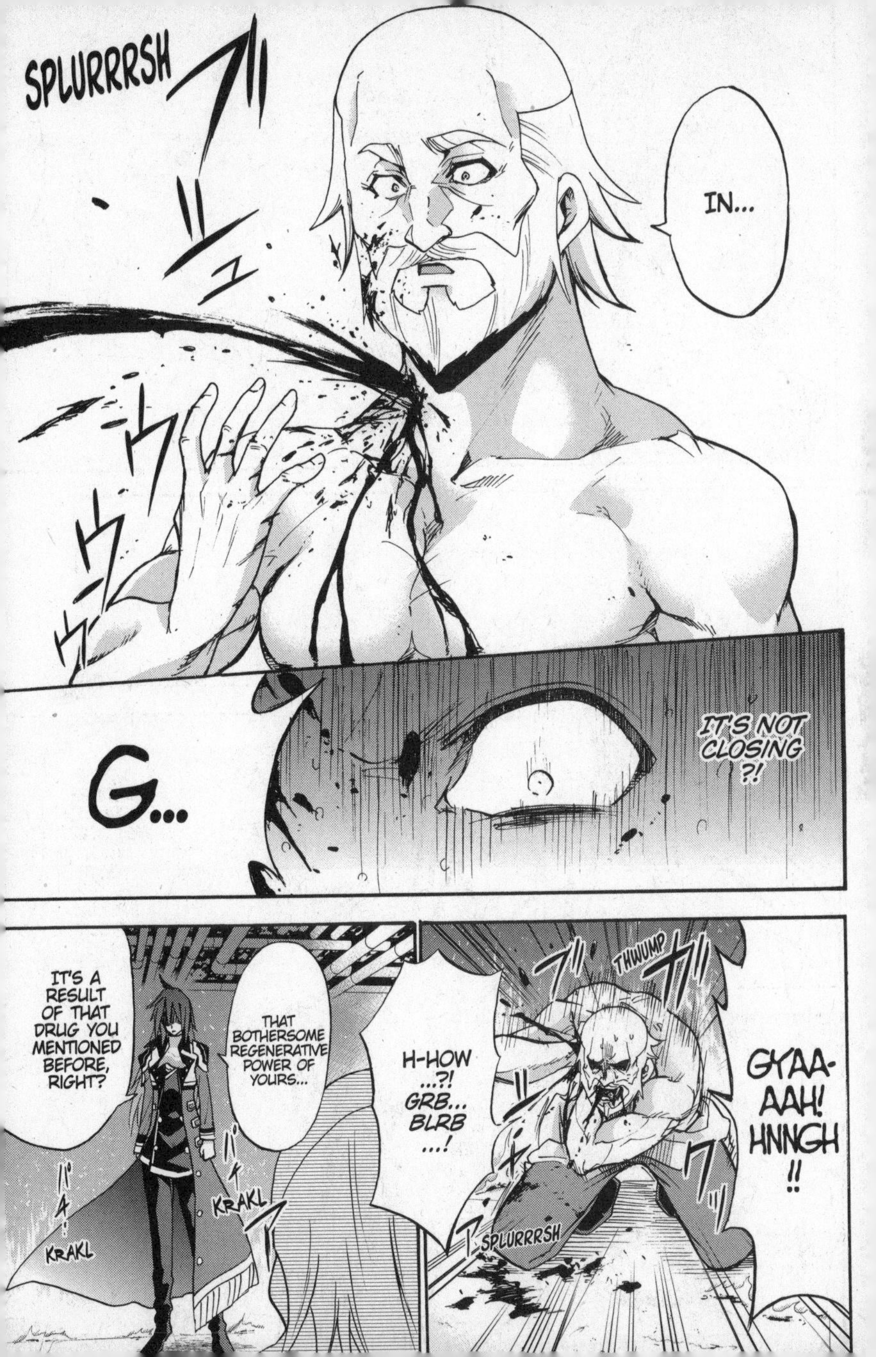
SPLURRRSH
IN...
IT'S NOT CLOSING ?!
G...
THWUMP
GYAA-AAH! HNNGH !!
H-HOW ...?! GRB... BLRB ...!
SPLURRRSH
THAT BOTHERSOME REGENERATIVE POWER OF YOURS...
IT'S A RESULT OF THAT DRUG YOU MENTIONED BEFORE, RIGHT?
KRAKL
KRAKL

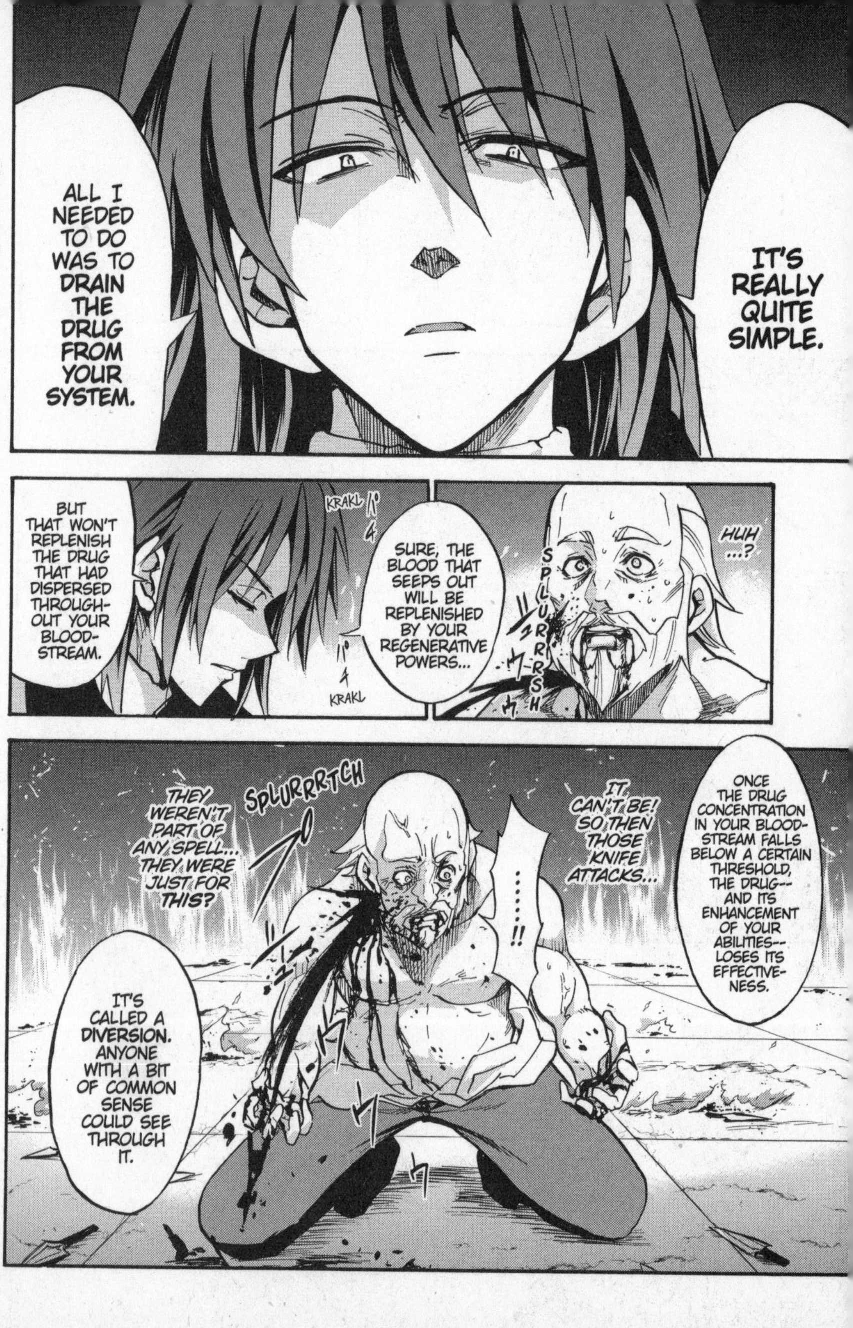
IT'S REALLY QUITE SIMPLE.
ALL I NEEDED TO DO WAS TO DRAIN THE DRUG FROM YOUR SYSTEM.
HUH ...?
SPLURRRSH
SURE, THE BLOOD THAT SEEPS OUT WILL BE REPLENISHED BY YOUR REGENERATIVE POWERS...
KRAKL
KRAKL
BUT THAT WON'T REPLENISH THE DRUG THAT HAD DISPERSED THROUGH-OUT YOUR BLOOD-STREAM.
ONCE THE DRUG CONCENTRATION IN YOUR BLOOD-STREAM FALLS BELOW A CERTAIN THRESHOLD, THE DRUG-- AND ITS ENHANCEMENT OF YOUR ABILITIES-- LOSES ITS EFFECTIVE-NESS.
......!!
IT CAN'T BE! SO THEN THOSE KNIFE ATTACKS...
THEY WEREN'T PART OF ANY SPELL... THEY WERE JUST FOR THIS?
SPLURRRTCH
IT'S CALLED A DIVERSION. ANYONE WITH A BIT OF COMMON SENSE COULD SEE THROUGH IT.

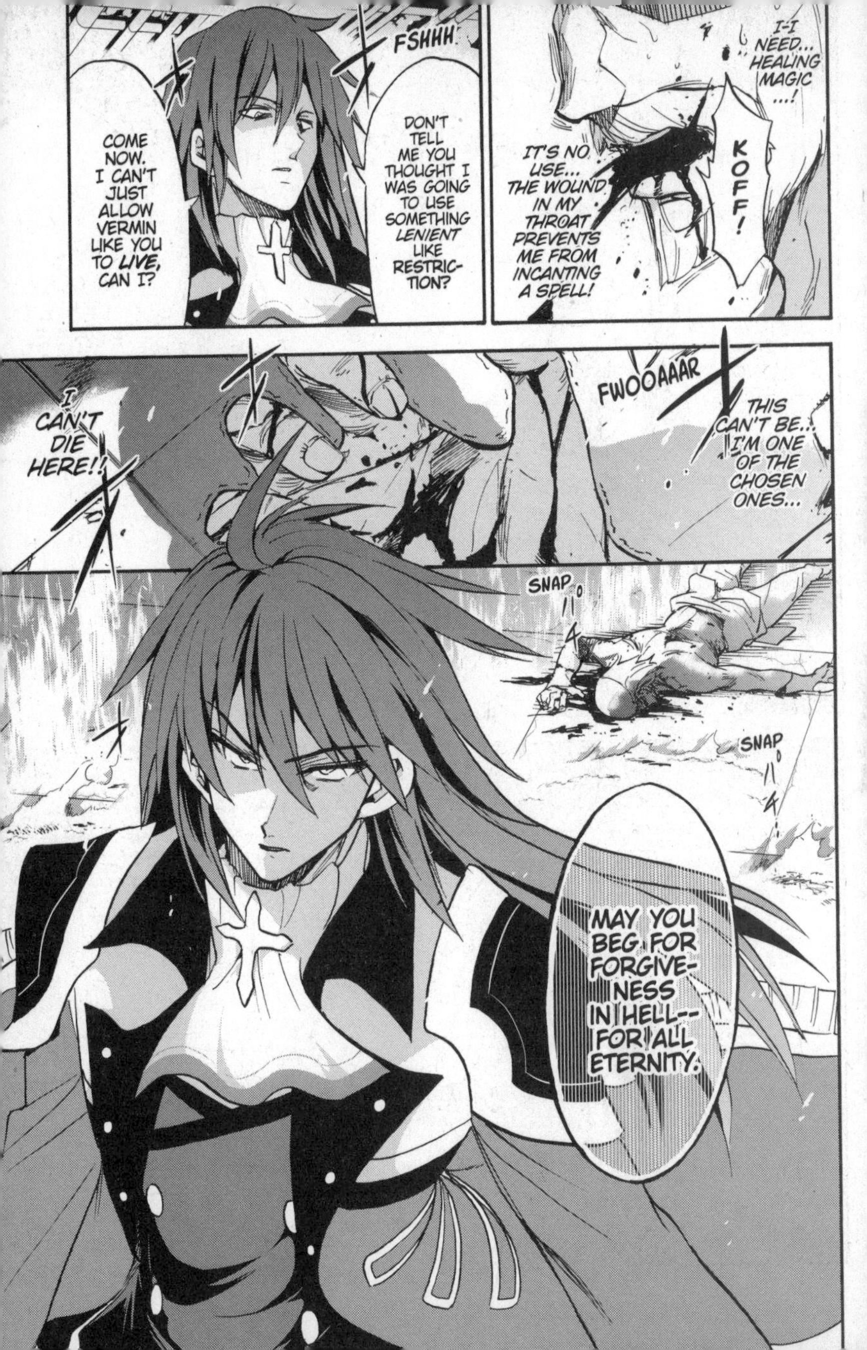
I-I NEED... HEALING MAGIC...!
KOFF!
IT'S NO USE... THE WOUND IN MY THROAT PREVENTS ME FROM INCANTING A SPELL!
FSHHH
DON'T TELL ME YOU THOUGHT I WAS GOING TO USE SOMETHING LENIENT LIKE RESTRICTION?
COME NOW. I CAN'T JUST ALLOW VERMIN LIKE YOU TO LIVE, CAN I?
FWOOAAAR
THIS CAN'T BE... I'M ONE OF THE CHOSEN ONES...
I CAN'T DIE HERE!!
SNAP
SNAP
MAY YOU BEG FOR FORGIVENESS IN HELL-- FOR ALL ETERNITY.

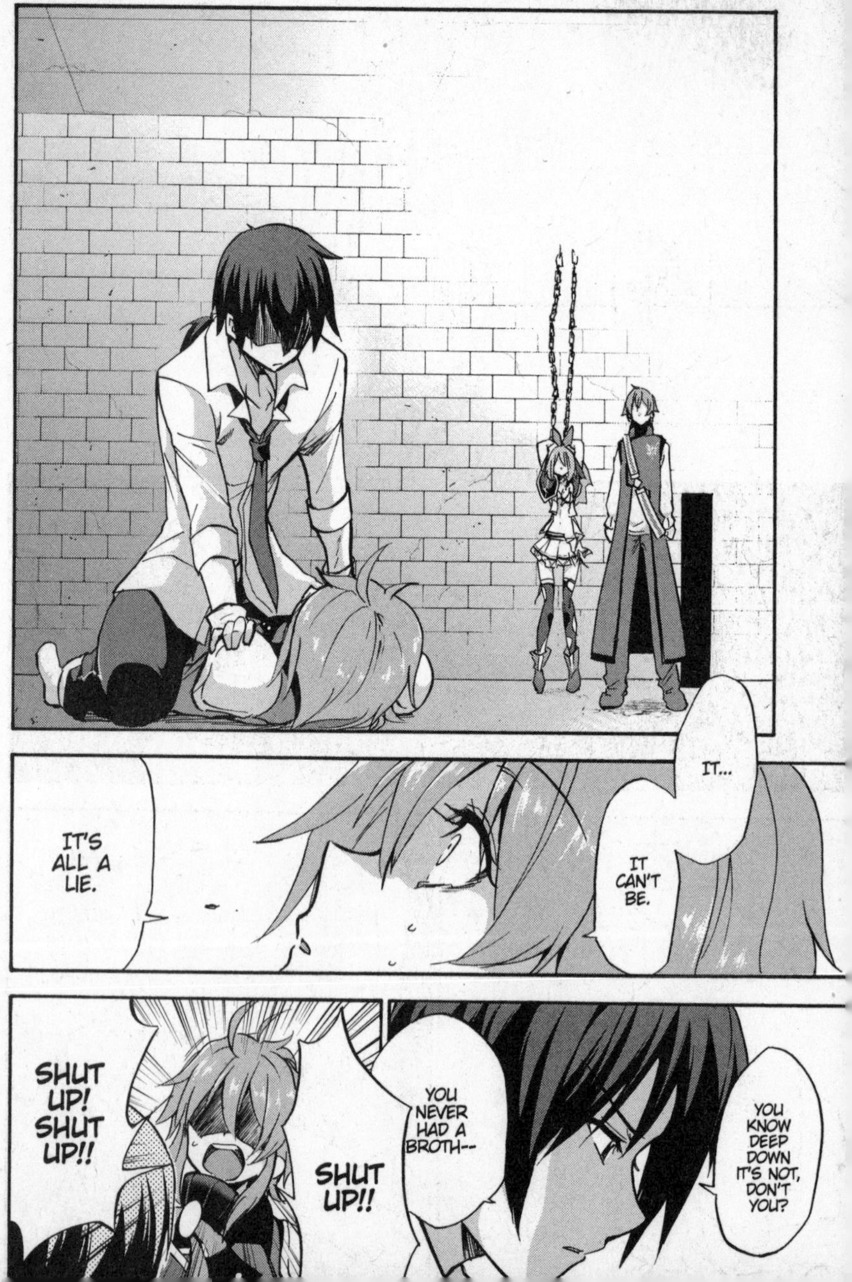
IT...
IT CAN'T BE.
IT'S ALL A LIE.
YOU KNOW DEEP DOWN IT'S NOT, DON'T YOU?
YOU NEVER HAD A BROTH--
SHUT UP!!
SHUT UP! SHUT UP!!

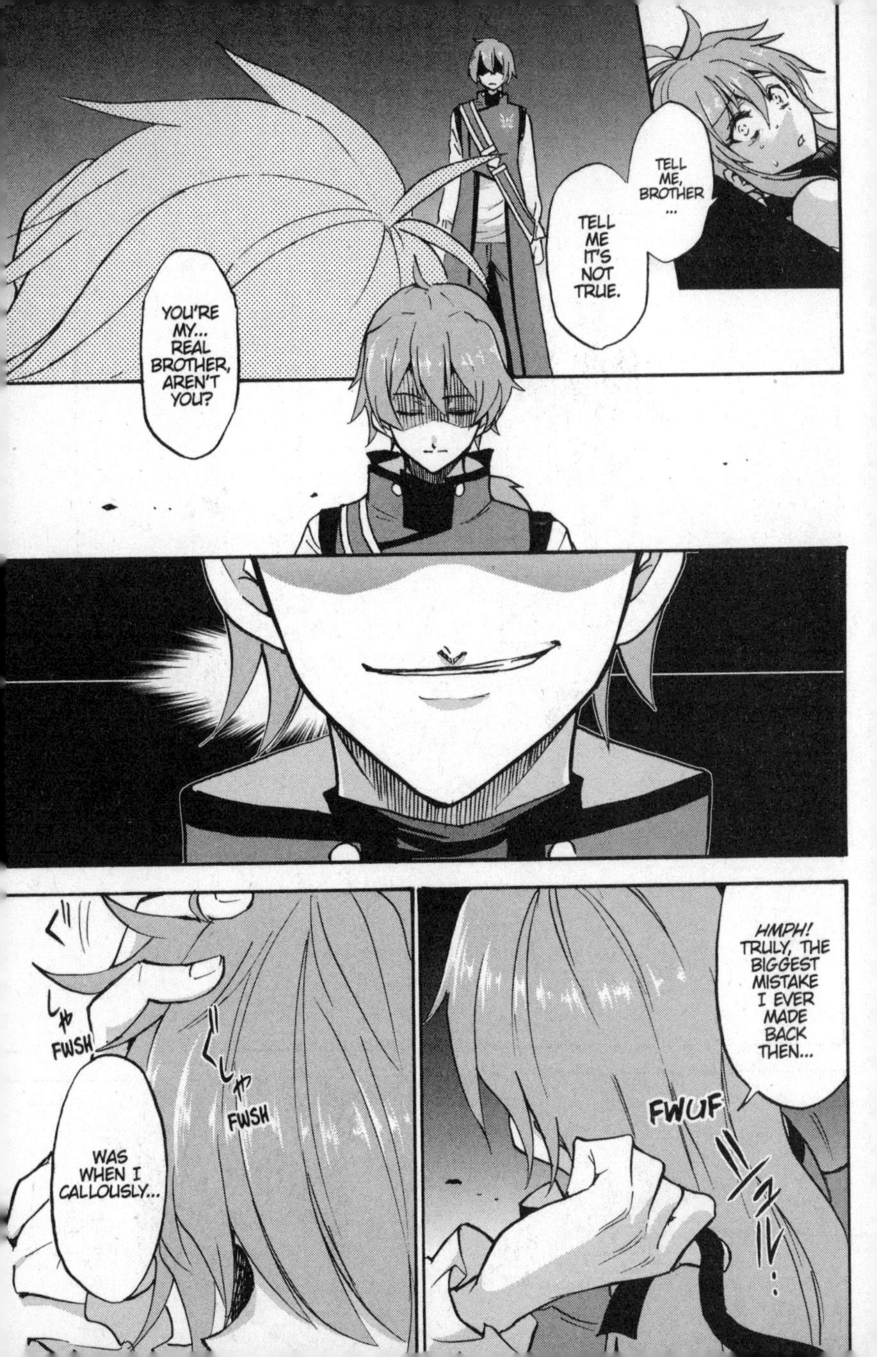
TELL ME, BROTHER...
TELL ME IT'S NOT TRUE.
YOU'RE MY... REAL BROTHER, AREN'T YOU?
HMPH! TRULY, THE BIGGEST MISTAKE I EVER MADE BACK THEN...
FWUF
FWSH
FWSH
WAS WHEN I CALLOUSLY...

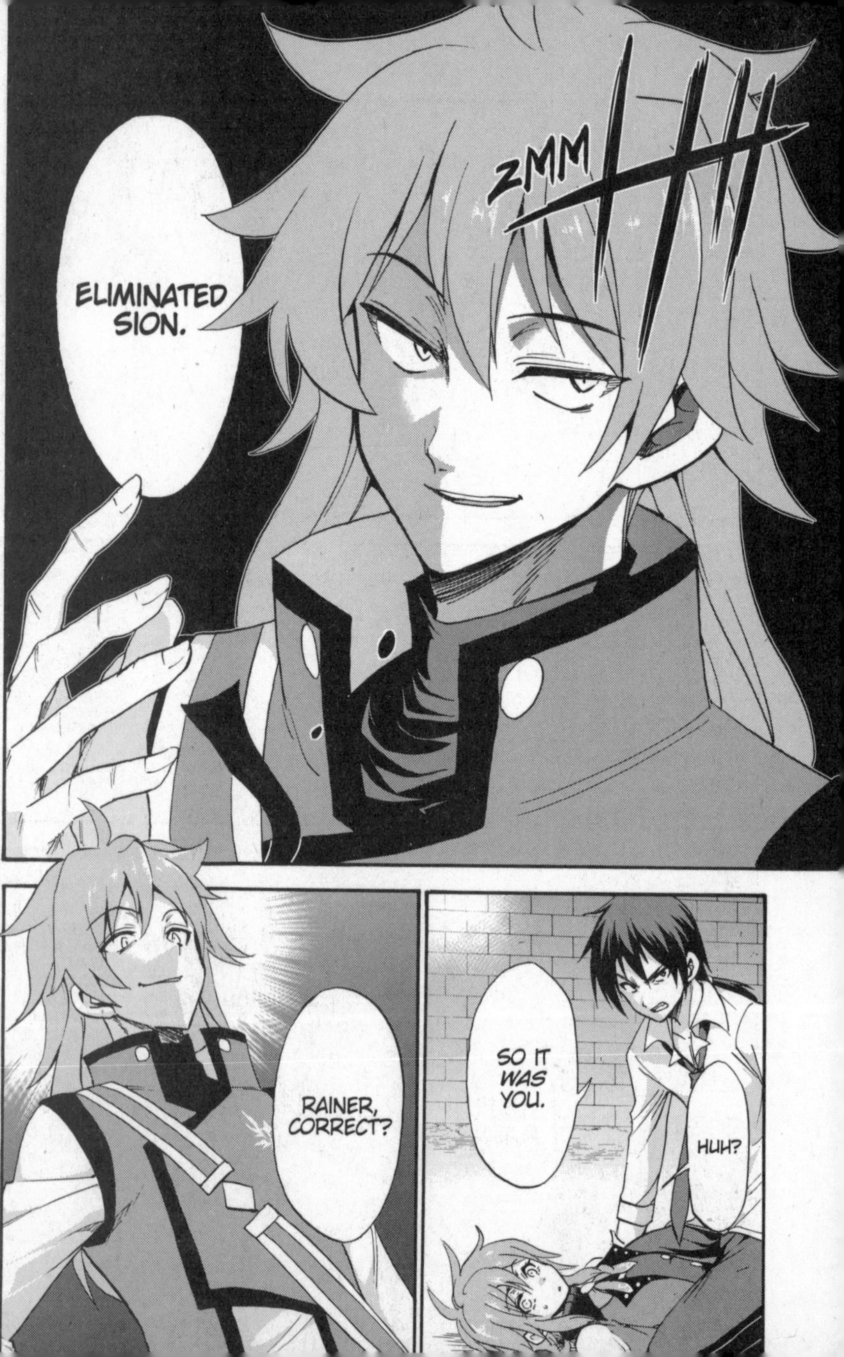
ZMM
ELIMINATED SION.
SO IT WAS YOU.
HUH?
RAINER, CORRECT?

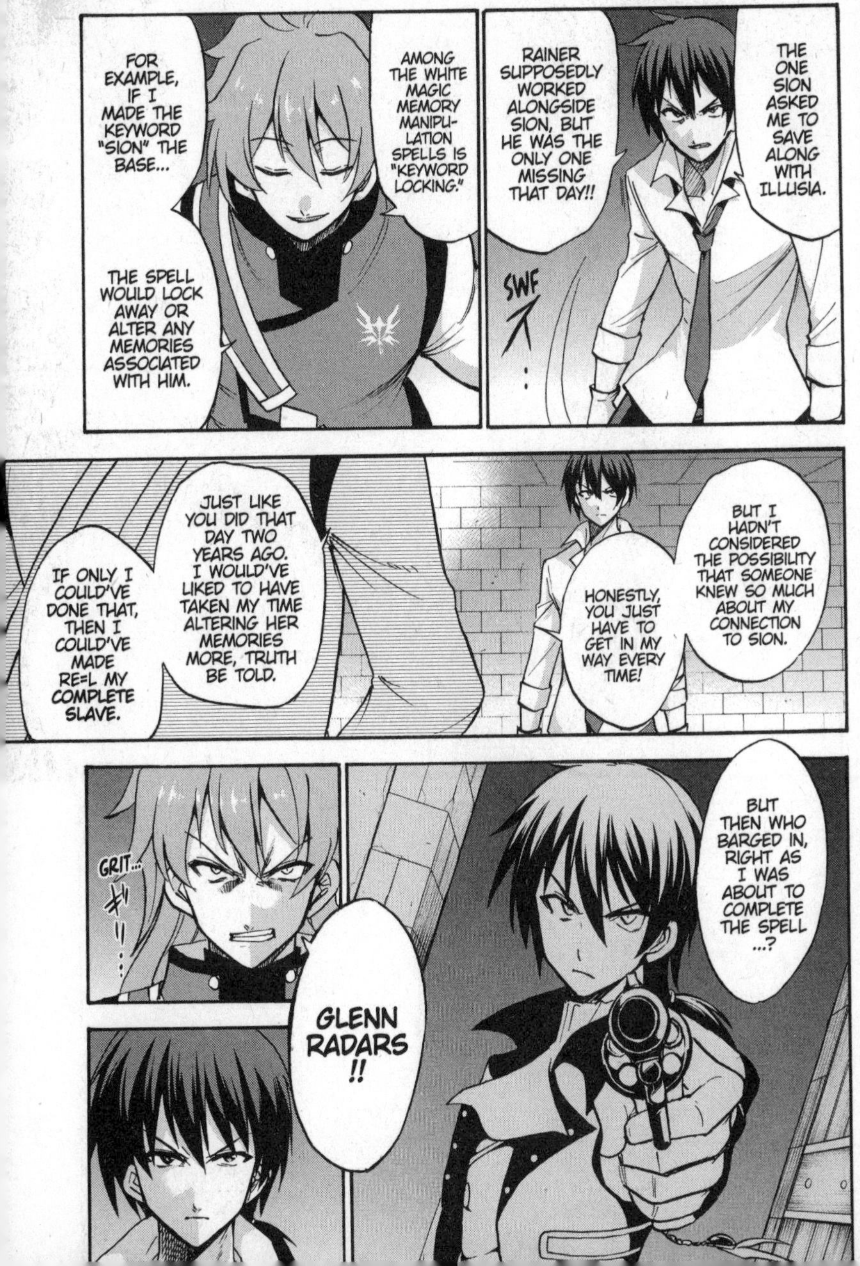
THE ONE SION ASKED ME TO SAVE ALONG WITH ILLUSIA.
RAINER SUPPOSEDLY WORKED ALONGSIDE SION, BUT HE WAS THE ONLY ONE MISSING THAT DAY!!
SWF
AMONG THE WHITE MAGIC MEMORY MANIPULATION SPELLS IS "KEYWORD LOCKING."
FOR EXAMPLE, IF I MADE THE KEYWORD "SION" THE BASE...
THE SPELL WOULD LOCK AWAY OR ALTER ANY MEMORIES ASSOCIATED WITH HIM.
BUT I HADN'T CONSIDERED THE POSSIBILITY THAT SOMEONE KNEW SO MUCH ABOUT MY CONNECTION TO SION.
HONESTLY, YOU JUST HAVE TO GET IN MY WAY EVERY TIME!
JUST LIKE YOU DID THAT DAY TWO YEARS AGO. I WOULD'VE LIKED TO HAVE TAKEN MY TIME ALTERING HER MEMORIES MORE, TRUTH BE TOLD.
IF ONLY I COULD'VE DONE THAT, THEN I COULD'VE MADE RE=L MY COMPLETE SLAVE.
BUT THEN WHO BARGED IN, RIGHT AS I WAS ABOUT TO COMPLETE THE SPELL...?
GRIT...
GLENN RADARS!!

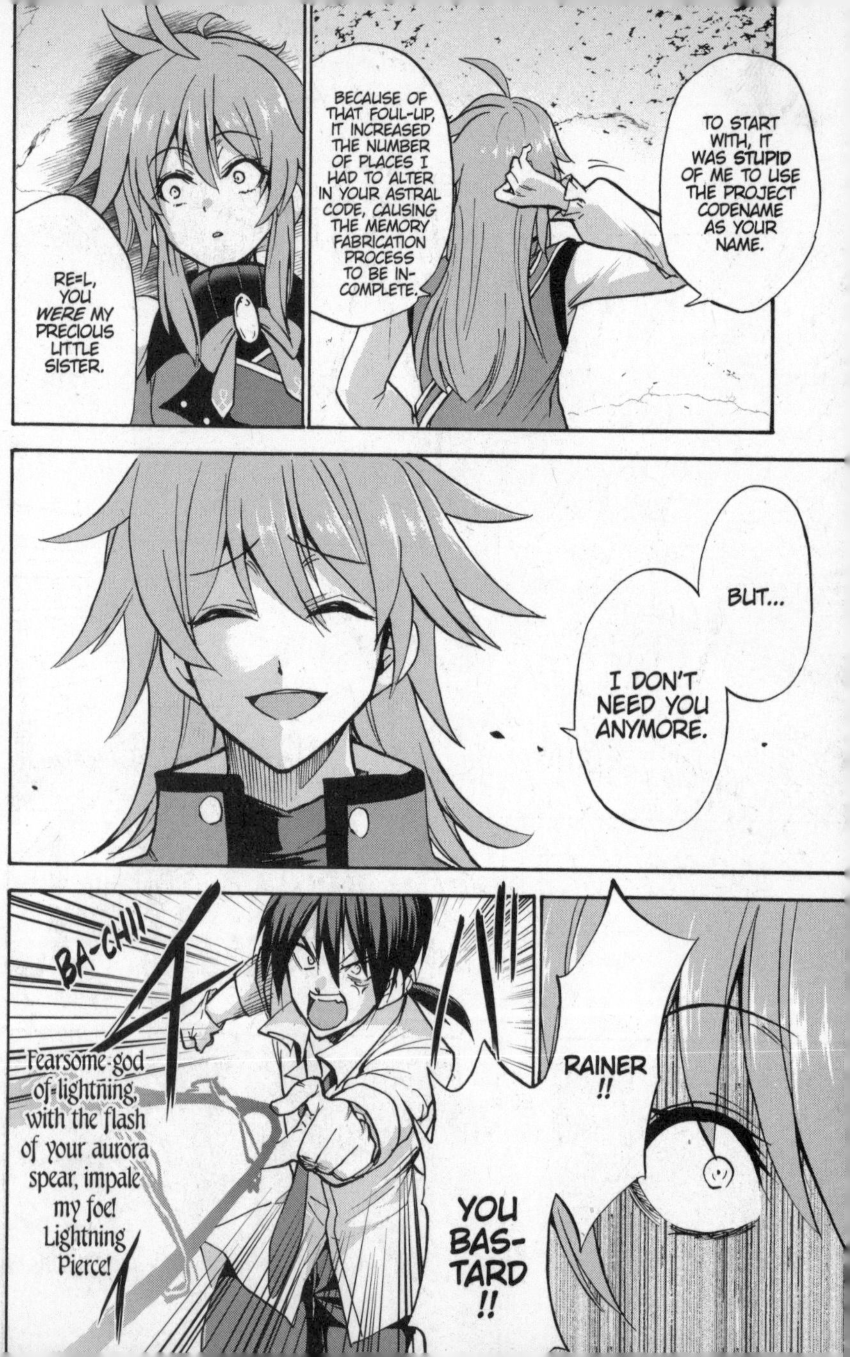
TO START WITH, IT WAS STUPID OF ME TO USE THE PROJECT CODENAME AS YOUR NAME.
BECAUSE OF THAT FOUL-UP, IT INCREASED THE NUMBER OF PLACES I HAD TO ALTER IN YOUR ASTRAL CODE, CAUSING THE MEMORY FABRICATION PROCESS TO BE IN-COMPLETE.
RE=L, YOU *WERE* MY PRECIOUS LITTLE SISTER.
BUT...
I DON'T NEED YOU ANYMORE.
RAINER!!
YOU BAS-TARD!!
BA-CHII
Fearsome god of lightning, with the flash of your aurora spear, impale my foe! Lightning Pierce!

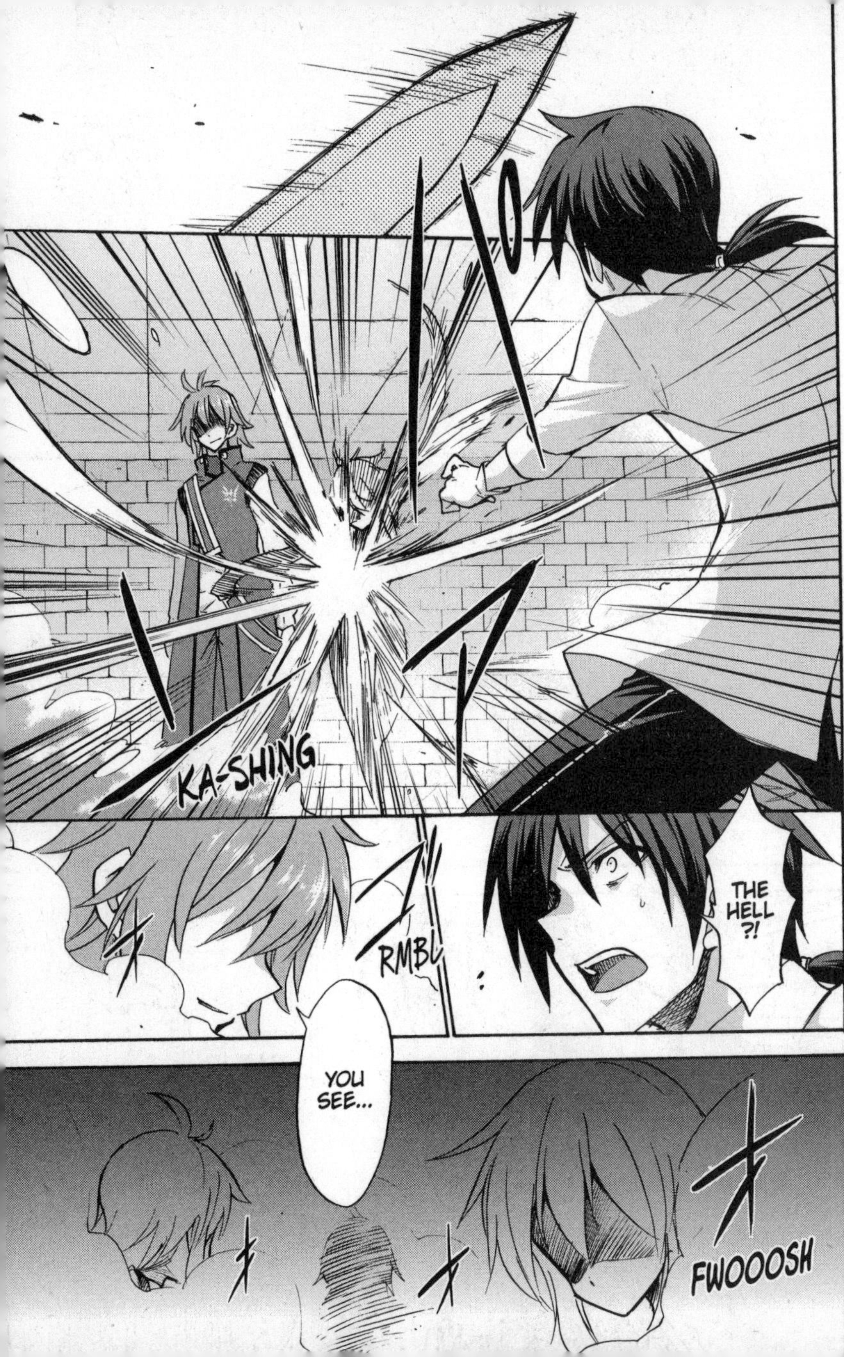
KA-SHING
THE HELL ?!
RMBL
YOU SEE...
FWOOOSH

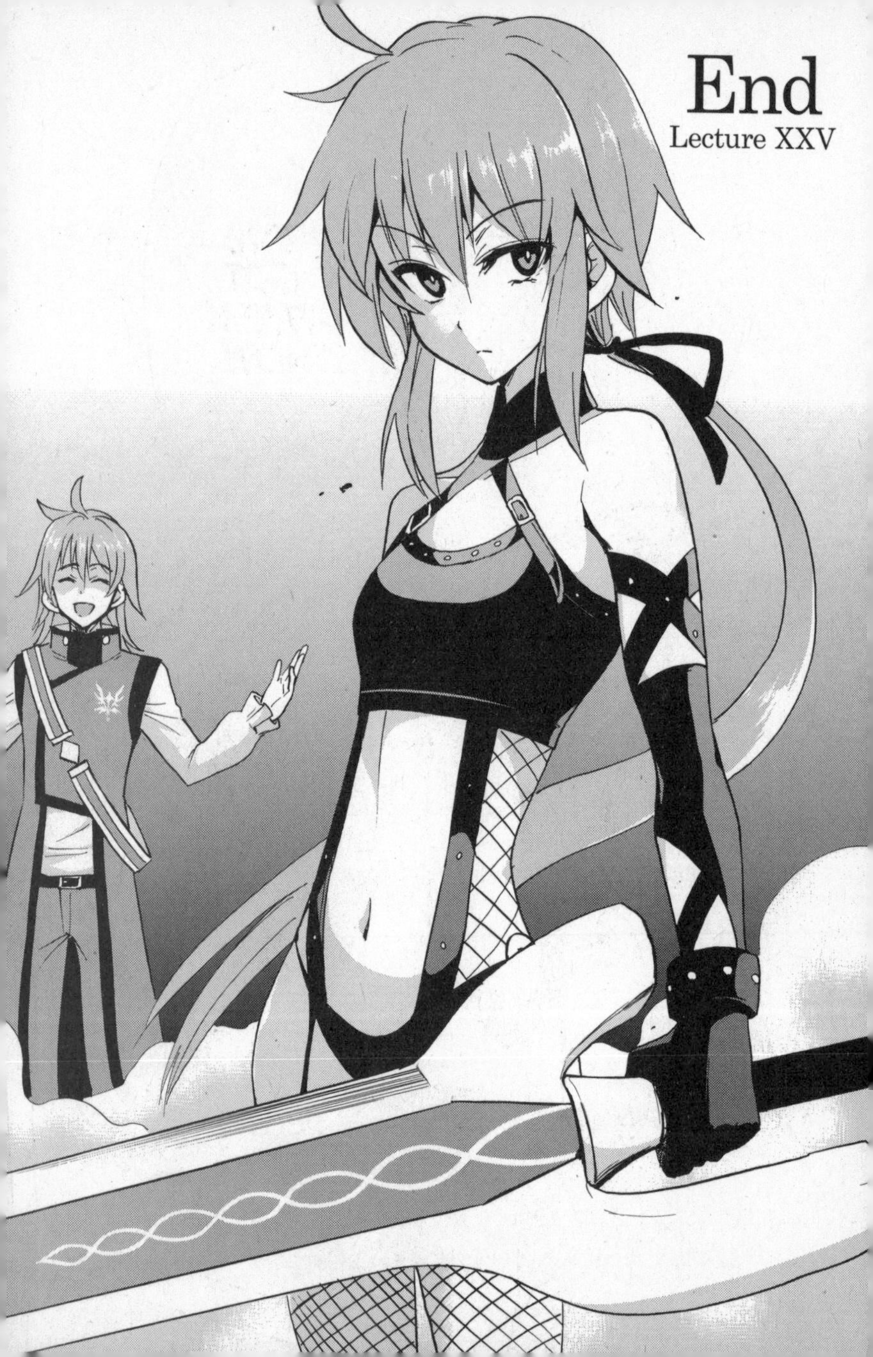
End
Lecture XXV

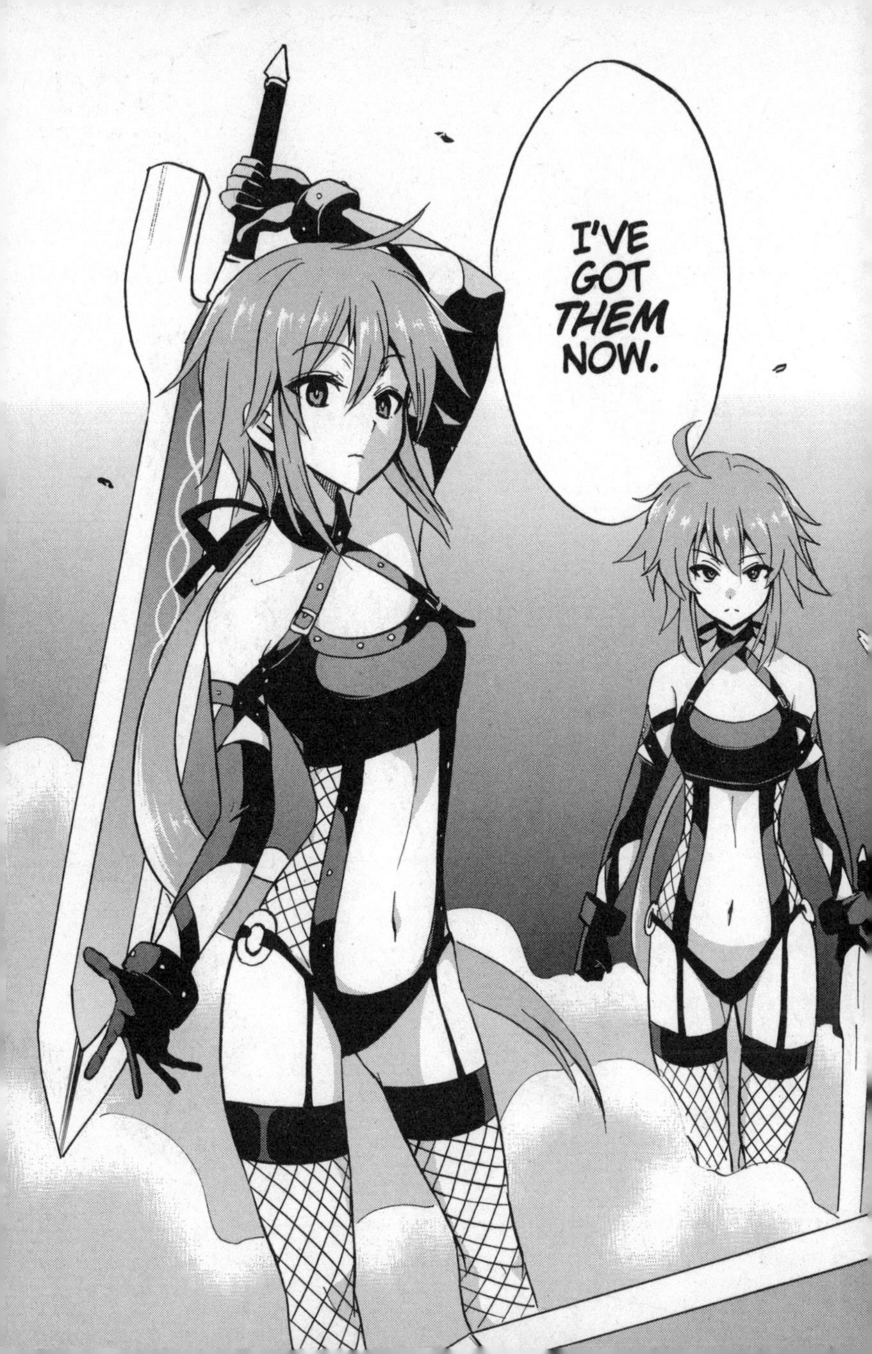
I'VE GOT THEM NOW.

Akashic Records

o f *Bastard* Magic *Instructor*

Lecture XXVI

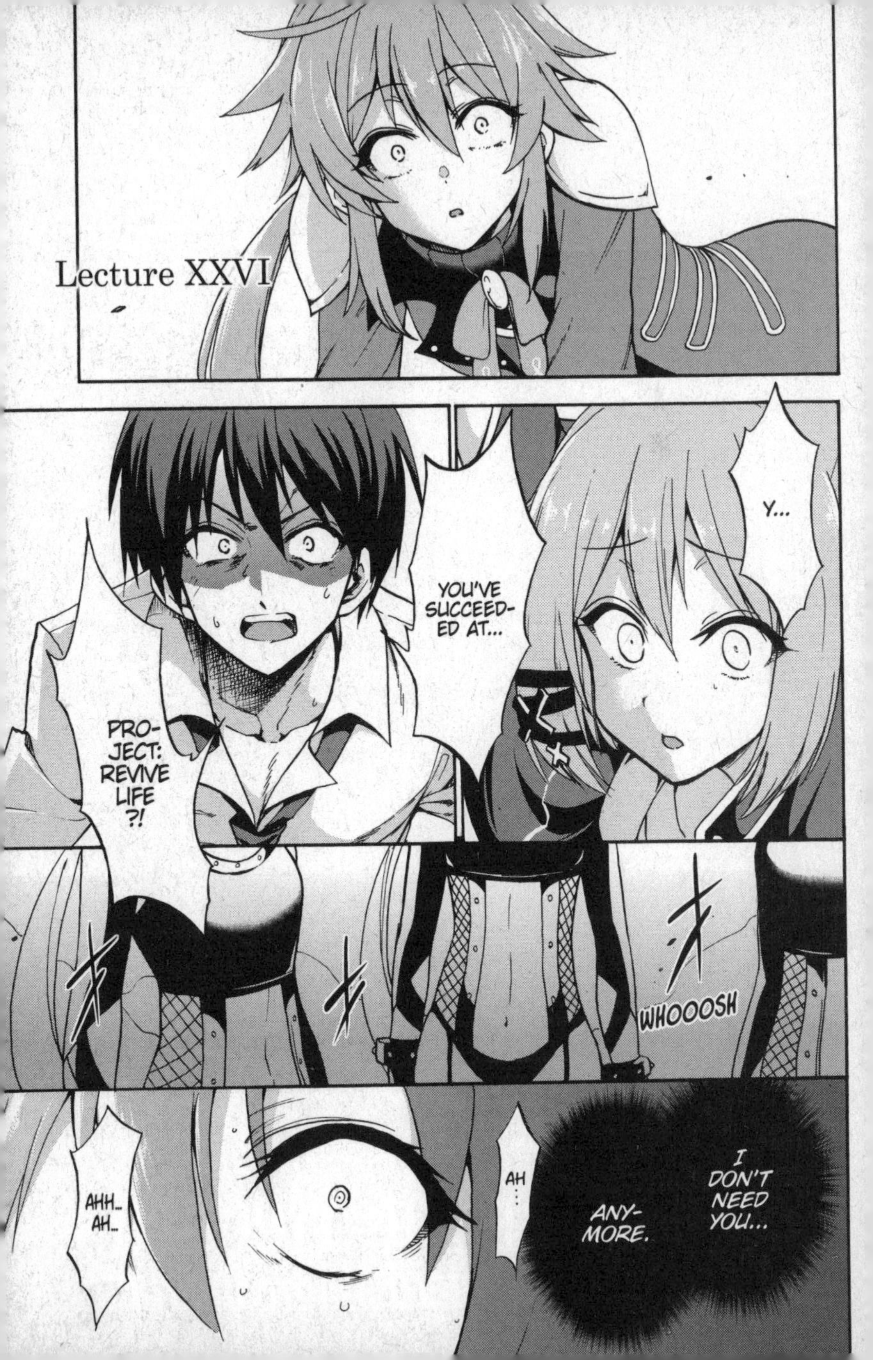

Y...
YOU'VE SUCCEEDED AT...
PROJECT: REVIVE LIFE ?!
WHOOOSH
I DON'T NEED YOU...
ANYMORE.
AH...
AHH.. AH...

Lecture XXVI

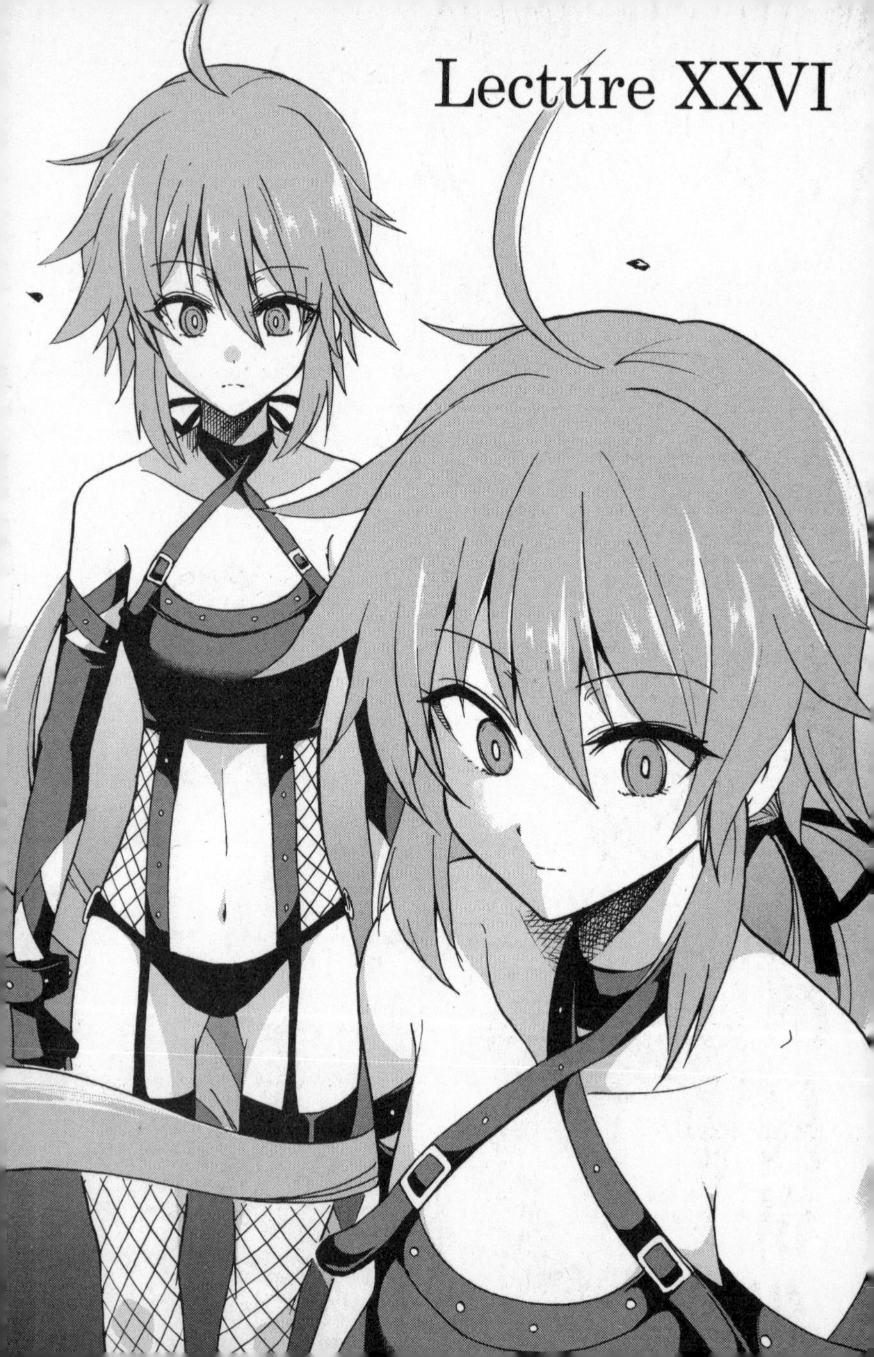

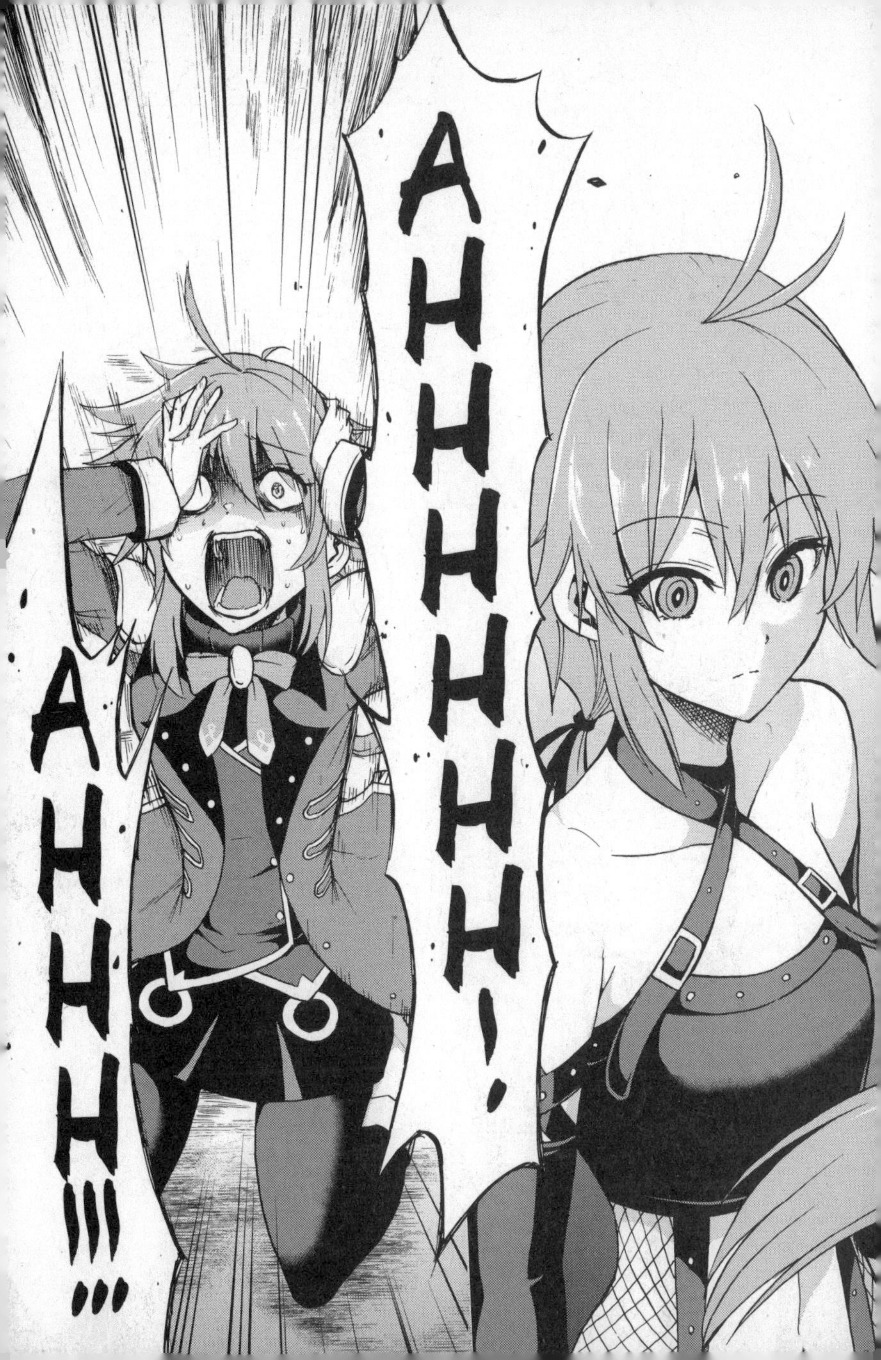
AHHHHHH!
AHHH!!!

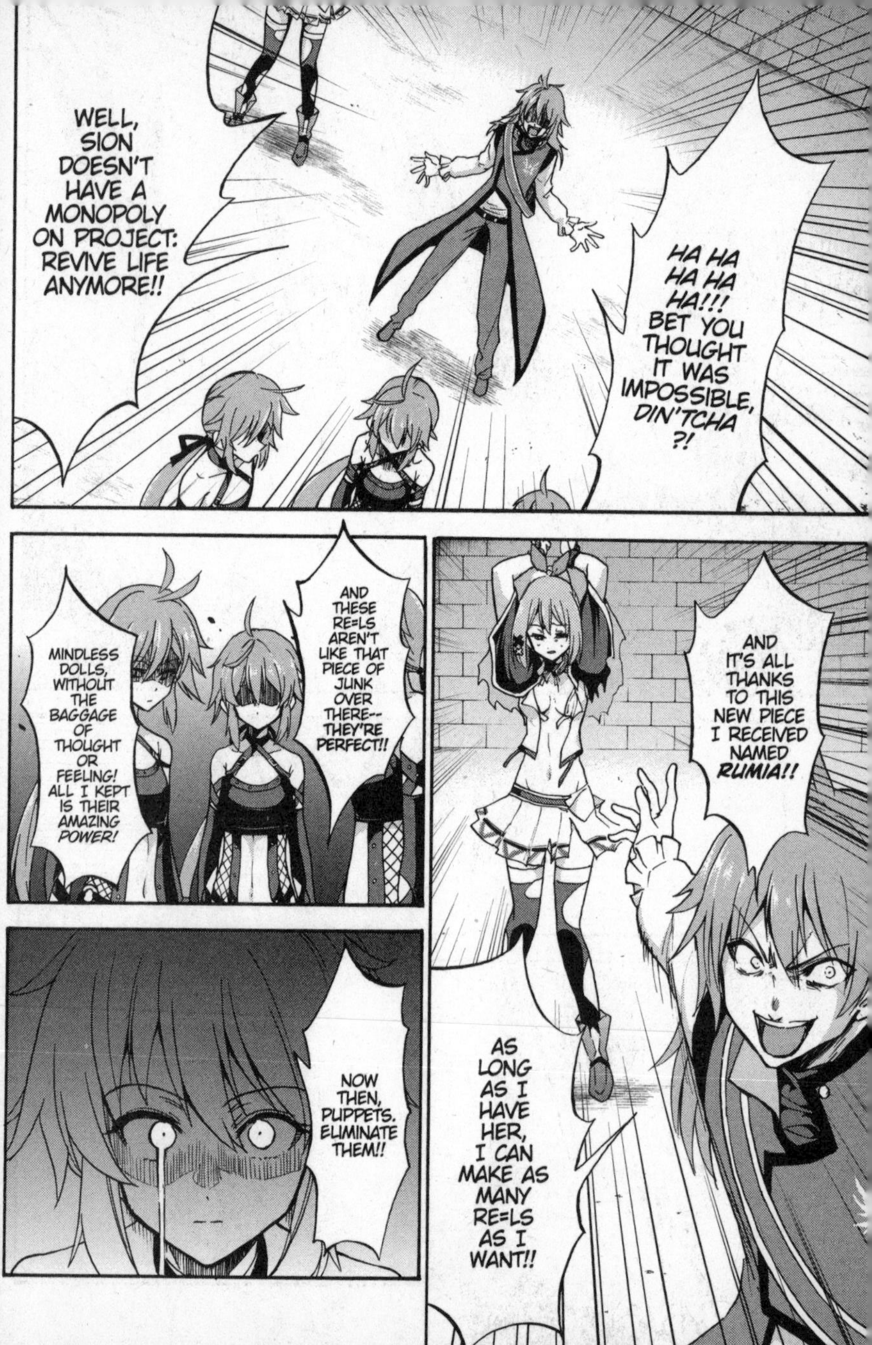
HA HA HA HA HA!!! BET YOU THOUGHT IT WAS IMPOSSIBLE, DIN'TCHA?!
WELL, SION DOESN'T HAVE A MONOPOLY ON PROJECT: REVIVE LIFE ANYMORE!!
AND IT'S ALL THANKS TO THIS NEW PIECE I RECEIVED NAMED RUMIA!!
AS LONG AS I HAVE HER, I CAN MAKE AS MANY RE=LS AS I WANT!!
AND THESE RE=LS AREN'T LIKE THAT PIECE OF JUNK OVER THERE-- THEY'RE PERFECT!!
MINDLESS DOLLS, WITHOUT THE BAGGAGE OF THOUGHT OR FEELING! ALL I KEPT IS THEIR AMAZING POWER!
NOW THEN, PUPPETS. ELIMINATE THEM!!

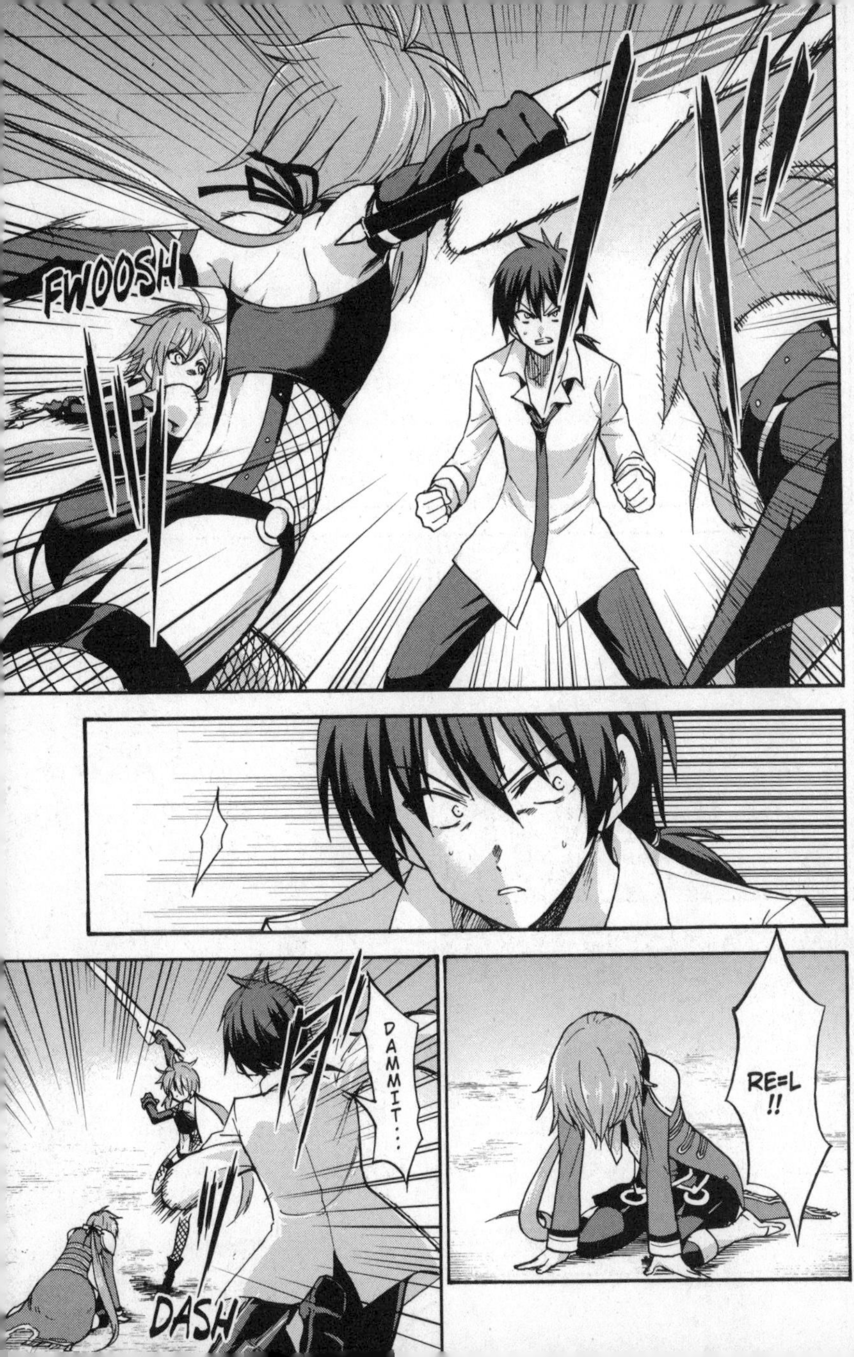
FWOOSH
RE=L !!
DAMMIT...
DASH

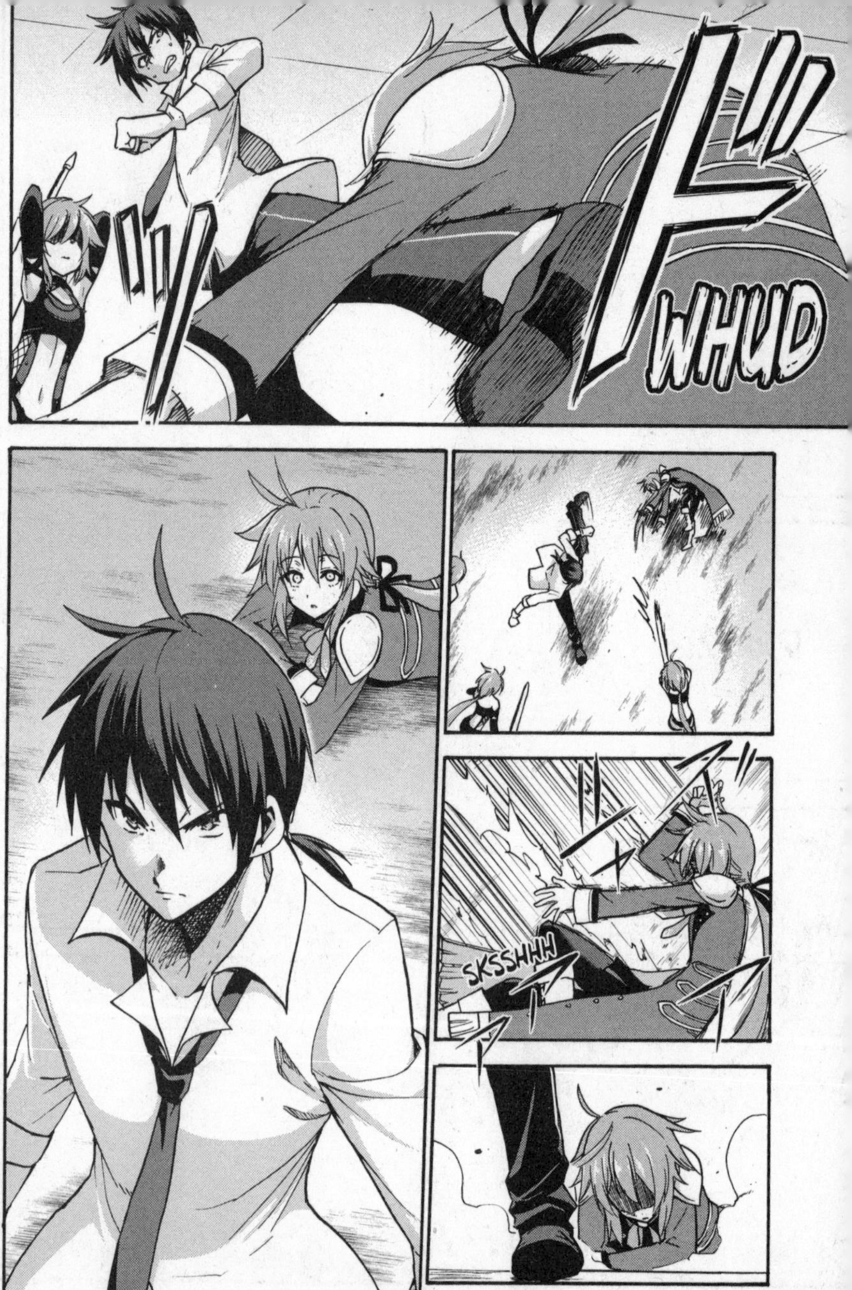
WHUD
SKSSHHH

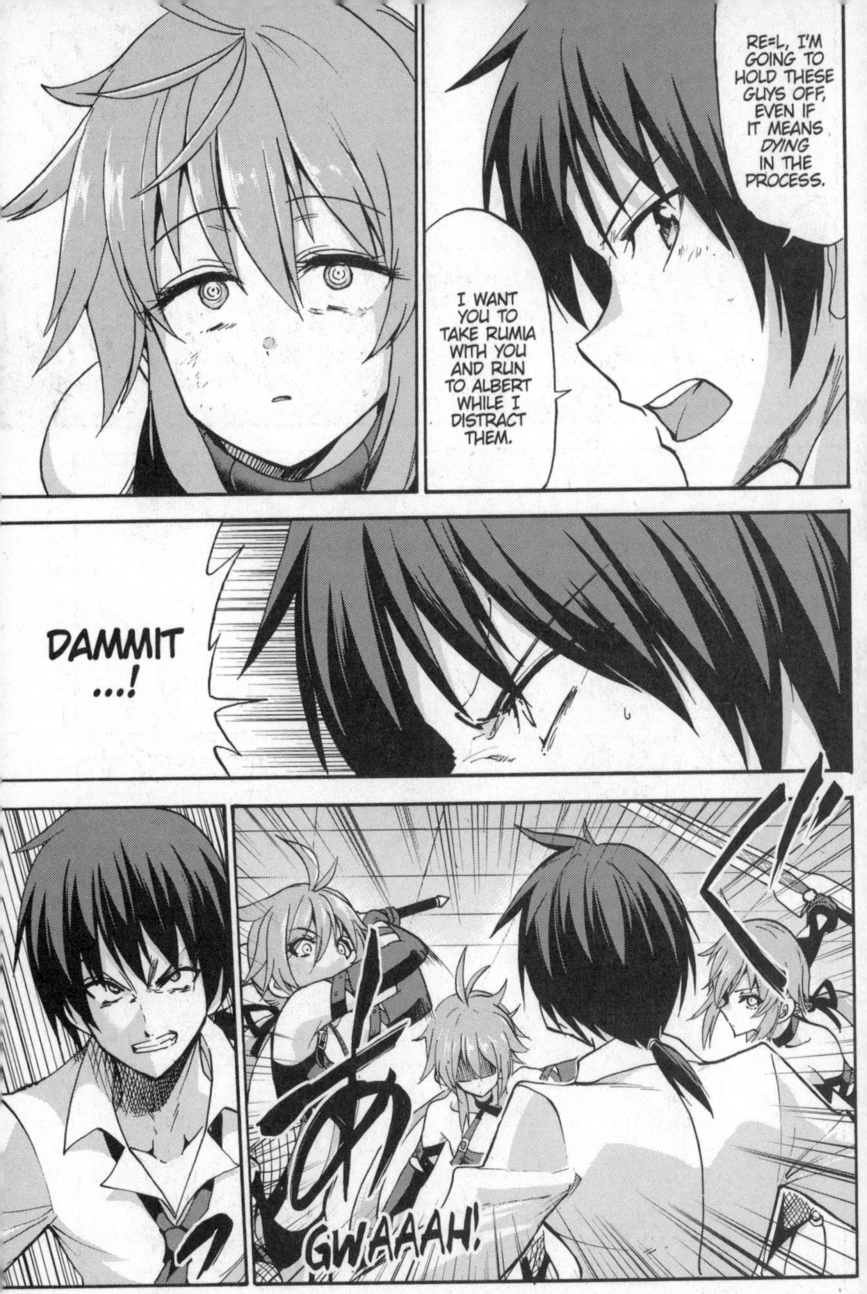
RE=L, I'M GOING TO HOLD THESE GUYS OFF, EVEN IF IT MEANS *DYING* IN THE PROCESS.
I WANT YOU TO TAKE RUMIA WITH YOU AND RUN TO ALBERT WHILE I DISTRACT THEM.
DAMMIT ...!
GWAAAH!

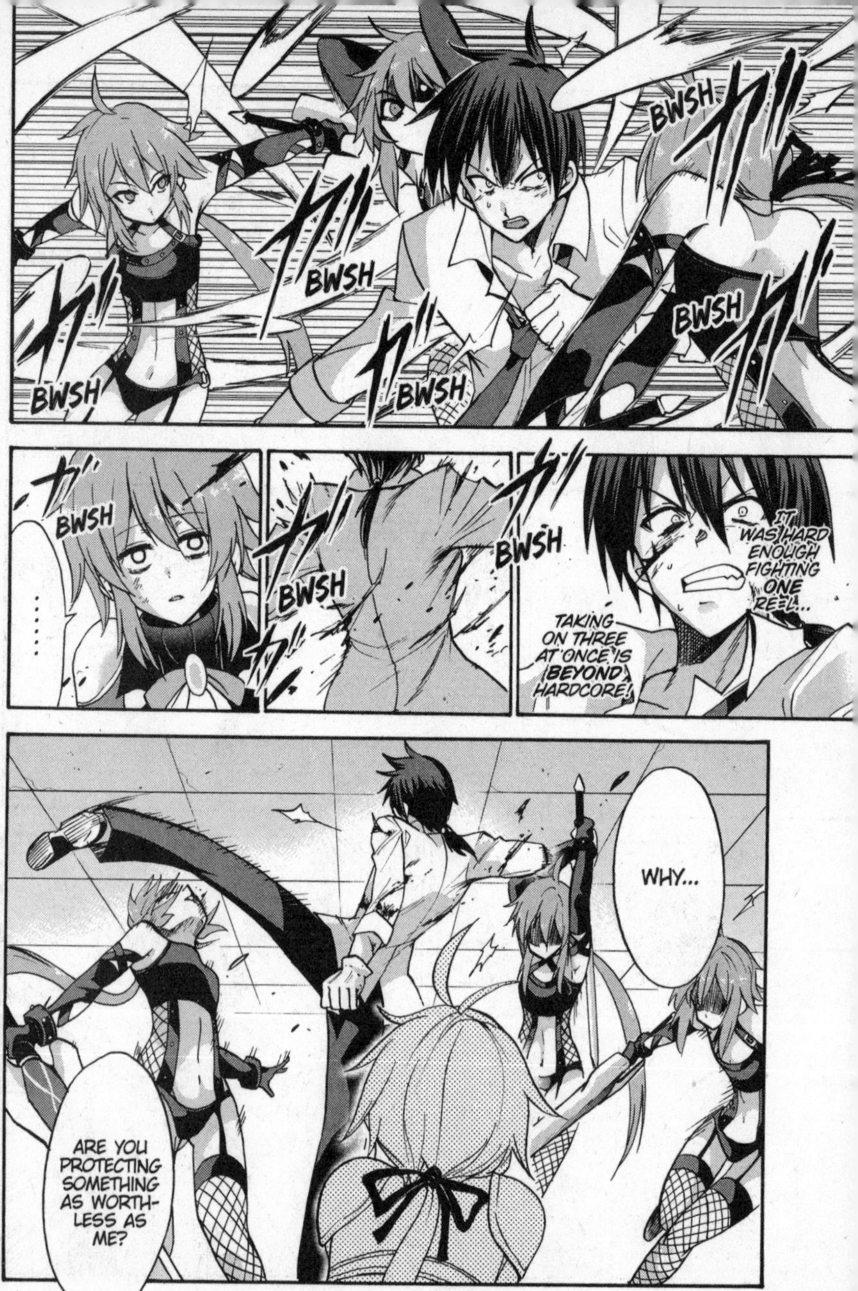
BWSH
BWSH
BWSH
BWSH
BWSH
BWSH
IT WAS HARD ENOUGH FIGHTING ONE REEL...
TAKING ON THREE AT ONCE IS BEYOND HARDCORE!
BWSH
BWSH
......
WHY...
ARE YOU PROTECTING SOMETHING AS WORTHLESS AS ME?

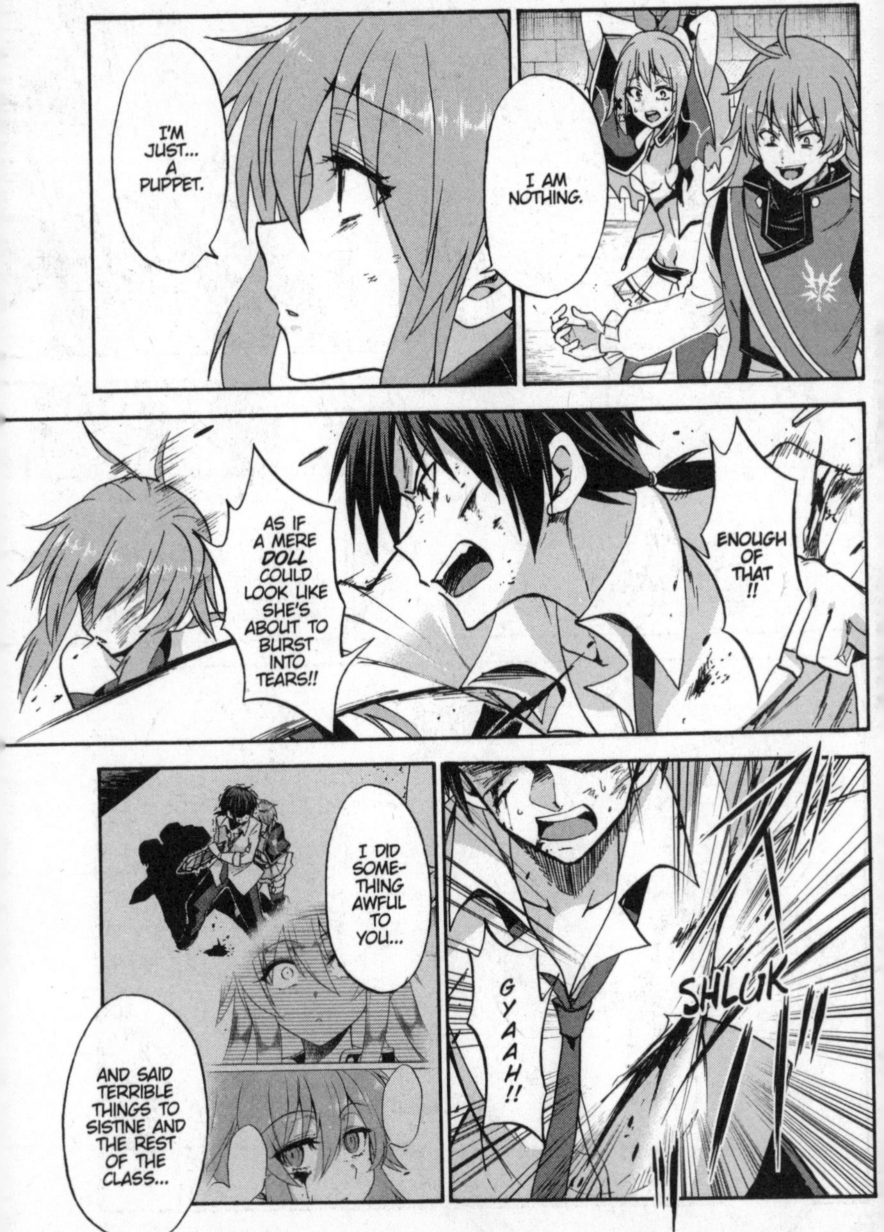
I AM NOTHING.
I'M JUST... A PUPPET.
ENOUGH OF THAT!!
AS IF A MERE DOLL COULD LOOK LIKE SHE'S ABOUT TO BURST INTO TEARS!!
SHLUK
GYAAAH!!
I DID SOMETHING AWFUL TO YOU...
AND SAID TERRIBLE THINGS TO SISTINE AND THE REST OF THE CLASS...

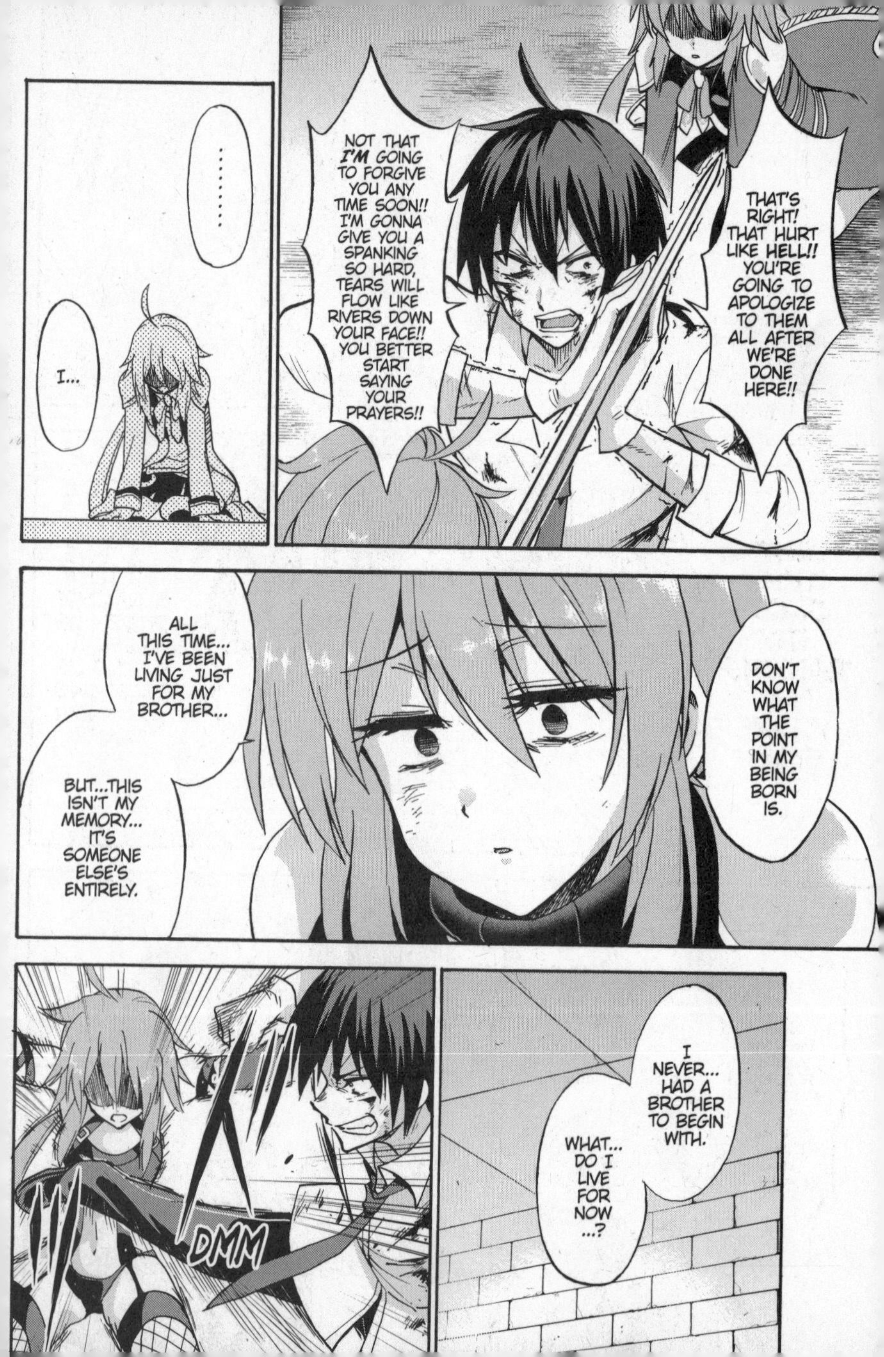
THAT'S RIGHT! THAT HURT LIKE HELL!! YOU'RE GOING TO APOLOGIZE TO THEM ALL AFTER WE'RE DONE HERE!!
NOT THAT *I'M* GOING TO FORGIVE YOU ANY TIME SOON!! I'M GONNA GIVE YOU A SPANKING SO HARD, TEARS WILL FLOW LIKE RIVERS DOWN YOUR FACE!! YOU BETTER START SAYING YOUR PRAYERS!!
......
I...
DON'T KNOW WHAT THE POINT IN MY BEING BORN IS.
ALL THIS TIME... I'VE BEEN LIVING JUST FOR MY BROTHER...
BUT...THIS ISN'T MY MEMORY... IT'S SOMEONE ELSE'S ENTIRELY.
I NEVER... HAD A BROTHER TO BEGIN WITH.
WHAT... DO I LIVE FOR NOW ...?
DMM

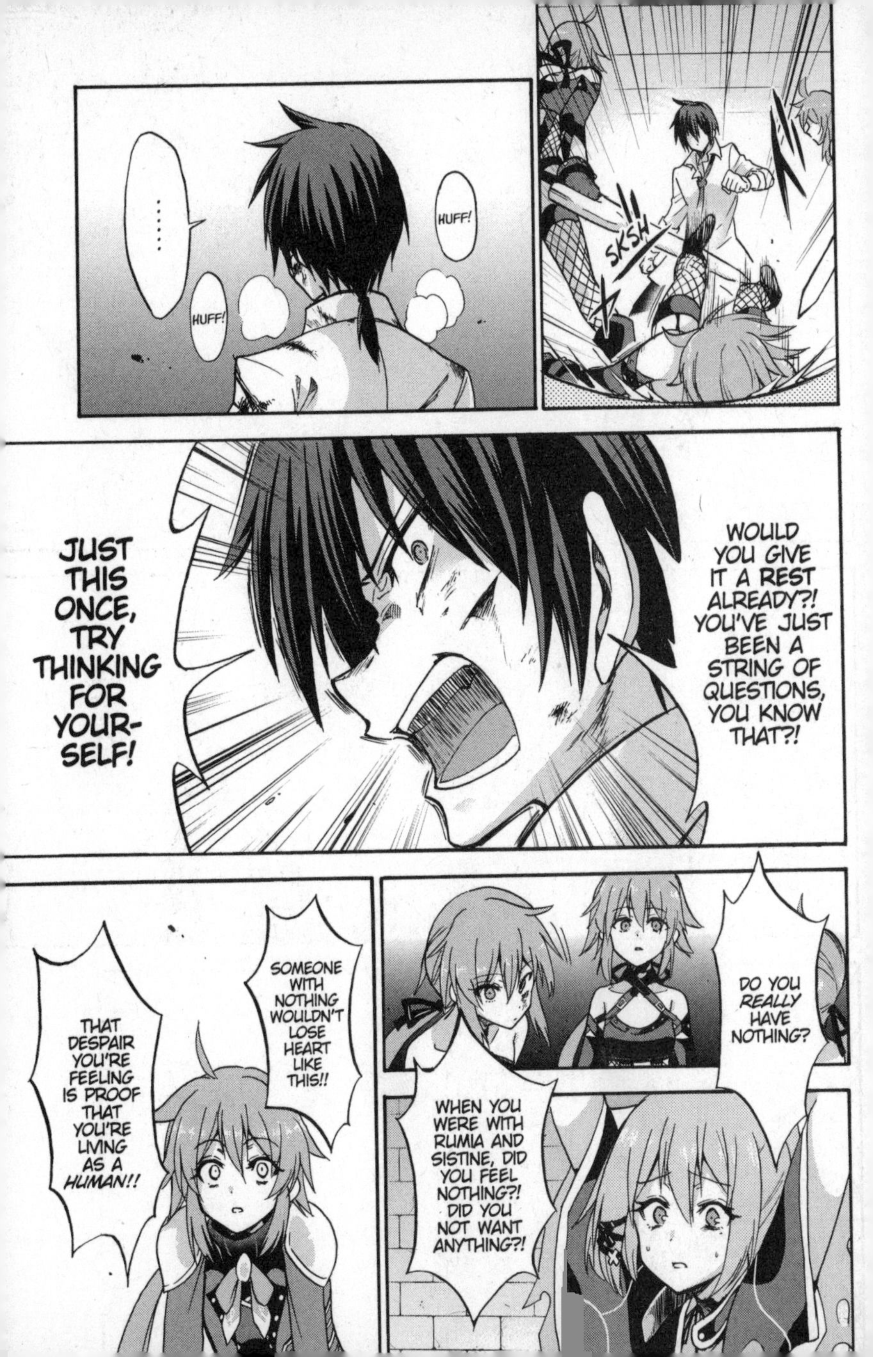
SKSH
HUFF!
......
HUFF!
WOULD YOU GIVE IT A REST ALREADY?! YOU'VE JUST BEEN A STRING OF QUESTIONS, YOU KNOW THAT?!
JUST THIS ONCE, TRY THINKING FOR YOUR-SELF!
DO YOU *REALLY* HAVE NOTHING?
WHEN YOU WERE WITH RUMIA AND SISTINE, DID YOU FEEL NOTHING?! DID YOU NOT WANT ANYTHING?!
SOMEONE WITH NOTHING WOULDN'T LOSE HEART LIKE THIS!!
THAT DESPAIR YOU'RE FEELING IS PROOF THAT YOU'RE LIVING AS A *HUMAN*!!

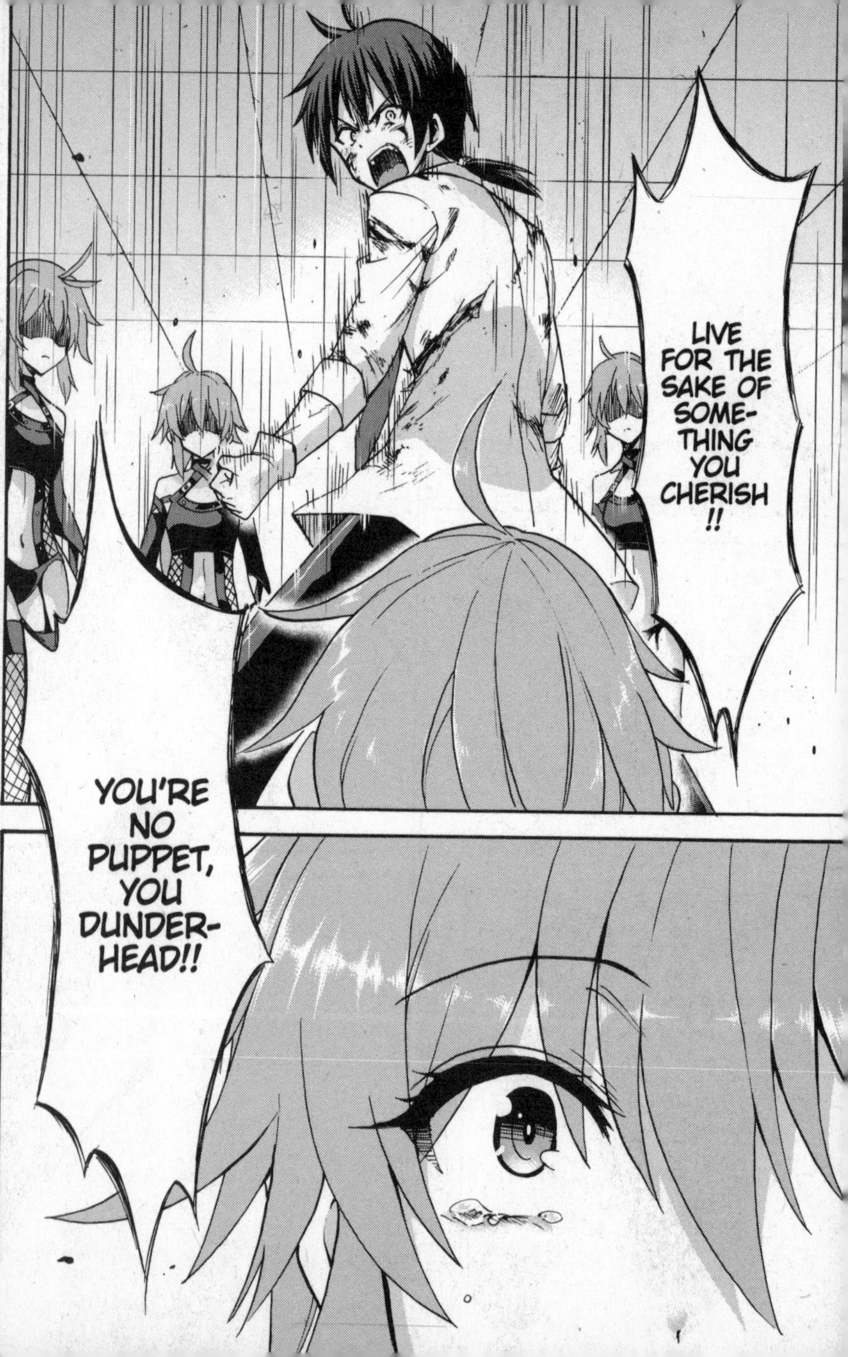
LIVE FOR THE SAKE OF SOME-THING YOU CHERISH !!
YOU'RE NO PUPPET, YOU DUNDER-HEAD!!

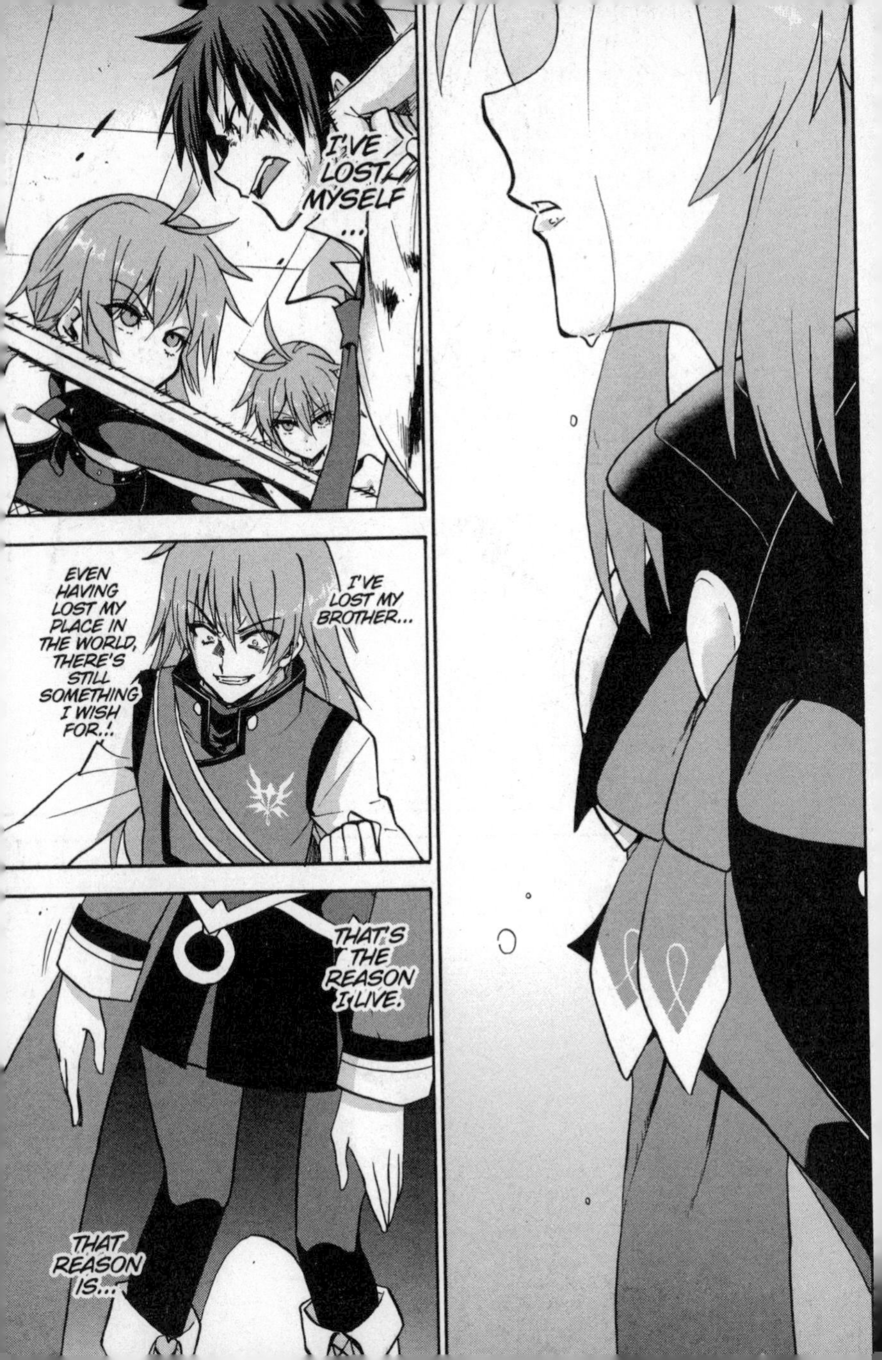
I'VE LOST MYSELF...
I'VE LOST MY BROTHER...
EVEN HAVING LOST MY PLACE IN THE WORLD, THERE'S STILL SOMETHING I WISH FOR..!
THAT'S THE REASON I LIVE.
THAT REASON IS...

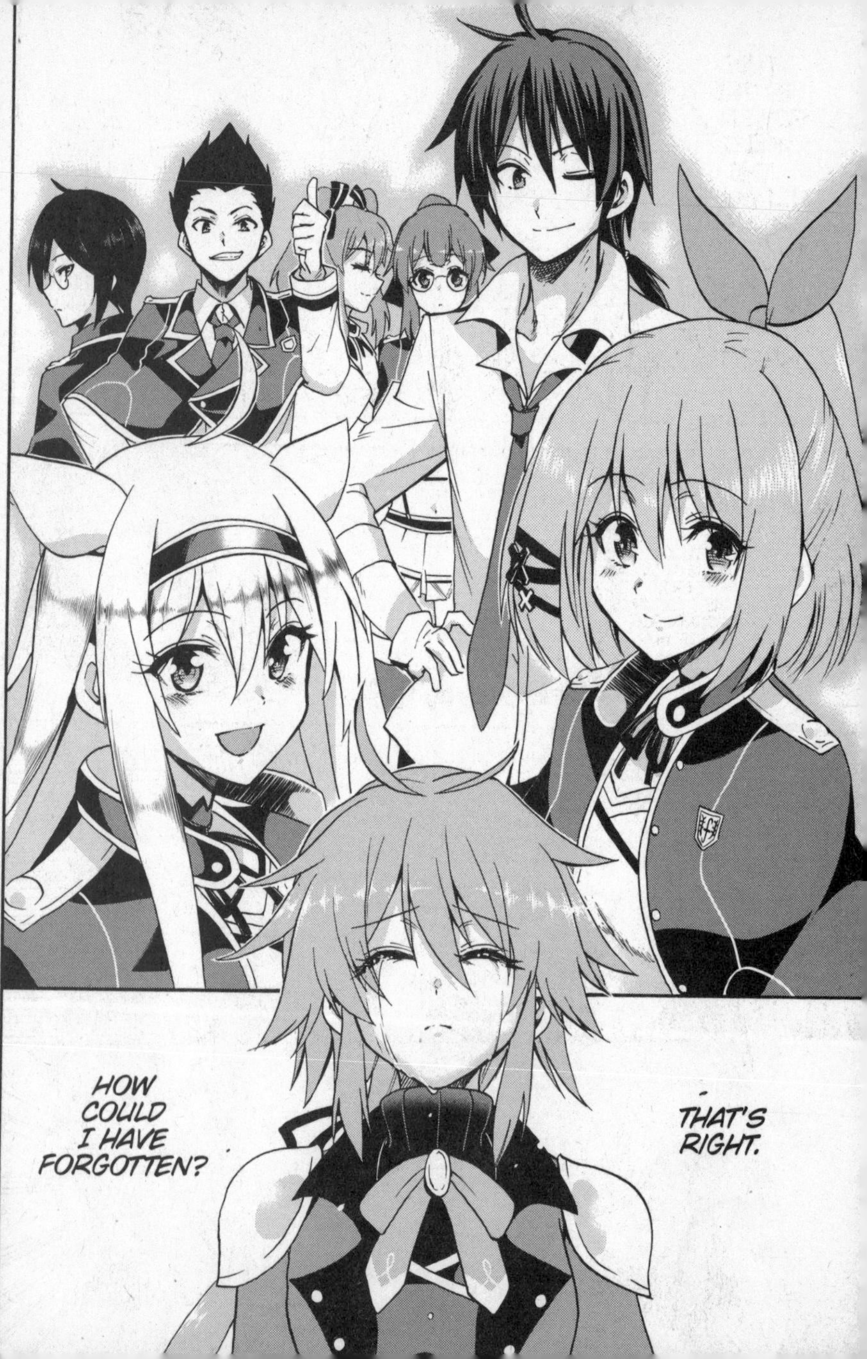
THAT'S RIGHT.
HOW COULD I HAVE FORGOTTEN?

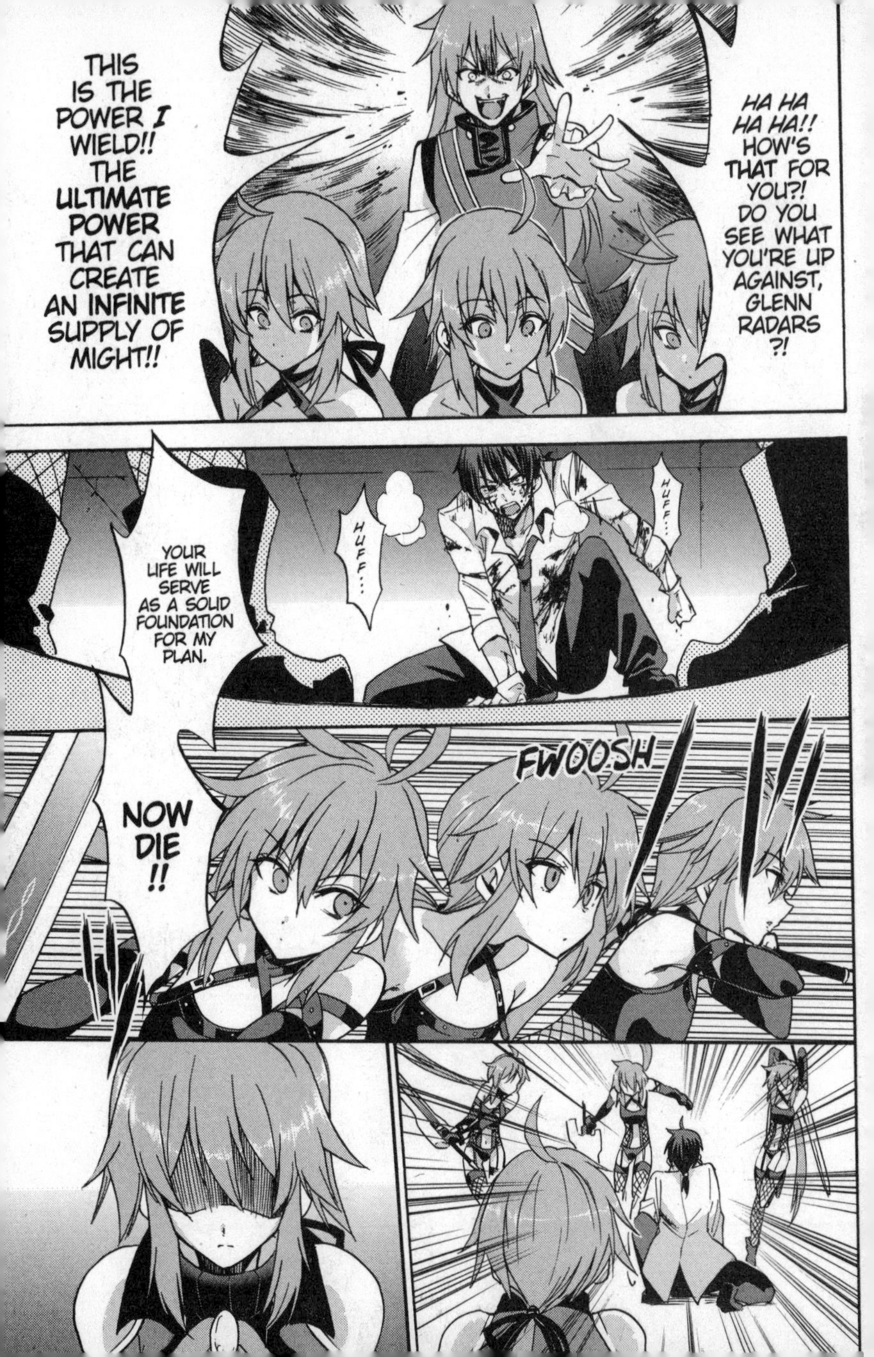
HA HA HA HA!! HOW'S THAT FOR YOU?! DO YOU SEE WHAT YOU'RE UP AGAINST, GLENN RADARS ?!
THIS IS THE POWER I WIELD!! THE ULTIMATE POWER THAT CAN CREATE AN INFINITE SUPPLY OF MIGHT!!
HUFF...
HUFF...
YOUR LIFE WILL SERVE AS A SOLID FOUNDATION FOR MY PLAN.
FWOOSH
NOW DIE !!

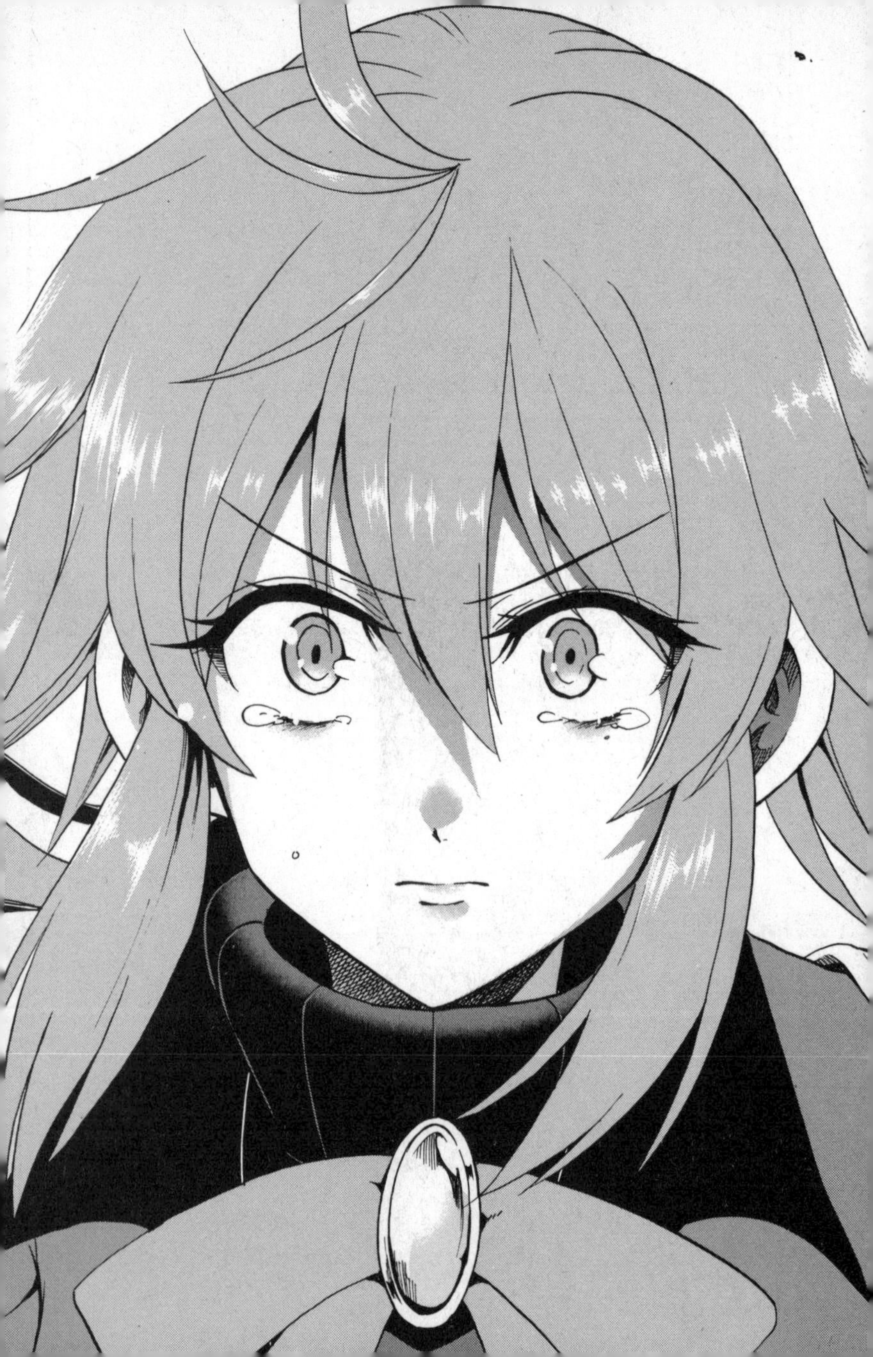

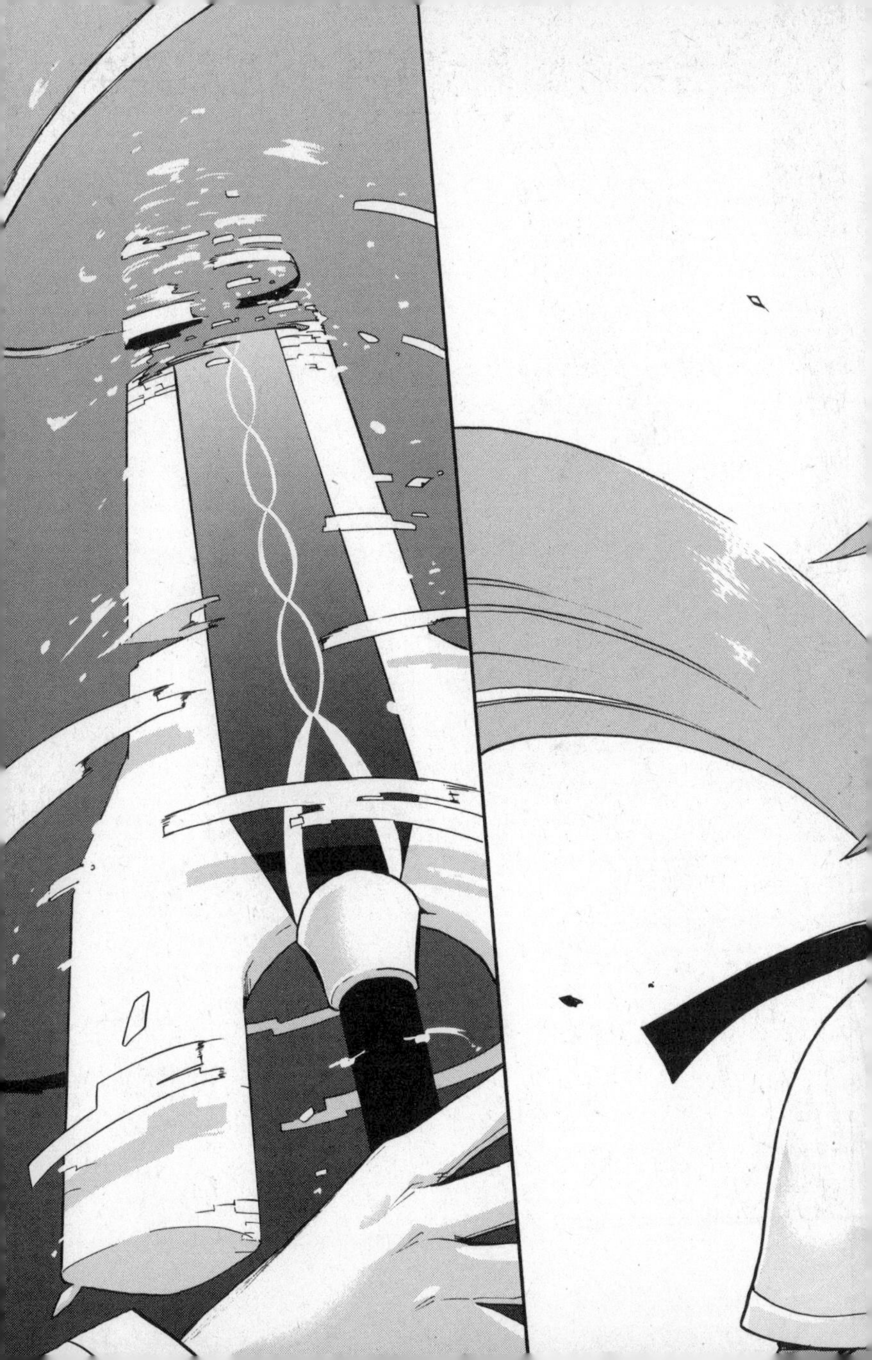

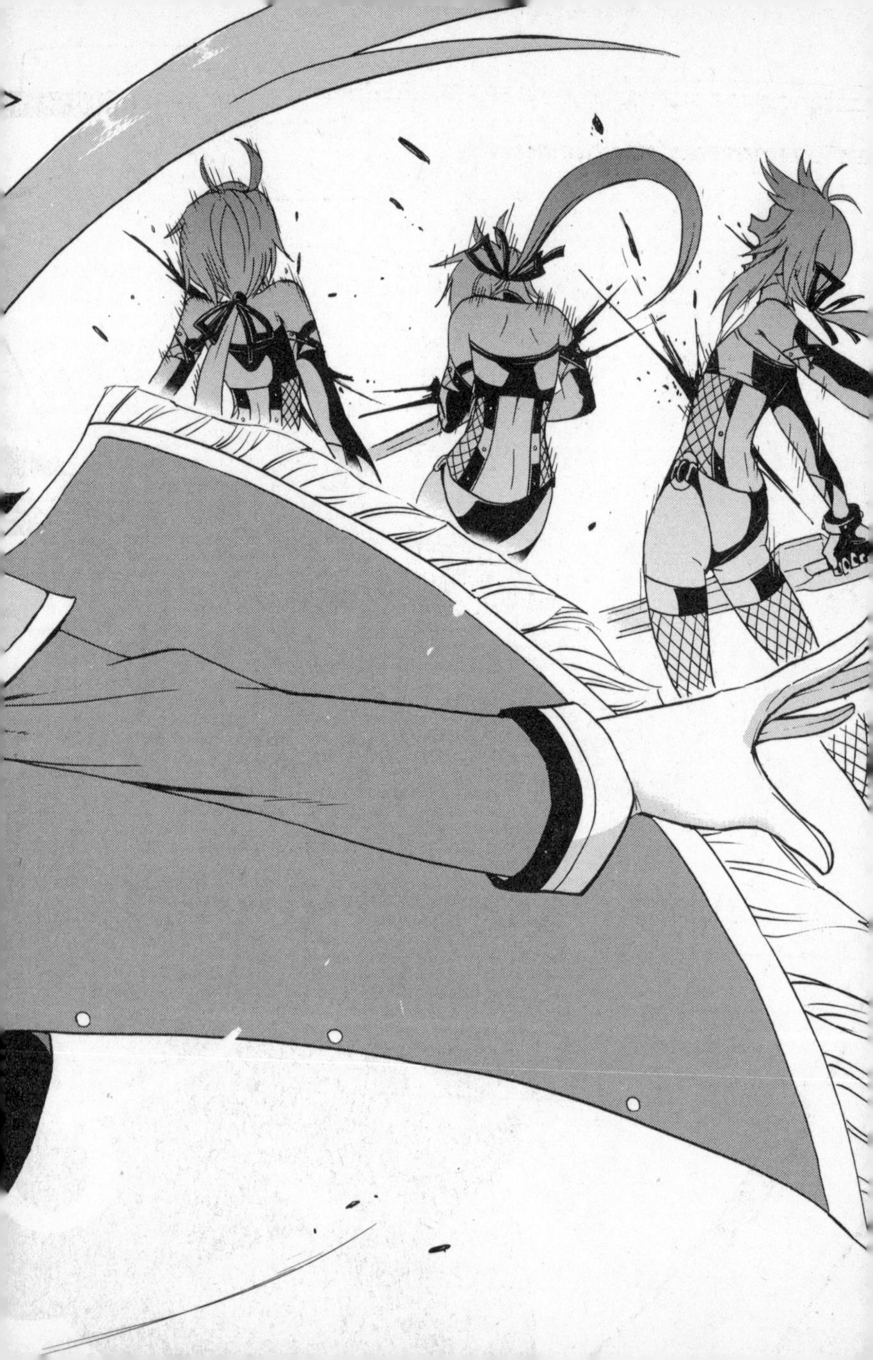

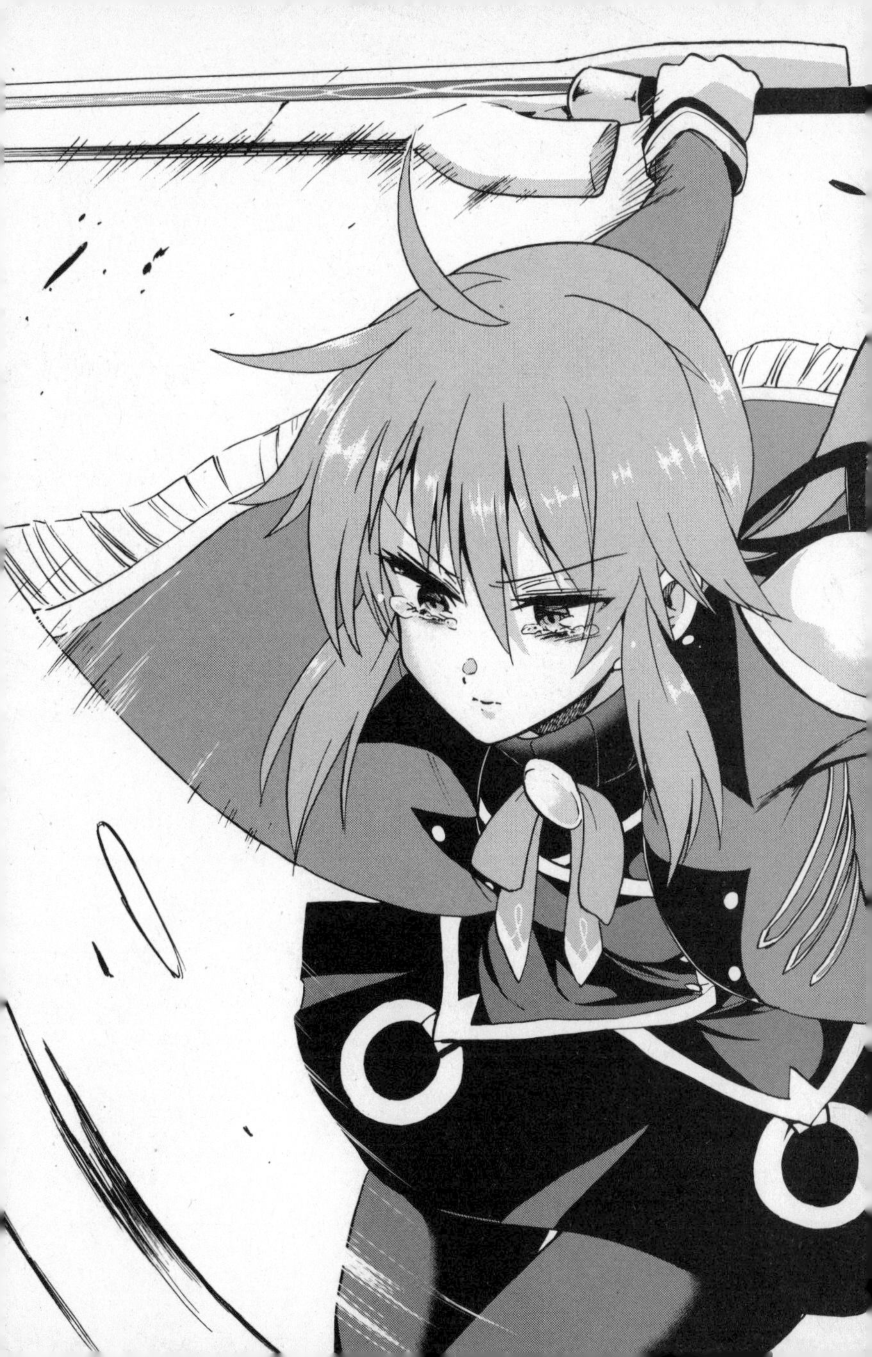

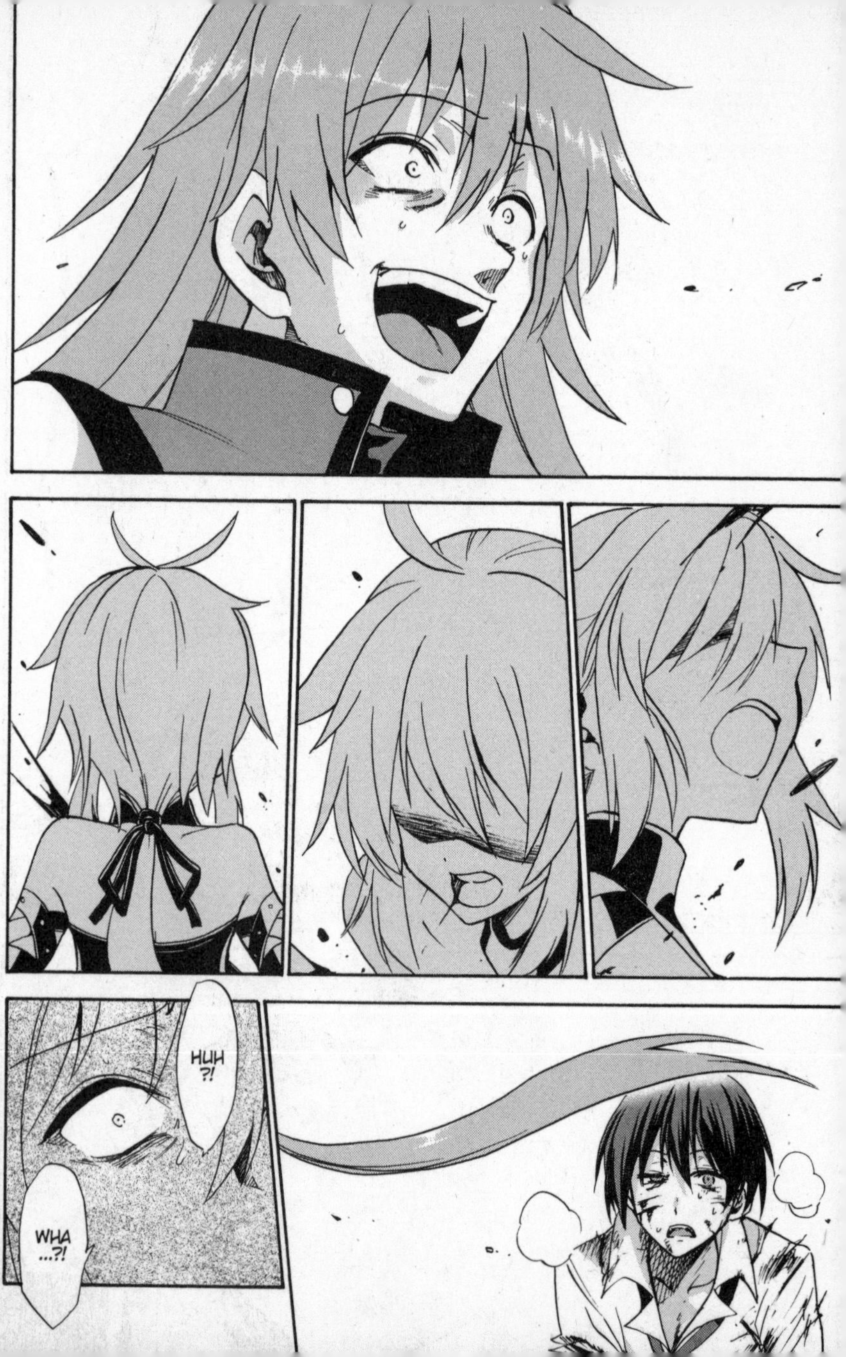
HUH ?!
WHA ...?!

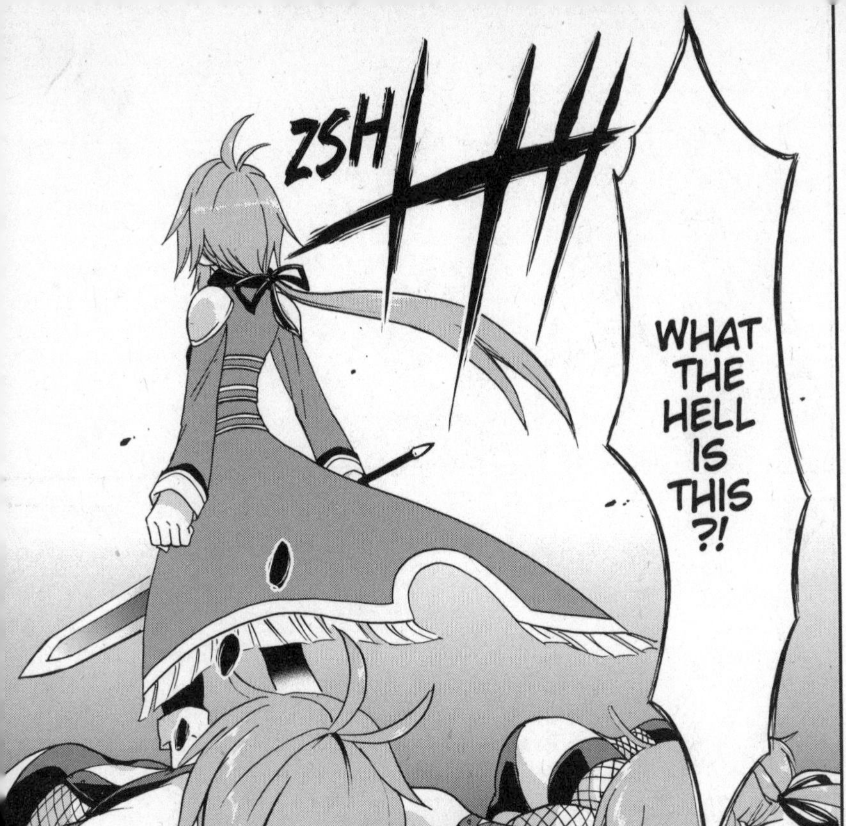
ZSH
WHAT THE HELL IS THIS?!
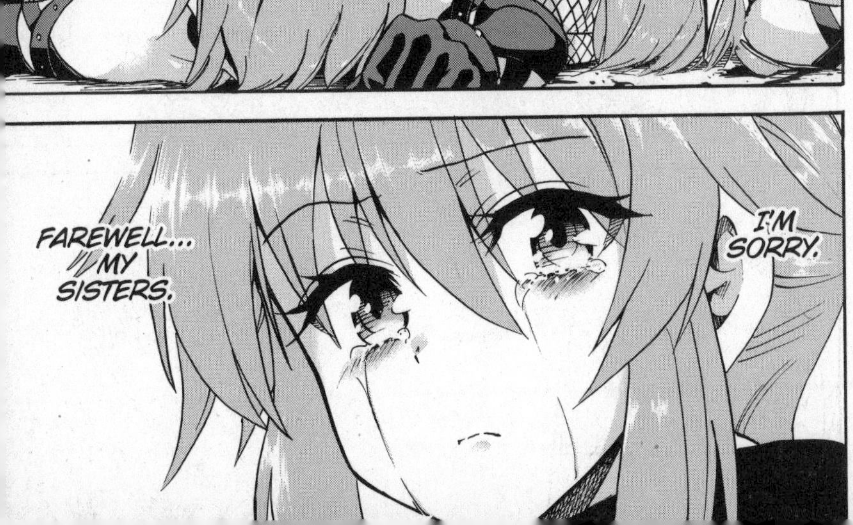
I'M SORRY.
FAREWELL... MY SISTERS.

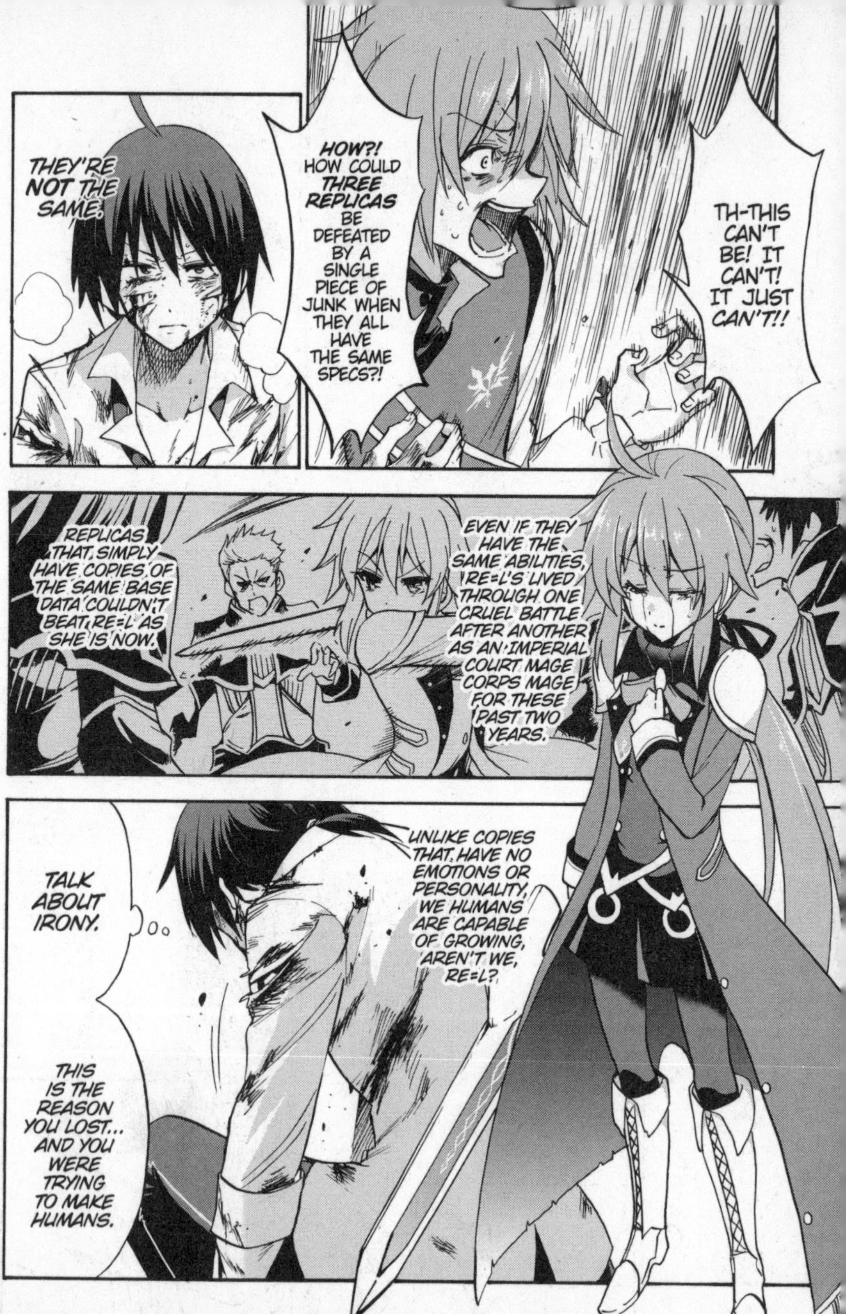
TH-THIS CAN'T BE! IT CAN'T! IT JUST CAN'T?!!
HOW?! HOW COULD THREE REPLICAS BE DEFEATED BY A SINGLE PIECE OF JUNK WHEN THEY ALL HAVE THE SAME SPECS?!
THEY'RE NOT THE SAME.
EVEN IF THEY HAVE THE SAME ABILITIES, RE=L'S LIVED THROUGH ONE CRUEL BATTLE AFTER ANOTHER AS AN IMPERIAL COURT MAGE CORPS MAGE FOR THESE PAST TWO YEARS.
REPLICAS THAT SIMPLY HAVE COPIES OF THE SAME BASE DATA COULDN'T BEAT RE=L AS SHE IS NOW.
UNLIKE COPIES THAT HAVE NO EMOTIONS OR PERSONALITY, WE HUMANS ARE CAPABLE OF GROWING, AREN'T WE, RE=L?
TALK ABOUT IRONY.
THIS IS THE REASON YOU LOST... AND YOU WERE TRYING TO MAKE HUMANS.

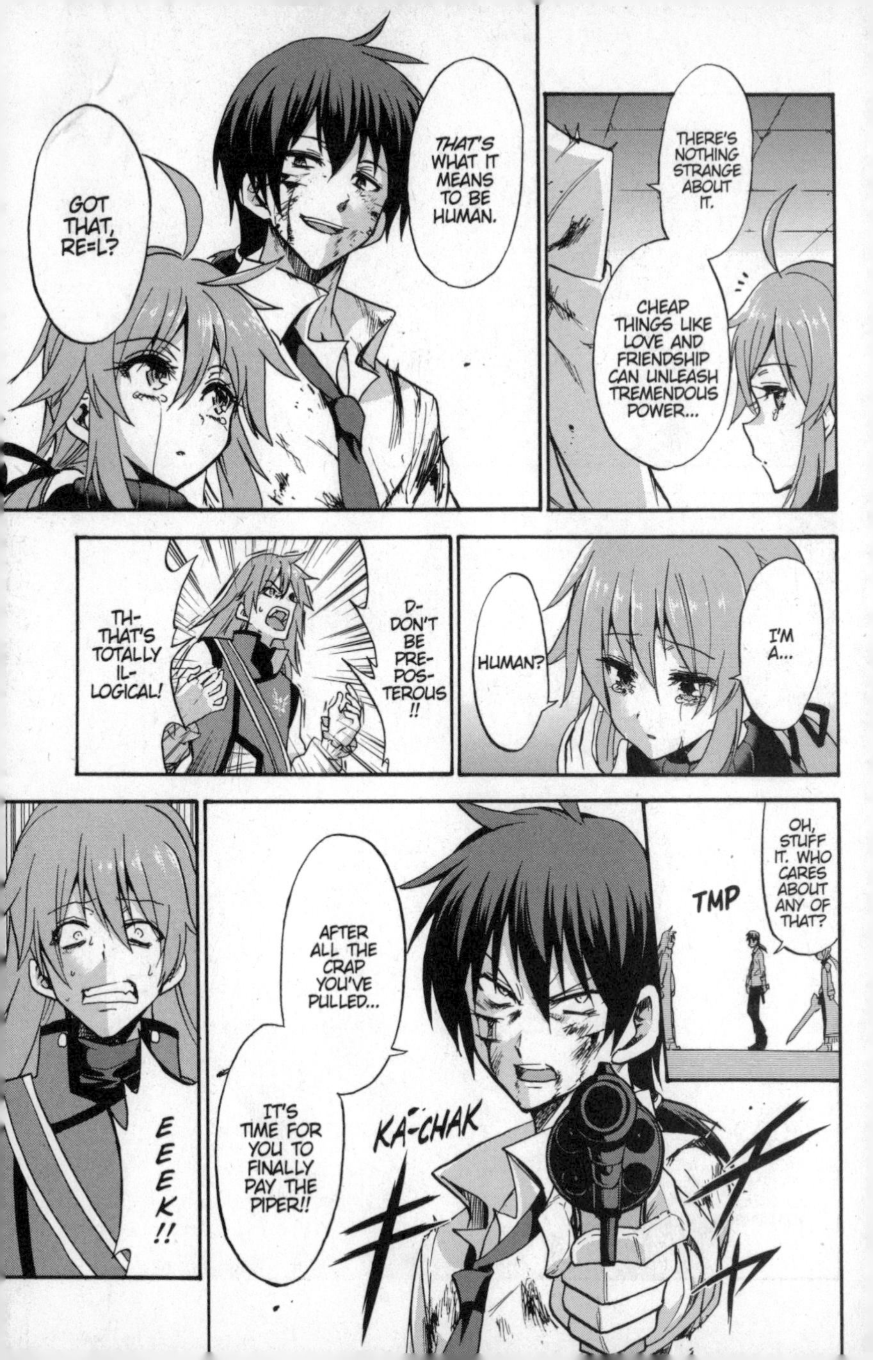
THERE'S NOTHING STRANGE ABOUT IT.
CHEAP THINGS LIKE LOVE AND FRIENDSHIP CAN UNLEASH TREMENDOUS POWER...
THAT'S WHAT IT MEANS TO BE HUMAN.
GOT THAT, RE=L?
I'M A...
HUMAN?
D-DON'T BE PRE-POS-TEROUS!!
TH-THAT'S TOTALLY IL-LOGICAL!
OH, STUFF IT. WHO CARES ABOUT ANY OF THAT?
TMP
AFTER ALL THE CRAP YOU'VE PULLED...
KA-CHAK
IT'S TIME FOR YOU TO FINALLY PAY THE PIPER!!
EEEK!!

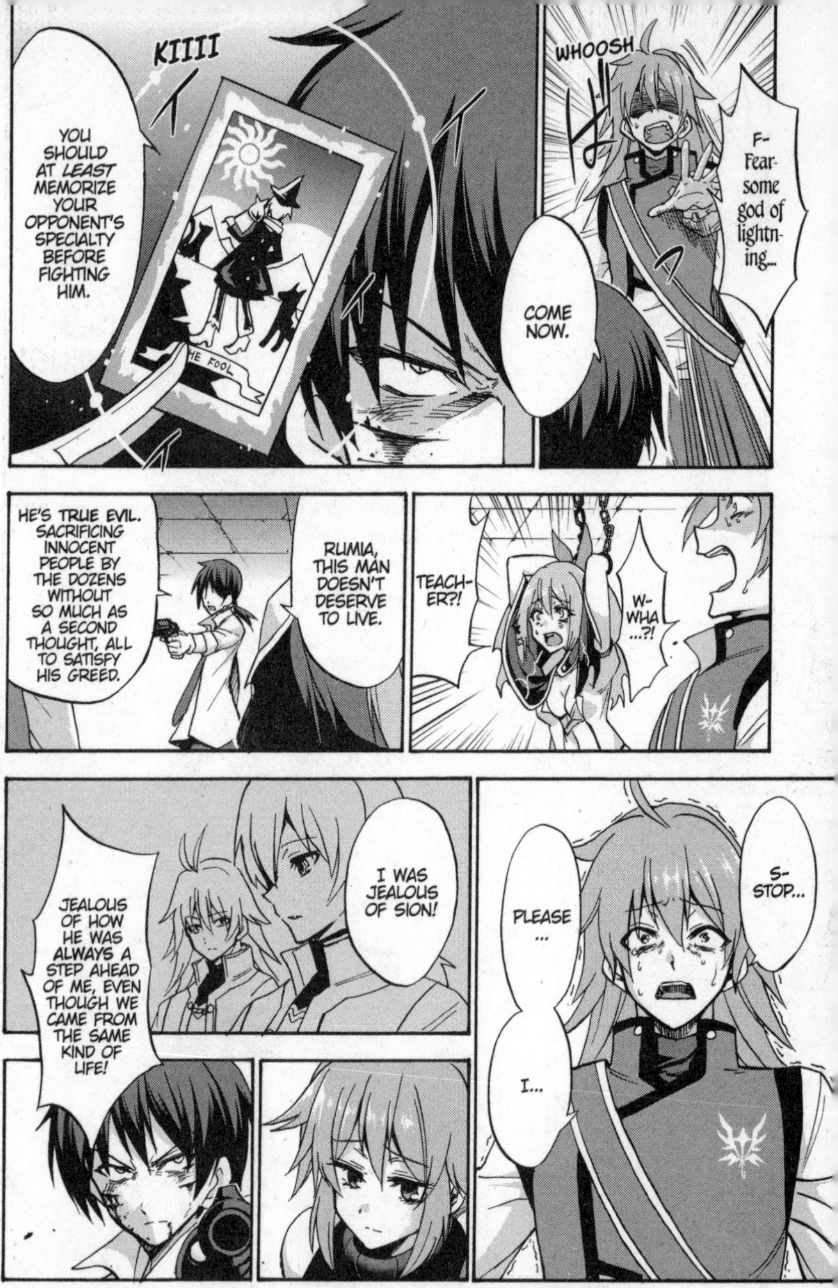
WHOOSH
F- Fear-some god of lightn-ing...
COME NOW.
KIIII
YOU SHOULD AT *LEAST* MEMORIZE YOUR OPPONENT'S SPECIALTY BEFORE FIGHTING HIM.
THE FOOL
W- WHA ...?!
TEACHER?!
RUMIA, THIS MAN DOESN'T DESERVE TO LIVE.
HE'S TRUE EVIL. SACRIFICING INNOCENT PEOPLE BY THE DOZENS WITHOUT SO MUCH AS A SECOND THOUGHT, ALL TO SATISFY HIS GREED.
S- STOP...
PLEASE ...
I...
I WAS JEALOUS OF SION!
JEALOUS OF HOW HE WAS ALWAYS A STEP AHEAD OF ME, EVEN THOUGH WE CAME FROM THE SAME KIND OF LIFE!

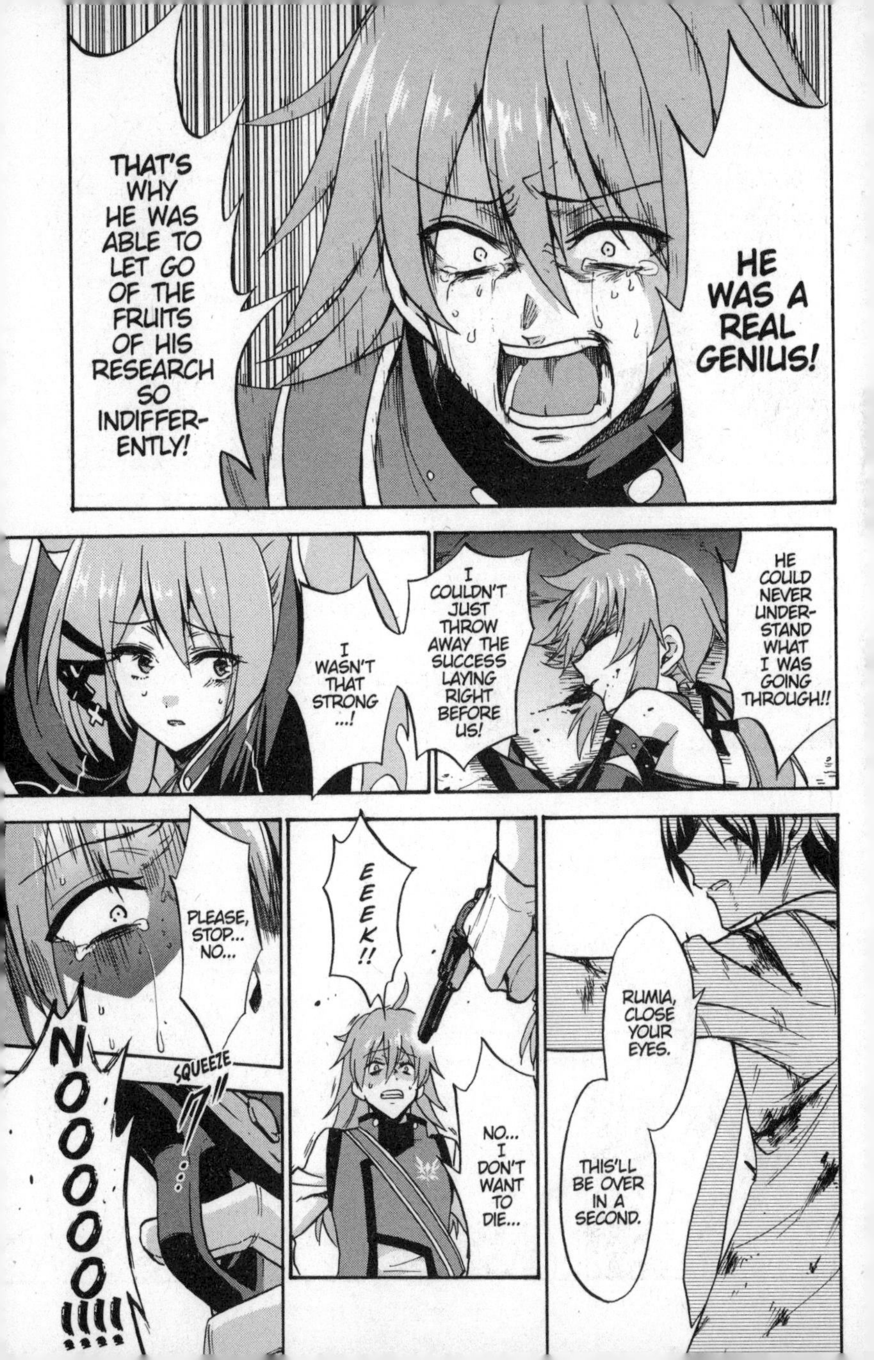
HE WAS A REAL GENIUS!
THAT'S WHY HE WAS ABLE TO LET GO OF THE FRUITS OF HIS RESEARCH SO INDIFFER-ENTLY!
HE COULD NEVER UNDER-STAND WHAT I WAS GOING THROUGH!!
I COULDN'T JUST THROW AWAY THE SUCCESS LAYING RIGHT BEFORE US!
I WASN'T THAT STRONG ...!
RUMIA, CLOSE YOUR EYES.
THIS'LL BE OVER IN A SECOND.
EEEK!!
NO... I DON'T WANT TO DIE...
PLEASE, STOP... NO...
SQUEEZE
NOOOOOO!!!!

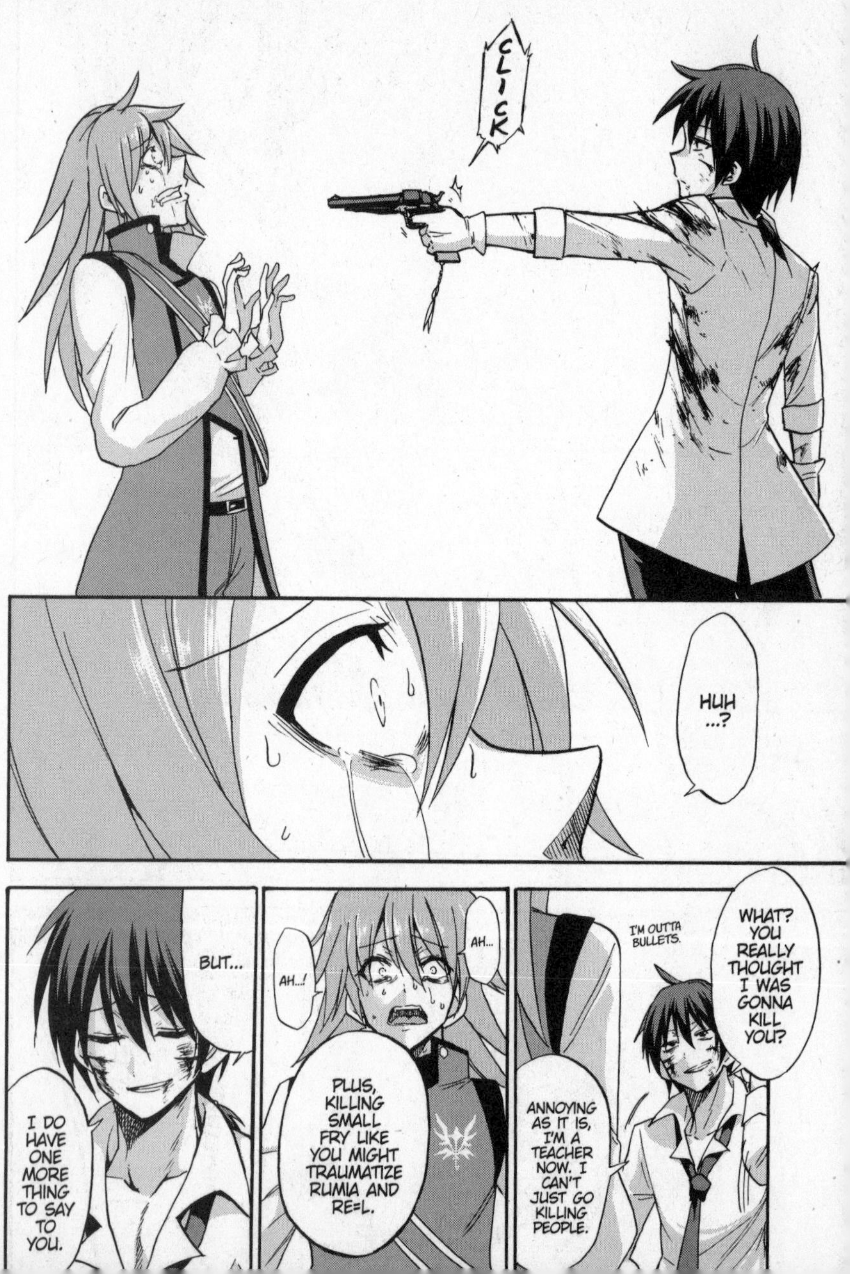
CLICK
HUH ...?
WHAT? YOU REALLY THOUGHT I WAS GONNA KILL YOU?
I'M OUTTA BULLETS.
ANNOYING AS IT IS, I'M A TEACHER NOW. I CAN'T JUST GO KILLING PEOPLE.
AH...
AH...!
PLUS, KILLING SMALL FRY LIKE YOU MIGHT TRAUMATIZE RUMIA AND RE=L.
BUT...
I DO HAVE ONE MORE THING TO SAY TO YOU.

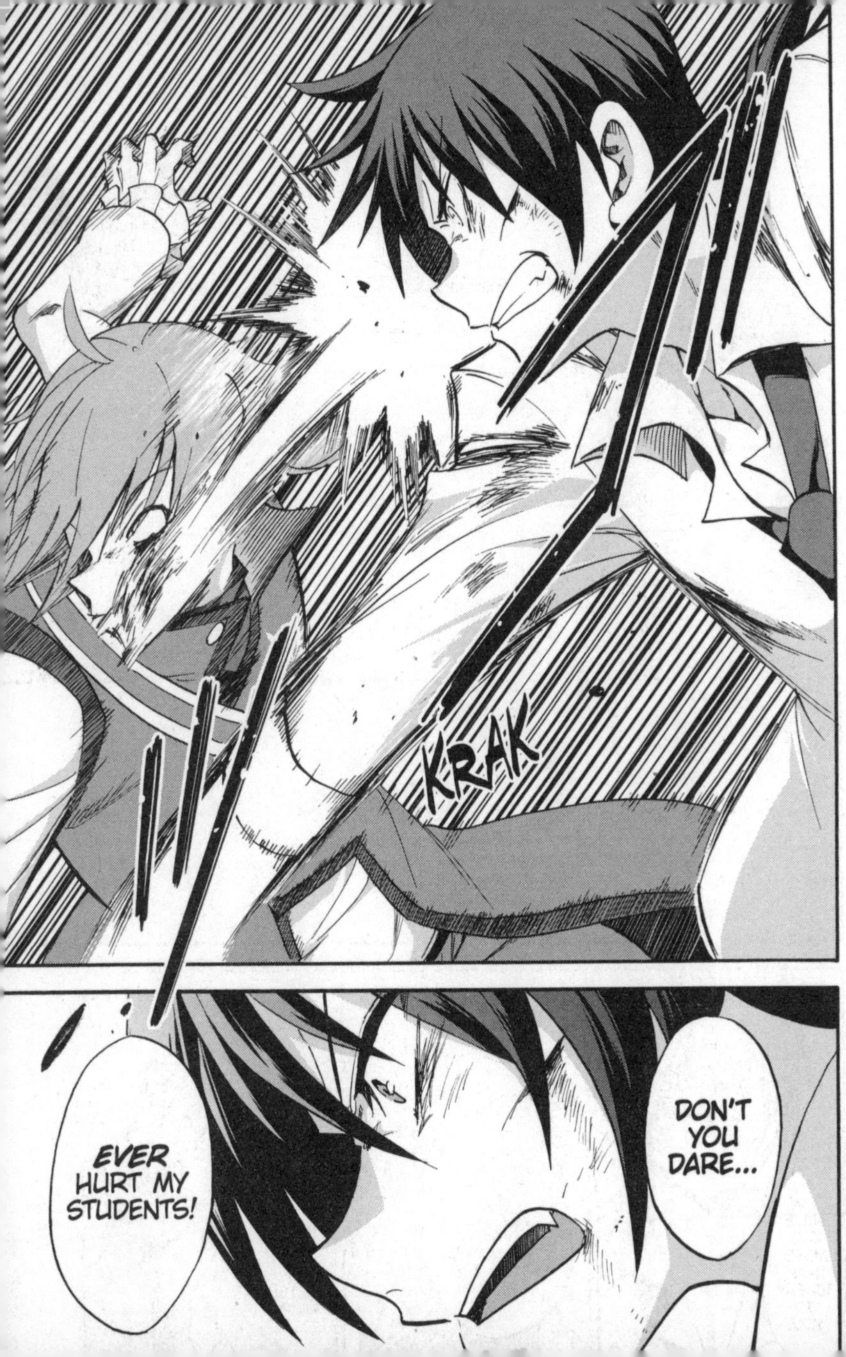
KRAK
DON'T YOU DARE...
EVER HURT MY STUDENTS!

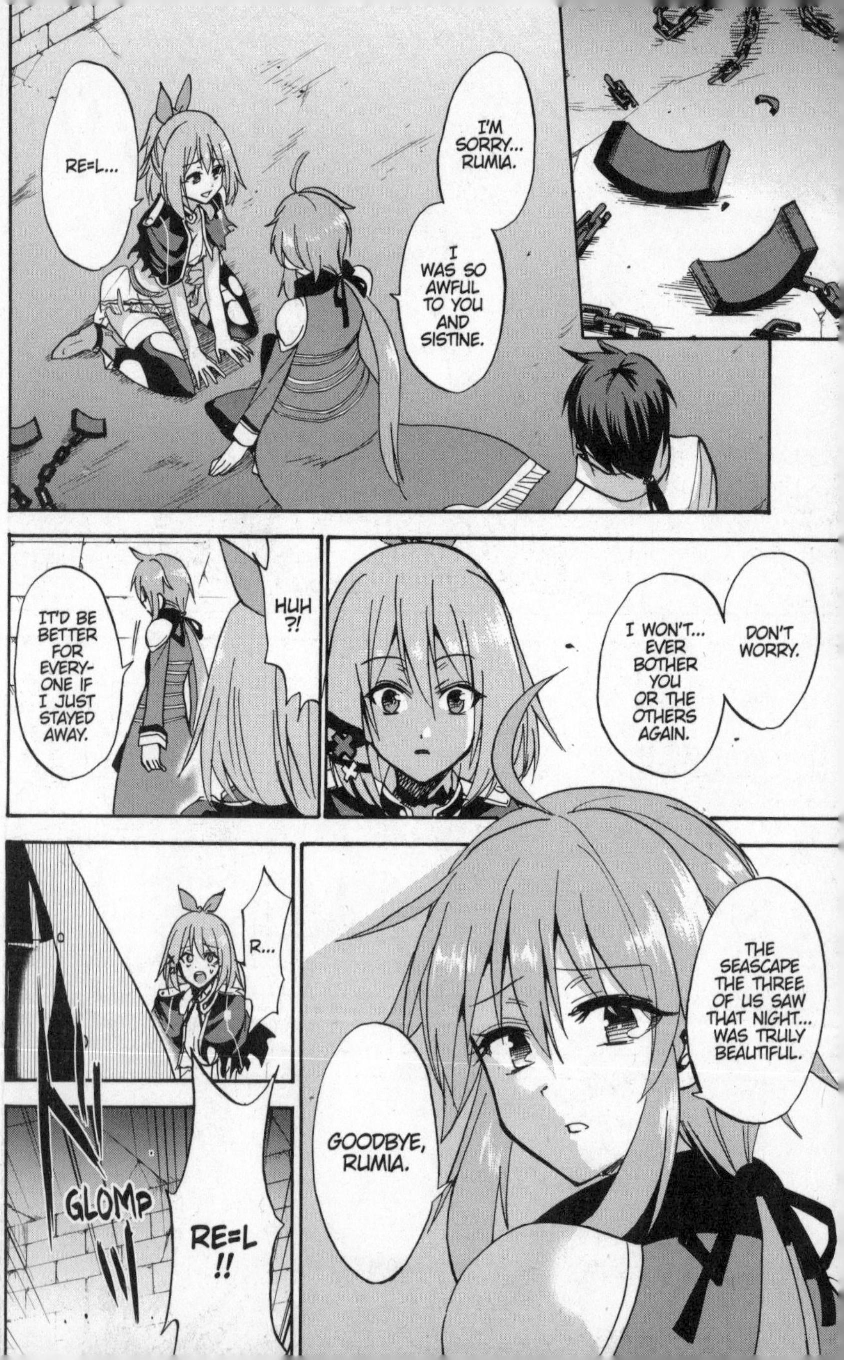
I'M SORRY... RUMIA.
I WAS SO AWFUL TO YOU AND SISTINE.
RE=L...
DON'T WORRY.
I WON'T... EVER BOTHER YOU OR THE OTHERS AGAIN.
HUH ?!
IT'D BE BETTER FOR EVERY-ONE IF I JUST STAYED AWAY.
THE SEASCAPE THE THREE OF US SAW THAT NIGHT... WAS TRULY BEAUTIFUL.
GOODBYE, RUMIA.
R...
GLOMP
RE=L !!

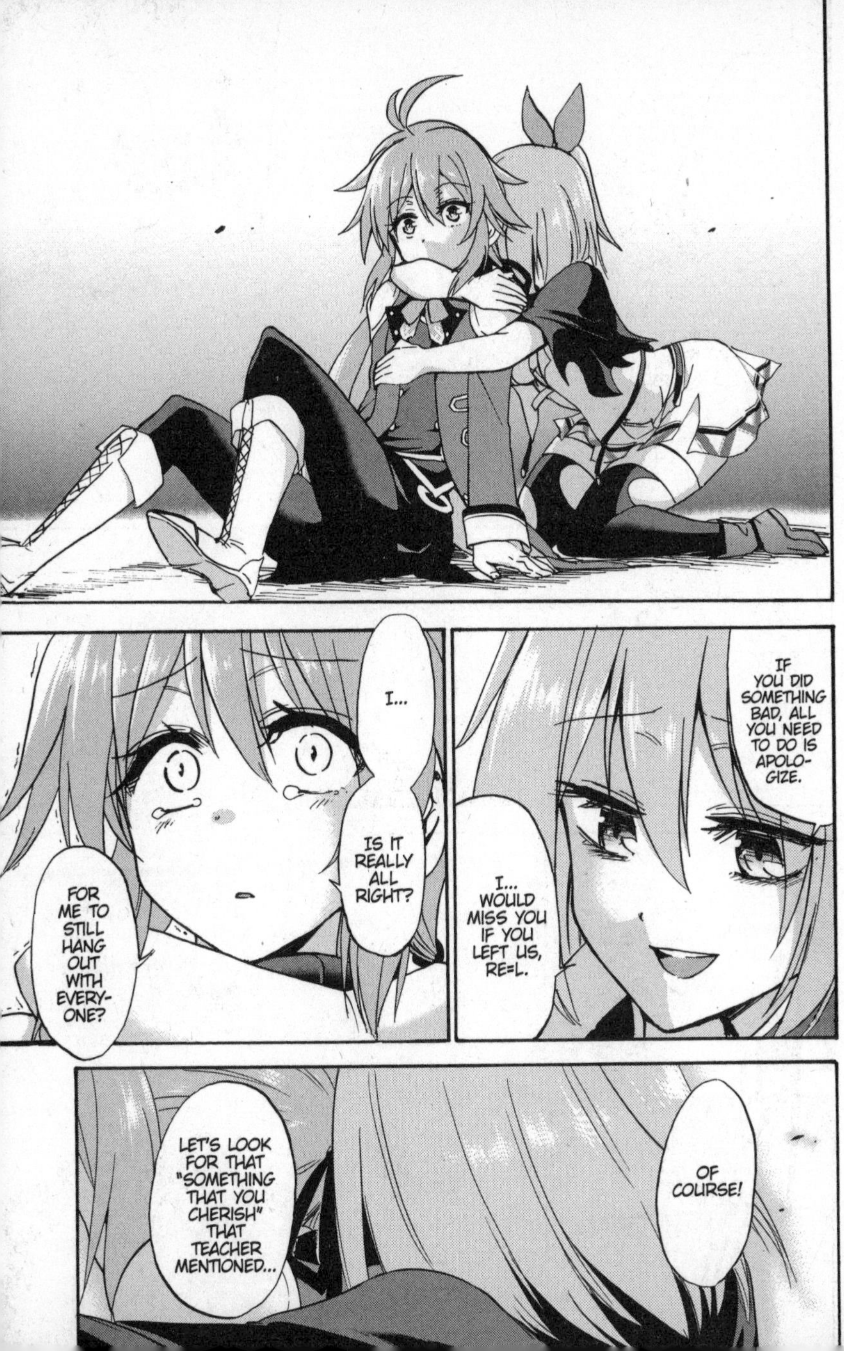
IF YOU DID SOMETHING BAD, ALL YOU NEED TO DO IS APOLO-GIZE.
I... WOULD MISS YOU IF YOU LEFT US, RE=L.
I...
IS IT REALLY ALL RIGHT?
FOR ME TO STILL HANG OUT WITH EVERY-ONE?
OF COURSE!
LET'S LOOK FOR THAT "SOMETHING THAT YOU CHERISH" THAT TEACHER MENTIONED...

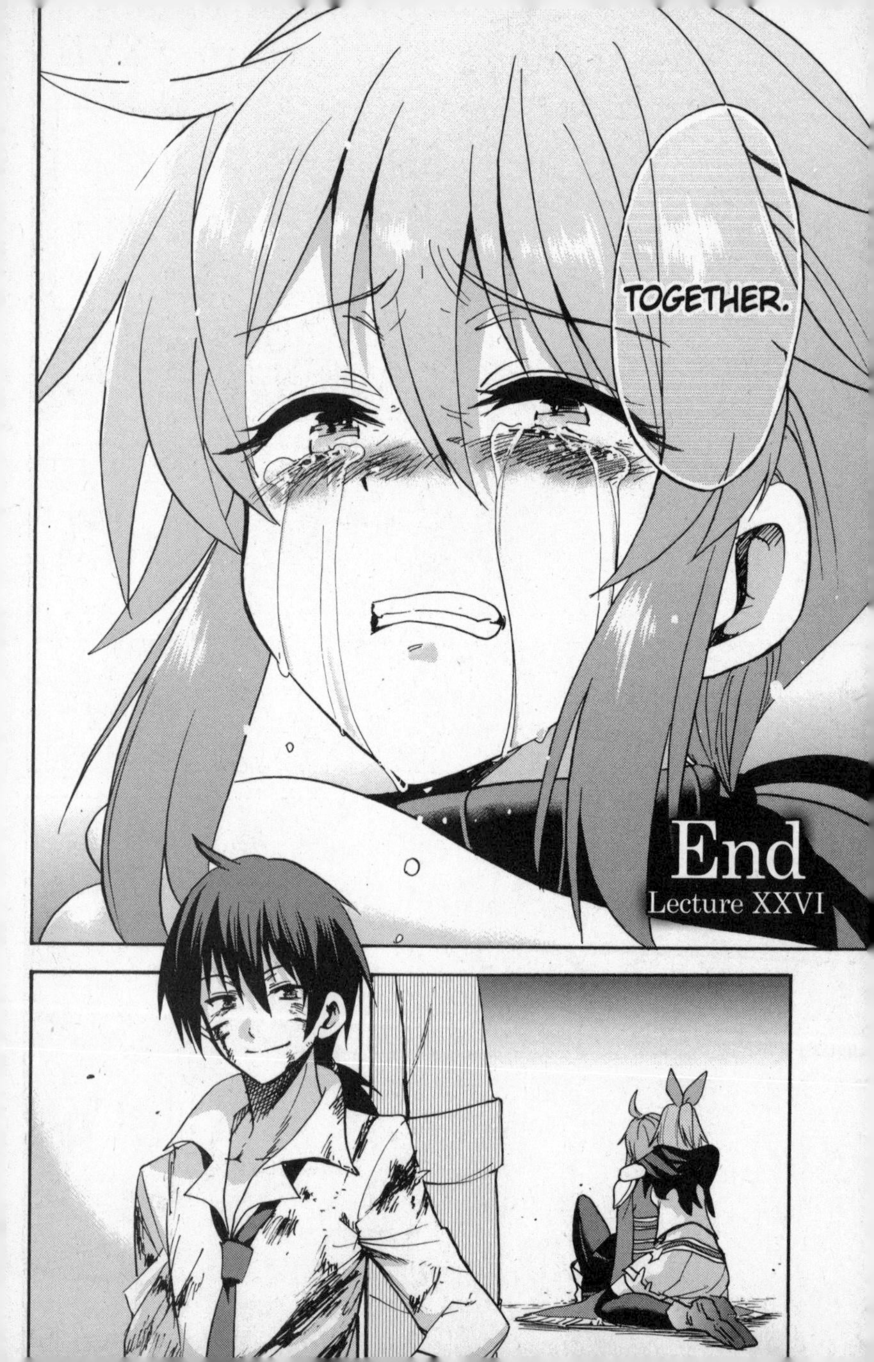

TOGETHER.
End
Lecture XXVI

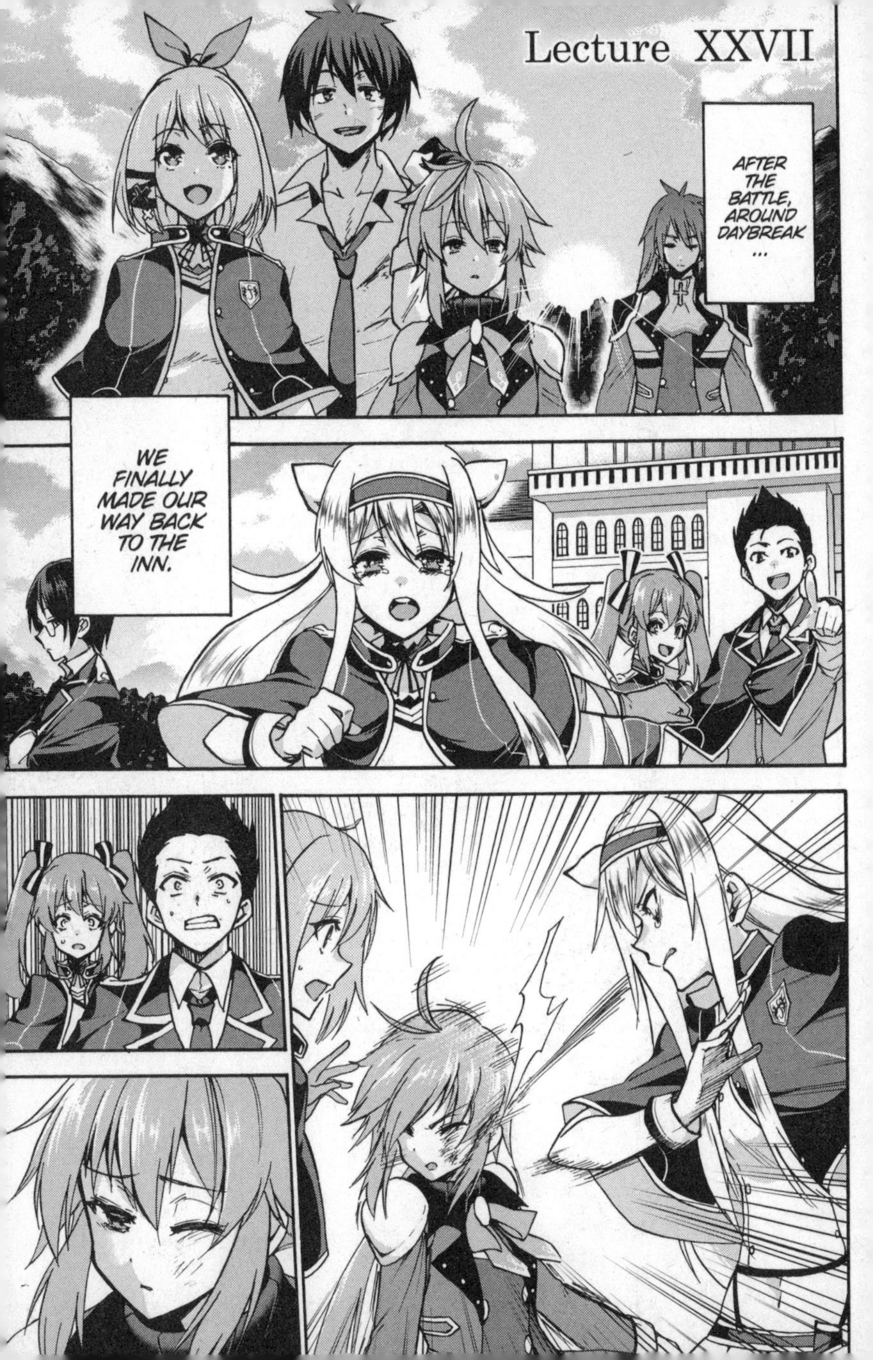
Lecture XXVII
AFTER THE BATTLE, AROUND DAYBREAK ...
WE FINALLY MADE OUR WAY BACK TO THE INN.

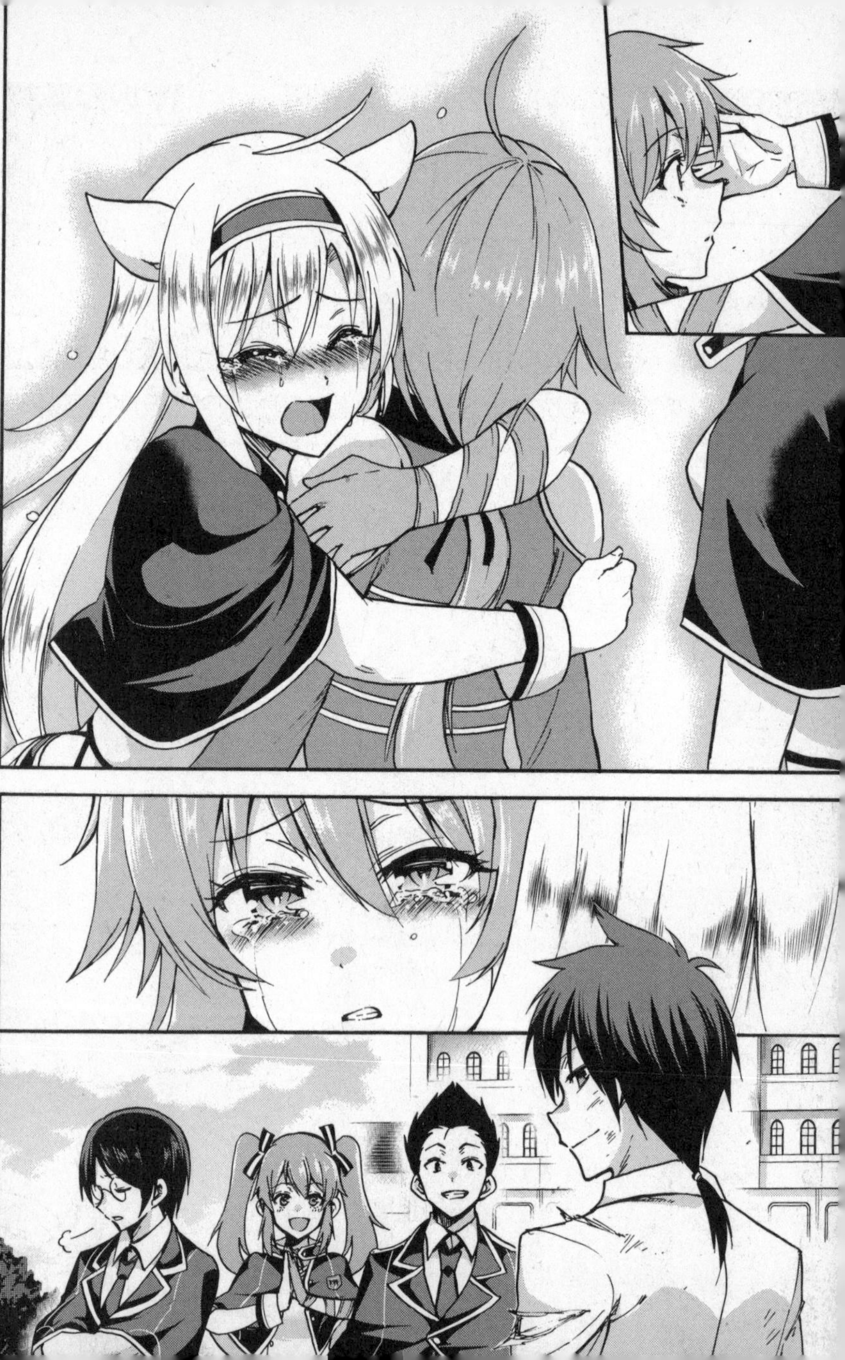

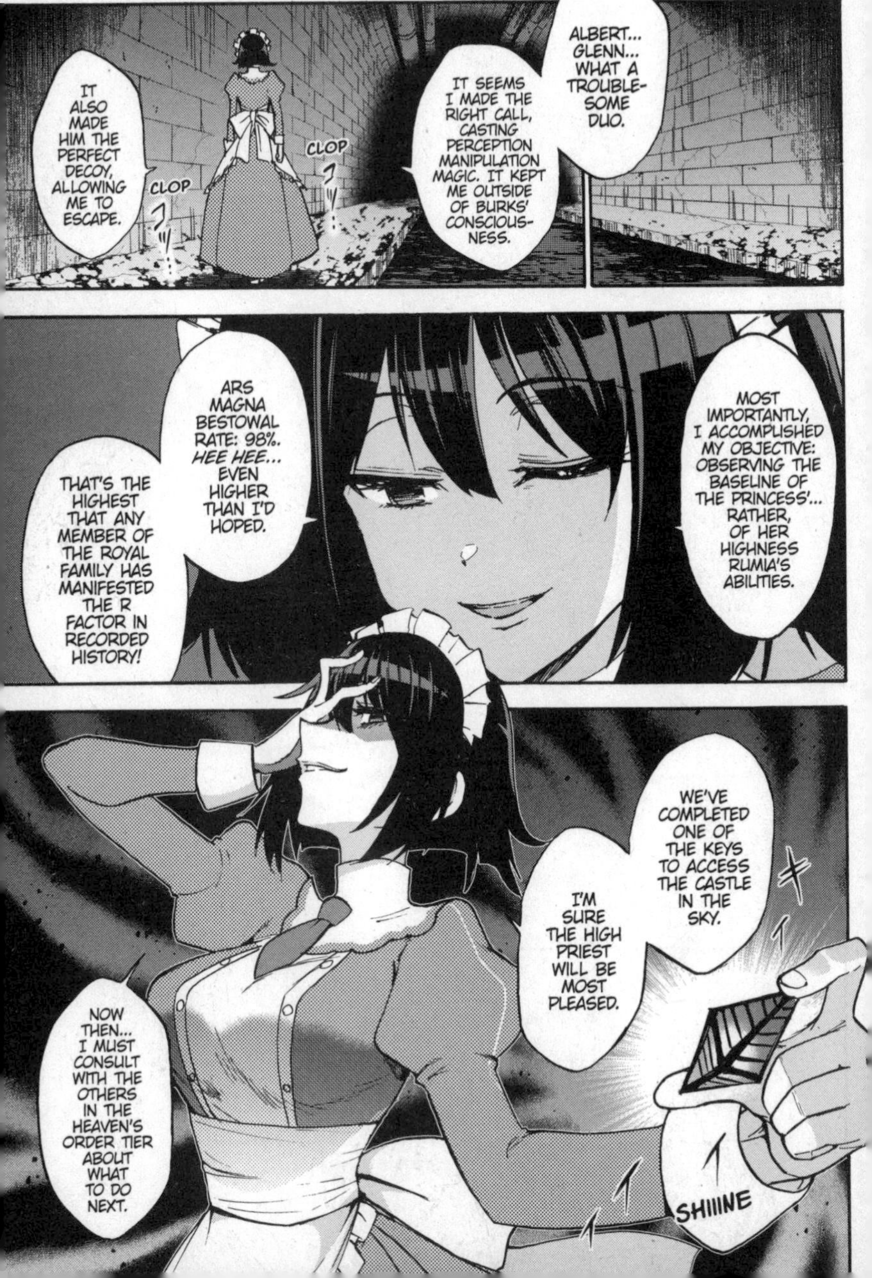
ALBERT... GLENN... WHAT A TROUBLE-SOME DUO.
IT SEEMS I MADE THE RIGHT CALL, CASTING PERCEPTION MANIPULATION MAGIC. IT KEPT ME OUTSIDE OF BURKS' CONSCIOUS-NESS.
CLOP
IT ALSO MADE HIM THE PERFECT DECOY, ALLOWING ME TO ESCAPE.
CLOP
MOST IMPORTANTLY, I ACCOMPLISHED MY OBJECTIVE: OBSERVING THE BASELINE OF THE PRINCESS'... RATHER, OF HER HIGHNESS RUMIA'S ABILITIES.
ARS MAGNA BESTOWAL RATE: 98%. *HEE HEE...* EVEN HIGHER THAN I'D HOPED.
THAT'S THE HIGHEST THAT ANY MEMBER OF THE ROYAL FAMILY HAS MANIFESTED THE R FACTOR IN RECORDED HISTORY!
WE'VE COMPLETED ONE OF THE KEYS TO ACCESS THE CASTLE IN THE SKY.
I'M SURE THE HIGH PRIEST WILL BE MOST PLEASED.
SHIIINE
NOW THEN... I MUST CONSULT WITH THE OTHERS IN THE HEAVEN'S ORDER TIER ABOUT WHAT TO DO NEXT.

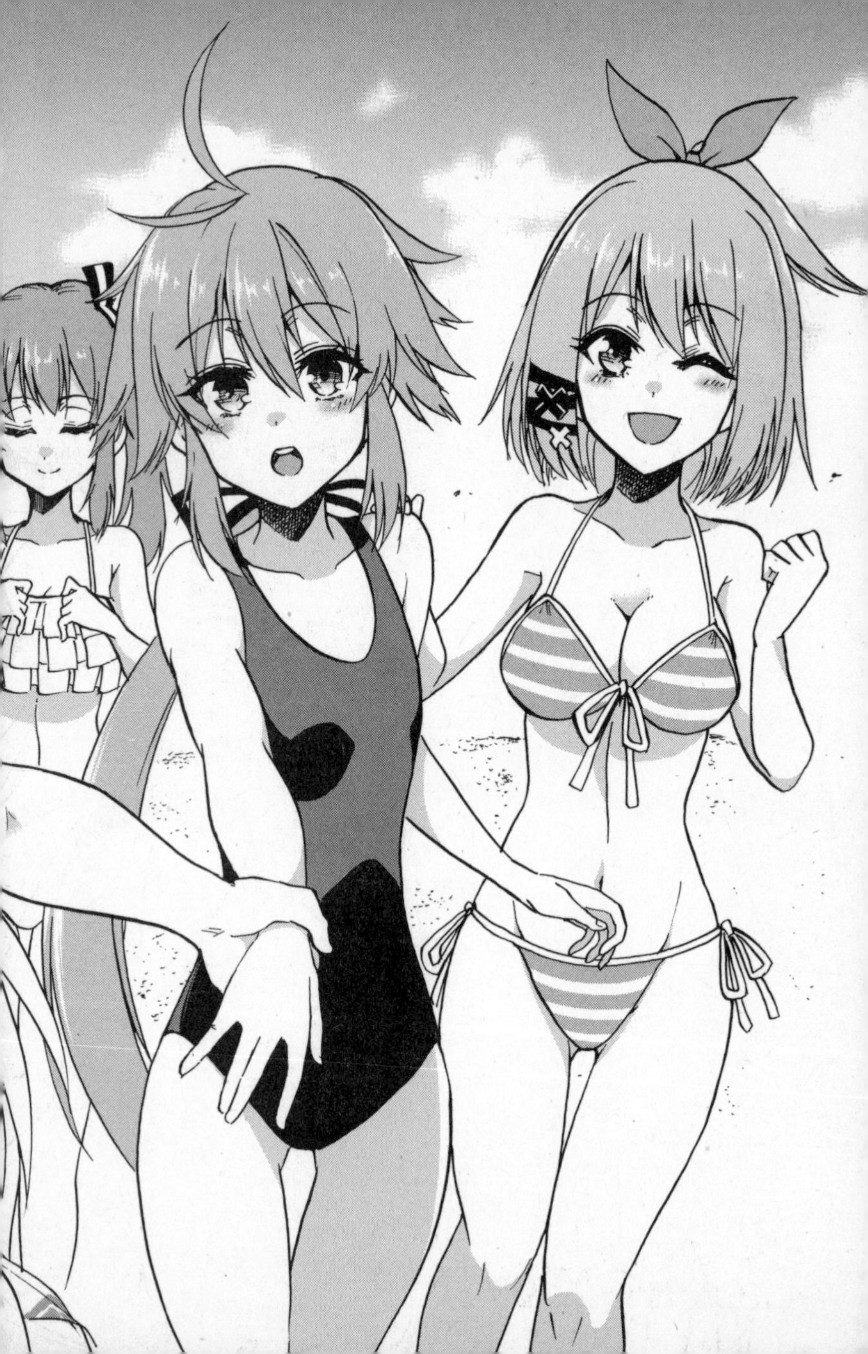

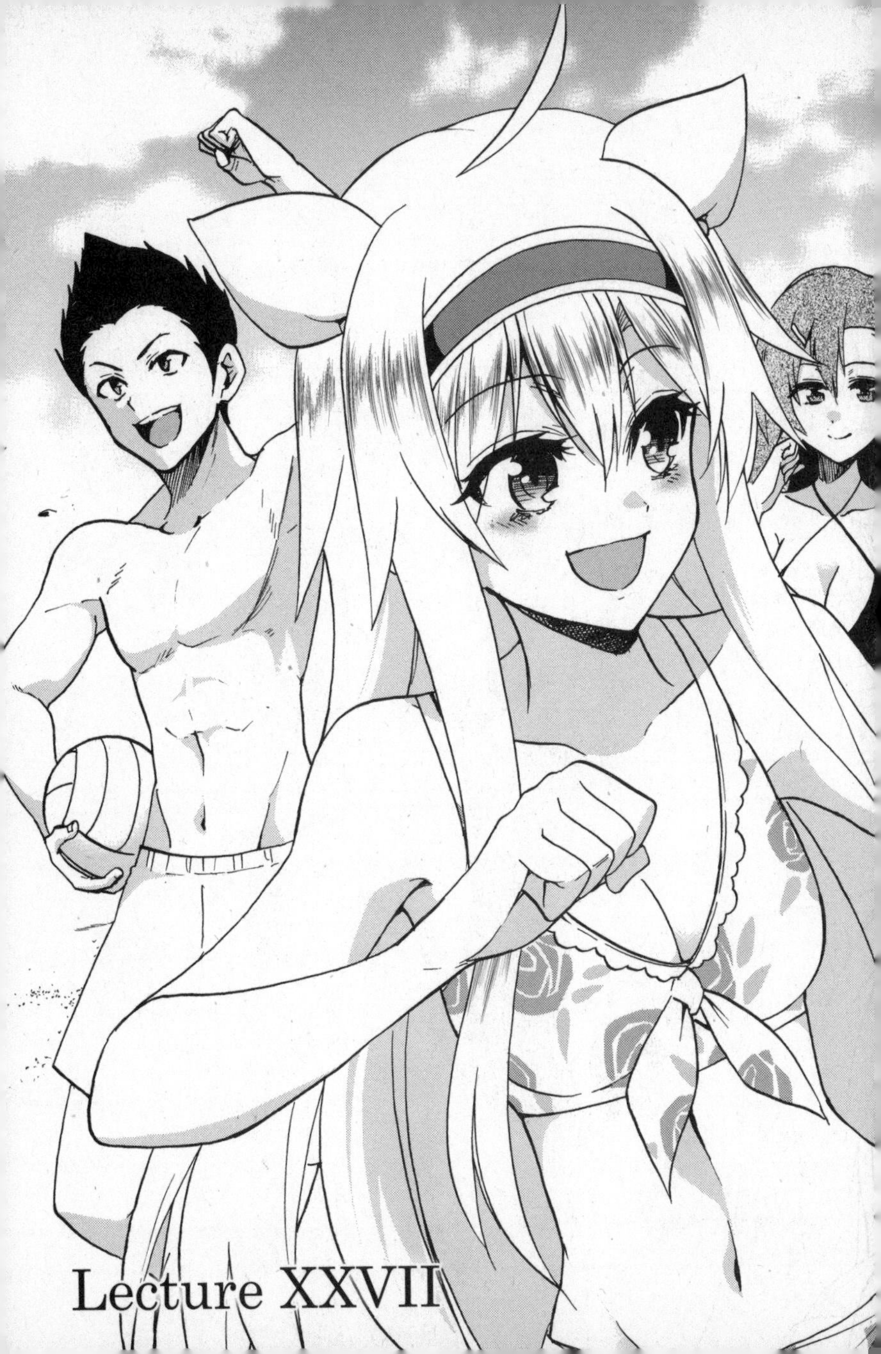
Lecture XXVII

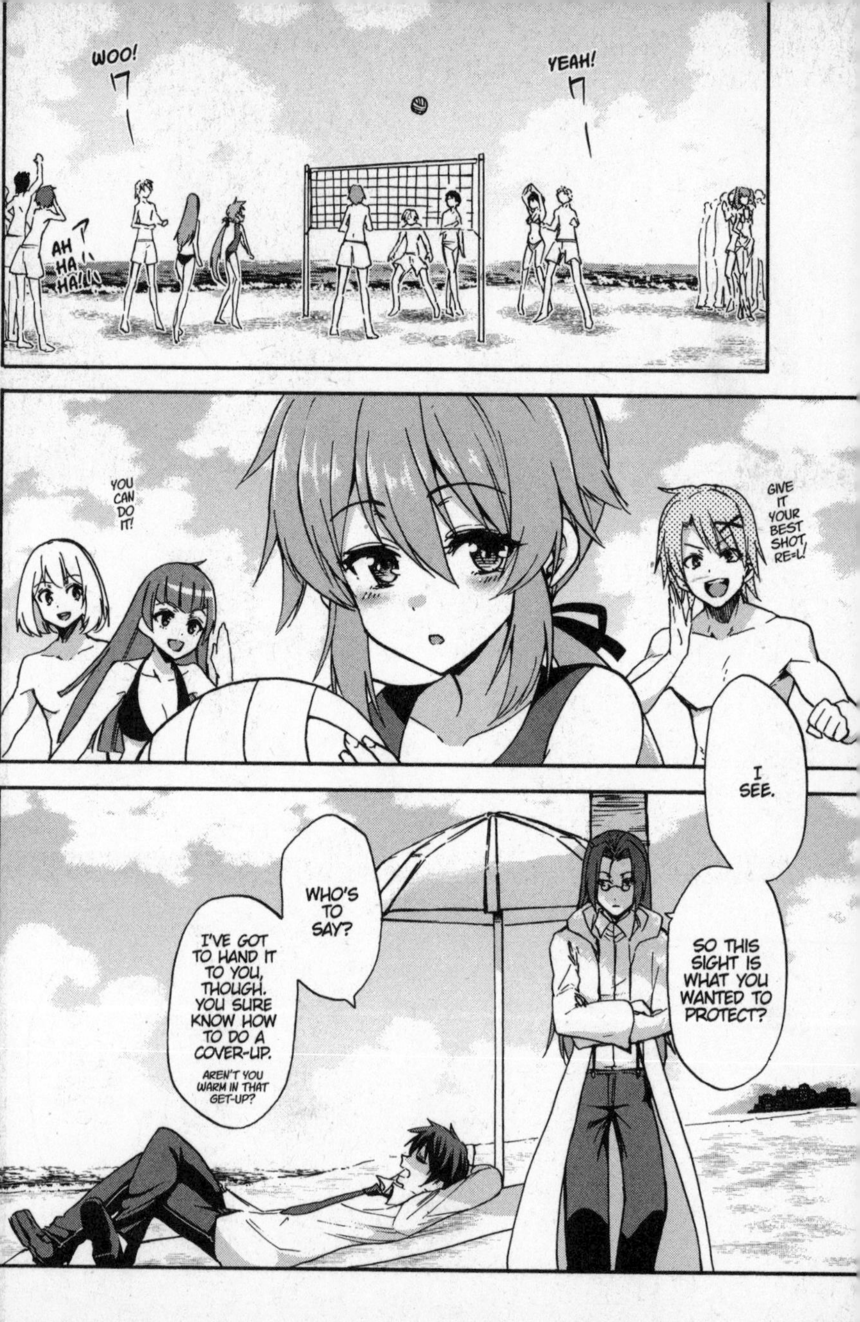
YEAH!
WOO!
AH HA HA!!
GIVE IT YOUR BEST SHOT, RE=L!
YOU CAN DO IT!
I SEE.
SO THIS SIGHT IS WHAT YOU WANTED TO PROTECT?
WHO'S TO SAY?
I'VE GOT TO HAND IT TO YOU, THOUGH. YOU SURE KNOW HOW TO DO A COVER-UP.
AREN'T YOU WARM IN THAT GET-UP?

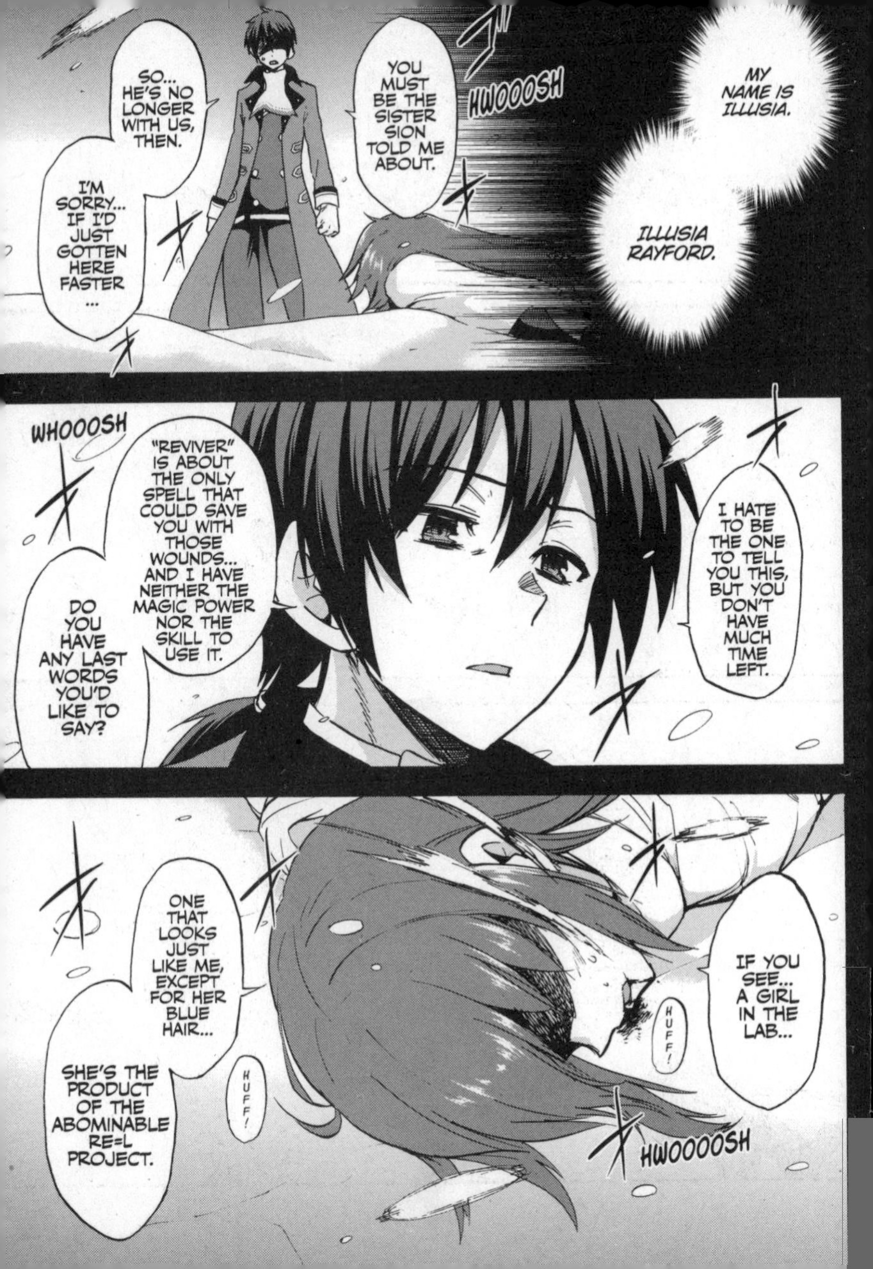
MY NAME IS ILLUSIA.
ILLUSIA RAYFORD.
HWOOOSH
YOU MUST BE THE SISTER SION TOLD ME ABOUT.
SO... HE'S NO LONGER WITH US, THEN.
I'M SORRY... IF I'D JUST GOTTEN HERE FASTER...
I HATE TO BE THE ONE TO TELL YOU THIS, BUT YOU DON'T HAVE MUCH TIME LEFT.
"REVIVER" IS ABOUT THE ONLY SPELL THAT COULD SAVE YOU WITH THOSE WOUNDS... AND I HAVE NEITHER THE MAGIC POWER NOR THE SKILL TO USE IT.
DO YOU HAVE ANY LAST WORDS YOU'D LIKE TO SAY?
WHOOOSH
IF YOU SEE... A GIRL IN THE LAB...
HUFF!
HWOOOOSH
ONE THAT LOOKS JUST LIKE ME, EXCEPT FOR HER BLUE HAIR...
HUFF!
SHE'S THE PRODUCT OF THE ABOMINABLE RE=L PROJECT.

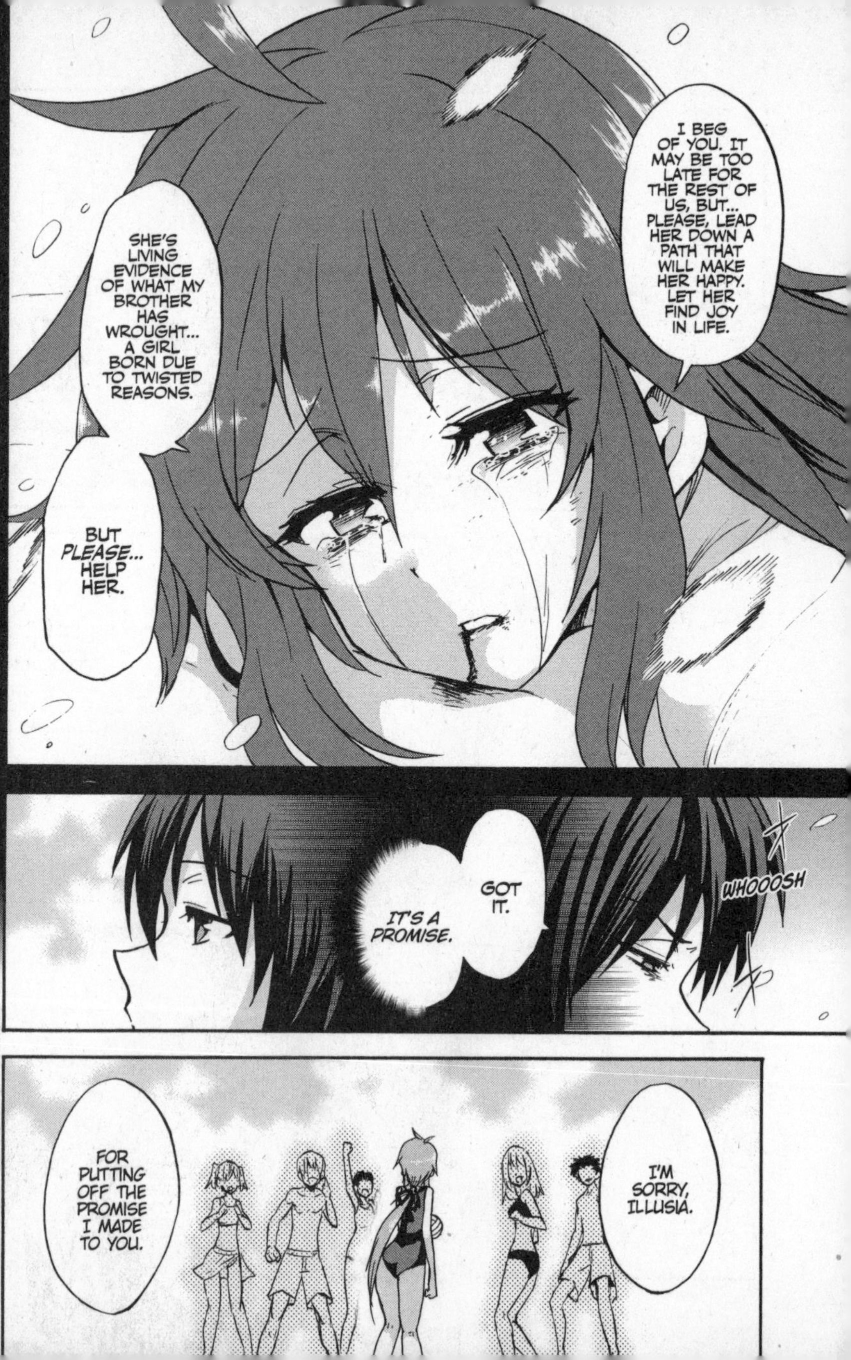
I BEG OF YOU. IT MAY BE TOO LATE FOR THE REST OF US, BUT... PLEASE, LEAD HER DOWN A PATH THAT WILL MAKE HER HAPPY. LET HER FIND JOY IN LIFE.
SHE'S LIVING EVIDENCE OF WHAT MY BROTHER HAS WROUGHT... A GIRL BORN DUE TO TWISTED REASONS.
BUT *PLEASE*... HELP HER.
WHOOOSH
GOT IT.
IT'S A PROMISE.
I'M SORRY, ILLUSIA.
FOR PUTTING OFF THE PROMISE I MADE TO YOU.

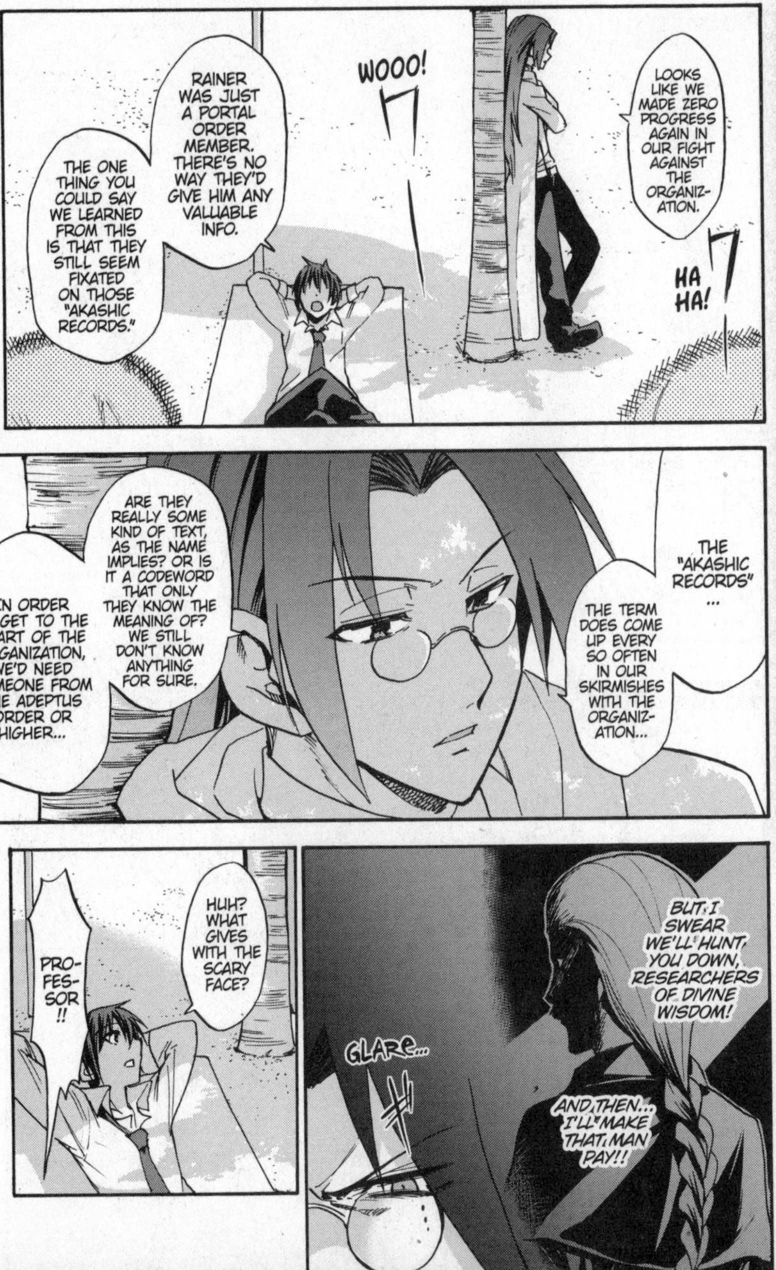
LOOKS LIKE WE MADE ZERO PROGRESS AGAIN IN OUR FIGHT AGAINST THE ORGANIZ-ATION.
HA HA!
WOOO!
RAINER WAS JUST A PORTAL ORDER MEMBER. THERE'S NO WAY THEY'D GIVE HIM ANY VALUABLE INFO.
THE ONE THING YOU COULD SAY WE LEARNED FROM THIS IS THAT THEY STILL SEEM FIXATED ON THOSE "AKASHIC RECORDS."
THE "AKASHIC RECORDS"...
THE TERM DOES COME UP EVERY SO OFTEN IN OUR SKIRMISHES WITH THE ORGANIZ-ATION...
ARE THEY REALLY SOME KIND OF TEXT, AS THE NAME IMPLIES? OR IS IT A CODEWORD THAT ONLY THEY KNOW THE MEANING OF? WE STILL DON'T KNOW ANYTHING FOR SURE.
IN ORDER TO GET TO THE HEART OF THE ORGANIZATION, WE'D NEED SOMEONE FROM THE ADEPTUS ORDER OR HIGHER...
BUT I SWEAR WE'LL HUNT YOU DOWN, RESEARCHERS OF DIVINE WISDOM!
GLARE...
AND THEN... I'LL MAKE THAT MAN PAY!!
HUH? WHAT GIVES WITH THE SCARY FACE?
PRO-FES-SOR!!

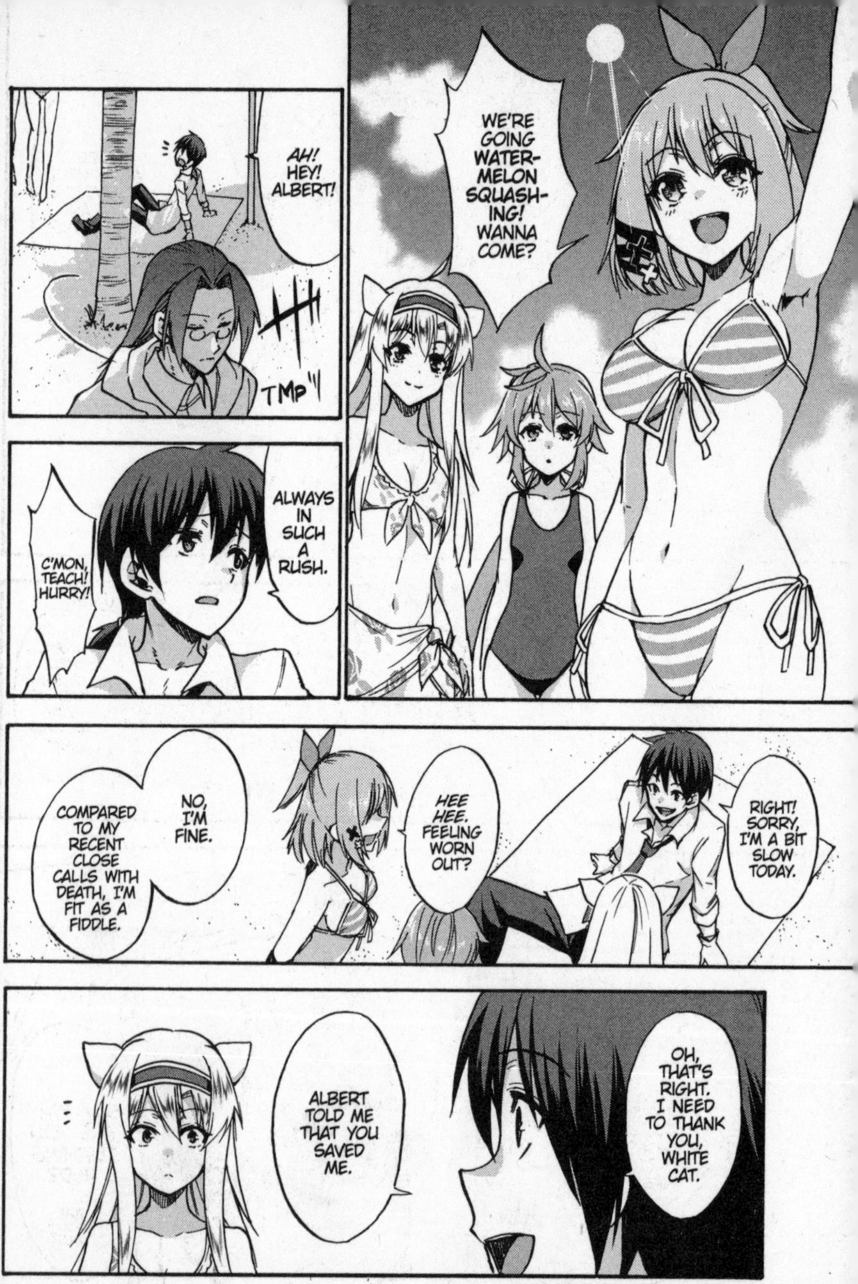
WE'RE GOING WATER-MELON SQUASH-ING! WANNA COME?
AH! HEY! ALBERT!
TMP
ALWAYS IN SUCH A RUSH.
C'MON, TEACH! HURRY!
RIGHT! SORRY, I'M A BIT SLOW TODAY.
HEE HEE. FEELING WORN OUT?
NO, I'M FINE.
COMPARED TO MY RECENT CLOSE CALLS WITH DEATH, I'M FIT AS A FIDDLE.
OH, THAT'S RIGHT. I NEED TO THANK YOU, WHITE CAT.
ALBERT TOLD ME THAT YOU SAVED ME.

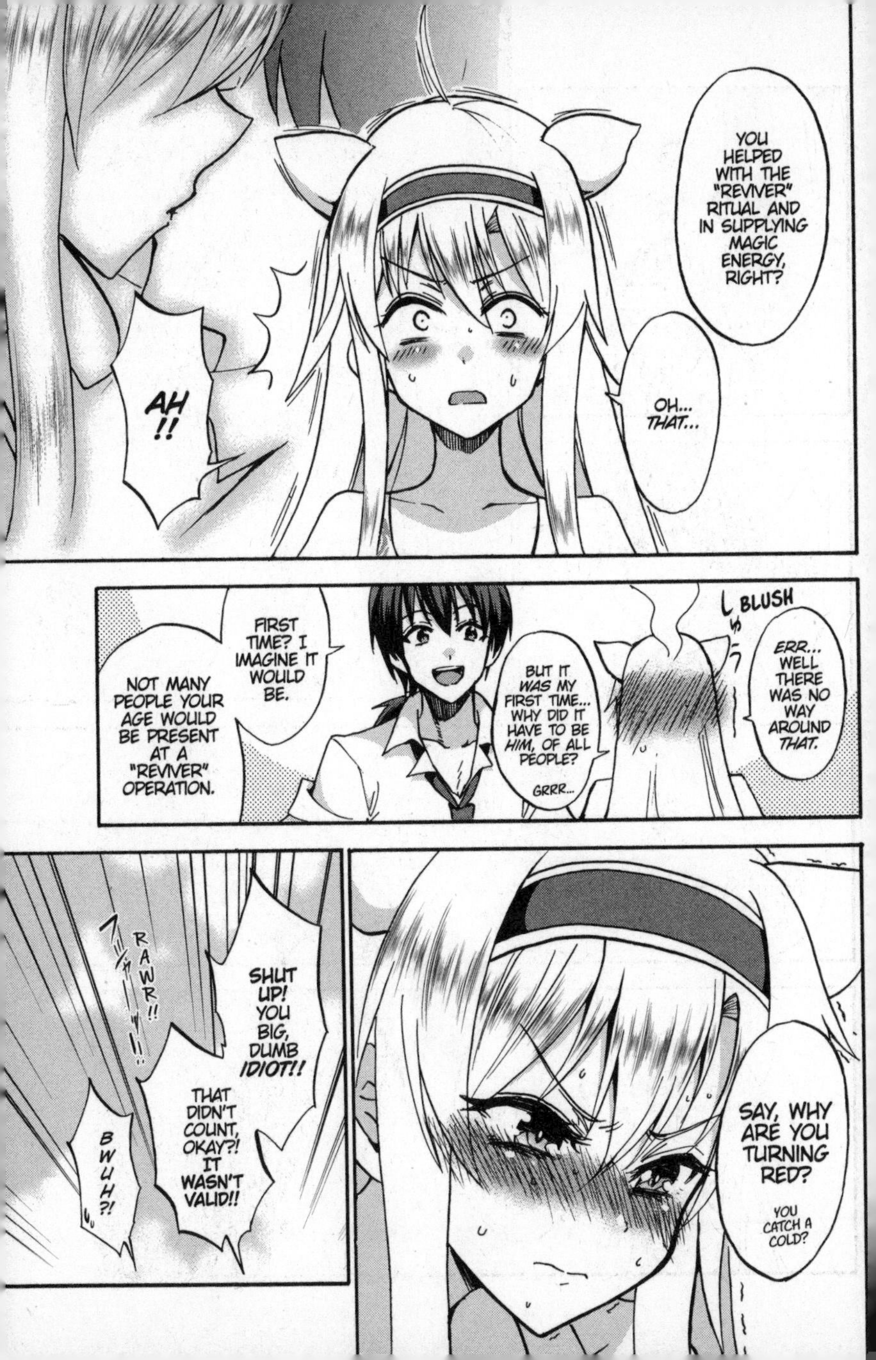
YOU HELPED WITH THE "REVIVER" RITUAL AND IN SUPPLYING MAGIC ENERGY, RIGHT?
OH... THAT...
AH!!
BLUSH
ERR... WELL THERE WAS NO WAY AROUND THAT.
BUT IT WAS MY FIRST TIME... WHY DID IT HAVE TO BE HIM, OF ALL PEOPLE?
GRRR...
FIRST TIME? I IMAGINE IT WOULD BE.
NOT MANY PEOPLE YOUR AGE WOULD BE PRESENT AT A "REVIVER" OPERATION.
SAY, WHY ARE YOU TURNING RED?
YOU CATCH A COLD?
SHUT UP! YOU BIG, DUMB IDIOT!!
RAWR!!
THAT DIDN'T COUNT, OKAY?! IT WASN'T VALID!!
BWUH?!

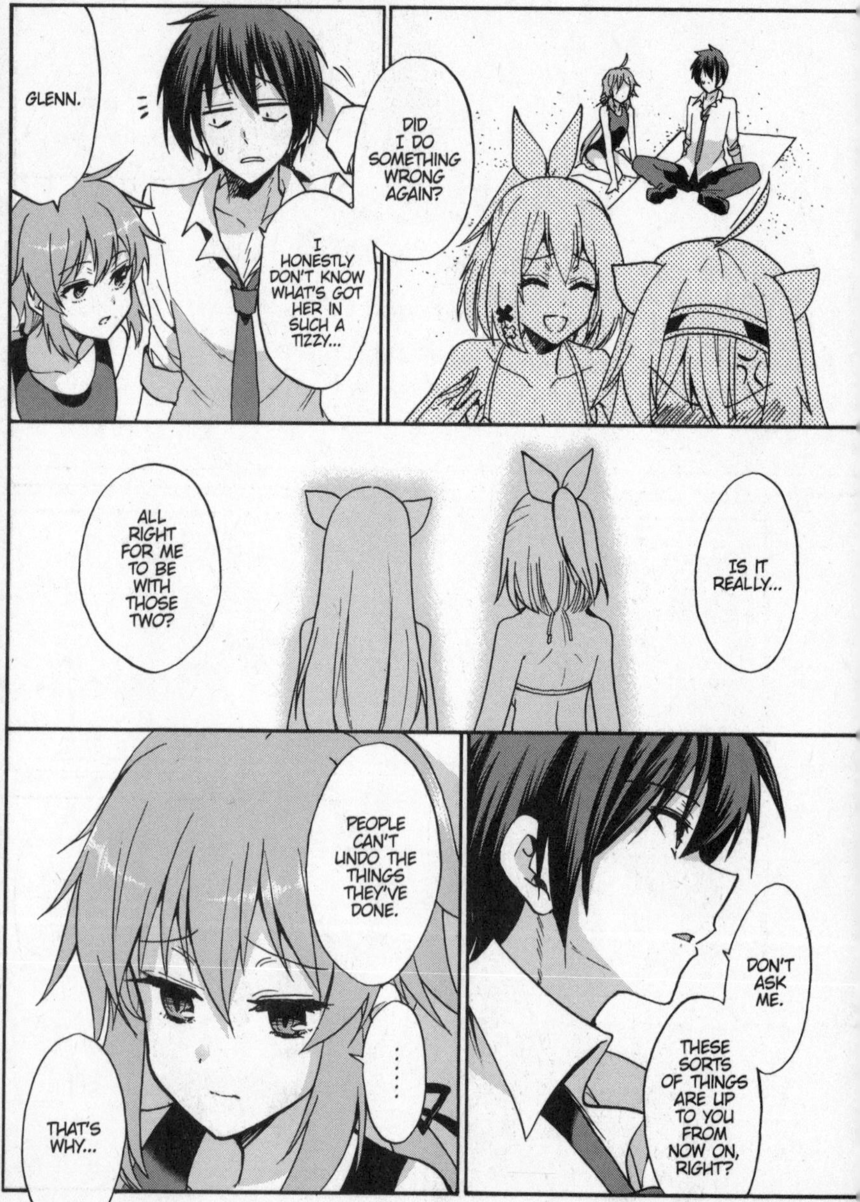
DID I DO SOMETHING WRONG AGAIN?
I HONESTLY DON'T KNOW WHAT'S GOT HER IN SUCH A TIZZY...
GLENN.
IS IT REALLY...
ALL RIGHT FOR ME TO BE WITH THOSE TWO?
DON'T ASK ME.
THESE SORTS OF THINGS ARE UP TO YOU FROM NOW ON, RIGHT?
PEOPLE CAN'T UNDO THE THINGS THEY'VE DONE.
......
THAT'S WHY...

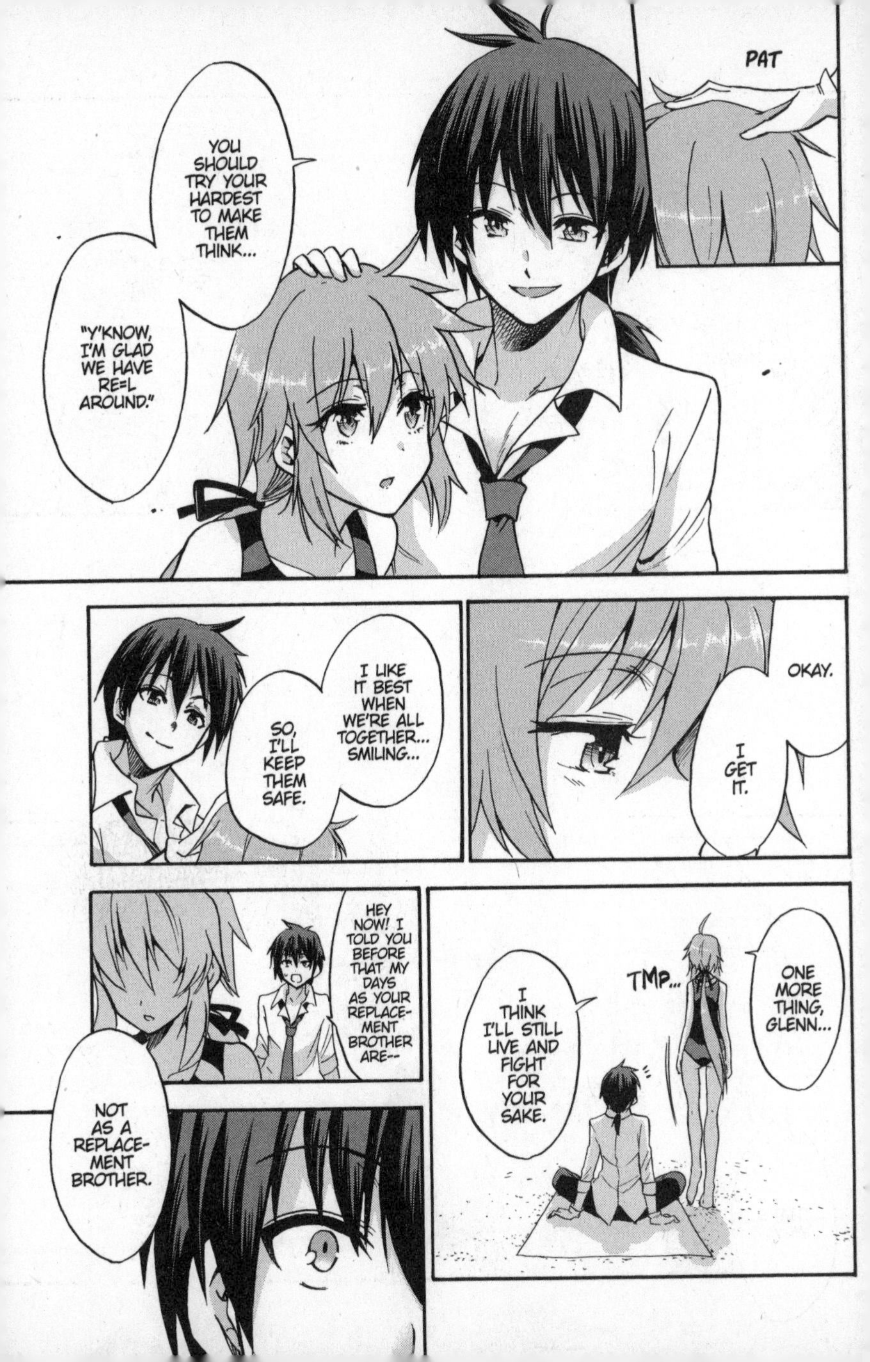
PAT
YOU SHOULD TRY YOUR HARDEST TO MAKE THEM THINK...
"Y'KNOW, I'M GLAD WE HAVE RE=L AROUND."
OKAY.
I GET IT.
I LIKE IT BEST WHEN WE'RE ALL TOGETHER... SMILING...
SO, I'LL KEEP THEM SAFE.
ONE MORE THING, GLENN...
TMP...
I THINK I'LL STILL LIVE AND FIGHT FOR YOUR SAKE.
HEY NOW! I TOLD YOU BEFORE THAT MY DAYS AS YOUR REPLACEMENT BROTHER ARE--
NOT AS A REPLACEMENT BROTHER.

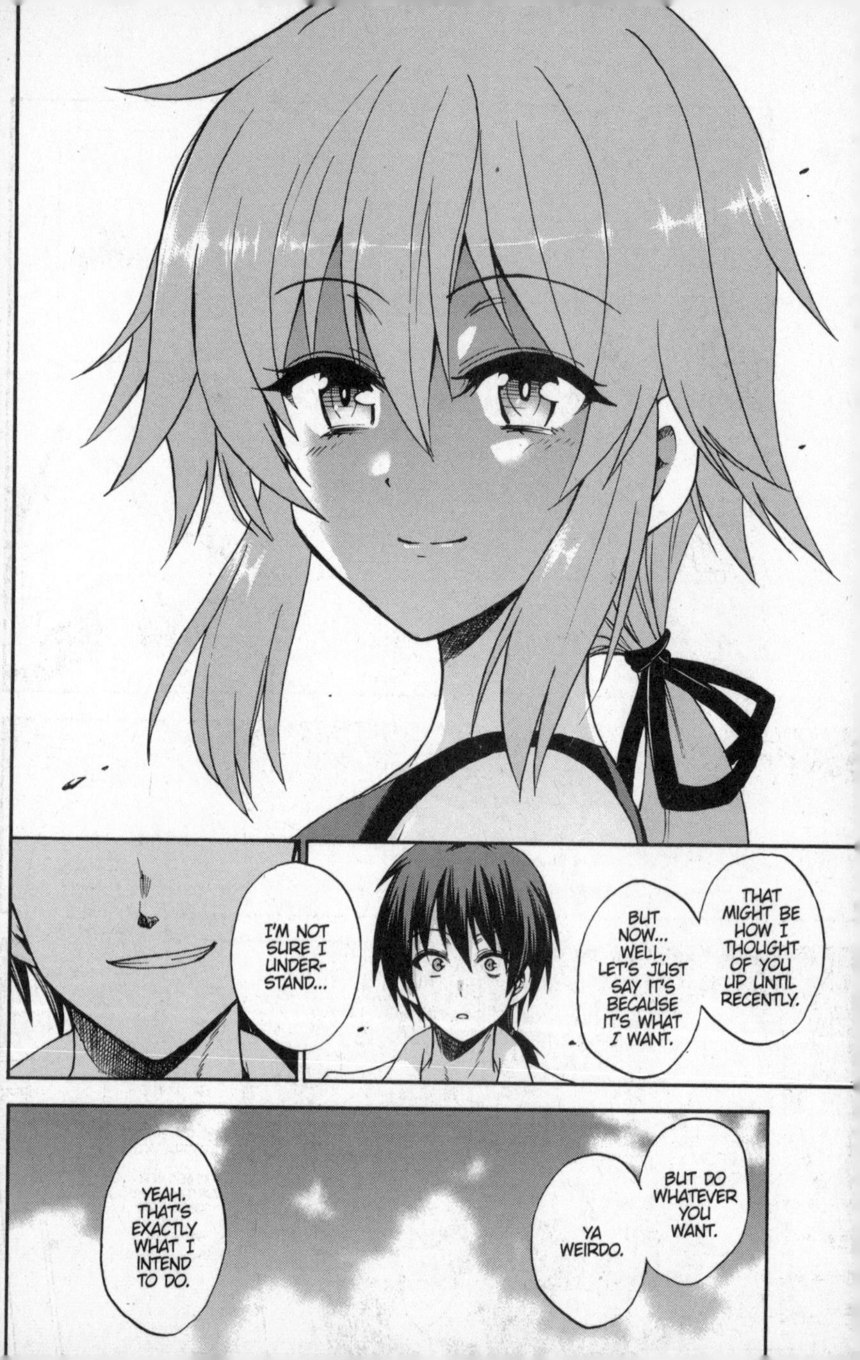
THAT MIGHT BE HOW I THOUGHT OF YOU UP UNTIL RECENTLY.
BUT NOW... WELL, LET'S JUST SAY IT'S BECAUSE IT'S WHAT *I* WANT.
I'M NOT SURE I UNDERSTAND...
BUT DO WHATEVER YOU WANT.
YA WEIRDO.
YEAH. THAT'S EXACTLY WHAT I INTEND TO DO.

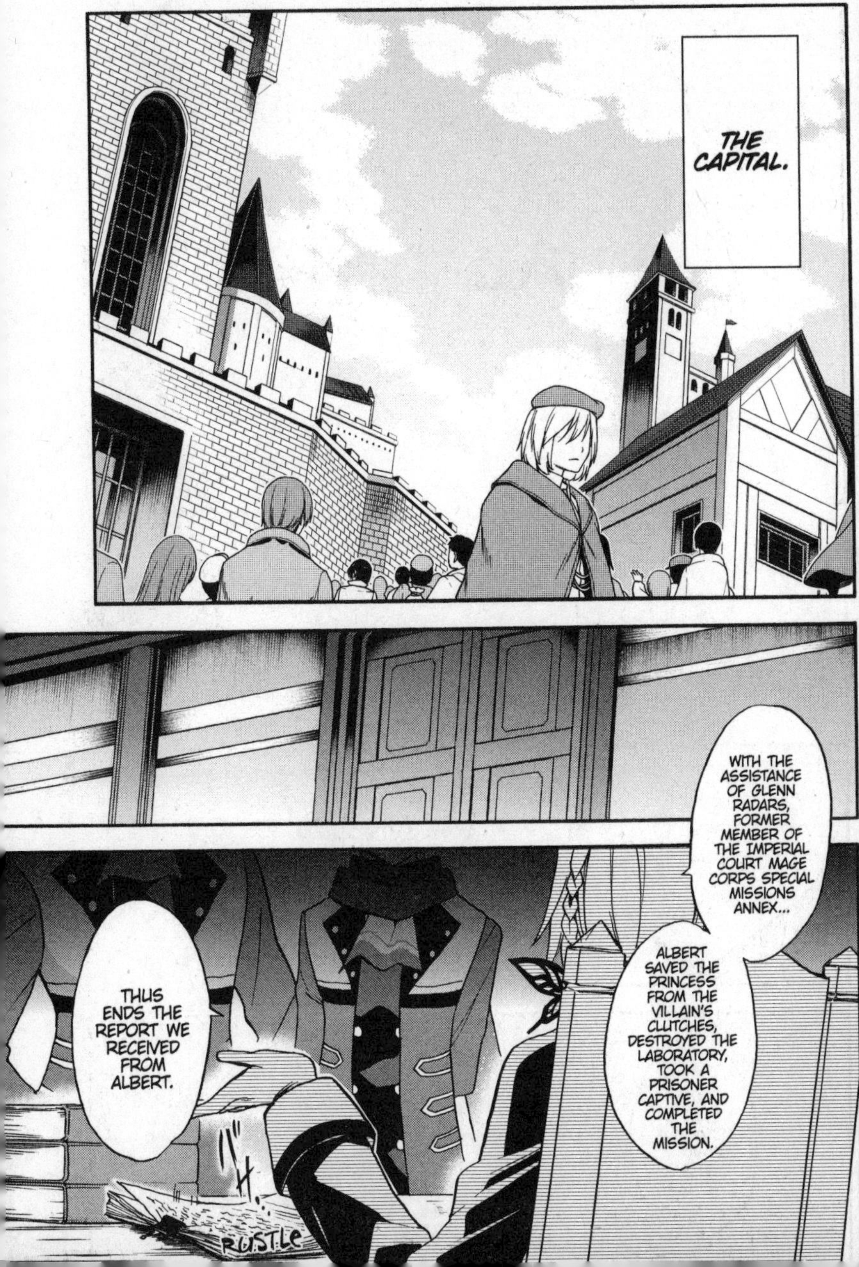
THE CAPITAL.
WITH THE ASSISTANCE OF GLENN RADARS, FORMER MEMBER OF THE IMPERIAL COURT MAGE CORPS SPECIAL MISSIONS ANNEX...
ALBERT SAVED THE PRINCESS FROM THE VILLAIN'S CLUTCHES, DESTROYED THE LABORATORY, TOOK A PRISONER CAPTIVE, AND COMPLETED THE MISSION.
THUS ENDS THE REPORT WE RECEIVED FROM ALBERT.
RUSTLE

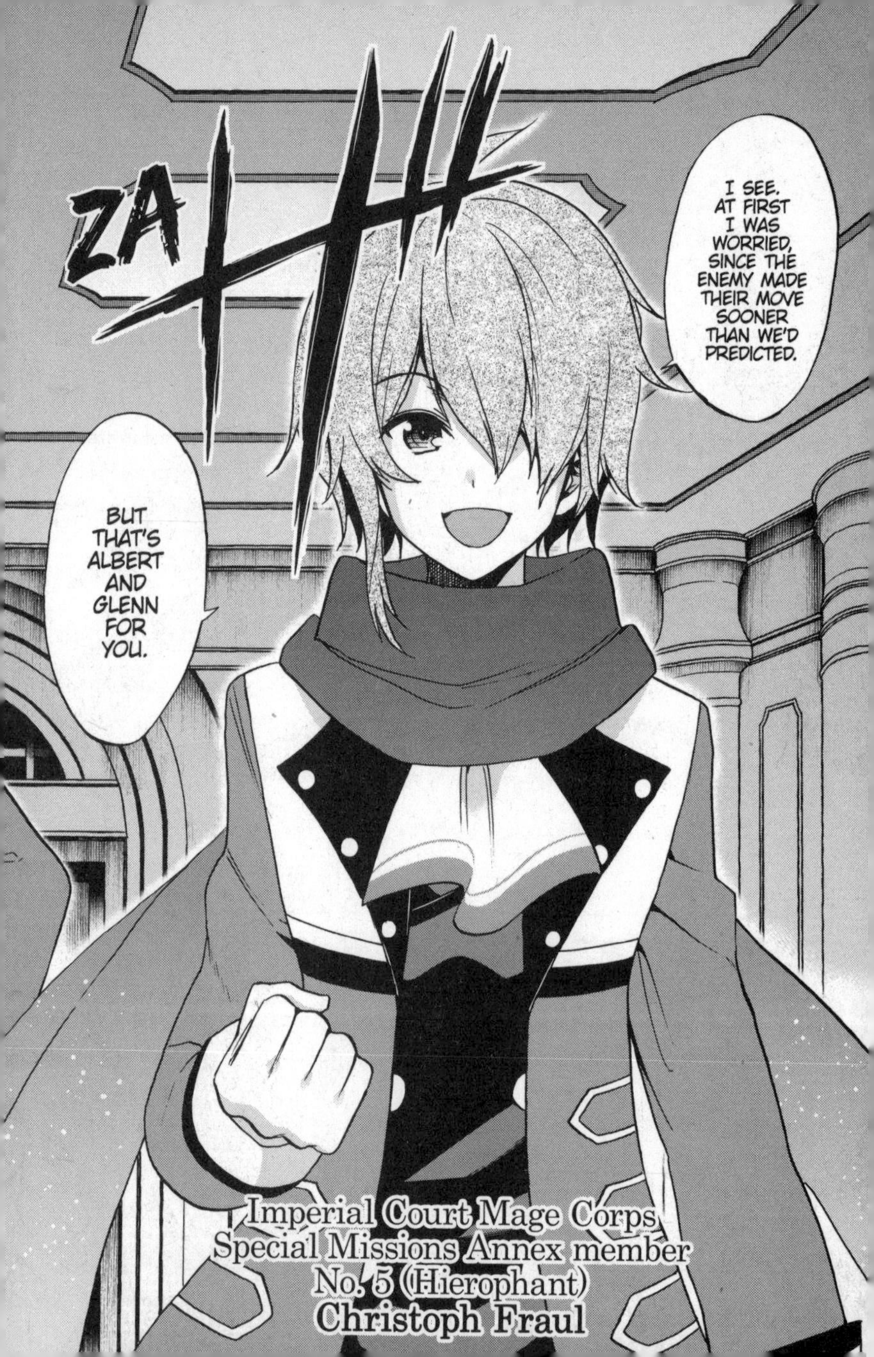
I SEE. AT FIRST I WAS WORRIED, SINCE THE ENEMY MADE THEIR MOVE SOONER THAN WE'D PREDICTED.
ZA
BUT THAT'S ALBERT AND GLENN FOR YOU.
Imperial Court Mage Corps Special Missions Annex member No. 5 (Hierophant) Christoph Fraul

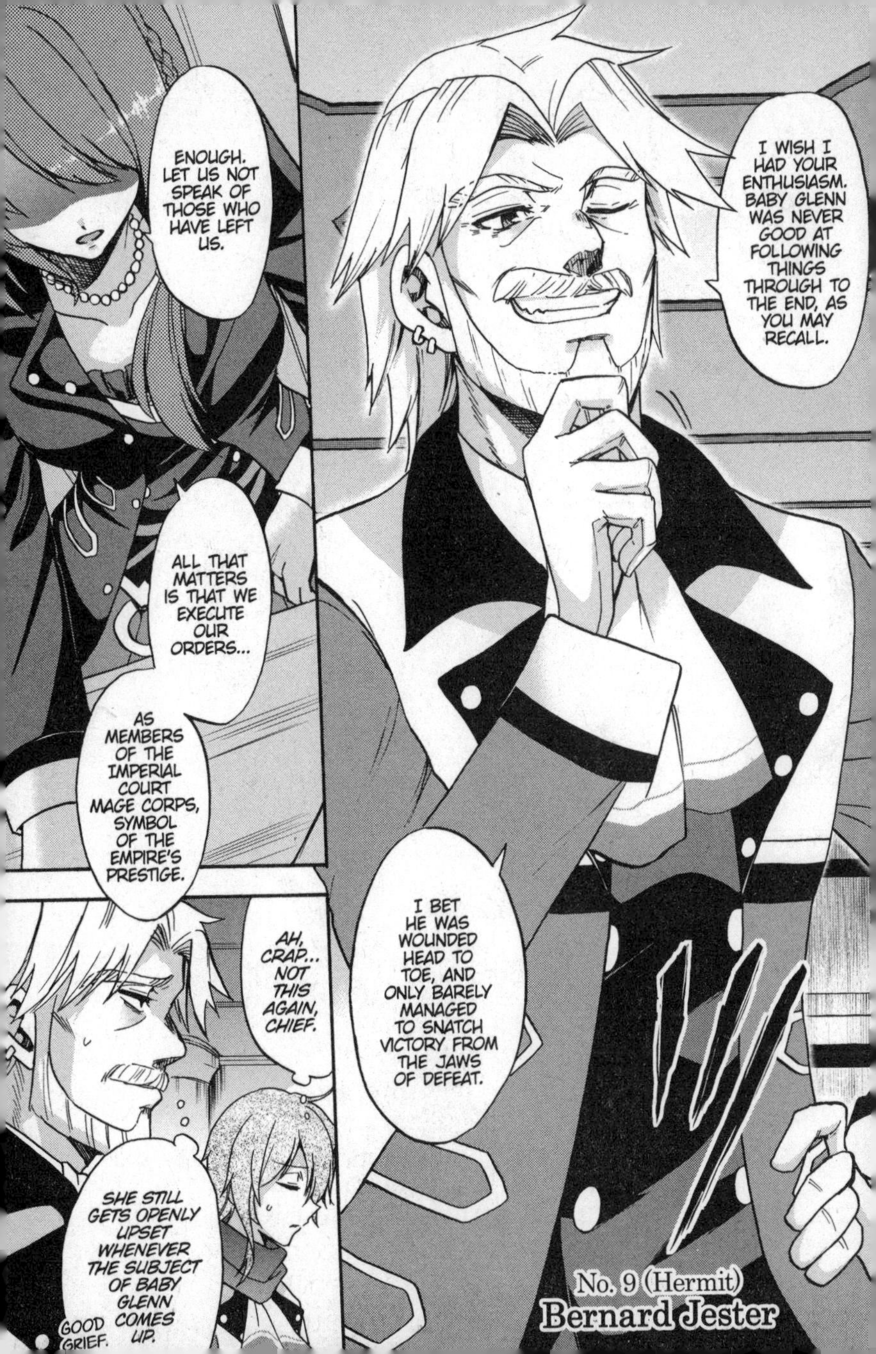
I WISH I HAD YOUR ENTHUSIASM. BABY GLENN WAS NEVER GOOD AT FOLLOWING THINGS THROUGH TO THE END, AS YOU MAY RECALL.
I BET HE WAS WOUNDED HEAD TO TOE, AND ONLY BARELY MANAGED TO SNATCH VICTORY FROM THE JAWS OF DEFEAT.
No. 9 (Hermit)
Bernard Jester
ENOUGH. LET US NOT SPEAK OF THOSE WHO HAVE LEFT US.
ALL THAT MATTERS IS THAT WE EXECUTE OUR ORDERS...
AS MEMBERS OF THE IMPERIAL COURT MAGE CORPS, SYMBOL OF THE EMPIRE'S PRESTIGE.
AH, CRAP... NOT THIS AGAIN, CHIEF.
SHE STILL GETS OPENLY UPSET WHENEVER THE SUBJECT OF BABY GLENN COMES UP.
GOOD GRIEF.

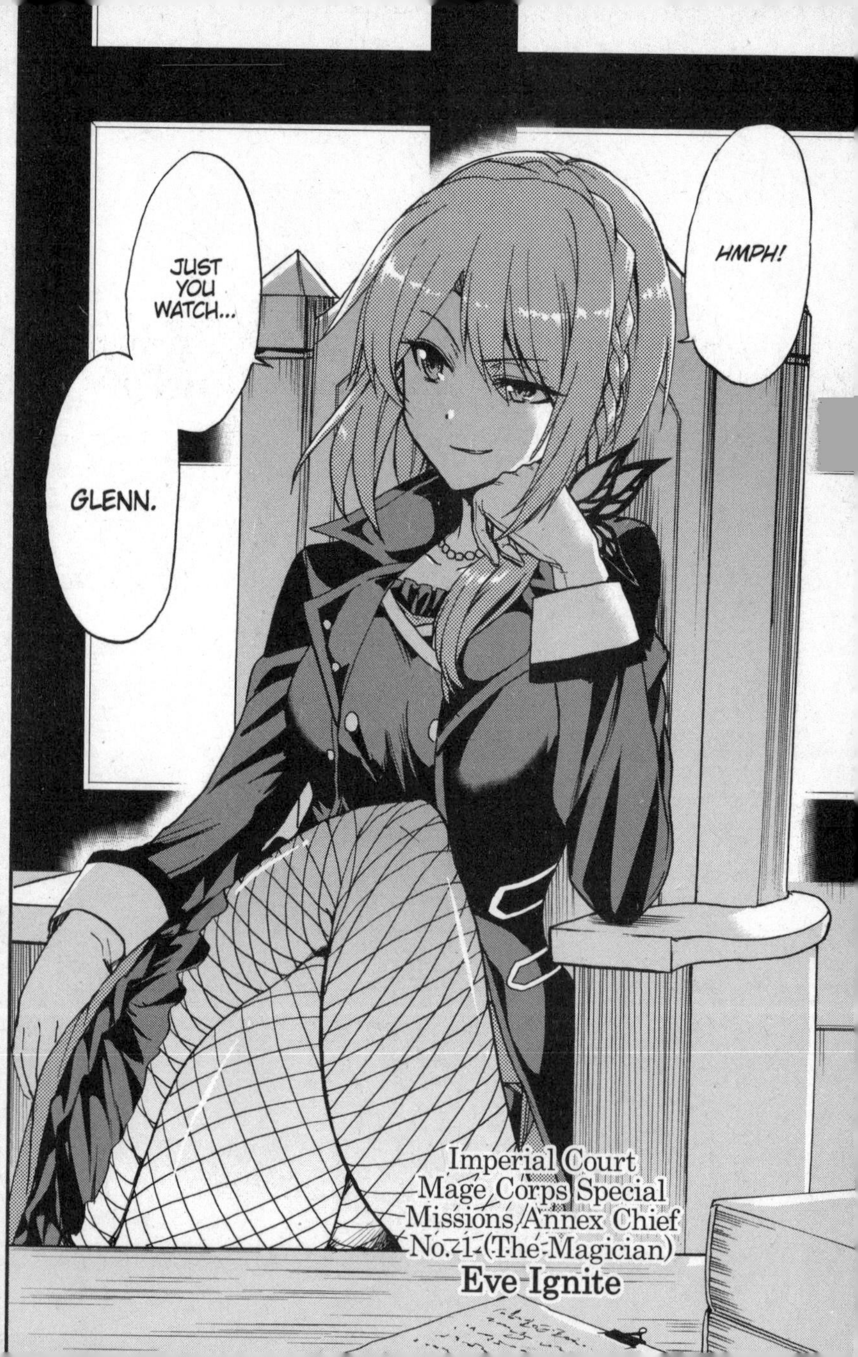
HMPH!
JUST YOU WATCH...
GLENN.
Imperial Court Mage Corps Special Missions Annex Chief No. 1 (The Magician)
Eve Ignite

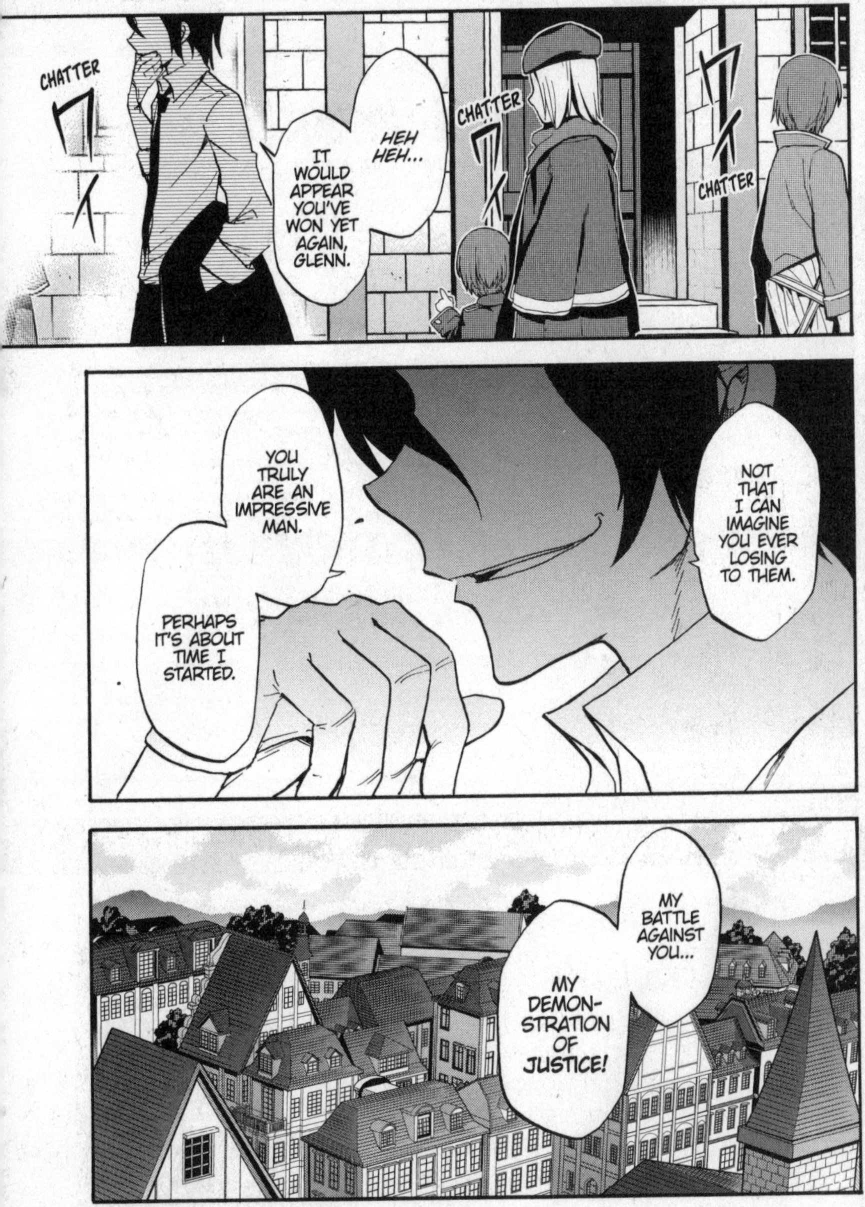

CHATTER
CHATTER
HEH HEH... IT WOULD APPEAR YOU'VE WON YET AGAIN, GLENN.
CHATTER
NOT THAT I CAN IMAGINE YOU EVER LOSING TO THEM.
YOU TRULY ARE AN IMPRESSIVE MAN.
PERHAPS IT'S ABOUT TIME I STARTED.
MY BATTLE AGAINST YOU...
MY DEMON-STRATION OF JUSTICE!

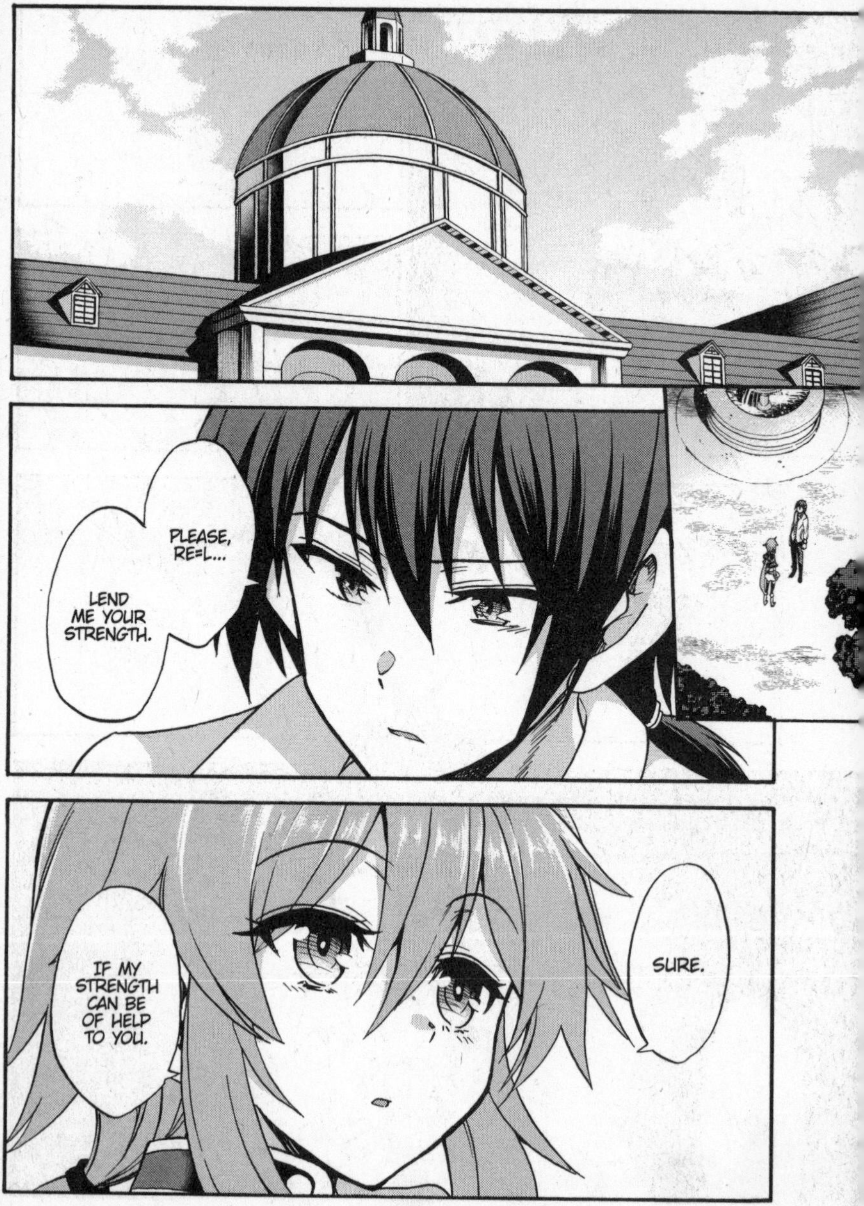
PLEASE, RE=L...
LEND ME YOUR STRENGTH.
SURE.
IF MY STRENGTH CAN BE OF HELP TO YOU.

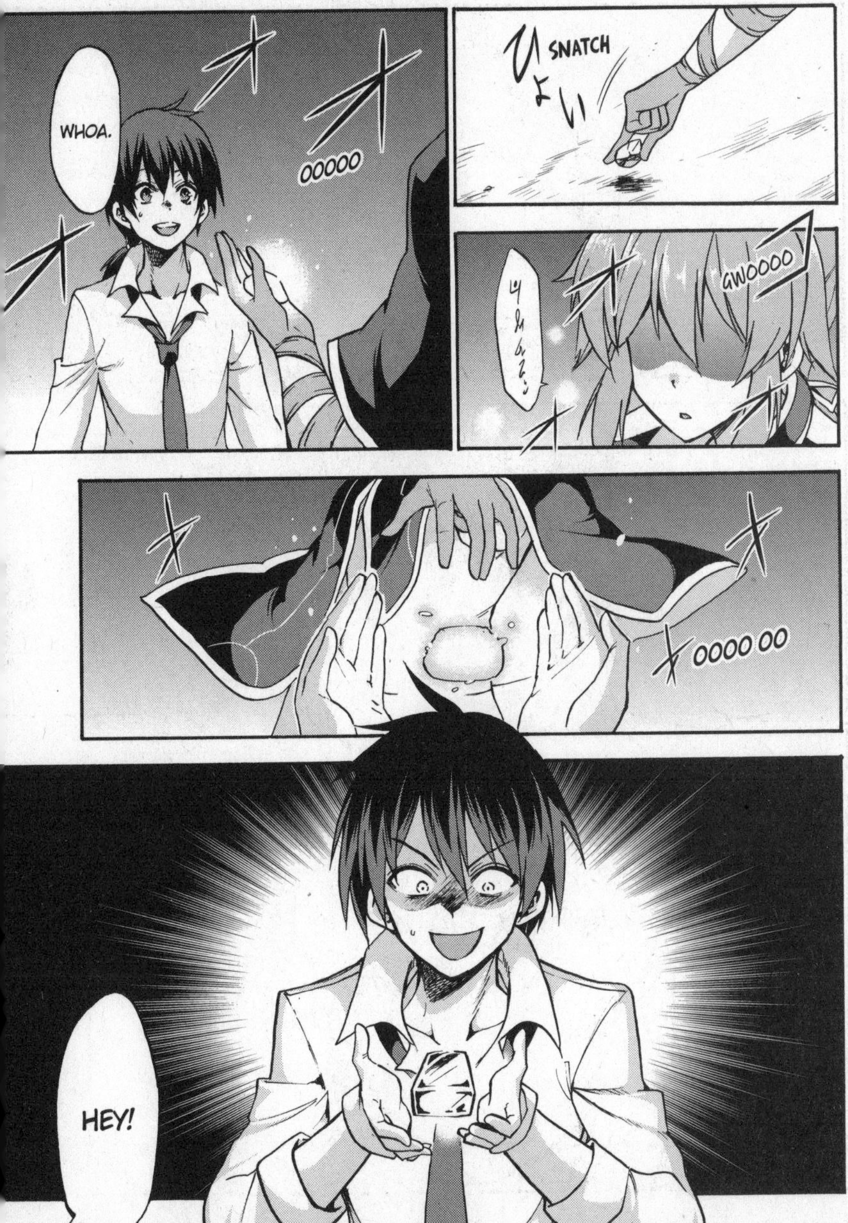
ひょい
SNATCH
GWOOOO
WHOA.
OOOOO
OOOO OO
HEY!

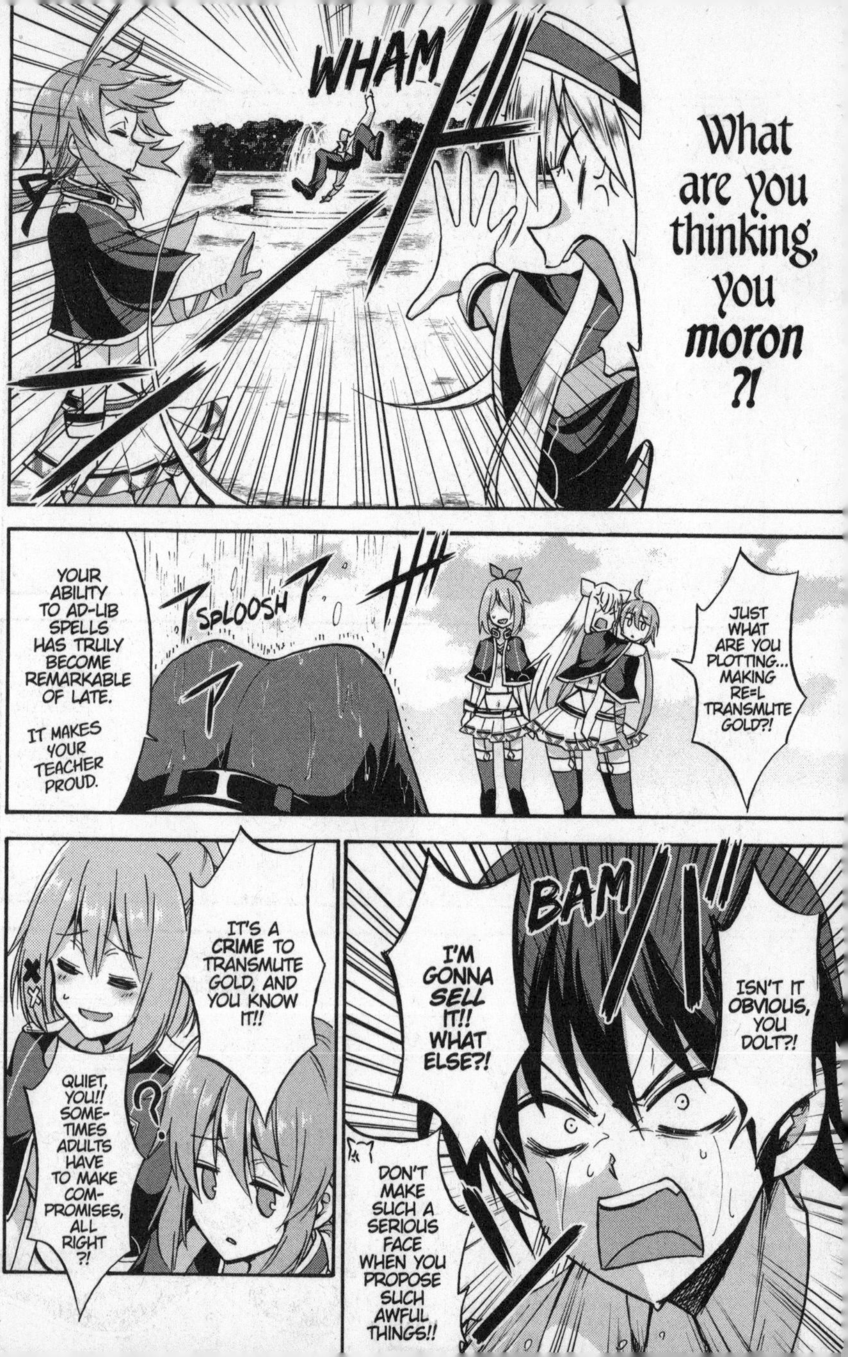
WHAM
What are you thinking, you moron?!
JUST WHAT ARE YOU PLOTTING... MAKING RE=L TRANSMUTE GOLD?!
SPLOOSH
YOUR ABILITY TO AD-LIB SPELLS HAS TRULY BECOME REMARKABLE OF LATE.
IT MAKES YOUR TEACHER PROUD.
BAM
ISN'T IT OBVIOUS, YOU DOLT?!
I'M GONNA SELL IT!! WHAT ELSE?!
DON'T MAKE SUCH A SERIOUS FACE WHEN YOU PROPOSE SUCH AWFUL THINGS!!
IT'S A CRIME TO TRANSMUTE GOLD, AND YOU KNOW IT!!
QUIET, YOU!! SOME-TIMES ADULTS HAVE TO MAKE COM-PROMISES, ALL RIGHT?!

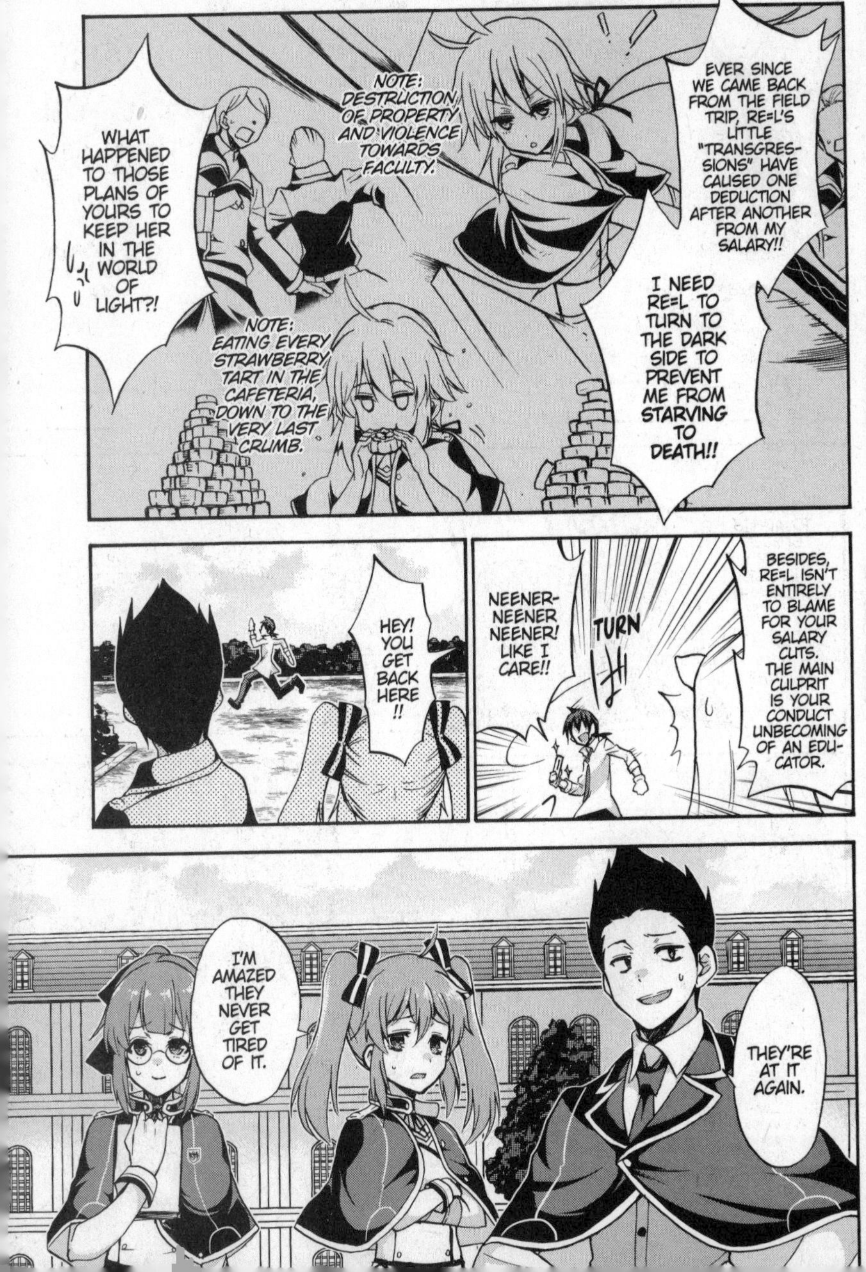
EVER SINCE WE CAME BACK FROM THE FIELD TRIP, RE=L'S LITTLE "TRANSGRES- SIONS" HAVE CAUSED ONE DEDUCTION AFTER ANOTHER FROM MY SALARY!!
NOTE: DESTRUCTION OF PROPERTY AND VIOLENCE TOWARDS FACULTY.
I NEED RE=L TO TURN TO THE DARK SIDE TO PREVENT ME FROM STARVING TO DEATH!!
WHAT HAPPENED TO THOSE PLANS OF YOURS TO KEEP HER IN THE WORLD OF LIGHT?!
NOTE: EATING EVERY STRAWBERRY TART IN THE CAFETERIA, DOWN TO THE VERY LAST CRUMB.
BESIDES, RE=L ISN'T ENTIRELY TO BLAME FOR YOUR SALARY CUTS. THE MAIN CULPRIT IS YOUR CONDUCT UNBECOMING OF AN EDU- CATOR.
TURN
NEENER- NEENER NEENER! LIKE I CARE!!
HEY! YOU GET BACK HERE !!
THEY'RE AT IT AGAIN.
I'M AMAZED THEY NEVER GET TIRED OF IT.

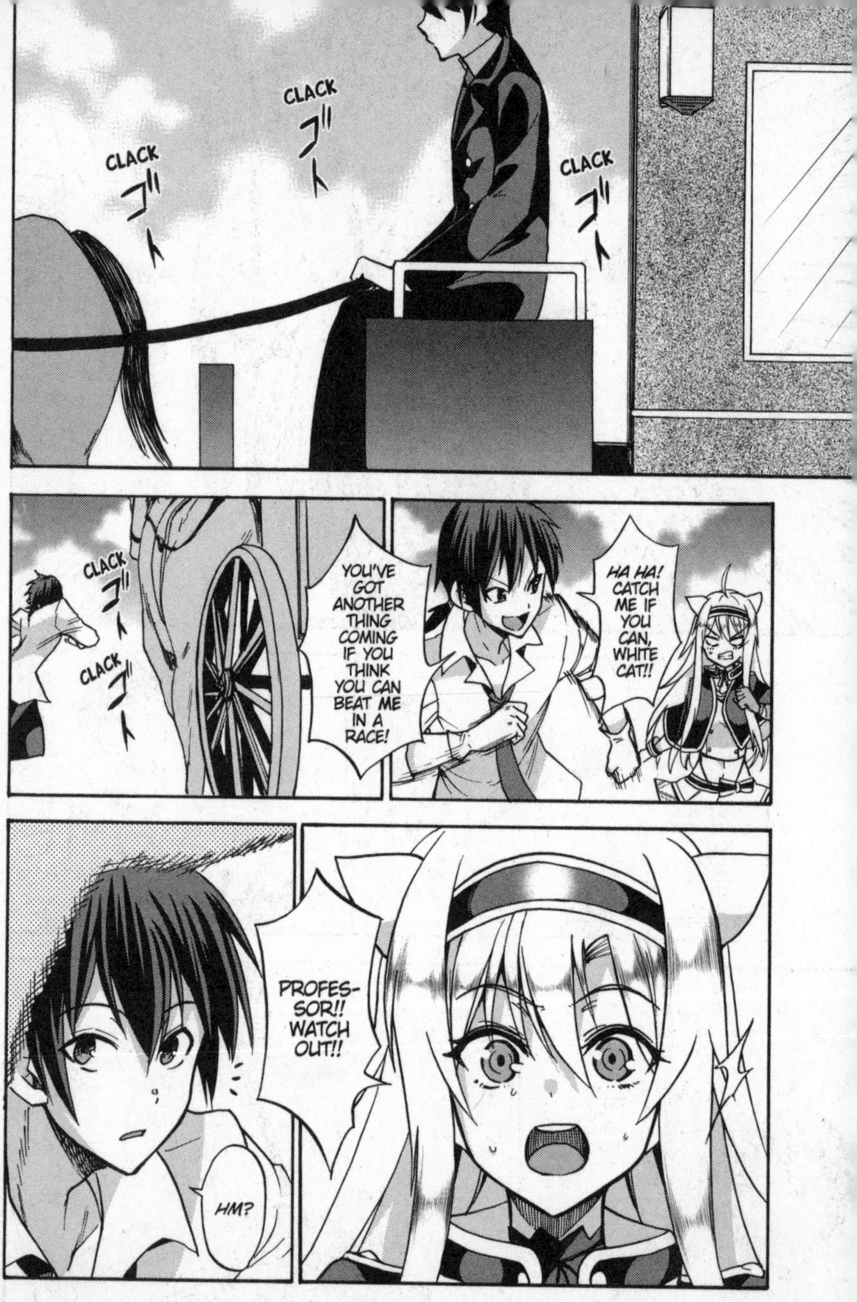
CLACK ゴト
CLACK ゴト
CLACK ゴト
HA HA! CATCH ME IF YOU CAN, WHITE CAT!!
YOU'VE GOT ANOTHER THING COMING IF YOU THINK YOU CAN BEAT ME IN A RACE!
CLACK ゴト
CLACK ゴト
PROFES-SOR!! WATCH OUT!!
HM?

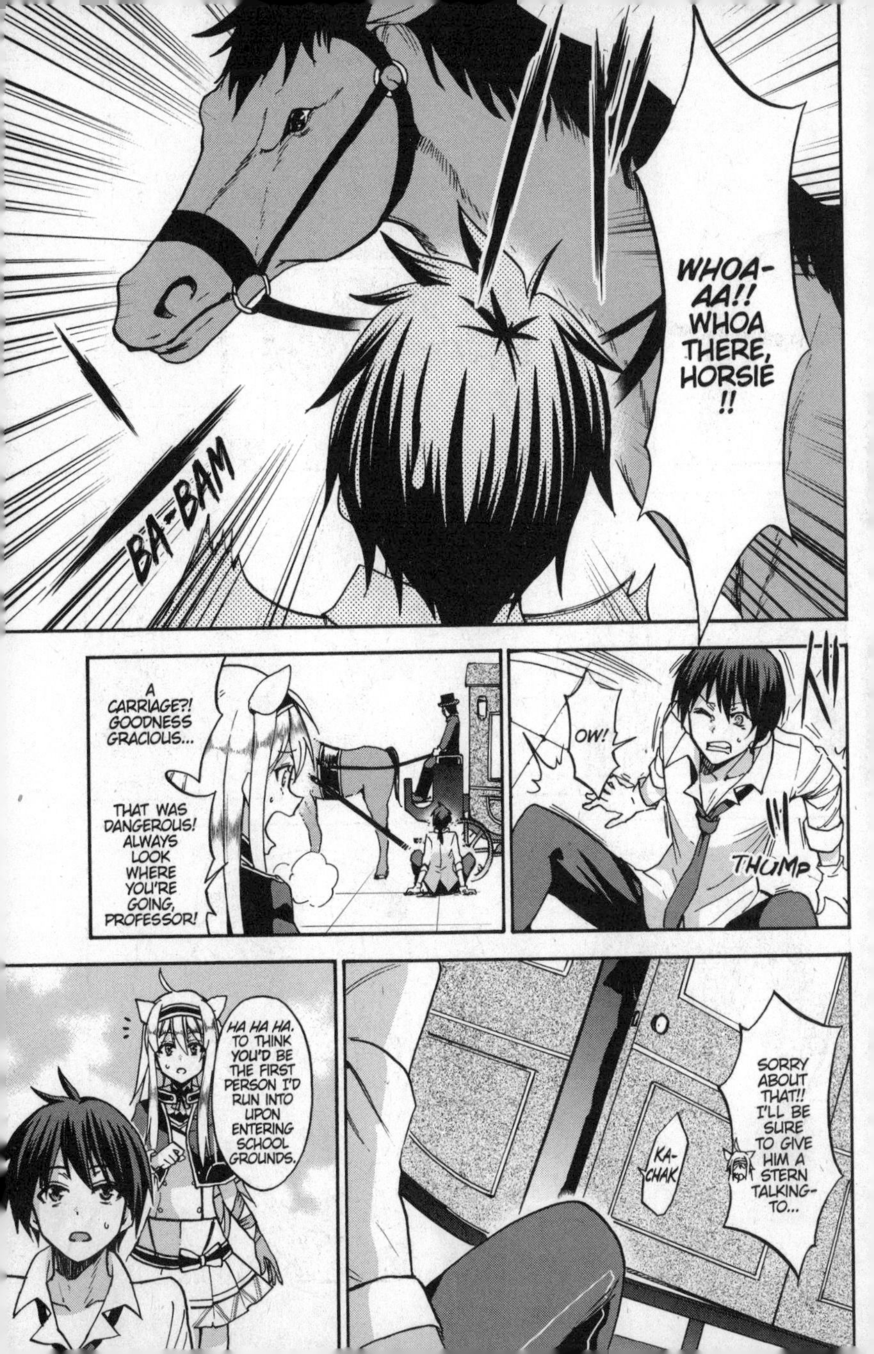
WHOA-AA!! WHOA THERE, HORSIE!!
BA-BAM
OW!
THUMP
A CARRIAGE?! GOODNESS GRACIOUS...
THAT WAS DANGEROUS! ALWAYS LOOK WHERE YOU'RE GOING, PROFESSOR!
SORRY ABOUT THAT!! I'LL BE SURE TO GIVE HIM A STERN TALKING-TO...
KA-CHAK
HA HA HA. TO THINK YOU'D BE THE FIRST PERSON I'D RUN INTO UPON ENTERING SCHOOL GROUNDS.

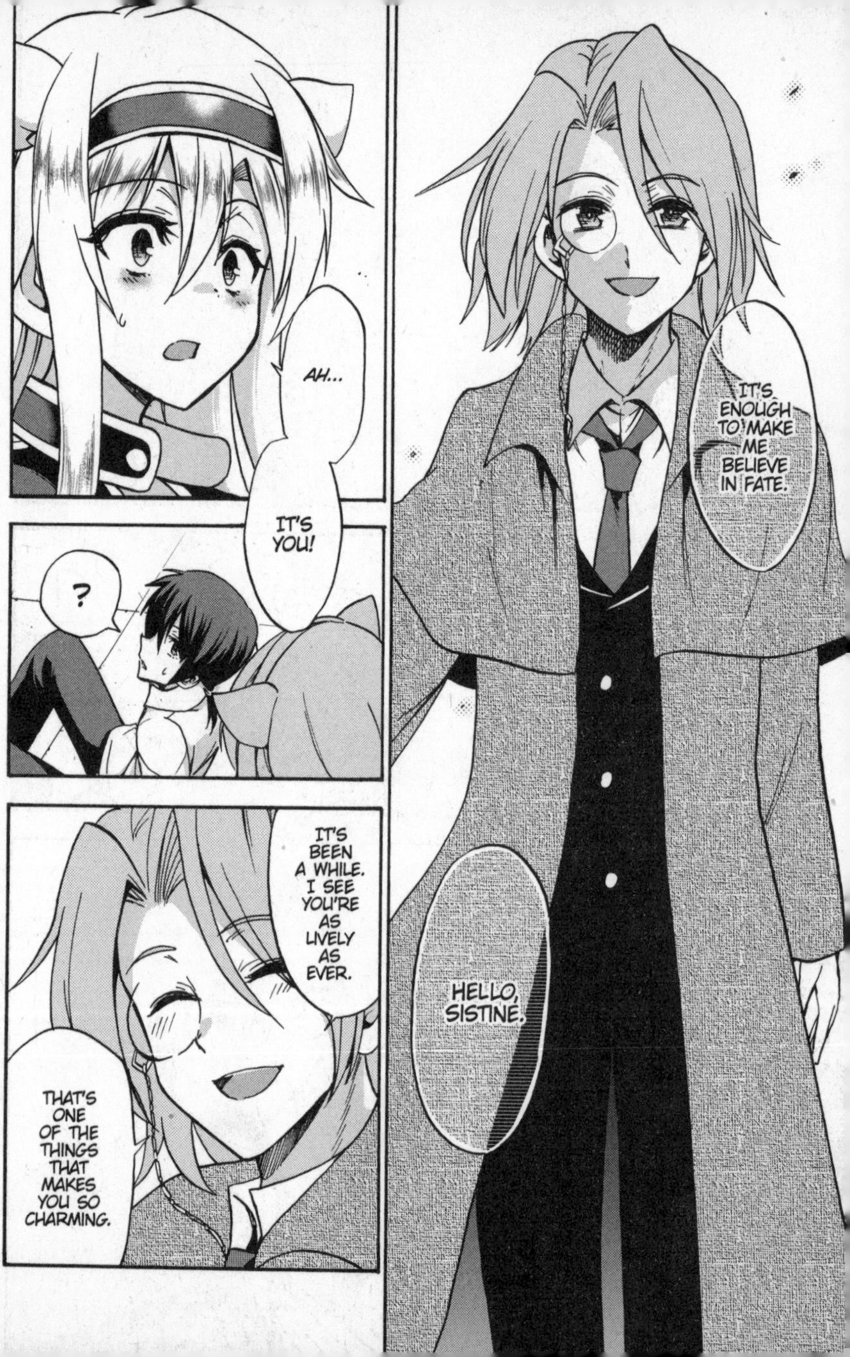
IT'S ENOUGH TO MAKE ME BELIEVE IN FATE.
HELLO, SISTINE.
AH...
IT'S YOU!
?
IT'S BEEN A WHILE. I SEE YOU'RE AS LIVELY AS EVER.
THAT'S ONE OF THE THINGS THAT MAKES YOU SO CHARMING.

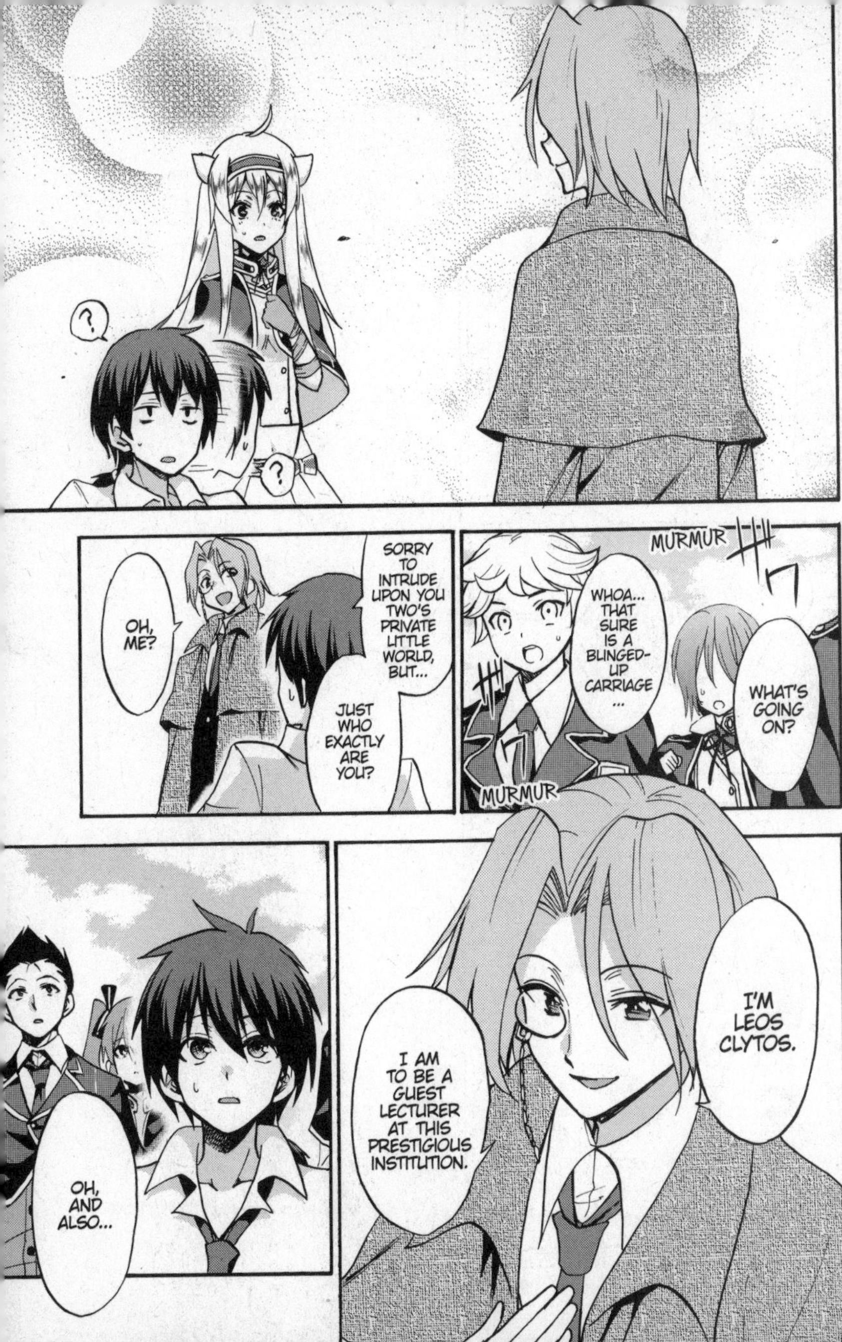
?
?
MURMUR
WHAT'S GOING ON?
WHOA... THAT SURE IS A BLINGED-UP CARRIAGE ...
MURMUR
SORRY TO INTRUDE UPON YOU TWO'S PRIVATE LITTLE WORLD, BUT...
JUST WHO EXACTLY ARE YOU?
OH, ME?
I'M LEOS CLYTOS.
I AM TO BE A GUEST LECTURER AT THIS PRESTIGIOUS INSTITUTION.
OH, AND ALSO...

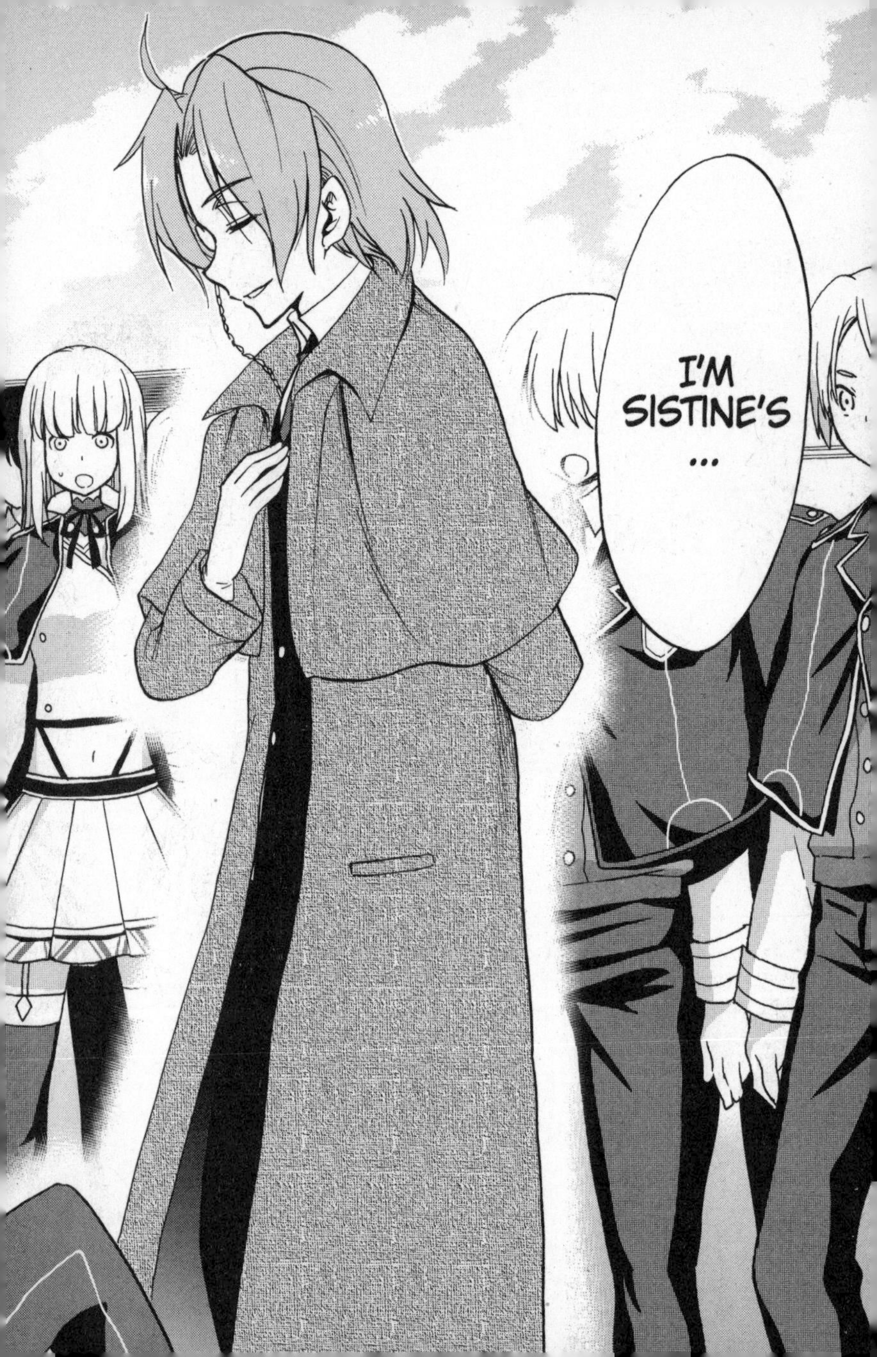
I'M SISTINE'S ...

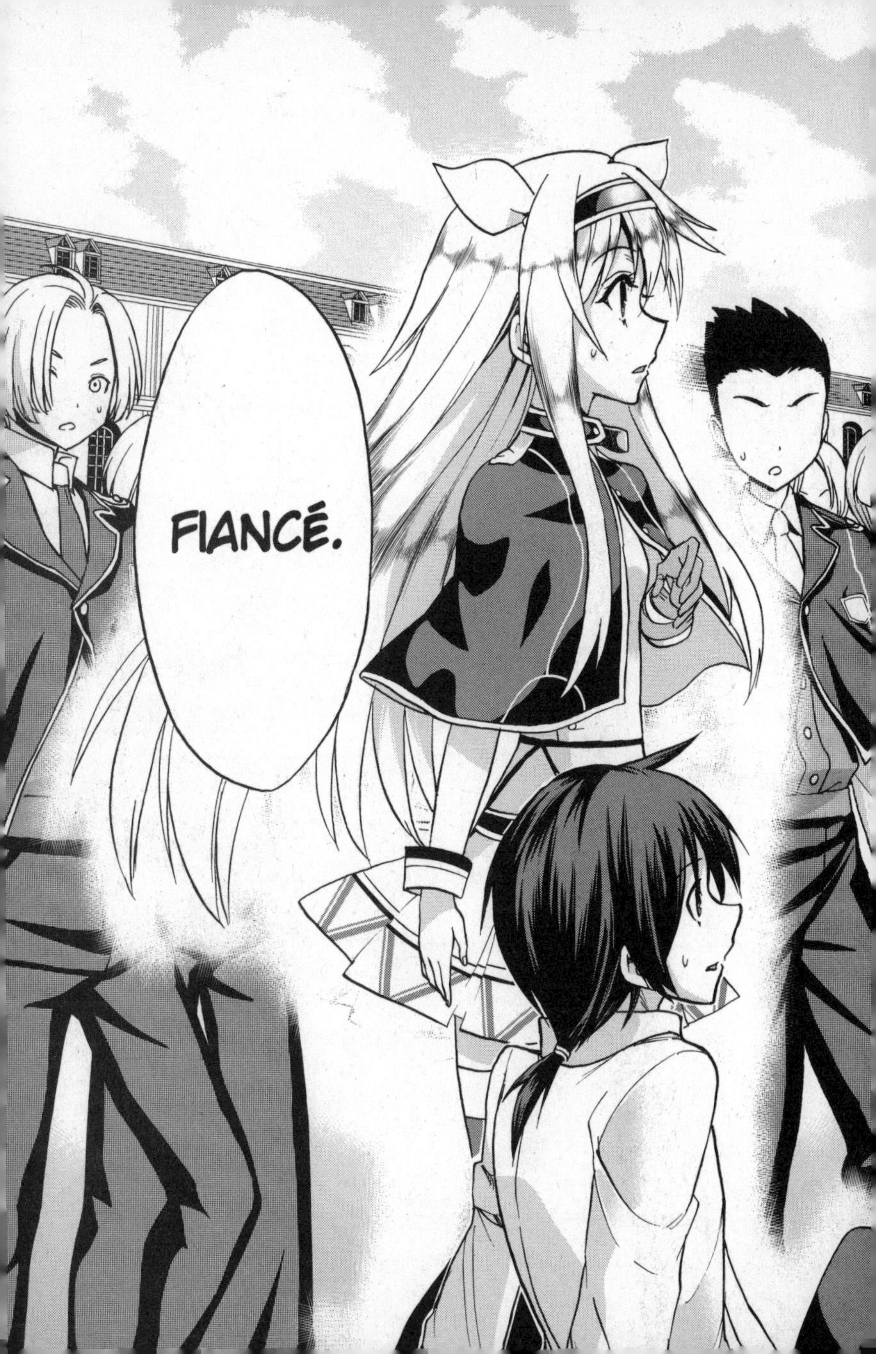
FIANCÉ.

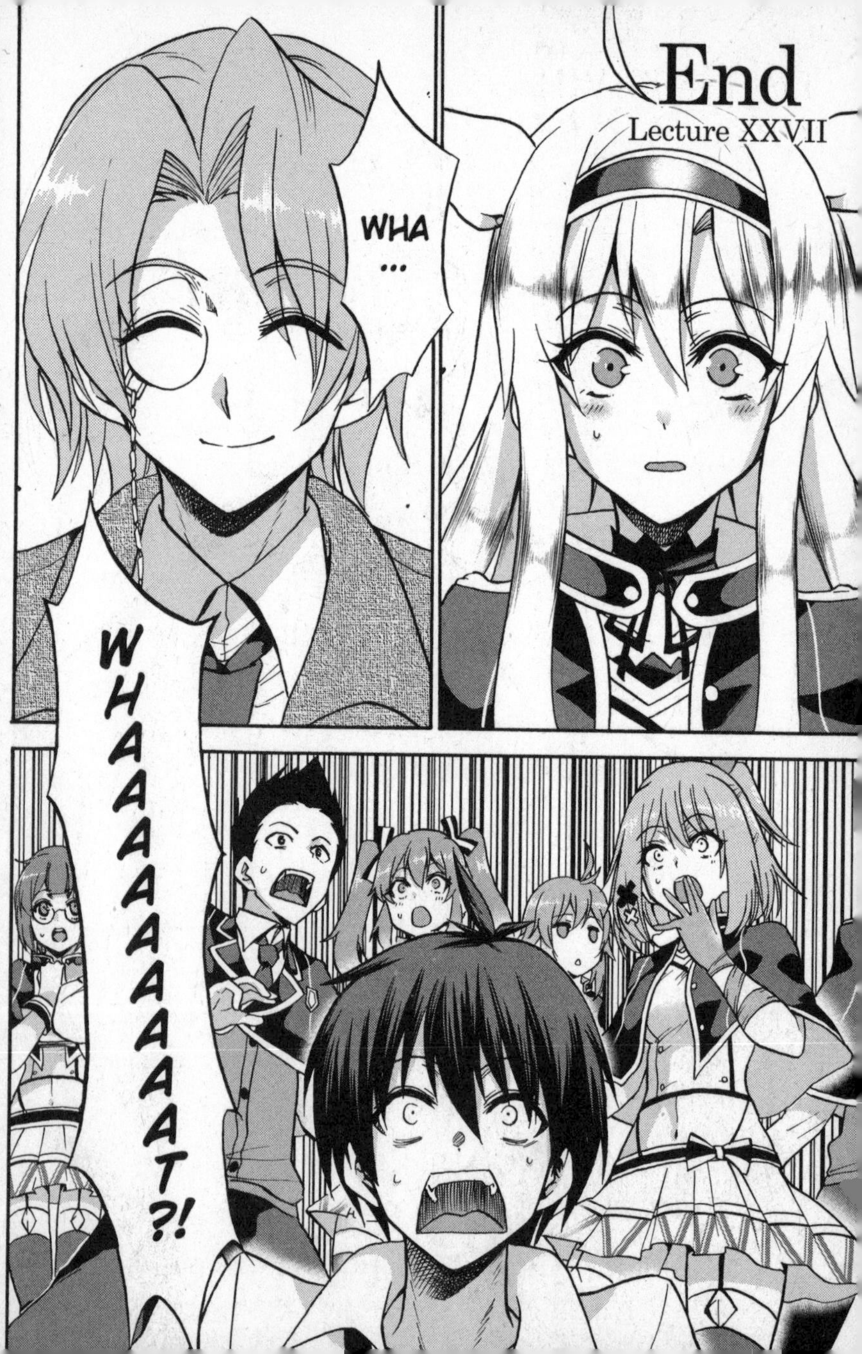
End
Lecture XXVII
WHA ...
WHAAAAAAAAAAT?!

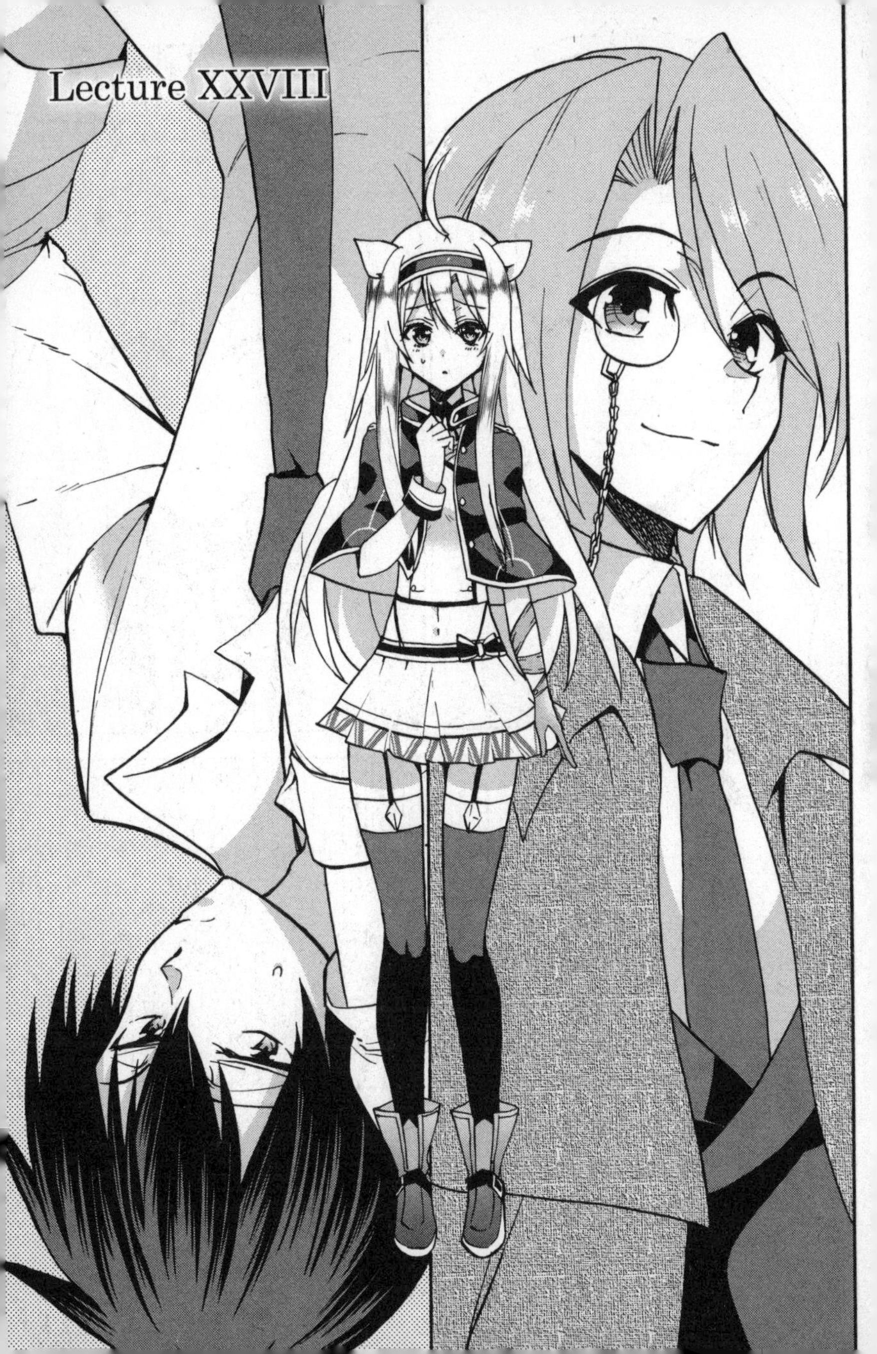
Lecture XXVIII

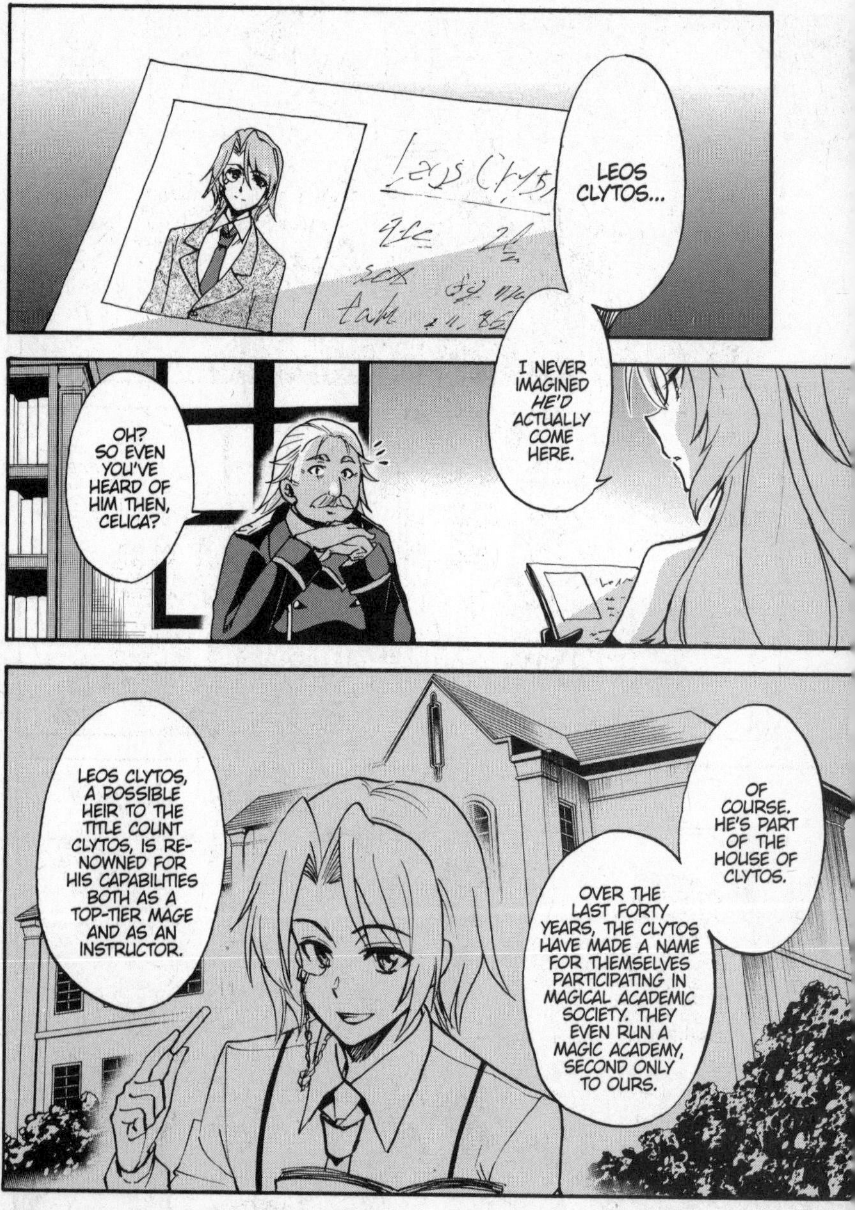
LEOS CLYTOS...
I NEVER IMAGINED HE'D ACTUALLY COME HERE.
OH? SO EVEN YOU'VE HEARD OF HIM THEN, CELICA?
OF COURSE. HE'S PART OF THE HOUSE OF CLYTOS.
OVER THE LAST FORTY YEARS, THE CLYTOS HAVE MADE A NAME FOR THEMSELVES PARTICIPATING IN MAGICAL ACADEMIC SOCIETY. THEY EVEN RUN A MAGIC ACADEMY, SECOND ONLY TO OURS.
LEOS CLYTOS, A POSSIBLE HEIR TO THE TITLE COUNT CLYTOS, IS RE-NOWNED FOR HIS CAPABILITIES BOTH AS A TOP-TIER MAGE AND AS AN INSTRUCTOR.

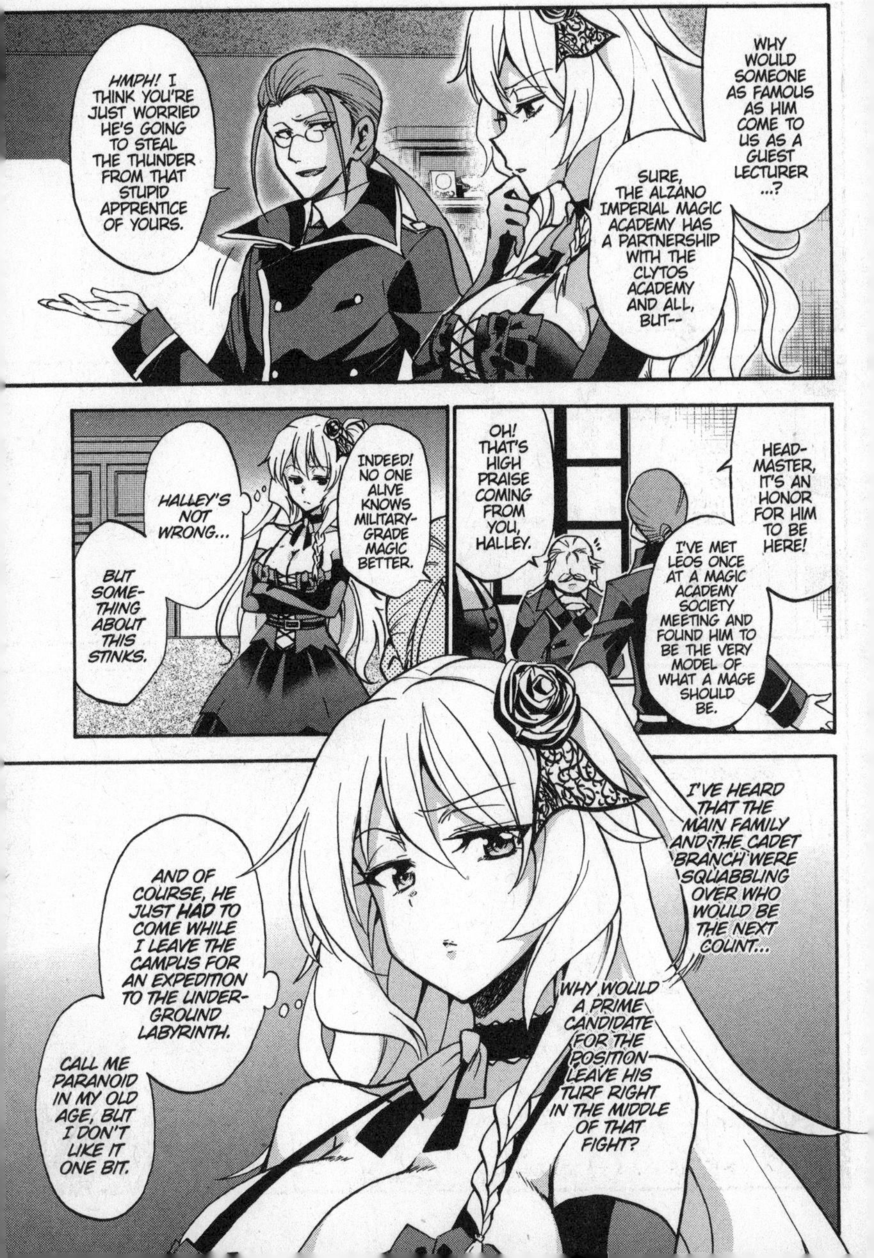
WHY WOULD SOMEONE AS FAMOUS AS HIM COME TO US AS A GUEST LECTURER ...?
SURE, THE ALZANO IMPERIAL MAGIC ACADEMY HAS A PARTNERSHIP WITH THE CLYTOS ACADEMY AND ALL, BUT--
HMPH! I THINK YOU'RE JUST WORRIED HE'S GOING TO STEAL THE THUNDER FROM THAT STUPID APPRENTICE OF YOURS.
HEAD-MASTER, IT'S AN HONOR FOR HIM TO BE HERE!
I'VE MET LEOS ONCE AT A MAGIC ACADEMY SOCIETY MEETING AND FOUND HIM TO BE THE VERY MODEL OF WHAT A MAGE SHOULD BE.
OH! THAT'S HIGH PRAISE COMING FROM YOU, HALLEY.
INDEED! NO ONE ALIVE KNOWS MILITARY-GRADE MAGIC BETTER.
HALLEY'S NOT WRONG...
BUT SOMETHING ABOUT THIS STINKS.
I'VE HEARD THAT THE MAIN FAMILY AND THE CADET BRANCH WERE SQUABBLING OVER WHO WOULD BE THE NEXT COUNT...
AND OF COURSE, HE JUST HAD TO COME WHILE I LEAVE THE CAMPUS FOR AN EXPEDITION TO THE UNDER-GROUND LABYRINTH.
WHY WOULD A PRIME CANDIDATE FOR THE POSITION LEAVE HIS TURF RIGHT IN THE MIDDLE OF THAT FIGHT?
CALL ME PARANOID IN MY OLD AGE, BUT I DON'T LIKE IT ONE BIT.

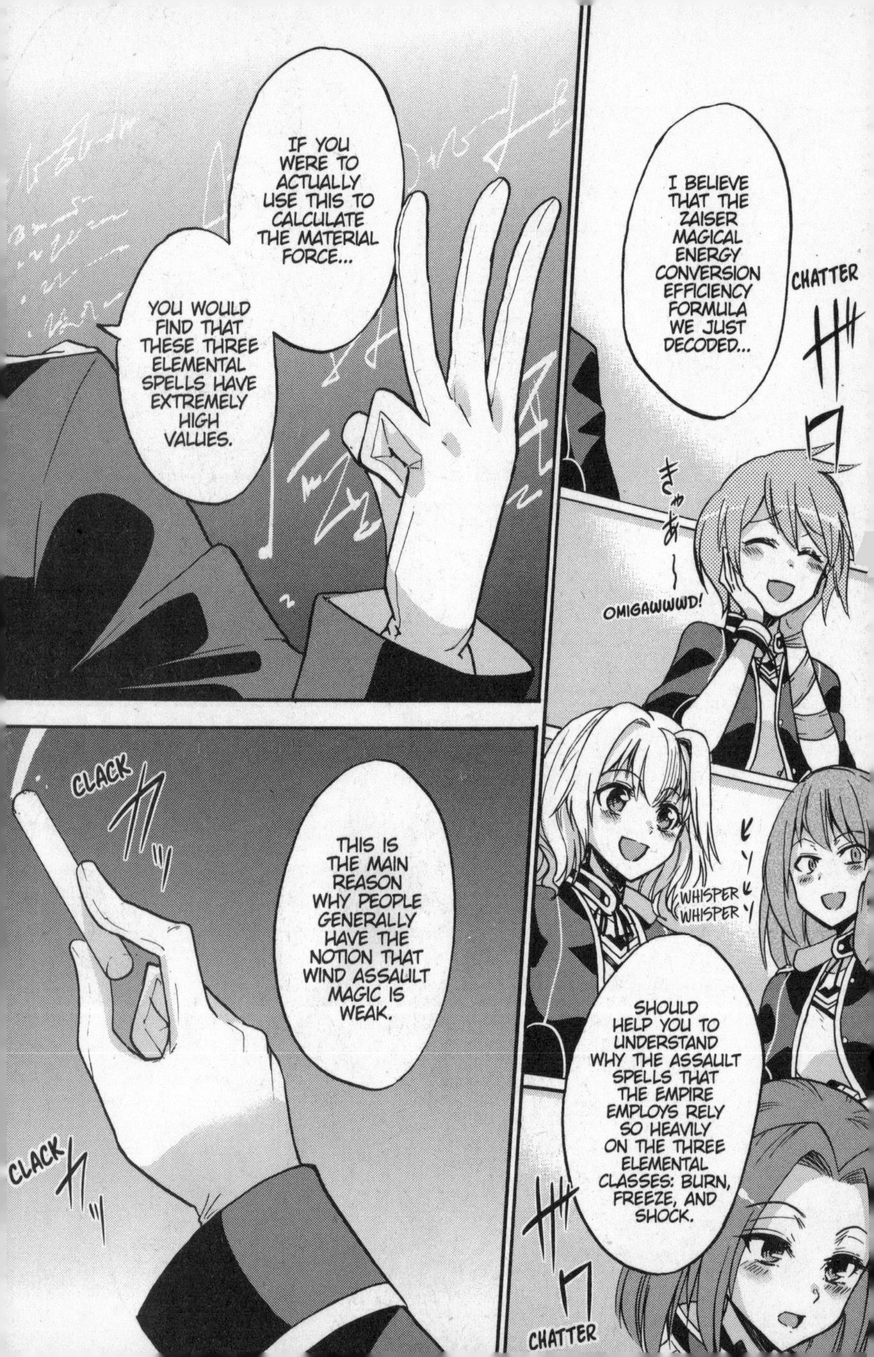
I BELIEVE THAT THE ZAISER MAGICAL ENERGY CONVERSION EFFICIENCY FORMULA WE JUST DECODED...
CHATTER
きゃあ～
OMIGAWWWD!
WHISPER WHISPER
SHOULD HELP YOU TO UNDERSTAND WHY THE ASSAULT SPELLS THAT THE EMPIRE EMPLOYS RELY SO HEAVILY ON THE THREE ELEMENTAL CLASSES: BURN, FREEZE, AND SHOCK.
CHATTER
IF YOU WERE TO ACTUALLY USE THIS TO CALCULATE THE MATERIAL FORCE...
YOU WOULD FIND THAT THESE THREE ELEMENTAL SPELLS HAVE EXTREMELY HIGH VALUES.
CLACK
THIS IS THE MAIN REASON WHY PEOPLE GENERALLY HAVE THE NOTION THAT WIND ASSAULT MAGIC IS WEAK.
CLACK

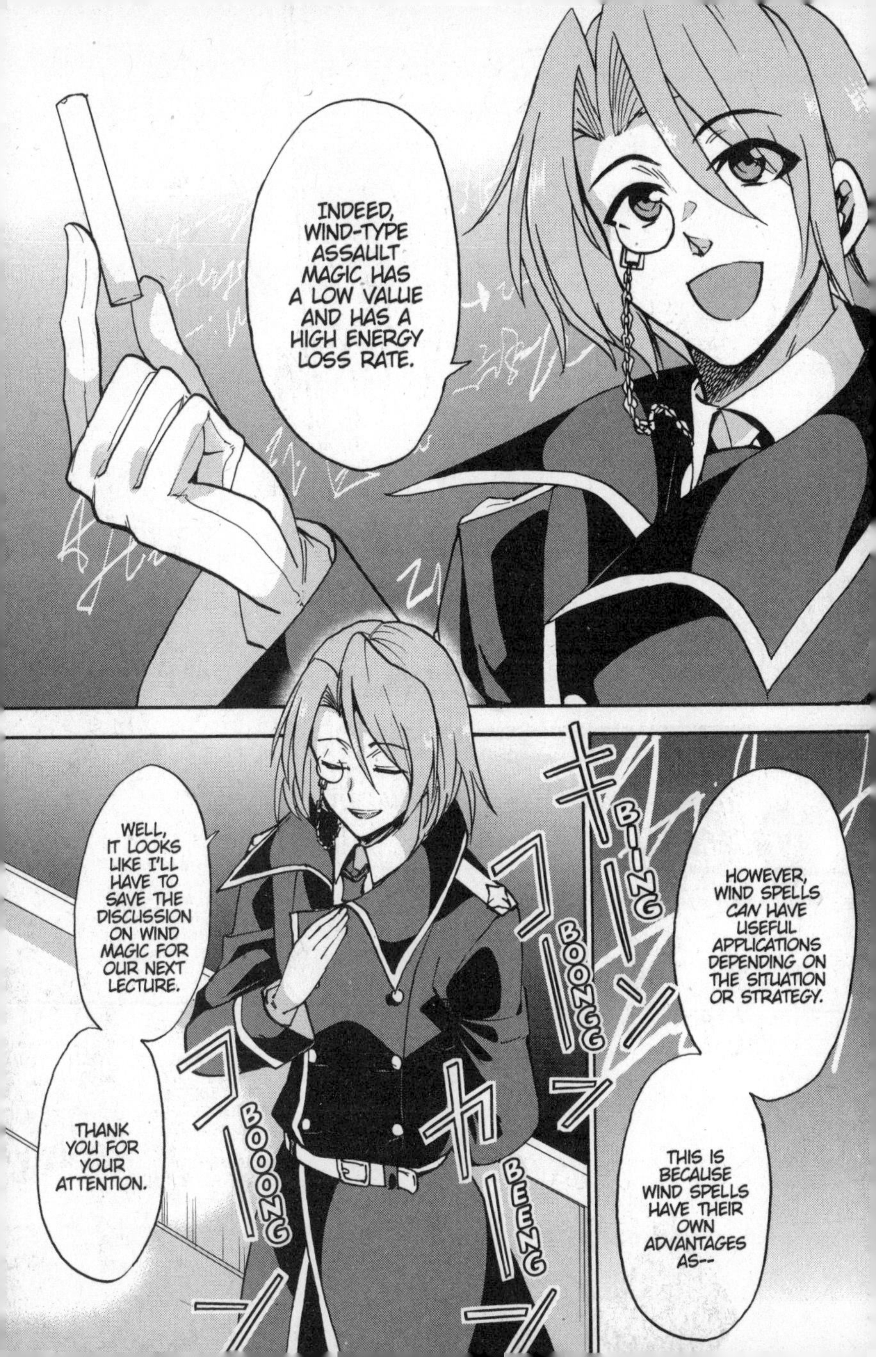

INDEED, WIND-TYPE ASSAULT MAGIC HAS A LOW VALUE AND HAS A HIGH ENERGY LOSS RATE.
HOWEVER, WIND SPELLS CAN HAVE USEFUL APPLICATIONS DEPENDING ON THE SITUATION OR STRATEGY.
THIS IS BECAUSE WIND SPELLS HAVE THEIR OWN ADVANTAGES AS--
BIING
BOONGG
WELL, IT LOOKS LIKE I'LL HAVE TO SAVE THE DISCUSSION ON WIND MAGIC FOR OUR NEXT LECTURE.
BEENG
BOOONG
THANK YOU FOR YOUR ATTENTION.

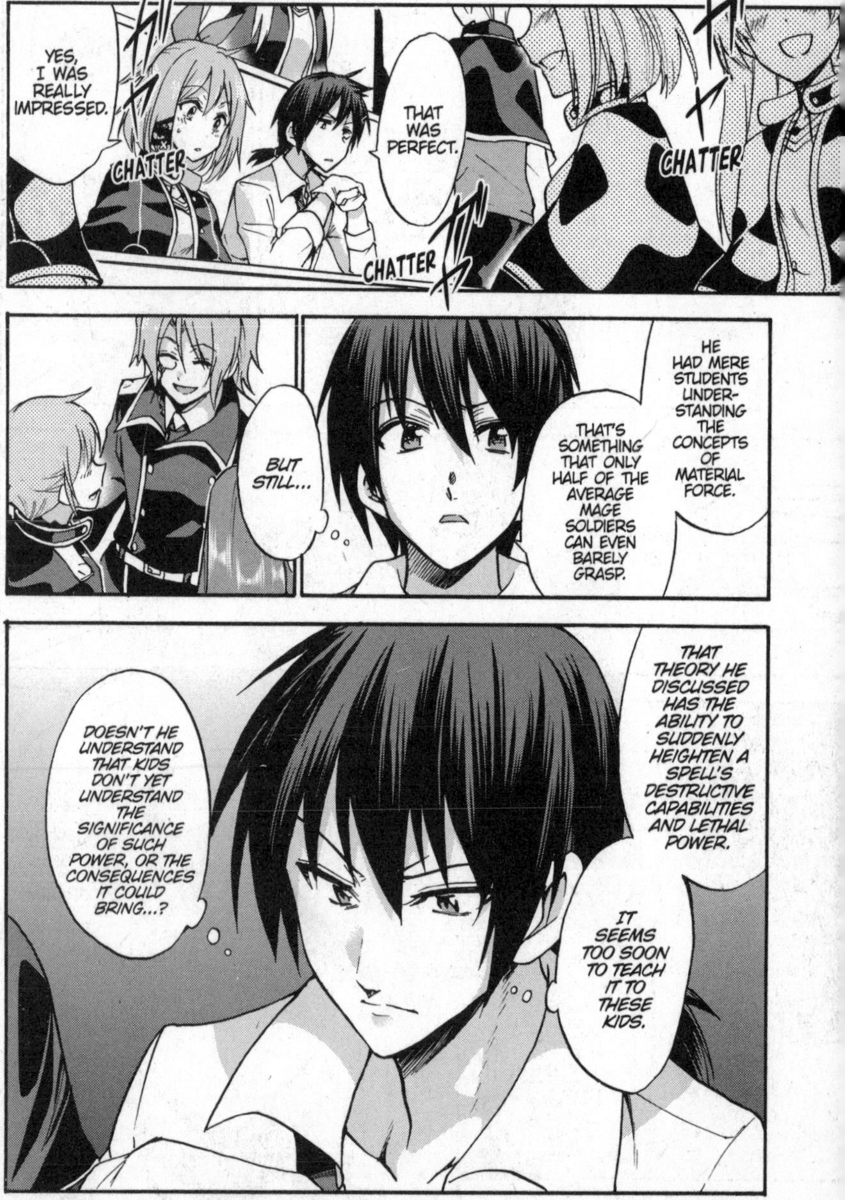
CHATTER
THAT WAS PERFECT.
YES, I WAS REALLY IMPRESSED.
CHATTER
CHATTER
HE HAD MERE STUDENTS UNDER-STANDING THE CONCEPTS OF MATERIAL FORCE.
THAT'S SOMETHING THAT ONLY HALF OF THE AVERAGE MAGE SOLDIERS CAN EVEN BARELY GRASP.
BUT STILL...
THAT THEORY HE DISCUSSED HAS THE ABILITY TO SUDDENLY HEIGHTEN A SPELL'S DESTRUCTIVE CAPABILITIES AND LETHAL POWER.
DOESN'T HE UNDERSTAND THAT KIDS DON'T YET UNDERSTAND THE SIGNIFICANCE OF SUCH POWER, OR THE CONSEQUENCES IT COULD BRING...?
IT SEEMS TOO SOON TO TEACH IT TO THESE KIDS.

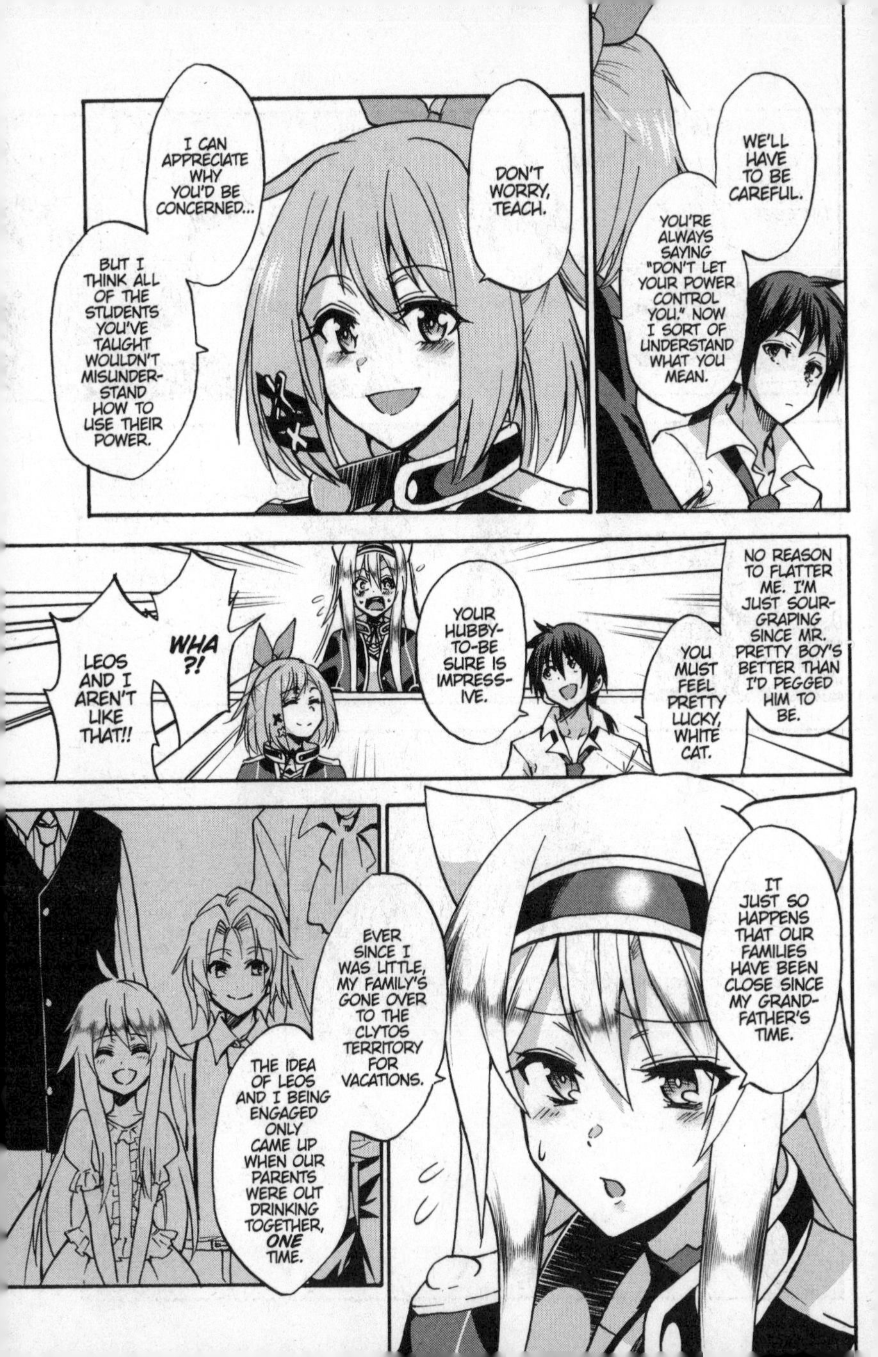

WE'LL HAVE TO BE CAREFUL.
YOU'RE ALWAYS SAYING "DON'T LET YOUR POWER CONTROL YOU." NOW I SORT OF UNDERSTAND WHAT YOU MEAN.
DON'T WORRY, TEACH.
I CAN APPRECIATE WHY YOU'D BE CONCERNED...
BUT I THINK ALL OF THE STUDENTS YOU'VE TAUGHT WOULDN'T MISUNDER-STAND HOW TO USE THEIR POWER.
NO REASON TO FLATTER ME. I'M JUST SOUR-GRAPING SINCE MR. PRETTY BOY'S BETTER THAN I'D PEGGED HIM TO BE.
YOU MUST FEEL PRETTY LUCKY, WHITE CAT.
YOUR HUBBY-TO-BE SURE IS IMPRESS-IVE.
WHA ?!
LEOS AND I AREN'T LIKE THAT!!
IT JUST SO HAPPENS THAT OUR FAMILIES HAVE BEEN CLOSE SINCE MY GRAND-FATHER'S TIME.
EVER SINCE I WAS LITTLE, MY FAMILY'S GONE OVER TO THE CLYTOS TERRITORY FOR VACATIONS.
THE IDEA OF LEOS AND I BEING ENGAGED ONLY CAME UP WHEN OUR PARENTS WERE OUT DRINKING TOGETHER, ***ONE*** TIME.

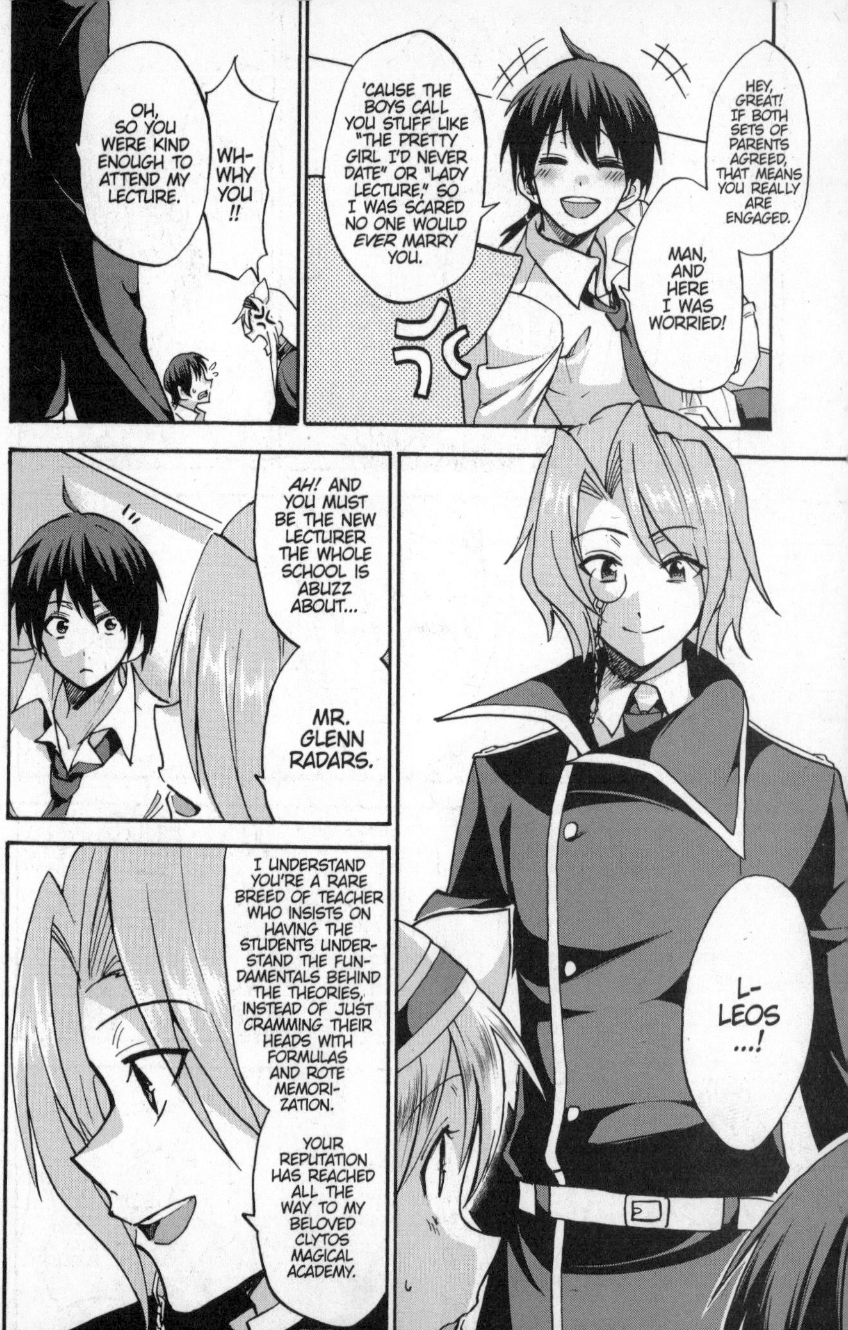
HEY, GREAT! IF BOTH SETS OF PARENTS AGREED, THAT MEANS YOU REALLY ARE ENGAGED.
MAN, AND HERE I WAS WORRIED!
'CAUSE THE BOYS CALL YOU STUFF LIKE "THE PRETTY GIRL I'D NEVER DATE" OR "LADY LECTURE," SO I WAS SCARED NO ONE WOULD *EVER* MARRY YOU.
WH-WHY YOU!!
OH, SO YOU WERE KIND ENOUGH TO ATTEND MY LECTURE.
L-LEOS...!
AH! AND YOU MUST BE THE NEW LECTURER THE WHOLE SCHOOL IS ABUZZ ABOUT...
MR. GLENN RADARS.
I UNDERSTAND YOU'RE A RARE BREED OF TEACHER WHO INSISTS ON HAVING THE STUDENTS UNDERSTAND THE FUNDAMENTALS BEHIND THE THEORIES, INSTEAD OF JUST CRAMMING THEIR HEADS WITH FORMULAS AND ROTE MEMORIZATION.
YOUR REPUTATION HAS REACHED ALL THE WAY TO MY BELOVED CLYTOS MAGICAL ACADEMY.

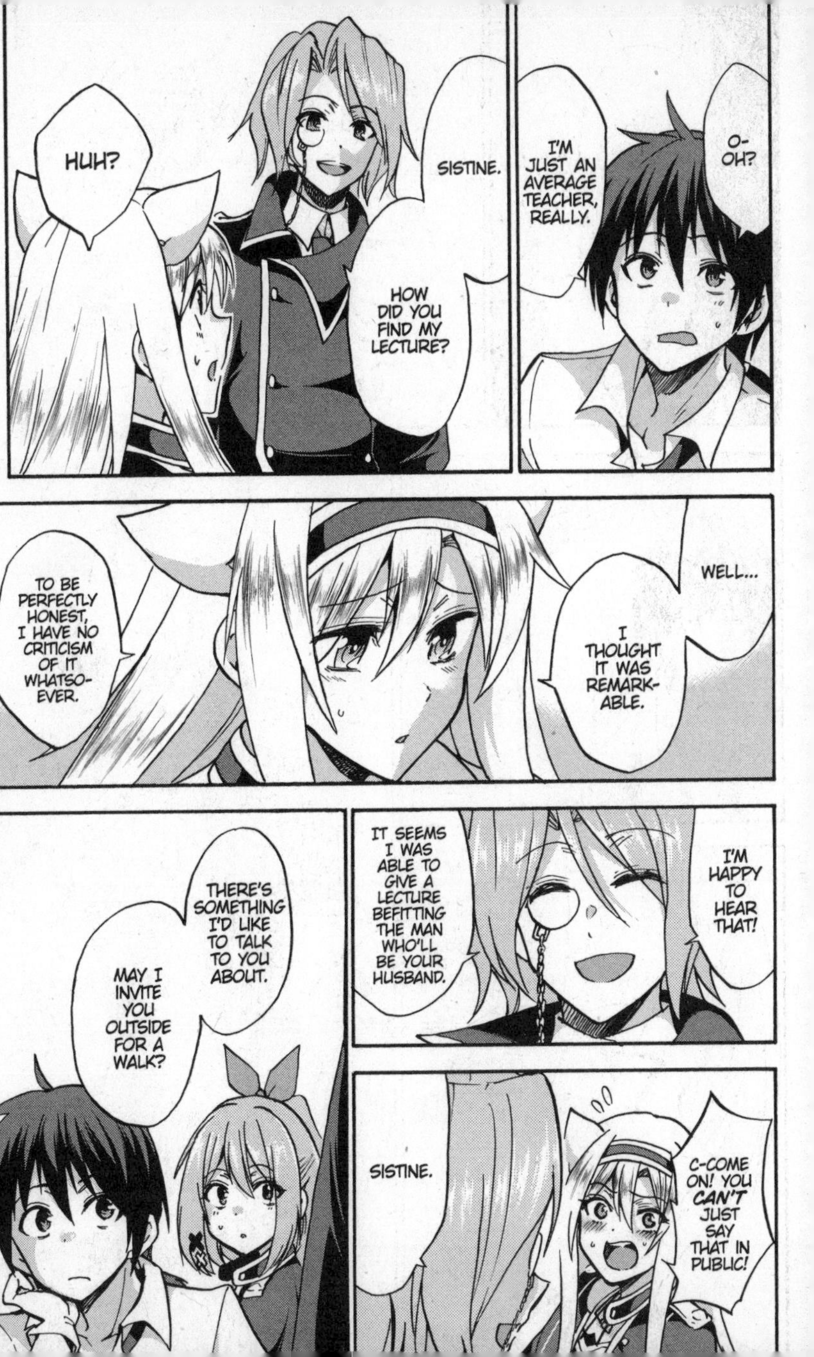
O-OH?
I'M JUST AN AVERAGE TEACHER, REALLY.
SISTINE.
HOW DID YOU FIND MY LECTURE?
HUH?
WELL...
I THOUGHT IT WAS REMARKABLE.
TO BE PERFECTLY HONEST, I HAVE NO CRITICISM OF IT WHATSOEVER.
I'M HAPPY TO HEAR THAT!
IT SEEMS I WAS ABLE TO GIVE A LECTURE BEFITTING THE MAN WHO'LL BE YOUR HUSBAND.
C-COME ON! YOU *CAN'T* JUST SAY THAT IN PUBLIC!
SISTINE.
THERE'S SOMETHING I'D LIKE TO TALK TO YOU ABOUT.
MAY I INVITE YOU OUTSIDE FOR A WALK?

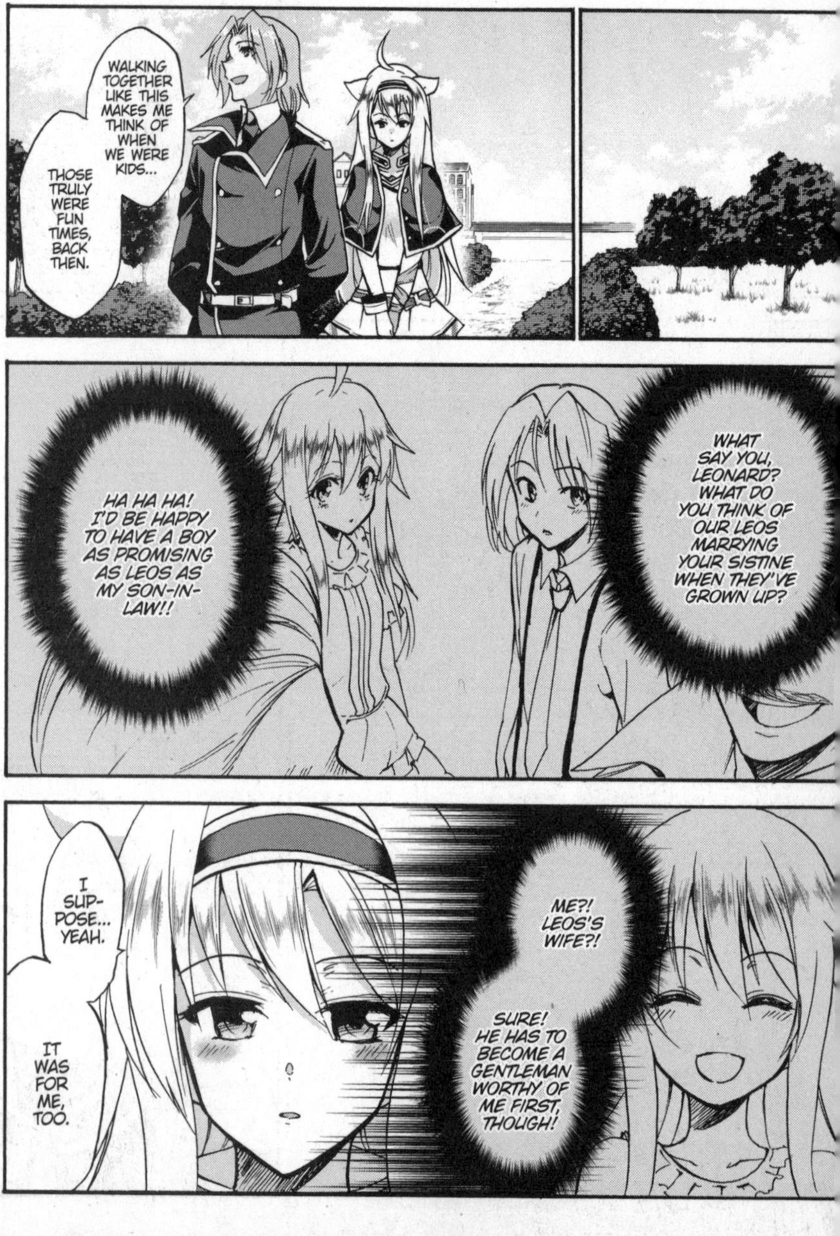
WALKING TOGETHER LIKE THIS MAKES ME THINK OF WHEN WE WERE KIDS...
THOSE TRULY WERE FUN TIMES, BACK THEN.
WHAT SAY YOU, LEONARD? WHAT DO YOU THINK OF OUR LEOS MARRYING YOUR SISTINE WHEN THEY'VE GROWN UP?
HA HA HA! I'D BE HAPPY TO HAVE A BOY AS PROMISING AS LEOS AS MY SON-IN-LAW!!
ME?! LEOS'S WIFE?!
SURE! HE HAS TO BECOME A GENTLEMAN WORTHY OF ME FIRST, THOUGH!
I SUP-POSE... YEAH.
IT WAS FOR ME, TOO.

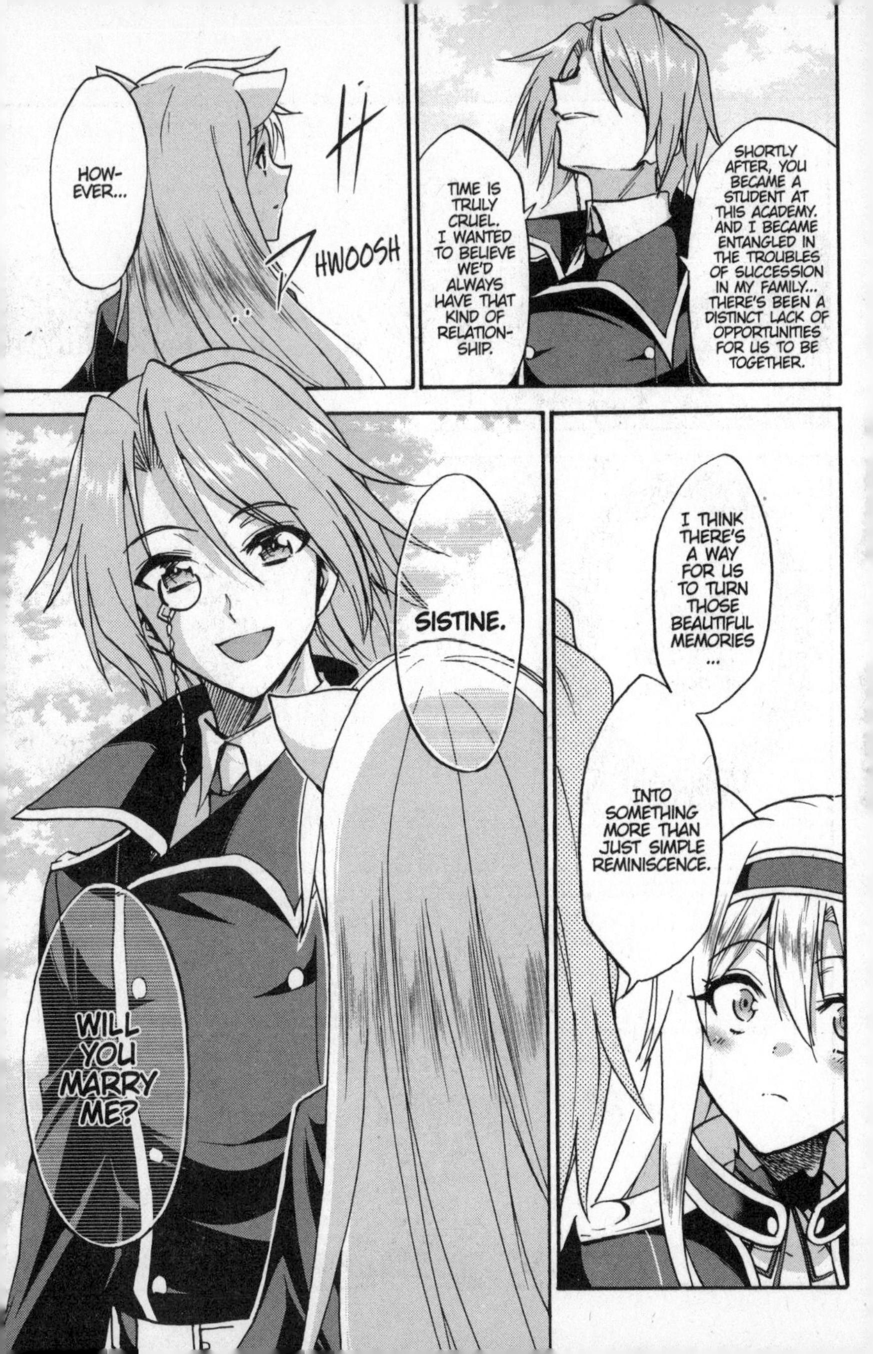
SHORTLY AFTER, YOU BECAME A STUDENT AT THIS ACADEMY. AND I BECAME ENTANGLED IN THE TROUBLES OF SUCCESSION IN MY FAMILY... THERE'S BEEN A DISTINCT LACK OF OPPORTUNITIES FOR US TO BE TOGETHER.
TIME IS TRULY CRUEL. I WANTED TO BELIEVE WE'D ALWAYS HAVE THAT KIND OF RELATION-SHIP.
HOW-EVER...
HWOOSH
I THINK THERE'S A WAY FOR US TO TURN THOSE BEAUTIFUL MEMORIES ...
INTO SOMETHING MORE THAN JUST SIMPLE REMINISCENCE.
SISTINE.
WILL YOU MARRY ME?

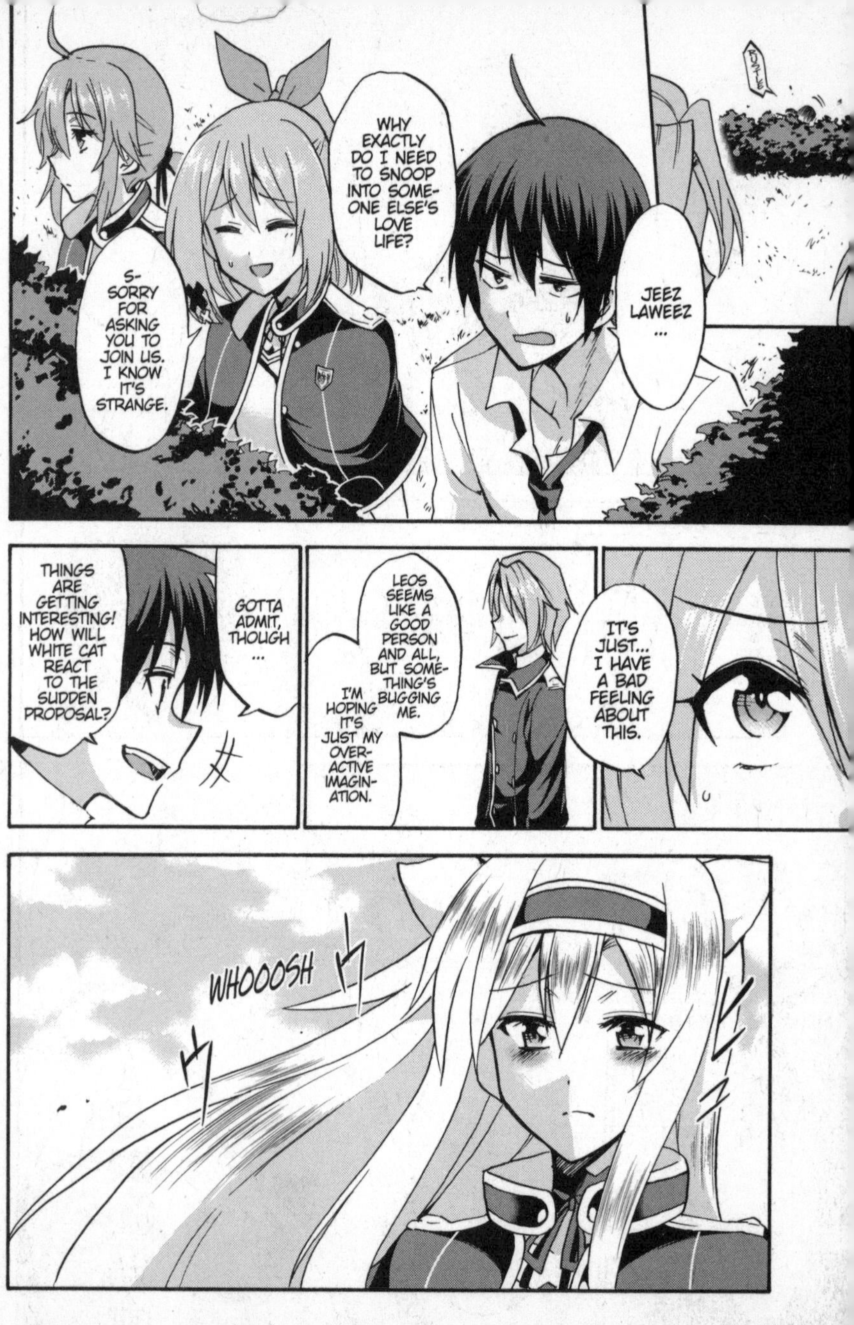
RUSTLE
JEEZ LAWEEZ ...
WHY EXACTLY DO I NEED TO SNOOP INTO SOMEONE ELSE'S LOVE LIFE?
S-SORRY FOR ASKING YOU TO JOIN US. I KNOW IT'S STRANGE.
IT'S JUST... I HAVE A BAD FEELING ABOUT THIS.
LEOS SEEMS LIKE A GOOD PERSON AND ALL, BUT SOMETHING'S BUGGING ME.
I'M HOPING IT'S JUST MY OVERACTIVE IMAGINATION.
GOTTA ADMIT, THOUGH ...
THINGS ARE GETTING INTERESTING! HOW WILL WHITE CAT REACT TO THE SUDDEN PROPOSAL?
WHOOOSH

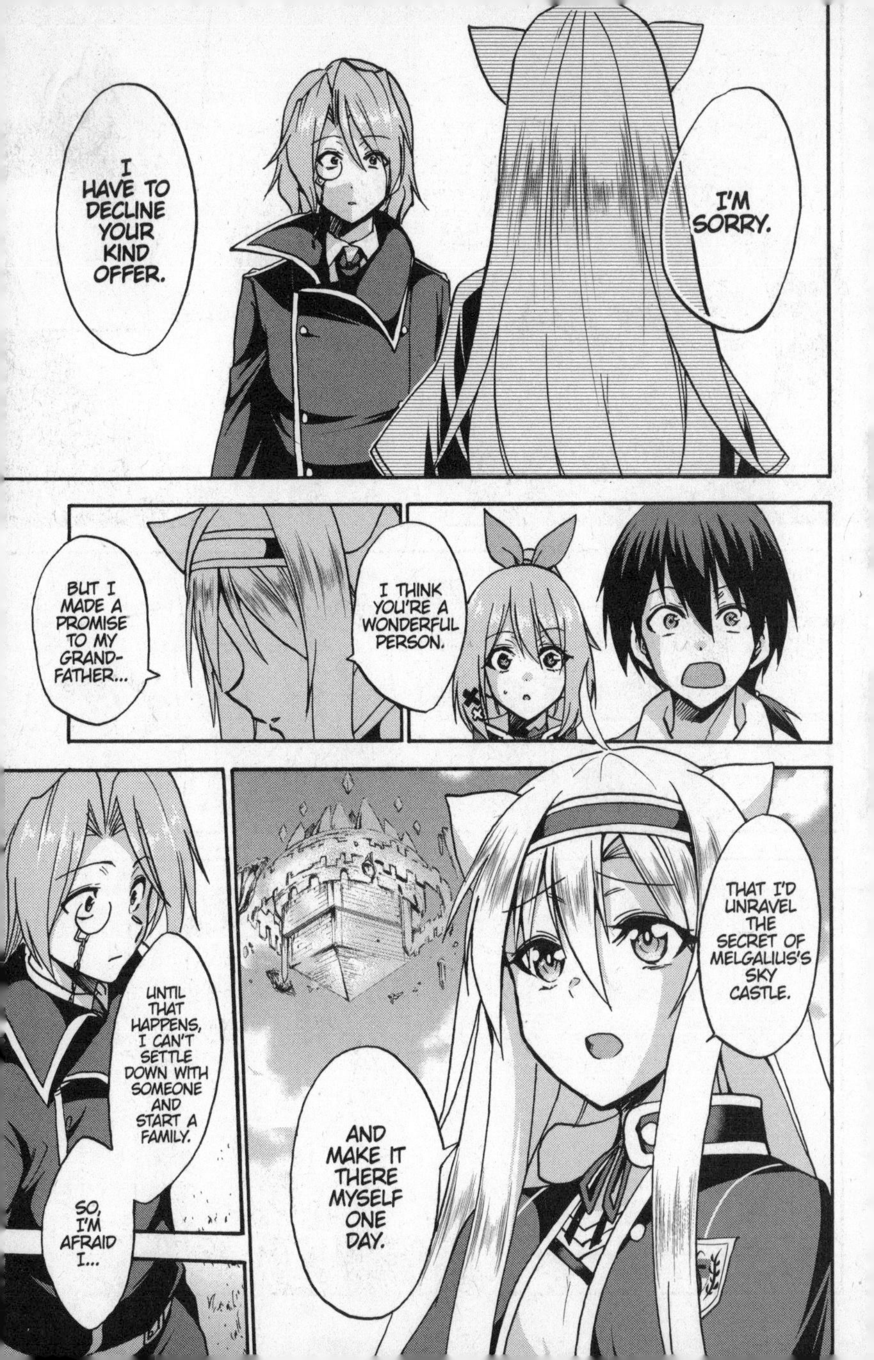
I'M SORRY.
I HAVE TO DECLINE YOUR KIND OFFER.
I THINK YOU'RE A WONDERFUL PERSON.
BUT I MADE A PROMISE TO MY GRAND-FATHER...
THAT I'D UNRAVEL THE SECRET OF MELGALIUS'S SKY CASTLE.
AND MAKE IT THERE MYSELF ONE DAY.
UNTIL THAT HAPPENS, I CAN'T SETTLE DOWN WITH SOMEONE AND START A FAMILY.
SO, I'M AFRAID I...

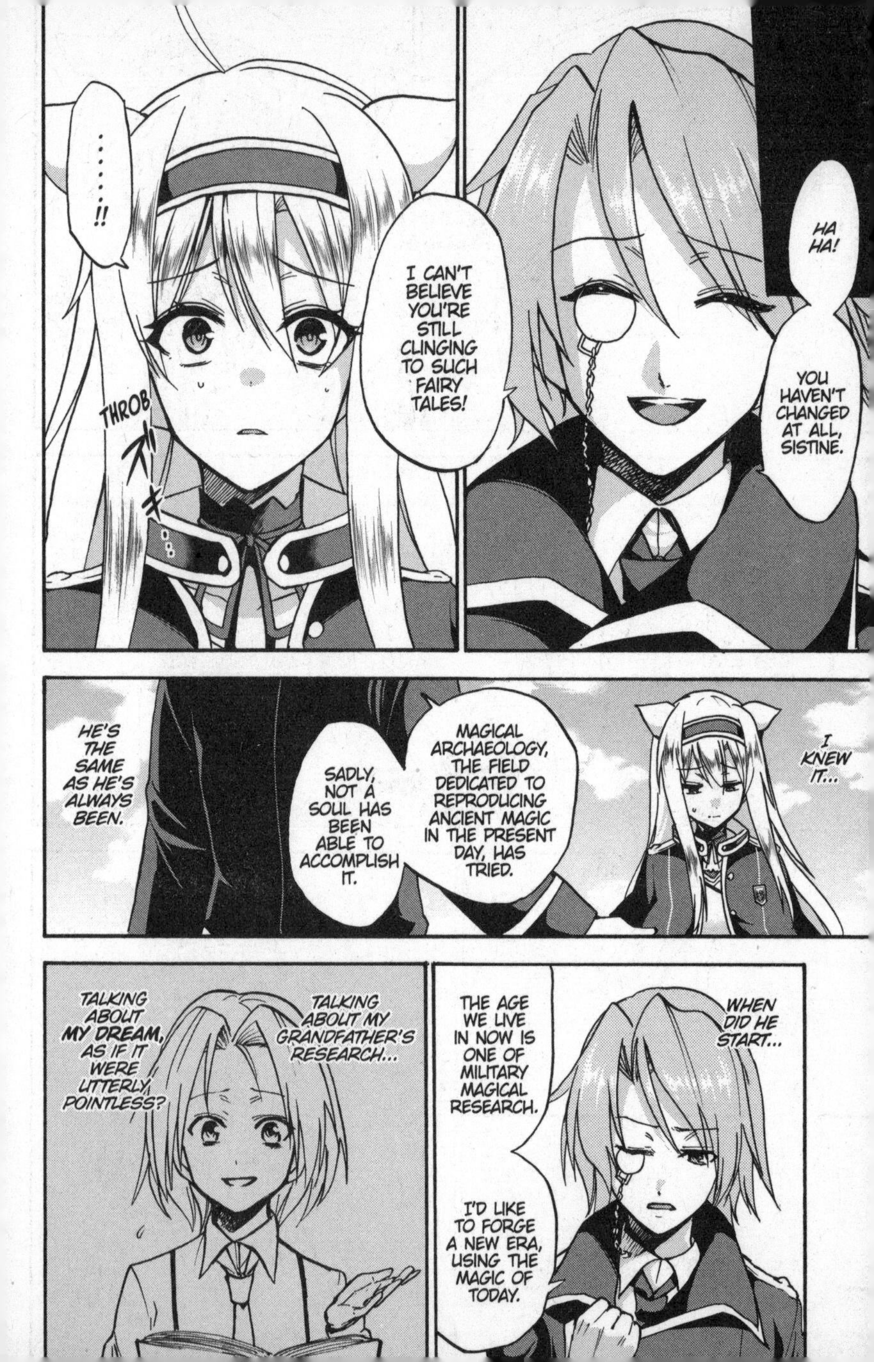
HA HA!
YOU HAVEN'T CHANGED AT ALL, SISTINE.
I CAN'T BELIEVE YOU'RE STILL CLINGING TO SUCH FAIRY TALES!
......!!
THROB
I KNEW IT...
MAGICAL ARCHAEOLOGY, THE FIELD DEDICATED TO REPRODUCING ANCIENT MAGIC IN THE PRESENT DAY, HAS TRIED.
SADLY, NOT A SOUL HAS BEEN ABLE TO ACCOMPLISH IT.
HE'S THE SAME AS HE'S ALWAYS BEEN.
WHEN DID HE START...
THE AGE WE LIVE IN NOW IS ONE OF MILITARY MAGICAL RESEARCH.
I'D LIKE TO FORGE A NEW ERA, USING THE MAGIC OF TODAY.
TALKING ABOUT MY GRANDFATHER'S RESEARCH...
TALKING ABOUT MY DREAM, AS IF IT WERE UTTERLY POINTLESS?

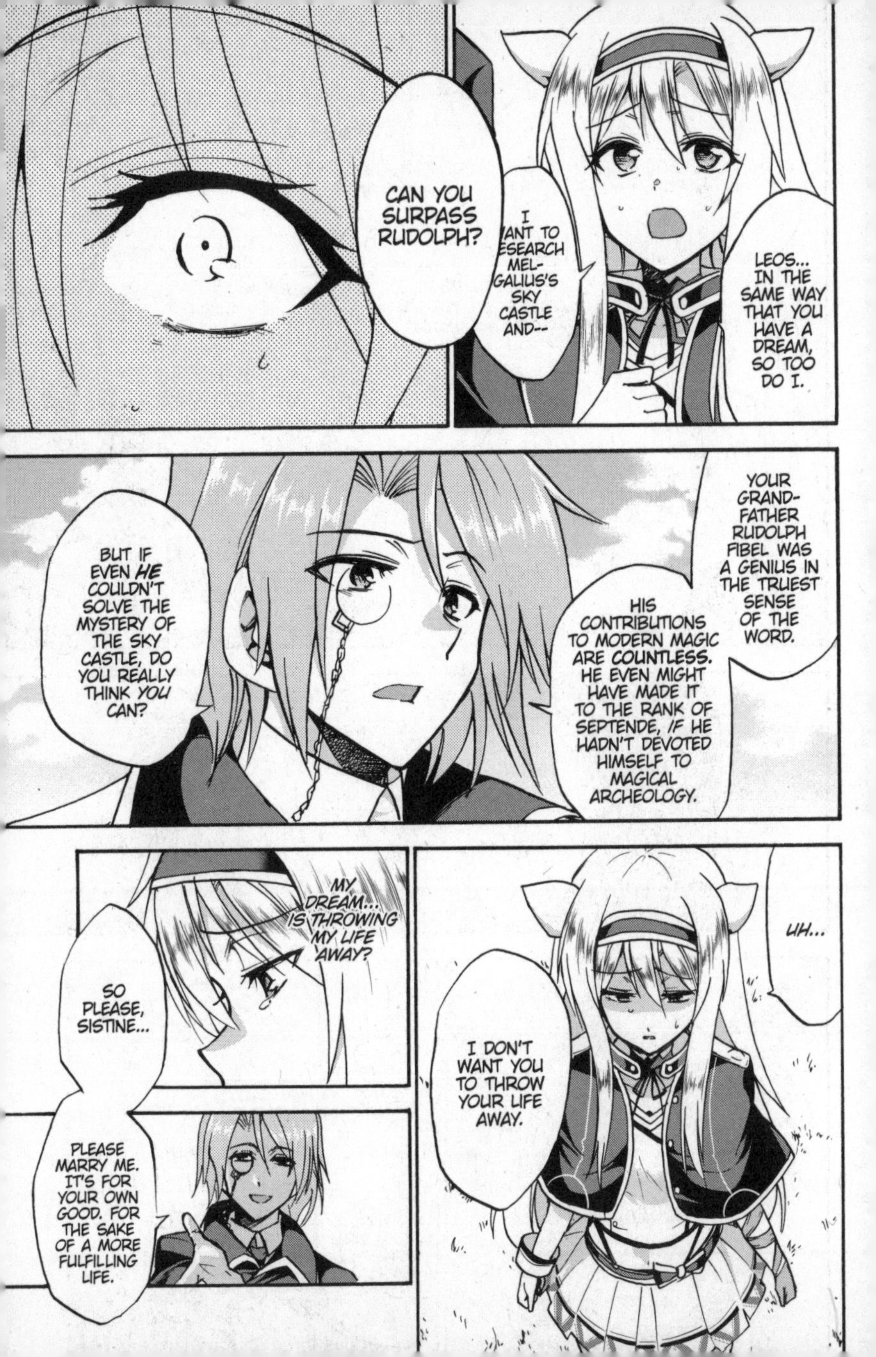
LEOS... IN THE SAME WAY THAT YOU HAVE A DREAM, SO TOO DO I.
I ANT TO ESEARCH MEL-GALIUS'S SKY CASTLE AND--
CAN YOU SURPASS RUDOLPH?
YOUR GRAND-FATHER RUDOLPH FIBEL WAS A GENIUS IN THE TRUEST SENSE OF THE WORD.
HIS CONTRIBUTIONS TO MODERN MAGIC ARE COUNTLESS. HE EVEN MIGHT HAVE MADE IT TO THE RANK OF SEPTENDE, *IF* HE HADN'T DEVOTED HIMSELF TO MAGICAL ARCHEOLOGY.
BUT IF EVEN *HE* COULDN'T SOLVE THE MYSTERY OF THE SKY CASTLE, DO YOU REALLY THINK *YOU* CAN?
UH...
I DON'T WANT YOU TO THROW YOUR LIFE AWAY.
MY DREAM... IS THROWING MY LIFE AWAY?
SO PLEASE, SISTINE...
PLEASE MARRY ME. IT'S FOR YOUR OWN GOOD. FOR THE SAKE OF A MORE FULFILLING LIFE.

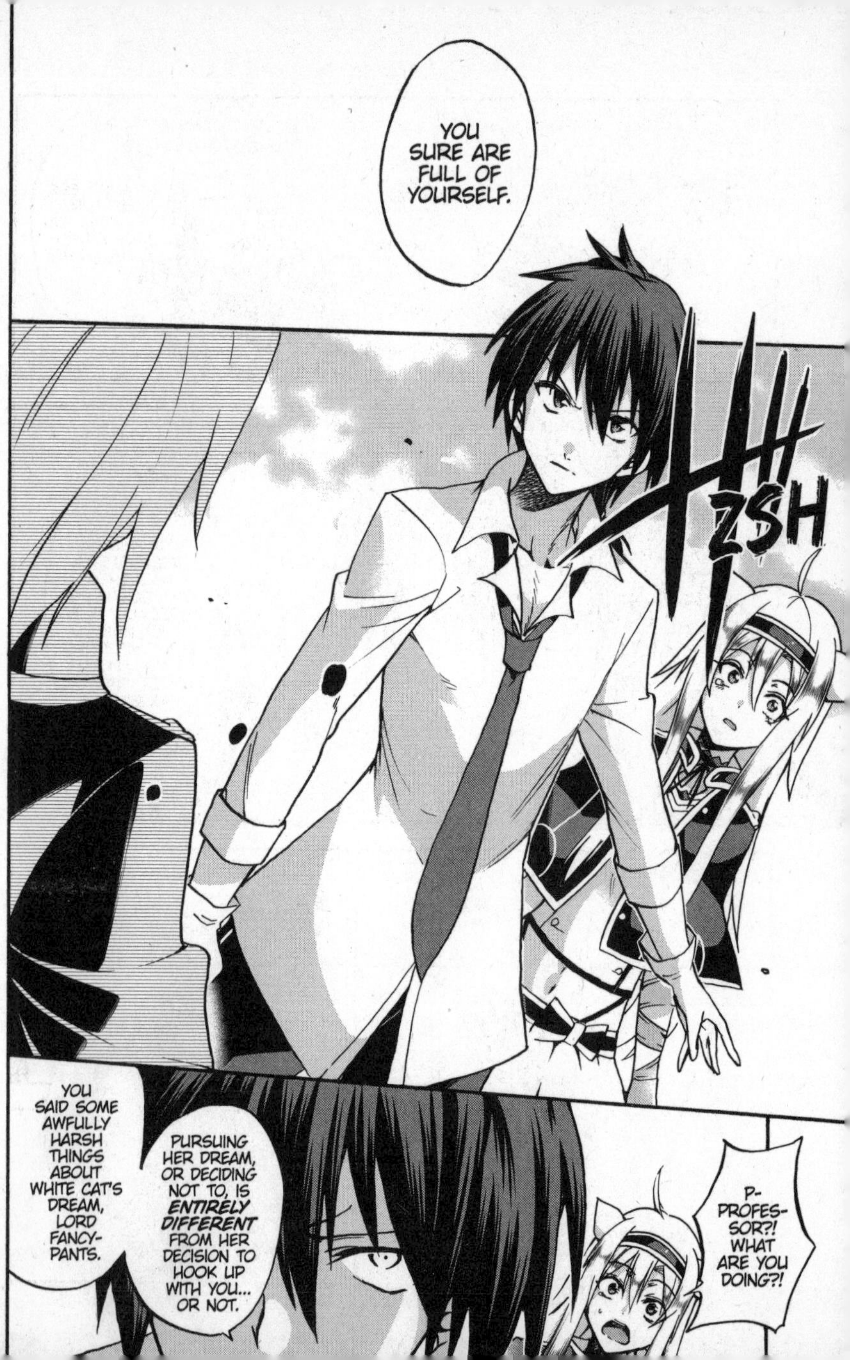
YOU SURE ARE FULL OF YOURSELF.
ZSH
P-PROFESSOR?! WHAT ARE YOU DOING?!
PURSUING HER DREAM, OR DECIDING NOT TO, IS ***ENTIRELY DIFFERENT*** FROM HER DECISION TO HOOK UP WITH YOU... OR NOT.
YOU SAID SOME AWFULLY HARSH THINGS ABOUT WHITE CAT'S DREAM, LORD FANCY-PANTS.

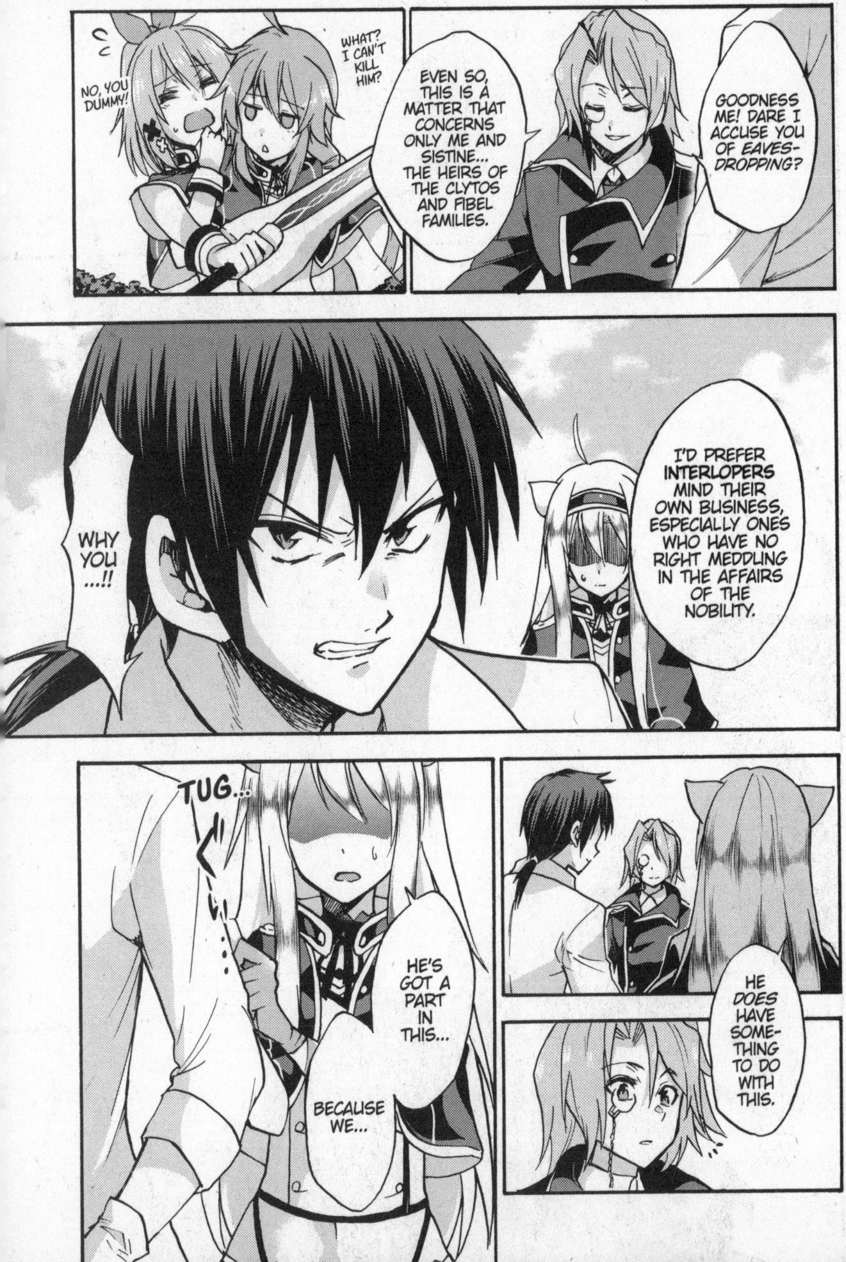
GOODNESS ME! DARE I ACCUSE YOU OF EAVES-DROPPING?
EVEN SO, THIS IS A MATTER THAT CONCERNS ONLY ME AND SISTINE... THE HEIRS OF THE CLYTOS AND FIBEL FAMILIES.
WHAT? I CAN'T KILL HIM?
NO, YOU DUMMY!
I'D PREFER INTERLOPERS MIND THEIR OWN BUSINESS, ESPECIALLY ONES WHO HAVE NO RIGHT MEDDLING IN THE AFFAIRS OF THE NOBILITY.
WHY YOU ...!!
HE DOES HAVE SOME-THING TO DO WITH THIS.
TUG...
HE'S GOT A PART IN THIS...
BECAUSE WE...

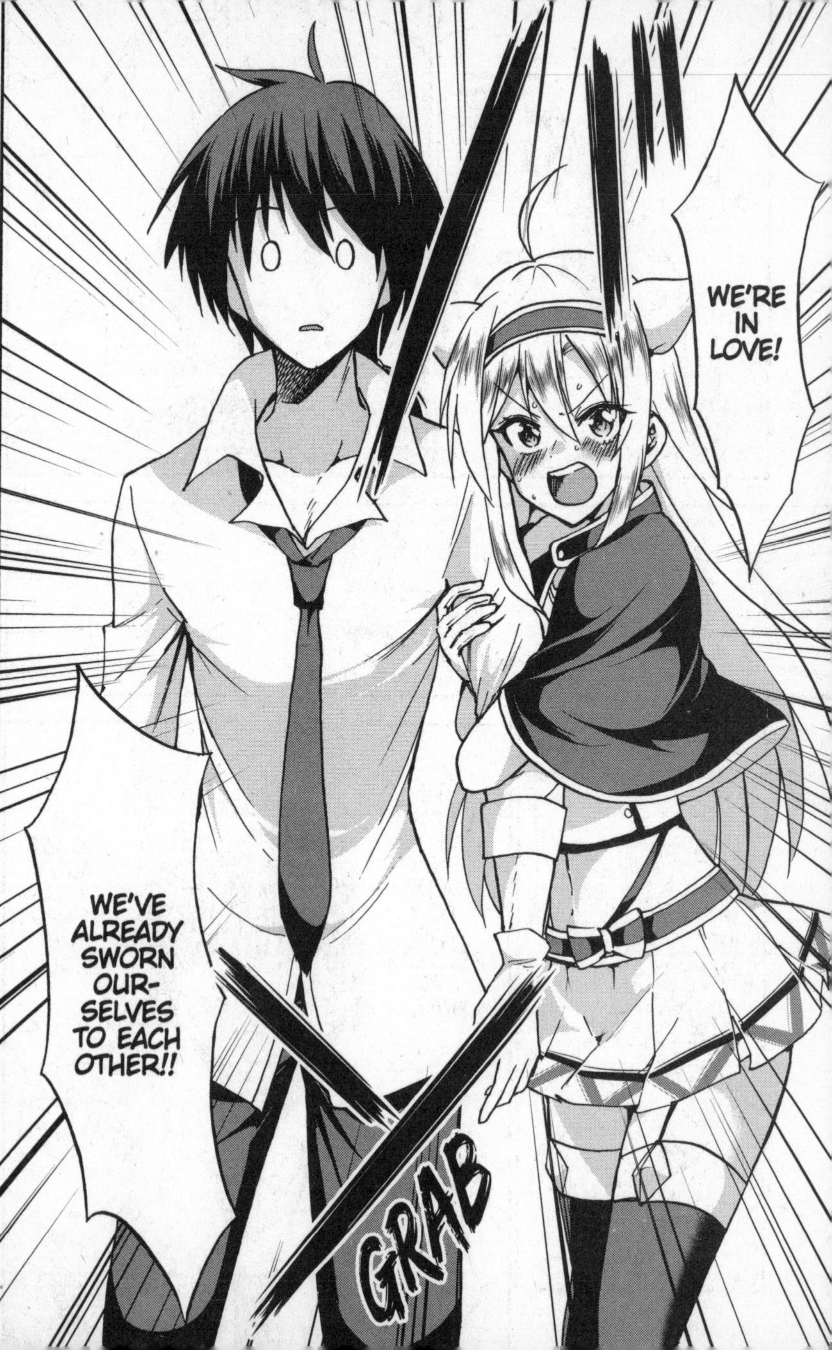
WE'RE IN LOVE!
WE'VE ALREADY SWORN OUR-SELVES TO EACH OTHER!!
GRAB

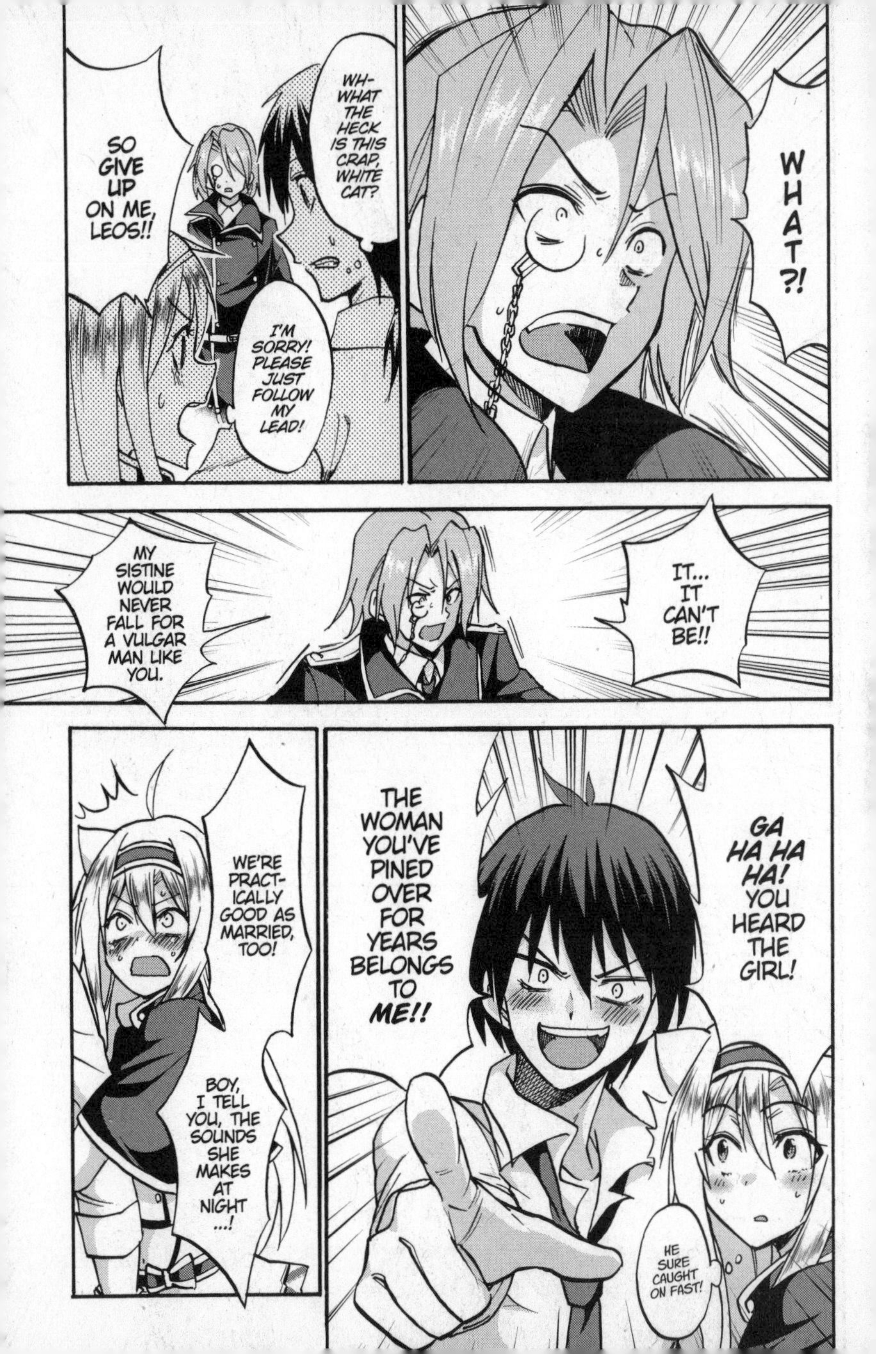
WHAT?!
WH-WHAT THE HECK IS THIS CRAP, WHITE CAT?
SO GIVE UP ON ME, LEOS!!
I'M SORRY! PLEASE JUST FOLLOW MY LEAD!
IT... IT CAN'T BE!!
MY SISTINE WOULD NEVER FALL FOR A VULGAR MAN LIKE YOU.
GA HA HA HA! YOU HEARD THE GIRL!
THE WOMAN YOU'VE PINED OVER FOR YEARS BELONGS TO ME!!
HE SURE CAUGHT ON FAST!
WE'RE PRACT-ICALLY GOOD AS MARRIED, TOO!
BOY, I TELL YOU, THE SOUNDS SHE MAKES AT NIGHT ...!

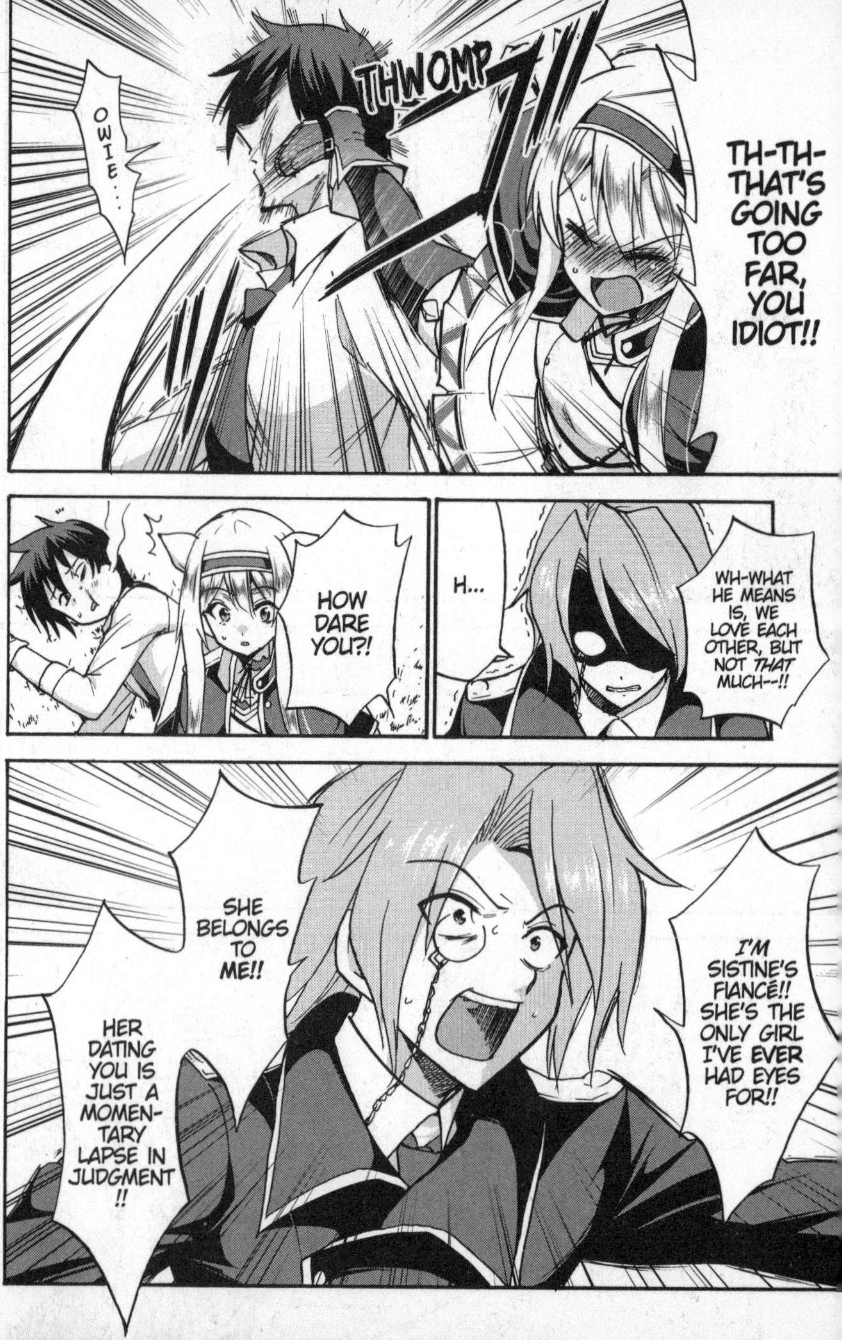
TH-TH-THAT'S GOING TOO FAR, YOU IDIOT!!
THWOMP
OWIE...
WH-WHAT HE MEANS IS, WE LOVE EACH OTHER, BUT NOT *THAT* MUCH--!!
H...
HOW DARE YOU?!
I'M SISTINE'S FIANCÉ!! SHE'S THE ONLY GIRL I'VE EVER HAD EYES FOR!!
SHE BELONGS TO ME!!
HER DATING YOU IS JUST A MOMENTARY LAPSE IN JUDGMENT!!

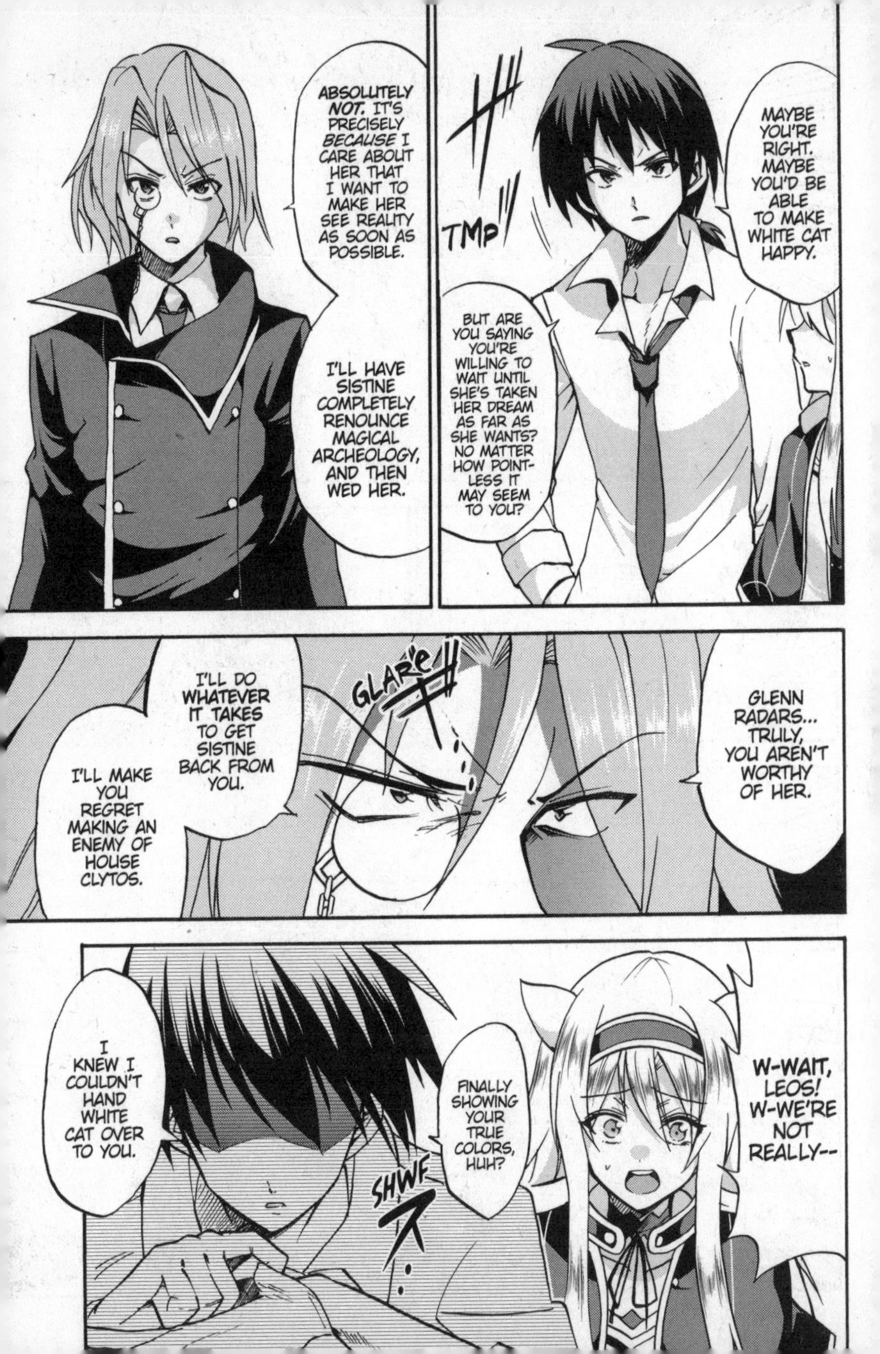
MAYBE YOU'RE RIGHT. MAYBE YOU'D BE ABLE TO MAKE WHITE CAT HAPPY.
TMP
BUT ARE YOU SAYING YOU'RE WILLING TO WAIT UNTIL SHE'S TAKEN HER DREAM AS FAR AS SHE WANTS? NO MATTER HOW POINT-LESS IT MAY SEEM TO YOU?
ABSOLUTELY *NOT.* IT'S PRECISELY *BECAUSE* I CARE ABOUT HER THAT I WANT TO MAKE HER SEE REALITY AS SOON AS POSSIBLE.
I'LL HAVE SISTINE COMPLETELY RENOUNCE MAGICAL ARCHEOLOGY, AND THEN WED HER.
GLENN RADARS... TRULY, YOU AREN'T WORTHY OF HER.
GLARE
I'LL DO WHATEVER IT TAKES TO GET SISTINE BACK FROM YOU.
I'LL MAKE YOU REGRET MAKING AN ENEMY OF HOUSE CLYTOS.
W-WAIT, LEOS! W-WE'RE NOT REALLY--
FINALLY SHOWING YOUR TRUE COLORS, HUH?
SHWF
I KNEW I COULDN'T HAND WHITE CAT OVER TO YOU.

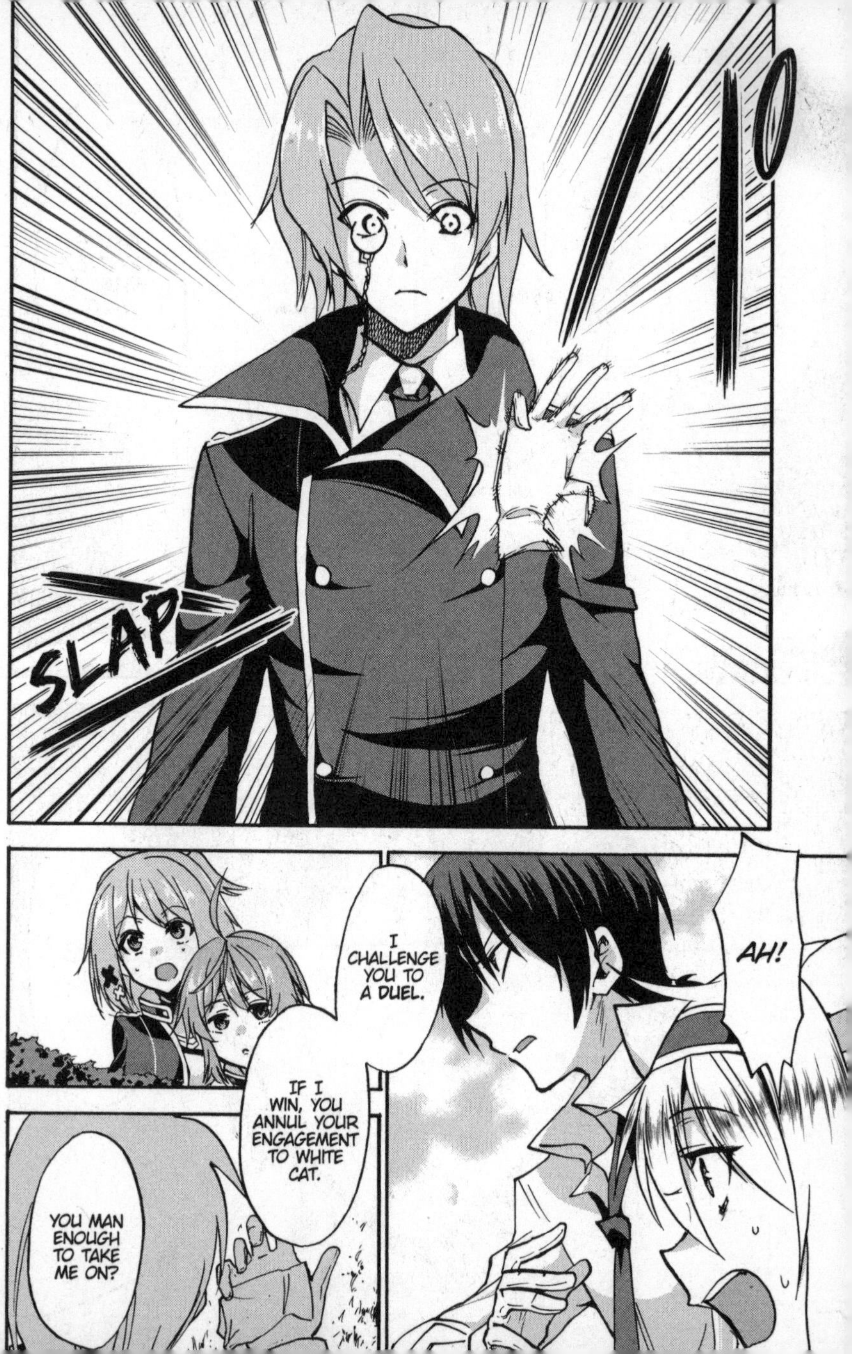
SLAP
AH!
I CHALLENGE YOU TO A DUEL.
IF I WIN, YOU ANNUL YOUR ENGAGEMENT TO WHITE CAT.
YOU MAN ENOUGH TO TAKE ME ON?

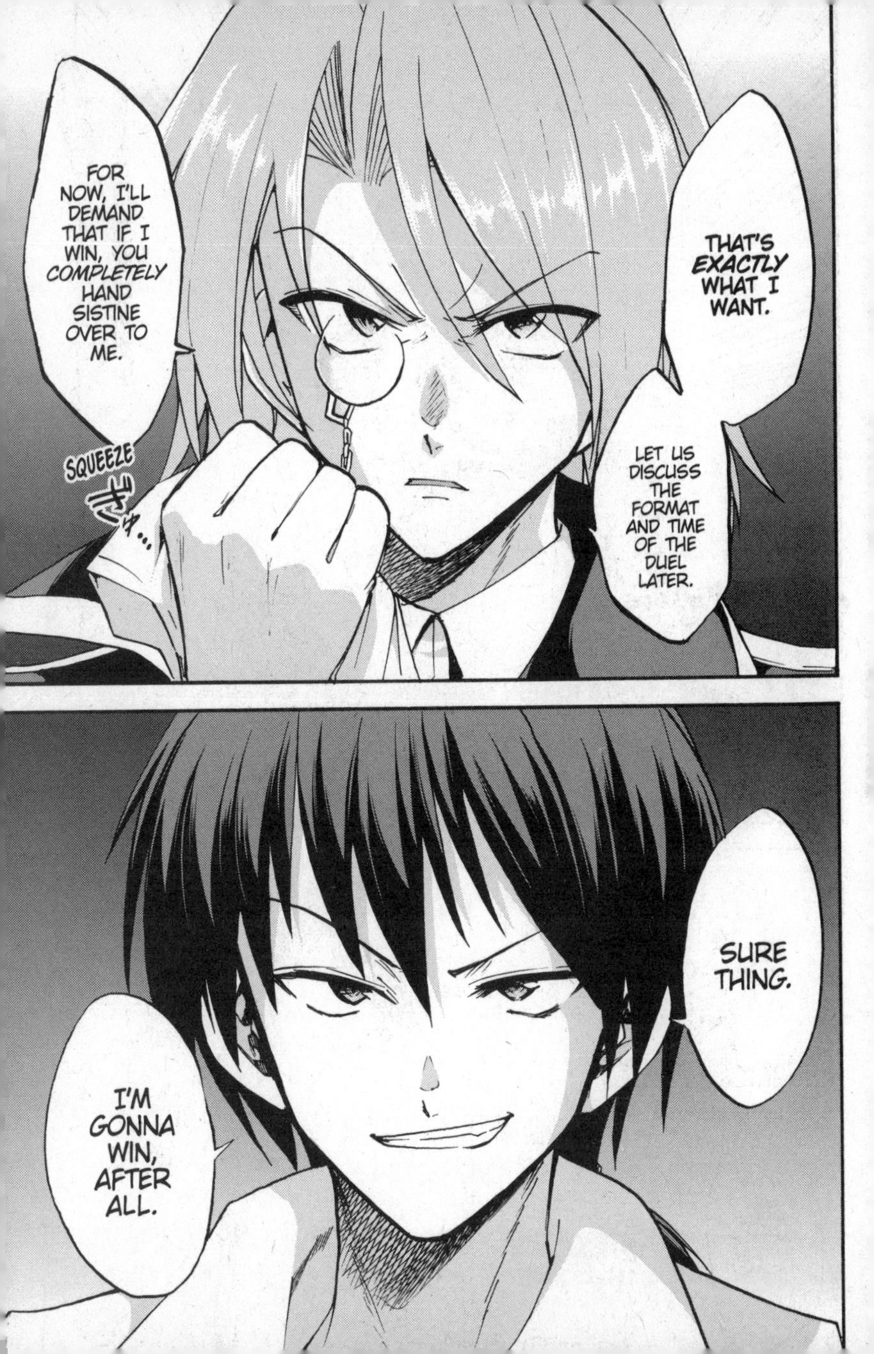
THAT'S EXACTLY WHAT I WANT.
LET US DISCUSS THE FORMAT AND TIME OF THE DUEL LATER.
FOR NOW, I'LL DEMAND THAT IF I WIN, YOU COMPLETELY HAND SISTINE OVER TO ME.
SQUEEZE
SURE THING.
I'M GONNA WIN, AFTER ALL.

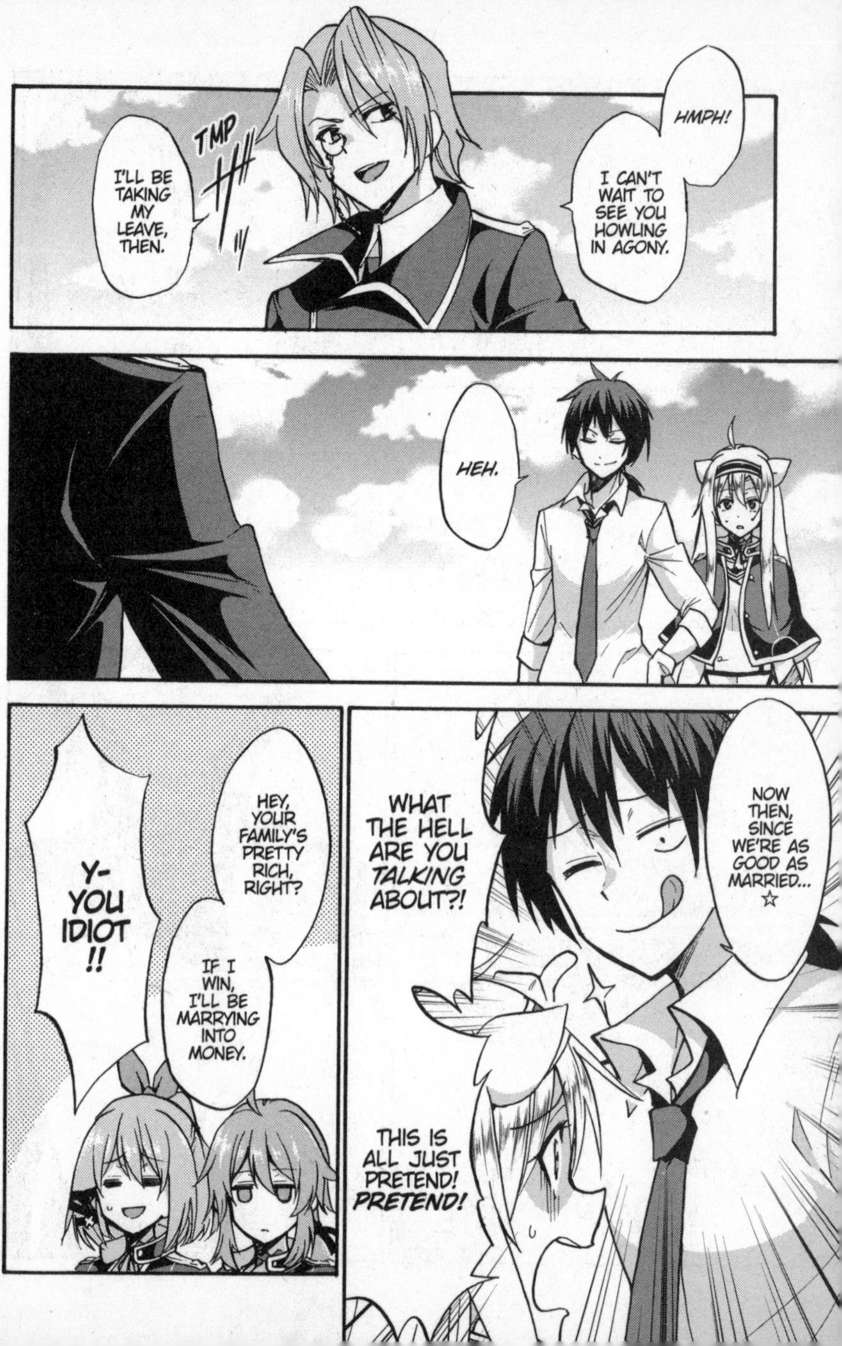
HMPH!
I CAN'T WAIT TO SEE YOU HOWLING IN AGONY.
TMP
I'LL BE TAKING MY LEAVE, THEN.
HEH.
NOW THEN, SINCE WE'RE AS GOOD AS MARRIED... ☆
WHAT THE HELL ARE YOU *TALKING* ABOUT?!
THIS IS ALL JUST PRETEND! ***PRETEND!***
HEY, YOUR FAMILY'S PRETTY RICH, RIGHT?
IF I WIN, I'LL BE MARRYING INTO MONEY.
Y-YOU IDIOT!!

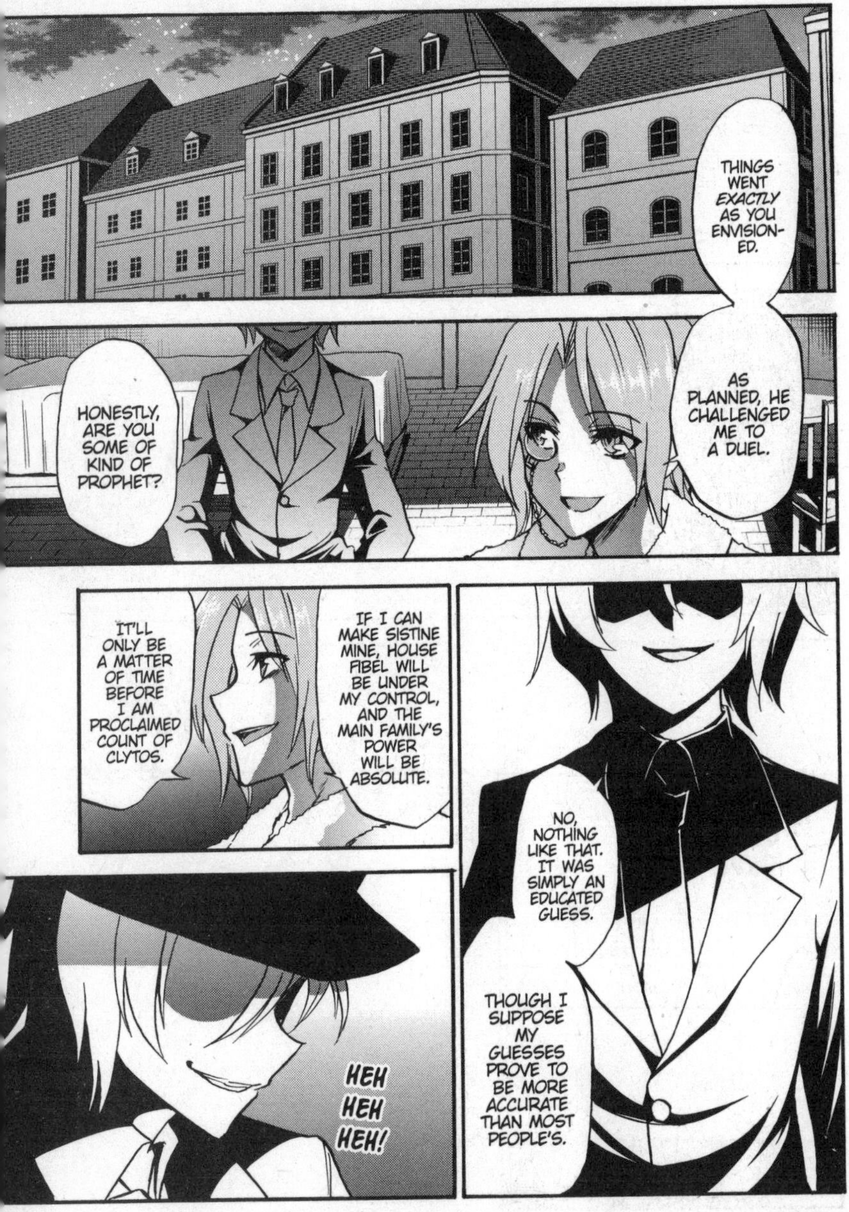
THINGS WENT *EXACTLY* AS YOU ENVISIONED.
AS PLANNED, HE CHALLENGED ME TO A DUEL.
HONESTLY, ARE YOU SOME OF KIND OF PROPHET?
NO, NOTHING LIKE THAT. IT WAS SIMPLY AN EDUCATED GUESS.
THOUGH I SUPPOSE MY GUESSES PROVE TO BE MORE ACCURATE THAN MOST PEOPLE'S.
IF I CAN MAKE SISTINE MINE, HOUSE FIBEL WILL BE UNDER MY CONTROL, AND THE MAIN FAMILY'S POWER WILL BE ABSOLUTE.
IT'LL ONLY BE A MATTER OF TIME BEFORE I AM PROCLAIMED COUNT OF CLYTOS.
HEH HEH HEH!

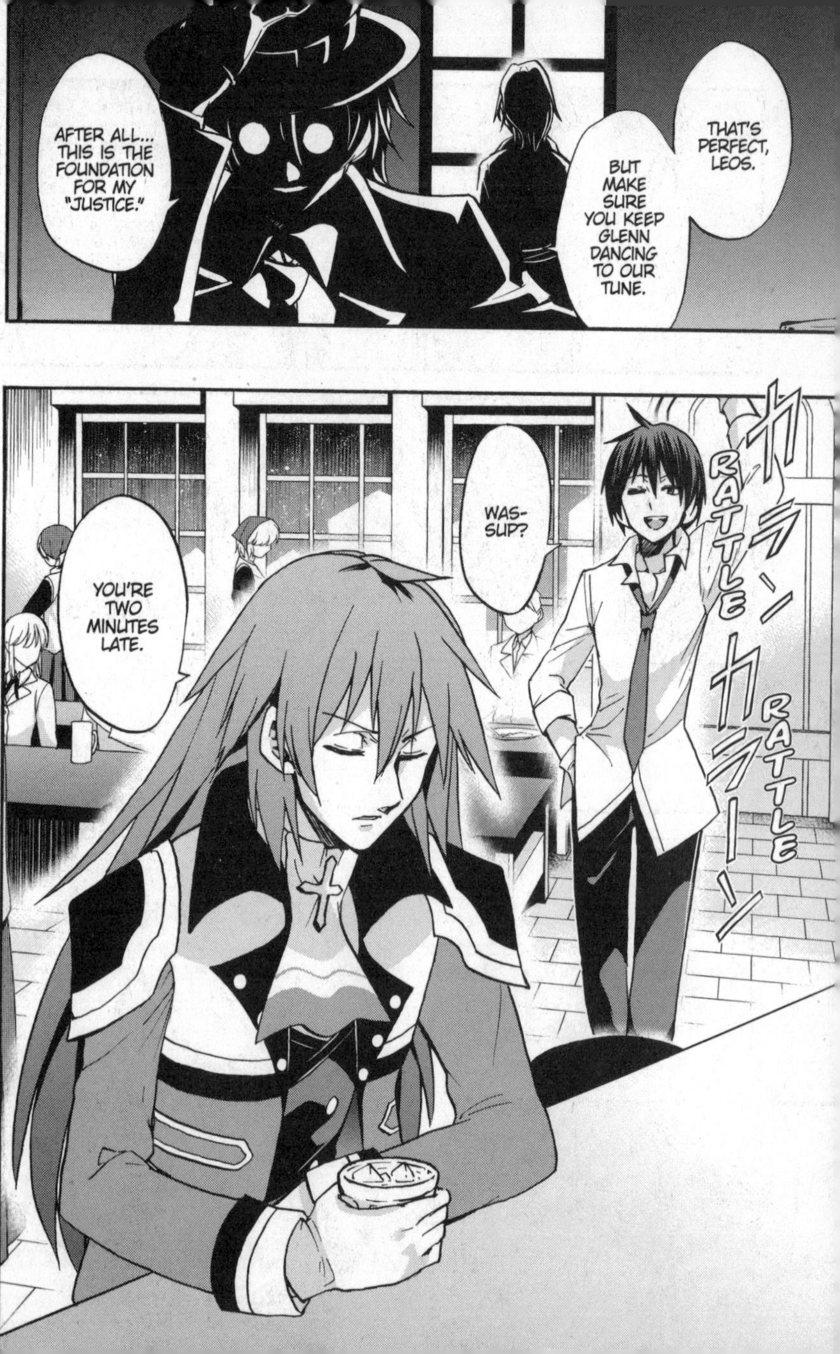
THAT'S PERFECT, LEOS.
BUT MAKE SURE YOU KEEP GLENN DANCING TO OUR TUNE.
AFTER ALL... THIS IS THE FOUNDATION FOR MY "JUSTICE."
カラン カラーン
RATTLE RATTLE
WAS-SUP?
YOU'RE TWO MINUTES LATE.

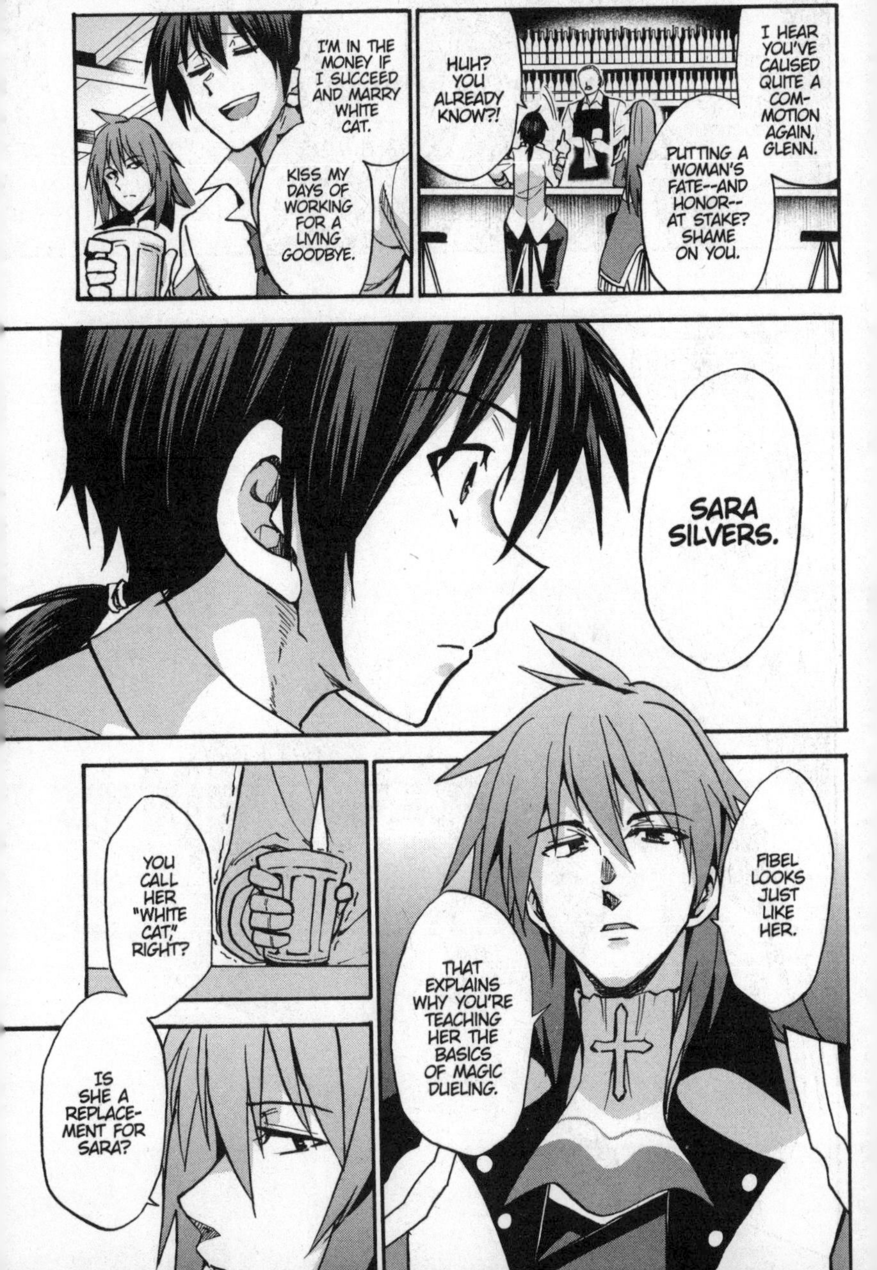
I HEAR YOU'VE CAUSED QUITE A COMMOTION AGAIN, GLENN.
PUTTING A WOMAN'S FATE--AND HONOR--AT STAKE? SHAME ON YOU.
HUH? YOU ALREADY KNOW?!
I'M IN THE MONEY IF I SUCCEED AND MARRY WHITE CAT.
KISS MY DAYS OF WORKING FOR A LIVING GOODBYE.
SARA SILVERS.
FIBEL LOOKS JUST LIKE HER.
THAT EXPLAINS WHY YOU'RE TEACHING HER THE BASICS OF MAGIC DUELING.
YOU CALL HER "WHITE CAT," RIGHT?
IS SHE A REPLACEMENT FOR SARA?

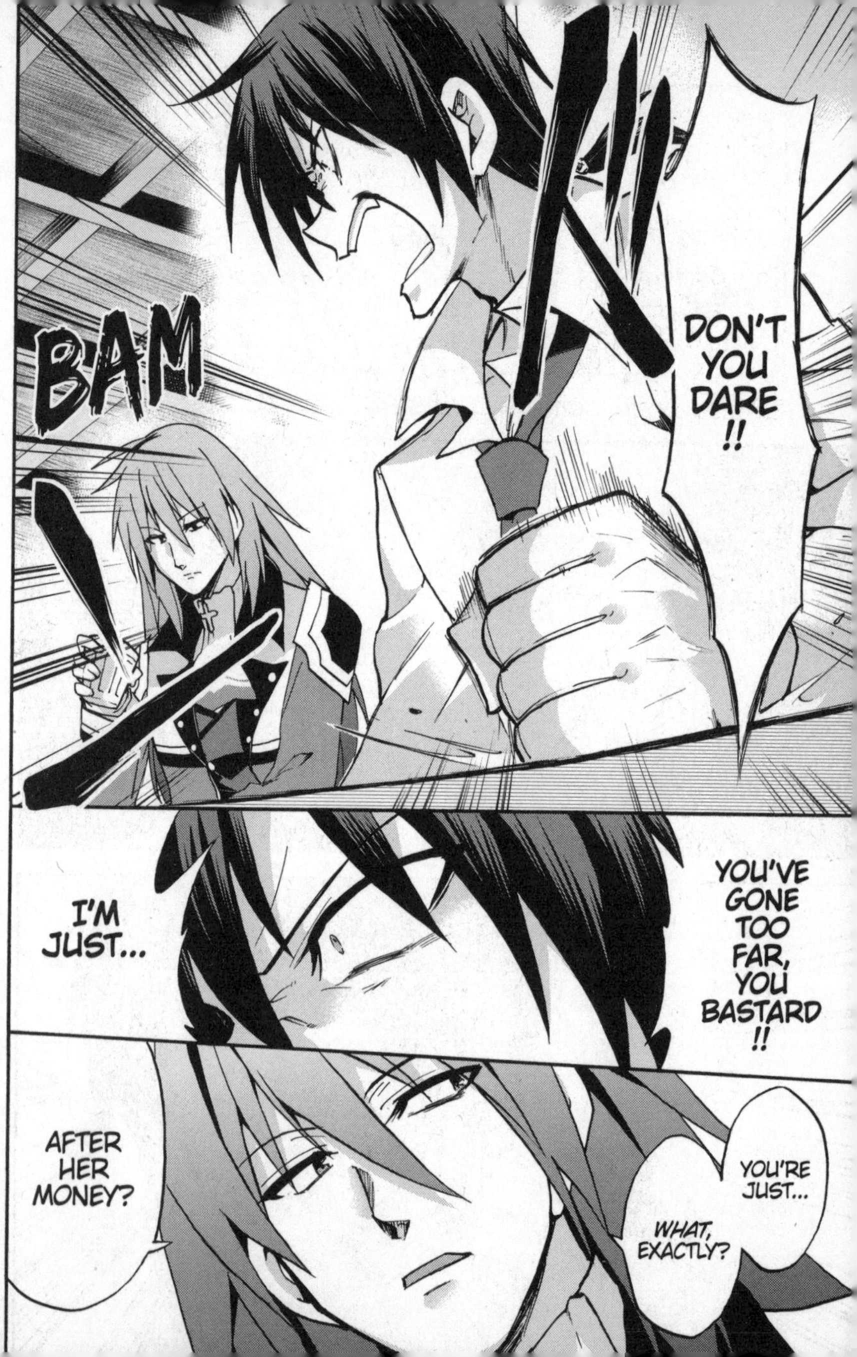
DON'T YOU DARE!!
BAM
YOU'VE GONE TOO FAR, YOU BASTARD!!
I'M JUST...
YOU'RE JUST...
WHAT, EXACTLY?
AFTER HER MONEY?

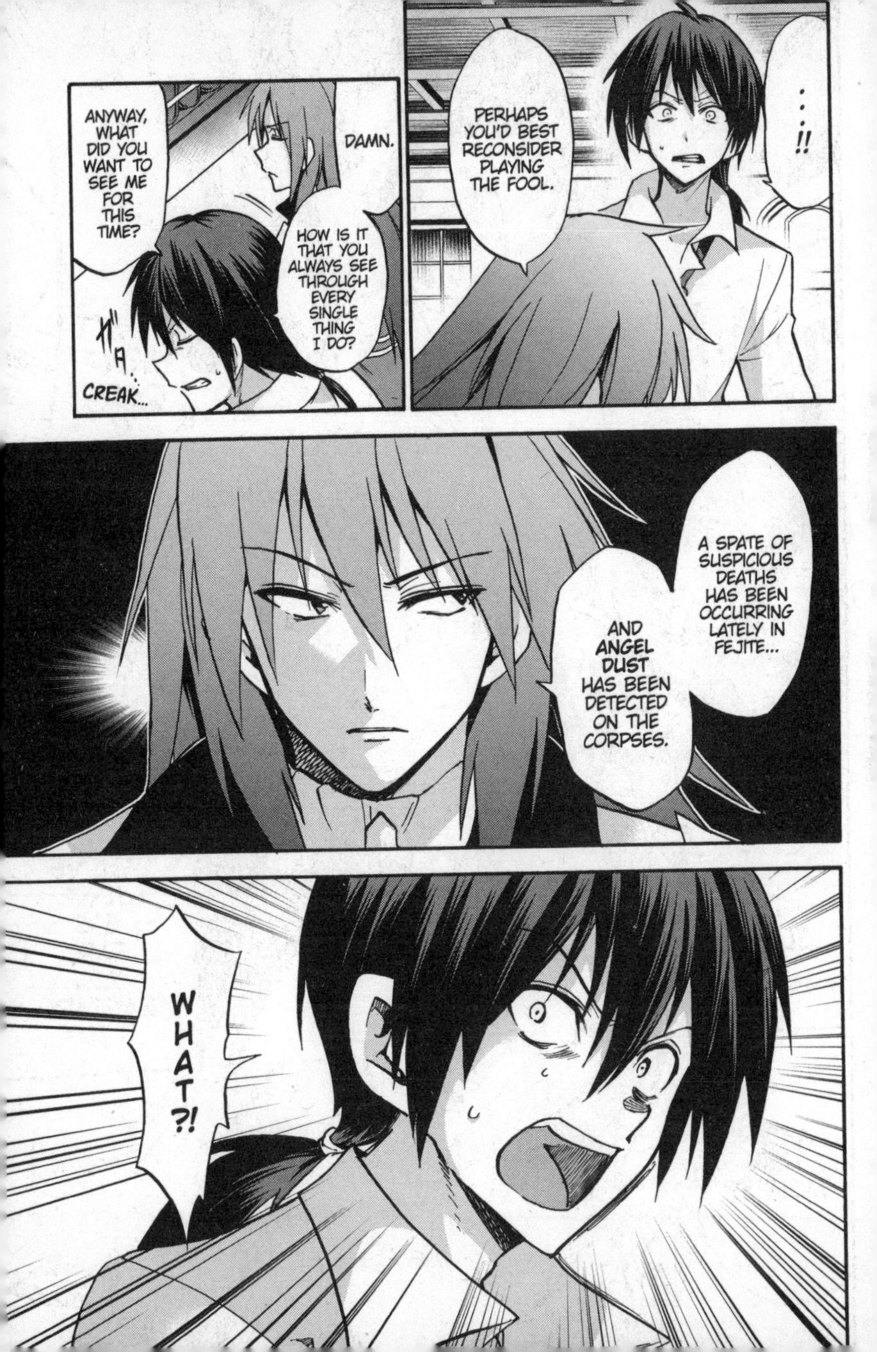
...!!
PERHAPS YOU'D BEST RECONSIDER PLAYING THE FOOL.
DAMN.
ANYWAY, WHAT DID YOU WANT TO SEE ME FOR THIS TIME?
HOW IS IT THAT YOU ALWAYS SEE THROUGH EVERY SINGLE THING I DO?
ガ
CREAK...
A SPATE OF SUSPICIOUS DEATHS HAS BEEN OCCURRING LATELY IN FEJITE...
AND ANGEL DUST HAS BEEN DETECTED ON THE CORPSES.
WHAT?!

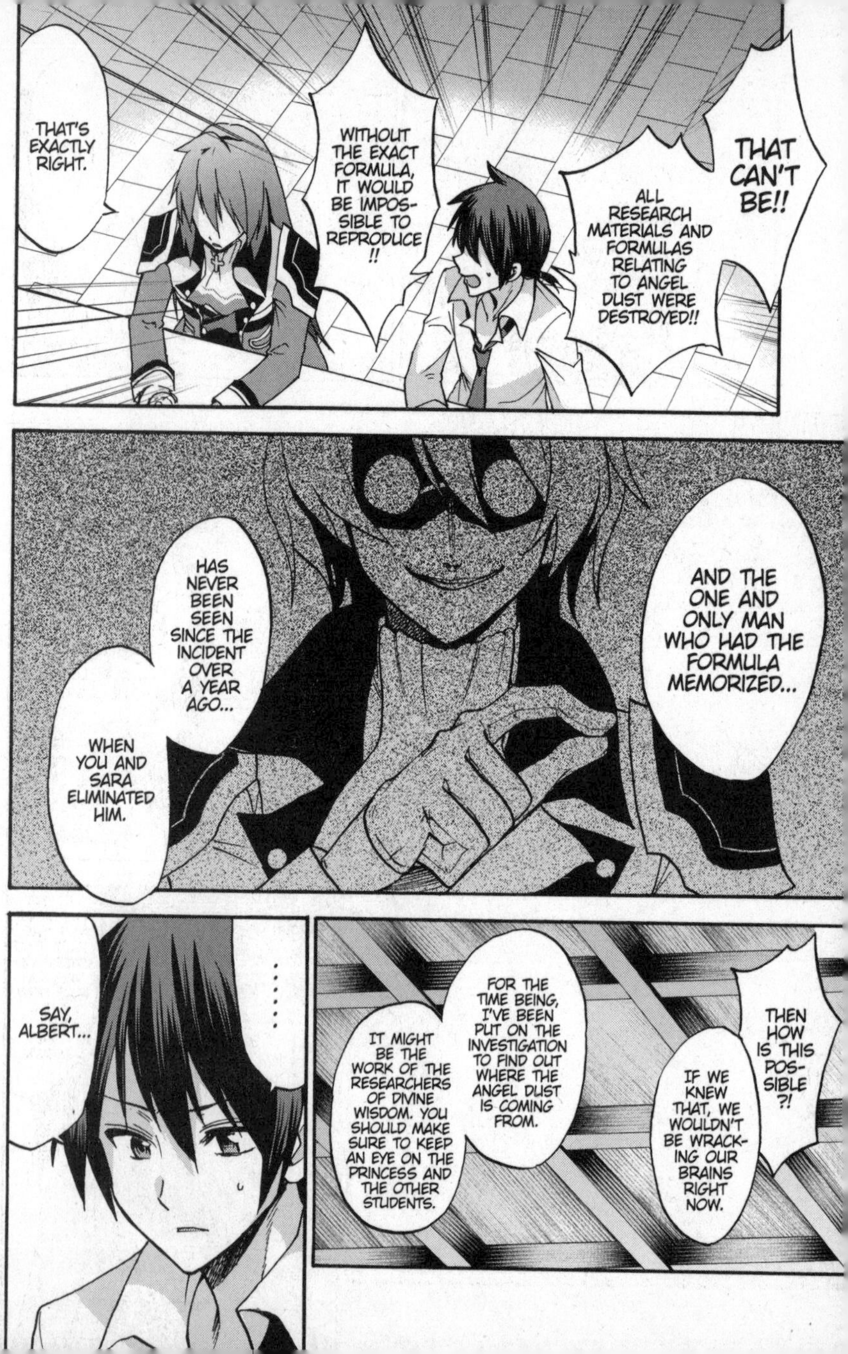
THAT CAN'T BE!!
ALL RESEARCH MATERIALS AND FORMULAS RELATING TO ANGEL DUST WERE DESTROYED!!
WITHOUT THE EXACT FORMULA, IT WOULD BE IMPOSSIBLE TO REPRODUCE!!
THAT'S EXACTLY RIGHT.
AND THE ONE AND ONLY MAN WHO HAD THE FORMULA MEMORIZED...
HAS NEVER BEEN SEEN SINCE THE INCIDENT OVER A YEAR AGO...
WHEN YOU AND SARA ELIMINATED HIM.
THEN HOW IS THIS POSSIBLE?!
IF WE KNEW THAT, WE WOULDN'T BE WRACKING OUR BRAINS RIGHT NOW.
FOR THE TIME BEING, I'VE BEEN PUT ON THE INVESTIGATION TO FIND OUT WHERE THE ANGEL DUST IS COMING FROM.
IT MIGHT BE THE WORK OF THE RESEARCHERS OF DIVINE WISDOM. YOU SHOULD MAKE SURE TO KEEP AN EYE ON THE PRINCESS AND THE OTHER STUDENTS.
......
SAY, ALBERT...

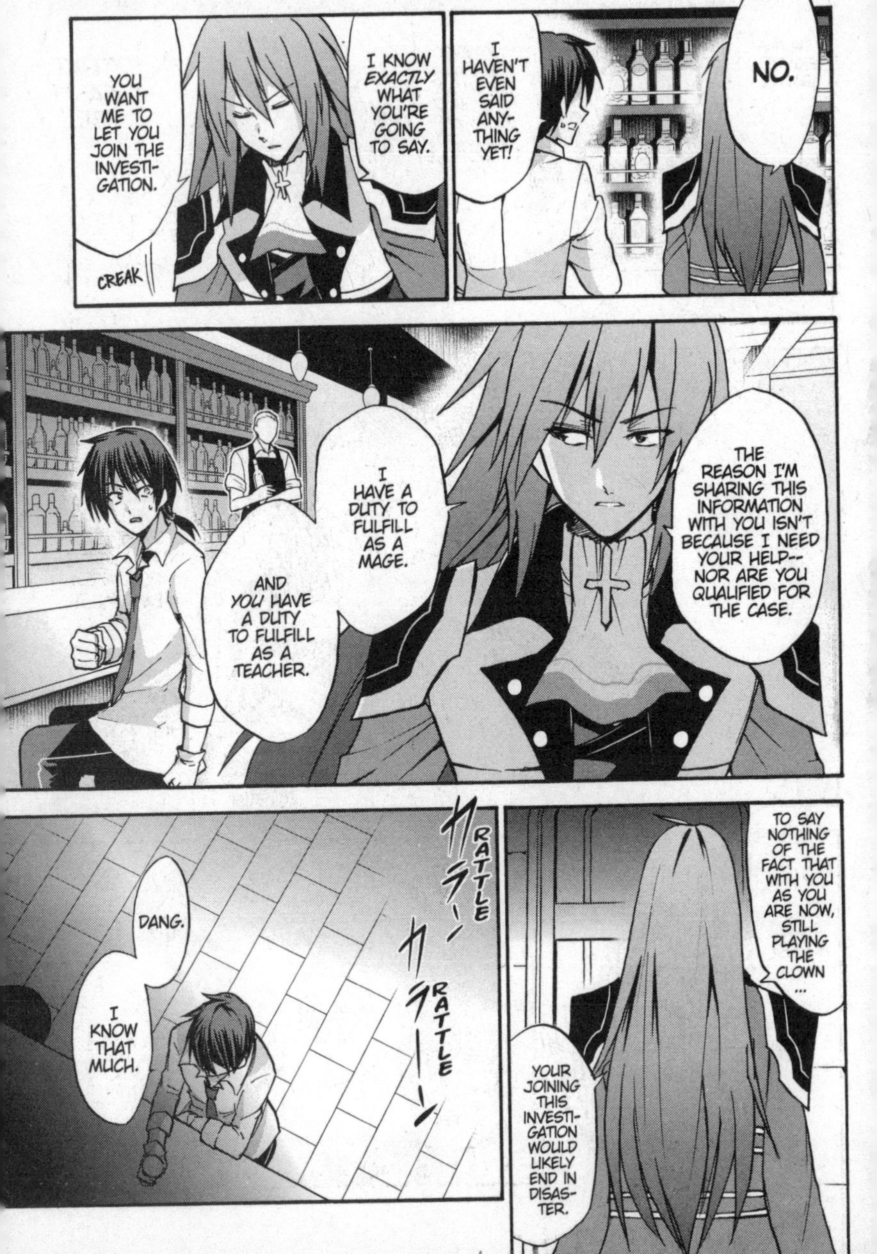
NO.
I HAVEN'T EVEN SAID ANYTHING YET!
I KNOW *EXACTLY* WHAT YOU'RE GOING TO SAY.
YOU WANT ME TO LET YOU JOIN THE INVESTIGATION.
CREAK
THE REASON I'M SHARING THIS INFORMATION WITH YOU ISN'T BECAUSE I NEED YOUR HELP-- NOR ARE YOU QUALIFIED FOR THE CASE.
I HAVE A DUTY TO FULFILL AS A MAGE.
AND *YOU* HAVE A DUTY TO FULFILL AS A TEACHER.
TO SAY NOTHING OF THE FACT THAT WITH YOU AS YOU ARE NOW, STILL PLAYING THE CLOWN ...
YOUR JOINING THIS INVESTIGATION WOULD LIKELY END IN DISASTER.
RATTLE
RATTLE
DANG.
I KNOW THAT MUCH.

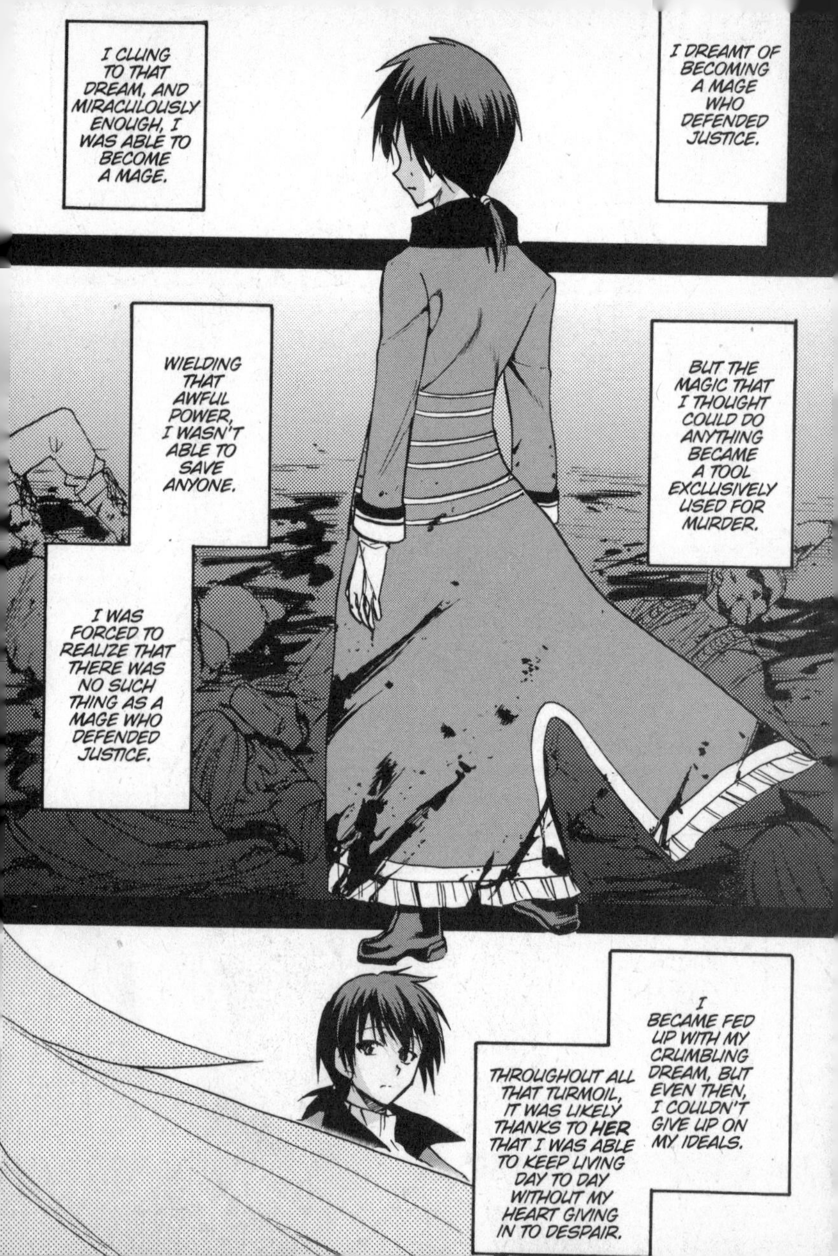
I DREAMT OF BECOMING A MAGE WHO DEFENDED JUSTICE.
I CLUNG TO THAT DREAM, AND MIRACULOUSLY ENOUGH, I WAS ABLE TO BECOME A MAGE.
BUT THE MAGIC THAT I THOUGHT COULD DO ANYTHING BECAME A TOOL EXCLUSIVELY USED FOR MURDER.
WIELDING THAT AWFUL POWER, I WASN'T ABLE TO SAVE ANYONE.
I WAS FORCED TO REALIZE THAT THERE WAS NO SUCH THING AS A MAGE WHO DEFENDED JUSTICE.
I BECAME FED UP WITH MY CRUMBLING DREAM, BUT EVEN THEN, I COULDN'T GIVE UP ON MY IDEALS.
THROUGHOUT ALL THAT TURMOIL, IT WAS LIKELY THANKS TO HER THAT I WAS ABLE TO KEEP LIVING DAY TO DAY WITHOUT MY HEART GIVING IN TO DESPAIR.

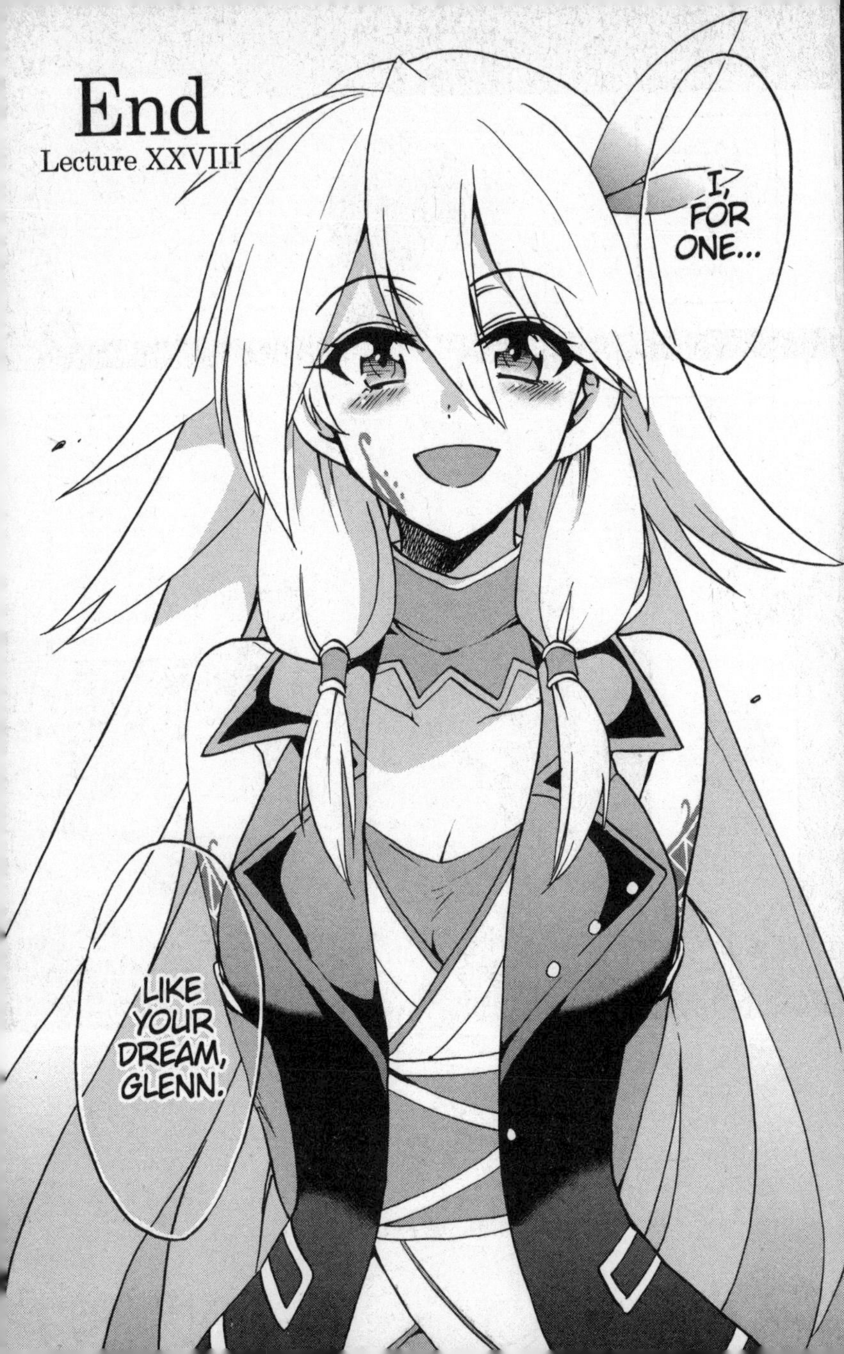
I, FOR ONE...
LIKE YOUR DREAM, GLENN.
End
Lecture XXVIII

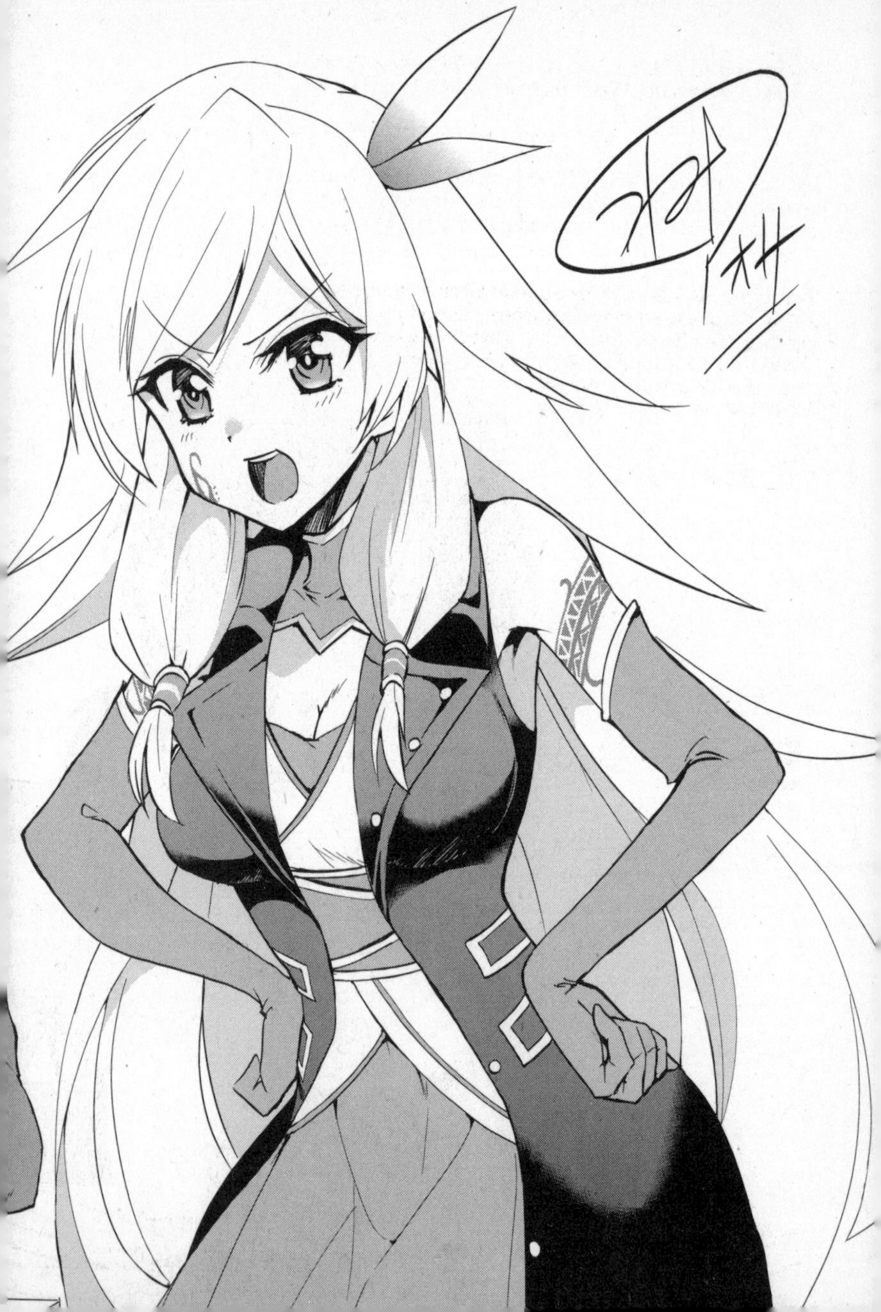

Thank you so much for purchasing volume 6 of *Akashic Records of Bastard Magic Instructor.* I'm Aosa Tsunemi.

The broadcast of the anime series seemed to finish just as soon as it started. My warm wishes to all the staff. I looked forward to seeing Glenn and the others moving around and talking each week. The manga will keep going strong, so I hope you readers continue to keep reading.

This time, Re=L's story came to a conclusion, we entered a new chapter, and new characters showed up one after another. It's always difficult to draw characters I'm not used to drawing, but I love drawing all kinds, and it's a great learning experience, so I'm always excited whenever newcomers show up.

Well then, see you next volume.

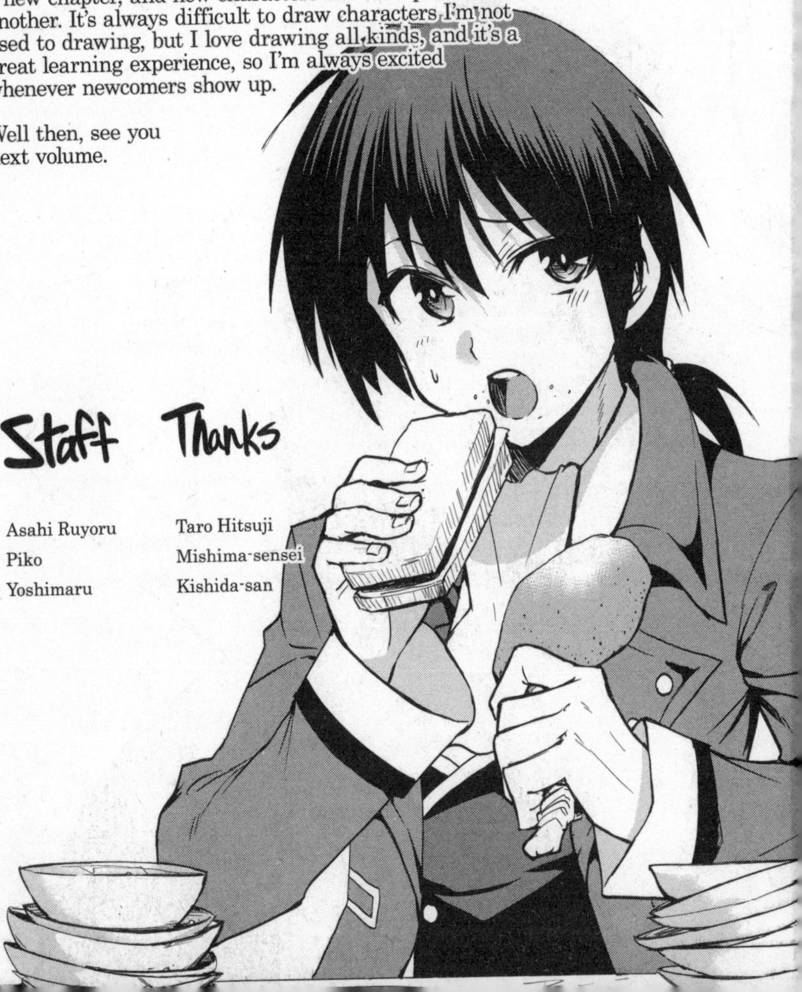

Staff Thanks

Asahi Ruyoru
Piko
Yoshimaru

Taro Hitsuji
Mishima-sensei
Kishida-san

SEVEN SEAS ENTERTAINMENT PRESENTS

Akashic Records
o f Bastard Magic Instructor VOLUME 6

story by **TARO HITSUJI**   art by **AOSA TSUNEMI**   original character designs by **KURONE MISHIMA**

TRANSLATION
Ryan Peterson

ADAPTATION
Bambi Eloriaga-Amago

LETTERING
Brandon Bovia

COVER DESIGN
KC Fabellon

PROOFREADER
Danielle King
Janet Houck

EDITOR
J.P. Sullivan

PRODUCTION ASSISTANT
CK Russell

PRODUCTION MANAGER
Lissa Pattillo

EDITOR-IN-CHIEF
Adam Arnold

PUBLISHER
Jason DeAngelis

ISBN: 978-1-64275-019-5

Printed in Canada

First Printing: April 2019

10 9 8 7 6 5 4 3 2 1

FOLLOW US ONLINE: www.sevenseasentertainment.com

READING DIRECTIONS

This book reads from *right to left*, Japanese style.
If this is your first time reading manga, you start
reading from the top right panel on each page and
take it from there. If you get lost, just follow the
numbered diagram here. It may seem backwards at
first, but you'll get the hang of it! Have fun!!

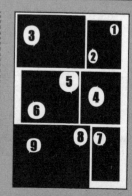